Disability in Local and Global Worlds

Disability in Local and Global Worlds

Edited by
BENEDICTE INGSTAD
SUSAN REYNOLDS WHYTE

University of California Press
BERKELEY   LOS ANGELES   LONDON

University of California Press, one of the most distinguished university presses in the United States, enriches lives around the world by advancing scholarship in the humanities, social sciences, and natural sciences. Its activities are supported by the UC Press Foundation and by philanthropic contributions from individuals and institutions. For more information, visit www.ucpress.edu.

University of California Press
Berkeley and Los Angeles, California

University of California Press, Ltd.
London, England

Library of Congress Cataloging-in-Publication Data

Disability in local and global worlds / edited by Benedicte Ingstad and Susan Reynolds Whyte.
       p.   cm.
   Includes bibliographical references and index.
   ISBN-13: 978-0-520-24616-4 (cloth, alk. paper)
   ISBN-13: 978-0-520-24617-1 (pbk., alk. paper)
   1. People with disabilities.   2. People with disabilities—Social conditions.   3. People with disabilities—Cross-cultural studies.
I. Ingstad, Benedicte.   II. Whyte, Susan Reynolds.

HV1568.D5687   2007
362.4—dc22   2007006678

Manufactured in the United States of America

16   15   14   13   12   11   10   09   08   07
10   9   8   7   6   5   4   3   2   1

This book is printed on New Leaf EcoBook 50, a 100% recycled fiber of which 50% is de-inked post-consumer waste, processed chlorine-free. EcoBook 50 is acid-free and meets the minimum requirements of ANSI/ASTM D5634-01 (Permanence of Paper).

Contents

Illustrations

Acknowledgments

We gratefully acknowledge permission from Duke University Press to republish "Disability and domestic citizenship: Voice, gender and the making of the subject" by Veena Das and Renu Addlakha, which originally appeared in *Public Culture*, Fall 2001, volume 13(3):511–31.

The Danish Ethnographic Society allowed us to republish "Dombá's spirit kidney: Transplant medicine and Suyá Indian cosmology" from *FOLK* (2003), volume 45:125–57.

The American Anthropological Association and the University of California Press granted permission to republish Matthew Kohrman's article "Why am I not disabled? Making state subjects, making statistics in post-Mao China" from *Medical Anthropology Quarterly*, March 2003, volume 17(1):5–24.

Introduction

Disability Connections

SUSAN REYNOLDS WHYTE AND BENEDICTE INGSTAD

The field of disability studies has flowered in the last decade, bringing together scholars and activists from many backgrounds and disciplines. With this book we offer a set of articles written by anthropologists. We believe that the study of disability challenges and enriches anthropology, and we take up issues that are currently of general interest in our branch of scholarly endeavor. But more than that, we would like to contribute to disability studies something that anthropology can provide, which may be of use and inspiration to others. This can be summed up as a combination of empirical commitment and comparative consciousness, what Geertz calls the "patient, modest, close-in work . . . sorting through concrete matters so as to develop circumstantial comparisons—specific inquiries into specific differences" (Geertz 2000:223). Circumstantial comparisons are those in which the surroundings (the time, place, conditions) of the phenomena compared are taken into account. The significance of circumstances is a fundamental principle of anthropology as is the importance of comparison, whether implicit or explicit, for reflecting and understanding.

The first collection of articles we edited, entitled *Disability and Culture* (Ingstad and Whyte 1995), was an attempt to show how cultural circumstances (such as assumptions about personhood) and social ones (such as the existence of disability institutions) shape the meaning of disability in different local worlds. Many of those contributions emphasized the different realities that constitute disability in different places: among the Punan Bah in Borneo or the Maasai in Tanzania. However, they also recognized the connections that bound local worlds to one another and to larger historical forces: the transfer of disability programs from Norway to Botswana, and the creation of a disability identity following the Sandinista revolution in Nicaragua.

1

In this volume we engage the issue of connections more thoroughly by moving from a concern with circumstances to a more explicit focus on context. Etymology can be suggestive. The Latin root of "circumstance" ("to stand around") implies static conditions that *are* there and must simply be recognized. That of "context" ("to weave together") suggests an intentional process of intertwining and interaction. Dilley (1999) invites us to think of context as a verb. To contextualize is to make connections between and within domains, to select from a range of possibilities those elements that help by their relevance to understand a phenomenon. Dilley uses the term "contextualizing moves" to focus attention on assertions of connectedness. This kind of meaning-making is undertaken by agents with purposes and interests, be they researchers or the social actors researchers study. No one is completely free to weave connections; it is a task of the researcher to examine the larger structures that shape the contextualizing possibilities in any situation.

Making disability connections, weaving links of relevance between located worlds, and between them and imagined ones of different scale: these are the projects of our contributors and also of their informants. We present these projects in two parts, which we call "Locating embodied identities" and "Localizing policy and technology," underlining the primacy of the local in the heuristic opposition of local and global worlds.

The chapters in Part 1 of the book explore subjectivities, the ways in which some-bodies experience themselves and their world through interacting with other subjects and imagining horizons. The examples are located, even though the point may be that they move from one locality to another, as do the participants in the Deaf World Games in Rome and the circumcised Somali women in London. The authors work close-in to situations where disability, identity, and subjectivity are managed: as a disfigured baby is brought home to Israeli parents who wanted to leave it at the hospital, as Indian and Egyptian couples confide experiences of infertility they cannot speak of publicly, as relatives enable or disable Delhi women as domestic and state citizens. But they also deploy comparison and reflection, stepping back from the details to analyze connections and disconnections in the weaving of embodied identities.

The chapters of Part 2 deal with technologies and policies—phenomena we often think of as "globalizable"—potentially flowing or being transferred from one part of the planet to another. The authors examine the specific connections or disconnections between the worlds in which people live and act, and the ways in which links are made (or not) to powerful broader visions and possibilities that might produce effects in the local world of social practice. The emphasis is on the particular processes by which techniques (like transplant medicine, mobility for polio survivors, making statistics about disability) are realized for some bodies (a Suyá "substance group") somewhere (eastern Ugandan border towns) sometime (in the last decade of Deng Xiaoping's life). In the case of genomics and prenatal screening, the debate is often disconnected and decontextualized, as we shall see. Policies for care of a growing population of disabled elderly and universal rules for securing the rights of disabled people, both in some sense abstract, are connected to moral worlds of families and care centers in northern Japan and the situations of families on the edge of the Kalahari in Botswana.

The basic approach is to start where people live, with their concerns and resources and the particular political ecology in which they are interacting. What is disabling for them there? This means that we do not necessarily assume the relevance of disability policy, declarations of rights, universal definitions, or identity politics for people's experience. Rather we ask how relations with powerful institutions, organizations, and media messages may affect their situations and their understandings of them. We are particularly interested in the uneven processes of change that can be traced as ideas and technologies spread.

Following our metaphor of weaving we devote this introduction to crosscutting themes and issues, linking the chapters to more general problems: the method of contextualizing, the uses of disability definitions, the effects of policy and technology, and the relation between subjectivity and citizenship. But first of all, we provide some political and scholarly background for this anthropological contribution to disability studies.

WHAT HAPPENED?

Stiker's history of disability, now translated into English (1999), traces Western formulations of normality and difference from biblical times, but stops short of the immensely important developments of the last few decades. Yet it is these recent political, legal, and social achievements that form the background for current scholarly interest in disability. Like the struggles for race and gender equality, the movement for disability rights was at once an effort for social justice and an inspiration to rethink and research: mobilizing, representing, and theorizing (Shakespeare and Watson 2001).

Although we think of the 1980s as the time when the United Nations weighed in on disability rights, there were already UN activities by the

1960s, as Bickenbach (2001:573) reports in his important review of disability human rights. In 1971, the UN adopted the first document on disability rights, the Declaration on the Rights of Mentally Retarded Persons, followed by the broader Declaration on the Rights of Disabled Persons in 1975. The World Programme of Action Concerning Disabled Persons came in 1982. The International Year (1981) and the Decade (1983–92) of Disabled Persons kept disability on the international agenda; African, Asian, and Arab decades were also declared.

The struggle was carried forward through the passage of the Americans with Disabilities Act (ADA) in 1990, the fruit of years of work by disability organizations. The ADA has been described as a "watershed event for disability rights on the international stage" (Braddock and Parish 2001:50). On the basis of clear findings of systematic exclusion and unequal treatment, the U.S. Congress barred discrimination in employment, public and private services, and accommodation. The link between scholarship and the history of disability rights is nowhere better illustrated than in the collection edited by Francis and Silvers (2000), in which a distinguished assembly of philosophers, jurists, political scientists, and sociologists explore the significance of the ADA.

National legislation was established in country after country in the 1990s. In the wealthier parts of the world Britain, Australia, Germany, Austria, Finland, Japan, and Hong Kong adopted laws or amended their constitutions to prohibit discrimination on the basis of disability. Similar steps were taken in some developing countries, including China, Brazil, the Philippines, South Africa, Malawi, and Uganda (Bickenbach 2001; Braddock and Parish 2001).

At the international level, efforts to create a legally binding convention on disability rights ran into difficulty. Instead the UN adopted the Standard Rules on the Equalization of Opportunities for Disabled Persons in 1994. Although this is an important instrument for monitoring and encouraging member states, it has no legal enforcement mechanisms. Disability-rights organizations pursued demands for a convention and in 2001 the Ad Hoc Committee was established by the UN General Assembly to consider proposals (DAA 2004). In August 2006 agreement was reached on the text of a Convention to Protect the Rights of Persons with Disabilities.

The common vision of disability and disability rights as a global issue has been strengthened by organizations such as Disabled Peoples' International, Rehabilitation International, and Disability Awareness in Action. At the same time, consciousness is growing on the part of policy makers including the World Bank, bilateral development agencies, and national governments that disability is a burgeoning political issue.

Sheer numbers of disabled people are increasing in developed countries as life expectancy lengthens and technological advances allow people to survive with impairments. Yet 80 percent of disabled people live in developing countries where longer life allows some to "achieve" the disabilities of old age, while diseases like AIDS, war, and inhuman work conditions produce disability for many millions more (Albrecht and Verbrugge 2000). Moreover, changes in demography, society, and economy mean that the broader social situation of people with disabilities has become more problematic (Ingstad 2001:789).

Coalitions of activists from the global North and South have made impressive achievements in promoting legislative change. They have also worked together to develop organizations, special education programs, and rehabilitation projects in developing countries. It is here most of all that differences in social worlds become evident. A recent contribution by Padmani Mendis (2004) examines the gap in assumptions between the independent-living movement, which has guided development in wealthier countries, and community-based rehabilitation programs that emphasize interdependence in resource-poor settings. Change interventions reveal differing suppositions about individuals in society. Even more, they entail (or should entail) confrontations with the realities of daily life for people with disabilities in particular worlds. Not only different values and conceptions of personhood but lack of resources, including social and health services, characterize the lifeworlds for which interventions are imagined (Ingstad 2001).

What has happened is that far-reaching changes have occurred in legislation, in disability activism, and in political awareness. One survey of 88 governments showed that "at least 80% of states had reformulated their thinking on disability issues in response to the UN rules" (Priestley 2001b:5). But the challenge is to see how much—or how little—the world has changed for the majority of disabled people and their families living in a great variety of particular situations. In invoking the perhaps overused contrast between local and global, we want to urge rethinking and research in the direction of greater differentiation and specificity. The conditions of life for most people with disabilities may not be changing as rapidly as political awareness.

DISABILITY SCHOLARSHIP

Scholarship and disability activism went hand in hand. The 1980s saw the emergence of disability studies as an important field of intellectual endeavor. As an interdisciplinary or multidisciplinary approach it reached across sociology, social psychology, political science, law, history, geography, development studies, public health, social work/policy, education, philosophy, literature, and the arts. It attracted people who wanted to make a difference: "Disability studies, like ethnic, women's and gay and lesbian studies, has developed from a position of engagement and activism rather than one of detachment" (Barnes et al. 2002:2).

In Britain, the United States, Canada, and Australia, disability-studies courses and programs began being offered at some universities. Two major journals were established. In the United States, the *Disability Studies Newsletter* (first published in 1980) became *Disability Studies Quarterly* in 1985 (Pfeiffer 2001:1). In Britain, *Disability, Handicap and Society* appeared in 1986 and was renamed *Disability and Society* in 1993. The proliferation of literature has been remarkable. The 852-page *Handbook of Disability Studies* (Albrecht et al. 2001), with its 34 chapters by prominent scholars, is a weighty landmark, but just one among other readers, collections, and special issues of journals (for example: L. Davis 1997; Jenkins 1998; Breckenridge and Vogler 2001; Priestley 2001a; Barnes et al. 2002; Corker and Shakespeare 2002).

Sociologists were early pioneers in the study of stigma, deviance, labeling, and chronic illness; and they continue to provide vital concepts for the study of disability. In their fine introductory book, Barnes and colleagues (1999) call for the application of C. Wright Mills's sociological imagination to the study of disability: that is, the exploration of "the links between structural conditions and people's lived experience of the process of disablement" (ibid.:211). While the concerns with policy, politics, and social mechanisms of differentiation remain central in the sociological approach, there is also an increasing phenomenological interest in the lived, embodied experience of disability (Michalko 1998,1999, 2002; Williams and Busby 2000; Corker and Shakespeare 2002).

Between anthropology and disability studies, a fruitful dialogue is under way in which the distinction between the two is being explored and shifted, drawn and blurred. On the one hand, disability studies is distinguished as a field in its own right and a special subfield within anthropology: "the growing field of disability studies in anthropology (part and parcel of the larger disability rights movement)," one of "the 'hottest' areas in medical anthropology today" (Inhorn 2004:132). On the other hand, anthropologists continue to produce penetrating ethnographies of great relevance to the study of disability, which are not explicitly identified as works of disability scholarship. These latter works can be sources of inspiration and challenge because they provide a variety of perspectives.

An institutional marking of the area occurred in the 1980s with the establishment of the Disability Research Interest Group under the Society for Medical Anthropology, a subsection of the American Anthropological Association (AAA). The group sponsors regular sessions on disability at the annual AAA meetings and also represents the interests of disabled anthropologists within the professional organization. A special issue of *Disability Studies Quarterly* (vol. 21, no. 3, 2001) was devoted to "engaging anthropology in disability studies." (See also Kasnitz and Shuttleworth 1999.) Testimony of that engagement is the recent issue of *Medical Anthropology Quarterly* (vol. 18, no. 2, 2004) honoring Joan Ablon, a pioneer in research on stigmatizing genetic conditions (for example, Ablon 1984).

People working at the interface between disability studies and anthropology emphasize the importance of ethnographic methods and the rich potential they offer (J. Davis 2000; Frank 2001; Shuttleworth and Kasnitz 2004:153). The last decade has seen the appearance of ethnographies that abundantly provide both empirical material on the lifeworlds and experience of disabled people, and fresh analytical perspectives. Some focus squarely on disability, such as Frank's (2000) cultural biography of Diane DeVries, a person without arms and legs who is a perfect example of an American woman. Breivik's (2001) research on the landscapes of deaf identification and belonging provides an example from Norway. Others take issues that lead on to disability through some particular technology or therapeutic approach, such as Rapp's (1999) monograph on amniocentesis in New York, or Mattingly's (1998) study of the narrative work of rehabilitation therapists.

Much of this research has been done in North America and Western Europe, but there is a growing body of work from other settings. Here too some scholars focus explicitly on disability, while others hardly mention the word although they make substantial contributions to the understanding of disability.

A prime example of the latter is Lawrence Cohen's (1998) monograph on Alzheimer's in India. Skillfully he contextualizes old age in India, drawing on fieldwork in poor neighborhoods of Varanasi and middle-class suburbs of Delhi. At the same time he keeps the comparative consciousness alert with discussions of the image of Alzheimer's in American tabloids and the history of geriatrics in biomedicine. One of the great strengths of the book is the combination of critical analysis of discourses on the social and biological aspects of dementia and the insistent grounding in real people and their families and the diversity of their situations.

Nor does Adriana Petryna (2002) identify herself as a disability scholar. Her book on biological citizenship after Chernobyl is an incisive portrayal of the interplay between the state, science, and Ukrainian citizens in the struggle for disability claims after the Chernobyl nuclear catastrophe. Her approach is from political economy, policy, and the specific characteristics of biomedicine in the Ukraine. Like Rapp's monograph on amniocentesis in New York, *Life Exposed* comes to disability issues through technology, in this case both medical and social. Making the "Chernobyl link" between symptom patterns and levels of exposure entitles one to claim a pension. Through portrayals of a whole range of people, Petryna shows what this can mean in the difficult circumstances of postsocialist transition. Her book is a singularly fine analysis of the way history intersects with biographies, the kind of sociological imagination of disability that Barnes and colleagues (1999) called for.

Like Petryna, Matthew Kohrman (2005) examines the relation between citizens and the state over a specific period of political history. His important monograph *Bodies of Difference* focuses squarely on disability as he traces the growth of institutional advocacy in modern China. He examines the relation between physically disabled people and what he calls "biobureaucracy," institutions responding to health and pathology in biological and biomedical terms (2005:3). His account of the growth of China's Disabled Persons' Federation is a national story, but his fieldwork in two very different sites (Beijing and the southeastern province of Hainan) and the attentiveness to gender and other social distinctions give his one story rich nuances. In his book, as in his chapter in this volume, he compellingly moves between the levels of lived experience and bureaucratic structure, showing how the organizational framework affects people's lives, and how it in turn is globally connected.

Disability studies in the global North takes an activist position. In the South, activism for change is often supported by development cooperation, whether through multilateral and bilateral programs or through the plethora of projects undertaken by NGOs, including DPOs—disabled people's organizations. Researchers working in developing countries are often concerned with different kinds of bodily disorders (the sequelae of leprosy and land mines, for instance) and different economic orders (scarce resources, weak state services). Community-based Rehabilitation (CBR), a fundamental policy in countries of the South, is hardly known in the North, where a stronger institutional infrastructure takes on the tasks communities are expected to manage in developing countries. Ingstad's (1997) monograph on CBR in Botswana is a rare in-depth ethnography.

The interest in using research to strengthen interventions by and for disabled people in the South and migrants to the North is reflected in the substantial collection edited by Holzer, Vreede, and Weigt (1999). Jeannine Coreil and colleagues (2003) have written a thoughtful study of an attempt to encourage support groups as an organizational form for poor Haitian women affected by the disabling tropical disease lymphatic filariasis. There is also an enormous gray literature on disability in developing countries, which is often an e-literature as more and more reports get posted on the Web. These kinds of studies offer insights into what activism is about in other settings and how scholarship can be applied critically and constructively in efforts for change.

Disability scholarship, including anthropological contributions, has grown immensely since our first edited collection appeared in 1995. Yet we feel there is still a need for work that provides a more radically comparative perspective through the juxtaposition of ethnographies and the questioning of global processes.

CONTEXTUALIZING MOVES IN LOCAL AND GLOBAL WORLDS

At first glance, the opposition "local and global worlds" in our title looks like a reference to two kinds of spaces or a description of two contrasting realities. But we would like to take the distinction as a heuristic device that can help us to ask questions rather than reinforce assumptions. Here the notion of contextualizing moves becomes useful. Instead of seeing the global as the given circumstances in which the local exists, we can ask in terms of the verb: "to contextualize," to weave together. What connections, and no less important, what disconnections are being made? By which actors? By ourselves as analysts? This means examining the positions from which people are speaking when they talk about the local and the global.

Bearing in mind the value of close-in work on concrete matters, there is one more point about context and the local and global that seems to us a good guideline: the need to be specific. As Strathern (1995a) argues, the focus on local worlds and society allows analytical discrimination and comparison, and the examination of connections. In contrast, the idea of global culture is totalizing and self-referential and closes off the possibility of examining relationships:

> Suppose we were to appropriate the epithet local for those locations where persons act, and act to make the world work. It would then be the point where they mobilise their resources, seek influence, labour,

> reproduce, spend energy, talk. The continuities people see between their
> actions—their effect on others, the reactions of colleagues, antecedents
> and futures, setting this in motion, in short the apprehension of a life
> that is larger than any of its moments—would be equally part of
> making the world work. (Strathern 1995b)

It is within such locations that we live and have a sense of scale against
which we can imagine a larger "global" world. And imagination of
expanded horizons has an "energizing effect," as Strathern goes on to say:
"The expanded horizon, like the world-view, is how things are made effective locally" (ibid.:180).

The injunction to be specific in problematizing the relation between
local and global worlds can be followed in two ways. First of all, we can ask
about the ways in which people imagine globality: to use Tsing's term, how
they invoke the global in connection with particular "projects" in the
worlds they are making work (Tsing 2000:347). This might mean calling
upon a universal set of values and ideals, such as the UN Standard Rules
for the Equalization of Opportunities for People with Disabilities. In
Uganda these have had an energizing effect on the commission that framed
the new constitution. Imagining an expanded horizon might mean not the
entire globe, but a vision of a larger world such as the state or the world of
white men's medicine. In any case, the discovery process is fruitful when
we ask who is imagining what and to which effect in a local world of
interaction.

Second, we can trace movements of people, things, images, ideas from
one local world to another. This means not only recognizing the flow of
phenomena but specifying—in Tsing's metaphor—the channels through
which they move and the landscape changes that such flows might bring
about. A number of scholars and activists have made the point that
"globalization" or "global flows" catch some people in their currents and not
others. We sometimes talk of technology as if it will spread out democrati-
cally and change lives; IVF treatment of infertility may be in the process of
globalization, but the channels through which it flows are not accessible to
the majority of infertile couples in Indian and Egyptian local worlds.

While all the chapters to follow are about conceptualizing moves by
researchers and the actors they study, Ingstad is the most explicit about the
problem of context. She takes a document, the UN Standard Rules, whose
vision is universal and asks how relevant that vision is for families with a
disability in Botswana's Kweneng District.[1] As she and her co-worker
revisit families they had met sixteen years earlier, they learn what has happened to their disabled members in terms of health, care, education,

employment, marriage, and children—areas for which the Standard Rules lay down a set of guidelines. In relating the situations in which they lived (and, for 26%, died), Ingstad makes connections to aspects of rural life in Botswana: the need for single mothers to leave their disabled children in the village with their grandmothers so that they can earn a living to support the family; high death rates from AIDS and other diseases; lack of transport to the nearest (minimally equipped) health centers. The UN Standard Rules are not located somewhere in the global; they were developed in major cities in the North and adopted in the UN General Assembly in New York. They are taken up or not in particular countries by lawmakers or organizations and used for advocacy or ornamentation. Ingstad draws attention to the lack of connection between disabled families in Kweneng District and any program or organization that might have invoked the UN rules. But she also shows that the rules themselves were developed in a context in which certain assumptions made sense—assumptions that did not necessarily hold for the families in Kweneng.

DEFINING DISABILITY

If "local" and "global" worlds are terms that raise questions, the other word in our title, "disability," is the object of intense debate. There are substantive questions about which diagnoses and prognoses should be included. Should one distinguish between chronic illness and disability? What kinds of conditions count? "Can a fat woman call herself disabled?" is the title of an article (Cooper 1997) in the journal *Disability and Society.* What about AIDS? What of incontinence? There are questions of degree and the interplay between impairment and a person's will and ability to participate in daily life. How poorly should someone see or hear to be reckoned disabled? Is a person born without a leg disabled if she has the combination of prosthesis and stamina to climb Kilimanjaro, as did a former mayor of Oslo?

These are not necessarily crucial questions for anthropologists. We are interested in people's own experiences of what is disabling in their world rather than in some universal definition. These experiences must be connected to (contextualized, woven together with) the process of defining disability and the shared criteria brought into play in particular settings. The chapters to follow do not restrict themselves to the conventional prototypes of sensory, motor, and intellectual disability. They include infertility, kidney insufficiency, facial birthmark, and disabilities of old age. Scheper-Hughes and Ferreira show how anomalies manifest at birth among Suyá and Mehinaku peoples of the Brazilian Amazon may be defined as inhuman, whereas conditions like that of their protagonist Dombá, which set in later in life, are valued indications of the person's ability to overcome adversity.

A clear example of such processes is unfolded in the chapter by Aud Talle on female circumcision in Somalia and London. In Somalia, women's bodies were complete and meaningful when they were closed, and the smoother the closure, the more beautiful. Pain and obstetric difficulties were part of women's lives, but on the marriage market, openness was more of a disability than closure. Fleeing war in Somalia, women who relocated to another world in London experienced the horrified gaze of doctors and the whispers of strangers. They learned that their bodies were defective (even mutilated) and in need of surgical rehabilitation, which was reckoned particularly successful in cases where a clitoris was discovered intact under scar tissue. Women who settled in London took up life not in a global world, but in a local one with neighborhoods, Western Union offices, family practitioners, the African Women's Clinic with its Somali gynecologist. However, they also met the powerful effect of globalism being invoked in the name of the campaign against "female genital mutilation." That was part of the context in which they experienced their bodies. What was equally important, as Talle points out, was their whole situation of exile and loss, which they connected to other corporal defects as well—obesity, diabetes, and heart problems. Shifting contexts meant different criteria for assessing bodies and different social identities, now marked with the stigmata of closure. Talle's example may have more general relevance, in that migration to new circumstances often leads to new awareness as people recontextualize their mindful bodies. Further research should examine how displacement is related to changing consciousness of disability.

So does it matter what kinds of definitions and classifications policy makers and authoritative experts establish? It matters a great deal to those who set themselves the task of producing statistics that can be compared within and across political units. The efforts that WHO has put into revising the International Classification of Impairments, Disabilities, and Handicaps (WHO 1980) bear witness to the significance of such a tool for the universalist project of comparison and technical assistance. It matters as well to disability activists in countries of the North who took issue with the implicit "medical model" underlying the first Classification and the neglect of social and cultural aspects, summarized as the "social model" (Pfeiffer 1998). What was at stake was the weight given to biomedical vis-à-vis social factors in disabling (and enabling) people. The argument was that focusing on factors in society and culture (in a sense, on context) would reveal barriers and facilitate change.

The revision, entitled the International Classification of Functioning, Disability, and Health and known as ICF (WHO 2001), tried to combine the two models. It adopted a universal view of disability as something everyone can experience in the course of a life, rather than a specific set of conditions embodied by minority groups and subject to identity politics (Bickenbach et al. 1999). Thus the new classification, even more explicitly than its predecessor, "democratizes" disability; many kinds of conditions qualify (which is also the principle we have adopted in this collection).

The ICF tried to avoid the pejorative connotations that disability activists had criticized in the first classification. The negative concepts "impairment," "disability," and "handicap" were replaced by the more neutral "body structures/functions," "activity" (ability or actual performance), and "participation" (involvement in life situations). A fourth level, "environmental factors," concerns physical, social, and attitudinal factors that form the background for a person's life. The term "disability" is thus freed for more general use, referring to functionality at all four levels (Lollar 2002). ICF is meant as a universal tool for classifying disability in a culturally neutral manner.

The studies that tested the cross-cultural applicability of the classification at 15 study sites in 13 countries are presented in a book published by WHO (Üstün et al. 2001) that also gives a thorough discussion of the methods used. On that basis, we can see several problems with the claim to cross-cultural applicability. The samples are drawn mainly from urban settings in developing, not least developed, countries (only one African example). The resource persons interviewed were mainly professionals, and the methods were biased toward disabled people with a relatively high degree of literacy. The focus was on the individual rather than the care unit, and on articulated opinions and attitudes expressed in interviews rather than practices and observations from field studies. Political economy, including factors like poverty and armed conflict, were not mentioned as causes and contexts of disability.

Importantly, the authors found great variation between the study sites as to whether different disabilities were stigmatized and how easily people having them could be integrated. But given the methodological problems of this project of definition, classification, and enumeration, we believe that in-depth studies in a wider variety of settings are absolutely necessary as supplements and correctives.

The process of defining disability and using a classification is the theme of Kohrman's chapter on making subjects and statistics in post-Mao China. Kohrman starts with the consequences that China's classification of disabilities had for Ma Zhun, a woman who had lost the toes on her right foot in an industrial accident. Because this impairment did not qualify her for a disability ID, she stood to lose her job at a small factory that was laying off workers but needed to meet a quota of 1.7 percent disabled staff. Ma Zhun wonders where these definitions of disability came from—and so does Kohrman. He reconstructs their genealogy with care, showing how at a particular juncture of political history a team of Chinese experts interacting with UN agencies designed and executed the National Sample Survey of Disability in 1987. The story could be read as one of globalization: disability criteria spread through UN channels in the period when awareness was high during the UN Decade for the Disabled. It could also be read as a story of modernity's or the state's fascination with statistics. But Kohrman does the "patient, close-in work" of finding out who actually developed the survey and what they were concerned about. He argues that the elite government actors were negotiating their own identities, positioning themselves in a changing political landscape and doing so partly with an eye to how the survey would represent China in the international scene. Kohrman's contextualizing moves are informative; the connections he makes leave us with an overwhelming impression of the historical contingency of the definition of disability—and of the consequent exclusion of Ma Zhun from the category that might have insured her job. His example also opens a whole set of questions about how bodily and mental differences are shaped and given meaning through policies and programs.

ORGANIZING IDENTITIES

The significance of disability depends on its context, and an important part of the context is the existence of "solutions" or programs for management of disability. It is not simply that disability is a "problem" and programs are put in place to solve it. Rather, the "solutions"—the programs and technologies that are being implemented, or that are imagined and planned—influence people's perception of what the problem is. In fact they play a role in identifying people and in shaping people's own self-understanding.

At an elementary level, programs sort people into different categories—as disabled, elderly, infertile, HIV-positive—although all might be considered people with disabilities. In Norway and Denmark, as in many other countries of the North, there is an enormous difference between the public support given to young adults with severe intellectual disabilities and older people with dementia. The "disabled" have rights to their own residence and caretaker, whereas the "elderly senile" must wait for a vacancy in a nursing home that is often understaffed (and elders who are "merely" physically impaired may not get any place at all). That people with similar needs on a functional level are perceived and treated so differently may be partly due to life experience and age of onset, but it is also a result of the way institutional structures make identity (and compatibility) seem natural (Breitenbach 2001).

The identity-shaping effects of institutions and programs have long fascinated sociologists from Goffman (1961) to the labeling theorists (Becker 1963; Scott 1970) who focused on the way identities as blind or mentally ill were formed in interaction with medical, social, and educational professionals and bureaucracies. As identity politics infused the understanding of disability in North America and Europe, it became evident that political activism as well as stigma could be the product of social processes (Anspach 1979). The challenge to sociology was forcefully put by a new generation of disability researchers who emphasized the importance of disabled peoples' self-organization (Barnes et al. 1999:153–80). However, some disability-studies scholars have expressed doubt about the extent to which disability can or should be a category like others (race, gender, sexual orientation) for pursuing identity politics (L. Davis 2001).

A more recent theoretical development of relevance for the issue of organization and identity brings anthropologists and sociologists together around the idea of biosociality advanced by Rabinow (1996). The formation of associational communities and collective identities around biomedical categories is particularly pronounced in the United States and Europe. Support and self-help groups are found for people with every kind of chronic condition or disability, including the results of medical interventions (colostomies, mastectomies). The age of genetics has witnessed the growth of groups (also online chat groups) for people with heritable conditions: "the mobilization of an identity anchored in a genetically marked category" (Rapp et al. 2001:393).

Rapp's work on support groups for parents of Down syndrome children in New York (Rapp 1999:285–303) shows that for some (mostly middle-class whites) there is a trajectory from the diagnosis to membership in a group that provides emotional and practical support as well as information. The idea of "biological citizenship" (Petryna 2002; Rose and Novas 2004)—that people's sense of belonging and relations to each other and the state may be based in a biological condition—does not necessarily mean that they accept the authority of biomedicine or science in general. They may be lobbying against what they perceive as hegemony or trying to influence the direction and use of scientific research. But in their very opposition they are organizing and identifying themselves in terms of a biomedical category.

Rabinow's discussion of biosociality and Rose and Novas's programmatic piece on biological citizenship are based in societies with well-developed biomedical systems. They concern that portion of the citizenry that has the social, cultural, and economic capital to engage in these kinds of associations. Recently these concepts have been used to analyze historical processes in other settings (Biehl 2004; Nguyen 2005). There are examples from developing countries of "post-test clubs" for people who have tested for HIV and a few more specialized organizations such as the Association of Parents of Children with Hydrocephalus and Spina Bifida in Uganda (Whyte 2004). But what is interesting for our purposes here is not to show the identity effects of biomedicine so much as to ask about how associational communities and disability identities might emerge and be used, and how they fit with other forms of sociality. From the point of view of people living in a local world, what kinds of connections are instrumental in developing a community and identity of disability?

There are surprisingly few answers to this question based on good empirical material. One of the best studies we know from a Southern setting is Silla's (1998) historical work on leprosy and identity in twentieth-century Mali. Silla shows how the establishment of leprosaria by missionaries and later the implementation of vertical treatment programs by WHO led to the transition from commonality to community. People with leprosy left their rural homes to move near clinics and remained in town with others like themselves after being cured. Silla shows that a group identity as lepers developed out of an interplay of institutional catalysts, a critical mass of similar disabled people, and common interests in survival strategies (including begging). In 1991 a formal association of leprosy patients emerged to overshadow earlier informal groupings, such as the one formed by women beggars. The new organization had more educated leaders, and it joined the national disability federation and took up an agenda of disability rights.

The chapter by Whyte and Muyinda traces the mobilization of people with mobility impairments in two border towns in eastern Uganda. Accused of being smugglers, they counter by asserting their rights as disabled people. In contrast to the situations in Mali and western Tanzania (Van den Bergh 1995), it was not treatment institutions or training programs that drew disabled people to town. They were seeking opportunities they did not have in their villages. In Jackson's words (2002:119), they were looking first of all for a life, not an identity. People used connections with relatives and friends to come to town from rural areas, and to obtain their most essential capital: a hand-crank tricycle. Physical mobility was necessary for social extension and political mobilization. Getting a life in the particular niche of cross-border trade that they were exploiting brought them together around common interests; they formed an association to support those interests and took advantage of the national requirement that disabled people be represented on district and municipal councils. While the political organization of people with disabilities is countrywide, some people identify themselves as disabled far more actively than others. In Busia and Malaba, men with motor impairments form the core of organization, whereas women and people with other disabilities are far less active. Whyte and Muyinda draw connections to the political economy of the border region, to the role of donors in supporting rehabilitation projects, and to Uganda's policy on disability.

Both the lepers in Mali and the mobility-disabled in eastern Uganda came together around common interests in particular local worlds. From there they made contacts to national and even international organizations; in Tsing's terms they could invoke the global in their rhetoric; they also connected with people from outside their immediate localities who passed on new ideas and new social technologies that they could use in their own local situations. Even in European countries, where institutions and organizations have been in place for some time to provide services or advocate for people with disabilities, the importance of grounding fellowship in specific projects and experiences of commonality should not be underestimated, as shown in Priestley's work (1995) on an organization of blind Asians in Leeds. Organizations do not determine practices and identities, but they facilitate them. What people do with the identity offered by a program or an organization varies enormously, as we shall see. A dramatic and instructive example, in relation to the theme of this book, is the celebration of fellowship at the Deaf World Games.

Haualand's use of the term "sacred occasion" to capture the meaning of the biennial Deaflympics is to the point. Not only is symbolism explicit, but the event has the qualities of a ritual as described by Geertz (1966) when the imagined world of ultimate reality is for a short time realized in this world. Inspired by Victor Turner's analysis of pilgrimages, Haualand's chapter shows how a sense of communitas is experienced by the deaf tourists, who come from many different countries, using different sign languages.

She suggests that the power of the sacred occasion lies in the experience of liberation from everyday constraints—in another place that is transformed for a short space of time. The diversity of participants highlights the commonality they celebrate: not so much their deafness as their form of communication and sense of a common culture. Like the other contributors Haualand traces particular connections being made by her interlocutors. This is not a global world in some abstract sense, but a two-week local world of their own creation in which they also make contacts to people living in other local worlds, with whom they may visit or correspond in the future. In their continuing connections, technologies of the internet, e-mail, and mobile-phone short text messages will play an important part. But again, as Haualand (referring to Bauman [1998]) reminds us, these are not global in the sense of universal, but selective in terms of who has access to them.

THE WINDING CHANNELS OF TECHNOLOGY

Like policies and programs, technology seems to have the capacity to identify, define, and transform the significance of disability.[2] The advent of tests for HIV, for example, makes it possible to know who has an impairment of the immune system; this knowledge can be used to disable someone, if passed to an employer who discriminates. For many people in wealthier countries, antiretroviral-drug technology makes AIDS a disability to be lived with rather than a death sentence. As in the case of policies, programs, and organizations, however, technology must be analyzed and understood within a social context. God's-eye views (or global announcements) of the transformative power of a given technology are not so much our concern here. Rather we examine the positions from which such announcements are made, the ways in which technology becomes accessible, and the implications it has in specific settings.

In her chapter, Lock confronts these problems directly in taking on the hype and hope of genomics, which promises to prevent certain types of hereditary impairments or by prenatal screening to allow selection by abortion. She is careful to link pronouncements on the significance of genomic research and technology to particular positions, and she emphasizes the need to contextualize. Technology in the broad sense of ideas, procedures, equipment, social relations, and discursive practices must be analyzed within the particular settings where it is developed and used. Many involved scientists, whether they are for or against germline engineering, have a universalistic vision of how new genetic technology might help insure health as a human right and avoid the suffering caused by some kinds of disability. However, practically none of them are discussing resource use or inequality of access within societies or between wealthier and poorer countries (the "health-genomics divide"). Examining the application and impact of genomic technology within families and communities is a pressing task; the implementation of genetic testing and screening has varied and sometimes unexpected consequences. What is particularly striking is the laissez-faire practice that leaves eugenic decisions to individuals and families in those countries where genetic screening is becoming routine.

Prenatal screening and eugenic technology are addressed critically by scholars within disability studies (Shakespeare 1998; Asch 2001; Wolbring 2001). They point to what they see as an underlying assumption that disabled lives are not worth living.[3] However, anthropologists working in this field underline the complexity of these issues for the families involved. Just as Lock challenges the tendency toward genetic reductionism that sees gene technology as the best way to improve human life, so can one also question the view that it is an absolute denial of the dignity and value of disabled people. For one thing, the kinds of impairments for which genetic technology is relevant are limited at the present and different from one another. To lump them all together as "disability" may be as deceptive as is counseling of pregnant women that does not include qualified information on life with the particular condition that has been diagnosed. Moreover, technology is realized within a lifeworld. Ethnographers like Rapp show that even within one city the implications of screening for Down syndrome are different for different people living different lives. Her hydraulic formulation fits well with the metaphors of flows and channels: "At stake in the analysis of the traffic between biomedical and familial discourses is an understanding of the inherently uneven seepage of science and its multiple uses and transformations into contemporary social life" (Rapp 1999:303). That unevenness of seepage is dramatically obvious in the case of another kind of reproductive technology, the treatment of infertility, now becoming possible for urban elites in developing countries.

In Egypt and in India, as in many countries of the South where kinship frames and bears social life, infertility is a disability in terms of most definitions, though it is seldom recognized as such by policy makers, researchers, or the public. In their chapter, Inhorn and Bharadwaj show how reproductive impairment is an impairment of personhood; just as inability to walk restricts social development and fulfillment in Uganda, so does inability to have children inhibit that extension of sociality that is fundamental to growth and life in these two pronatal countries. The stigma of this basic and intimate deficit is so great that those who bear it find it difficult to speak of it—though others talk too much. Neither the positive acceptance of child-free living nor adoption are endorsed as responses to fertility impairment in Egypt and India. Nor are support groups an option for the silent women who also take on the stigma when the impairment lies with their husbands. But the advent of new reproductive technologies has far-reaching implications. So far the winding channels that bring IVF to Egypt and India are accessible to urban more than rural residents, and to middle-class and upper-class more than poor treatment seekers. Yet in both countries, the new medical procedures were accompanied by media publicity about "test-tube babies"; they drew attention to the problem of infertility while providing a new discourse about it. New technology helps to break the silence, but it also medicalizes disability by defining it as a disease that can be treated (at private clinics!) rather than a difference that can be accepted and lived with.

One of the most important dimensions in the study of technological change is its implications for patterns of sociality. We have seen that laissez-faire eugenics seems to leave weighty existential decisions to individual women in North America. Each must take responsibility for determining whether a genetically impaired and possibly disabled child should be brought into the world. New reproductive technology in Egypt and India also seems to treat persons as individuals (although Inhorn and Bharadwaj make the interesting point that the seekers of "rehabilitation" are often couples who share the burden of silence and support one another more sympathetically than many spouses who have children). In any case, they are not motivated to form associations, but act instead as patients and customers if they are able. In eastern Uganda, mobility technology (tricycles are also new technology there) had the opposite effect of facilitating association based on common interests and problems. In trying to understand these different social aspects of technology, scholars weave together elements such as the characteristics of the impairment, the techniques and equipment available, the political economy of disability, and the morality and values of personhood, on a loom of historical contingency.

Scheper-Hughes and Ferreira spin a strong story of technology and sociality out of the stuff of a kidney transplant and a cosmology of partible substance. The account in their chapter is mostly in the words of Dombá, a Suyá from Brazil's Xingu Indigenous Park who twines the narrative of his increasing disability onto the web of relationships that make up his world: to his wife, his father and brother-in-law, both shamans who took the form of birds to visit him in the hospital, his relatives, his surgeon, the animals of which he dreams, and the kidney spirit of the young white man who died in a car crash. People in many societies are concerned about the relation between an organ donor and recipient; sometimes this concern extends to the family of a deceased donor to whom a debt of gratitude is felt. Scheper-Hughes and Ferreira write of changes in the corporeal imaginary—perhaps we could say the social ontology of the body—as transplant technology becomes routine and people think of body parts as spares that can be separated from selves and sold or circulated. What is unique about Dombá's corporal imaginary is his embeddedness in a group where relatedness is conceived as exchanging and sharing substances. Not only he but his entire substance group incorporated a white man's kidney, and to a certain extent they all have to live with the side effects of immunosuppressive drugs. They all observe dietary restrictions, and they share the dangers and powers of the white man's spirit kidney. This is a tale of the appropriation of technology in a local Amazonian world that expands to embrace the tenth floor of a prestigious São Paulo hospital. In a sense, as Scheper-Hughes and Ferreira suggest, it is also a subtle critique of biomedical fundamentalisms.

EMBODIED SUBJECTS AND CITIZENS

We have suggested that authoritative identifications of people as disabled, as well as technologies of eugenics, treatment, and rehabilitation, can have far-reaching consequences for the lives of people with disabilities and their families. They *can* have, but when and how *do* they have effects on identities and life chances? This question problematizes assumptions about the formation of subjects and subjectivities and the related notion of citizenship. If citizenship is about how people as subjects are defined and shaped by authority, it is also about how they in turn understand themselves and act to make claims, demand protection, communicate, and seek information. Investigating it requires close-in work in specific settings and a comparative consciousness of differences.

The notions of biosociality and biological citizenship in countries of the North depend, as Das and Addlakha point out in their chapter, on locating subjects within a liberal political regime in which individuals can form associations in civil society to influence the state and the course of scientific research. They propose a "productive disturbance" to this approach by examining the way citizenship can be performed as belonging—not only in relation to the state but also with regard to the domestic sphere. Instead of seeing the domestic as the private in contrast to the public, they suggest that different kinds of public are created in relation to families with disabled members. The research task is to trace the ways that domestic belonging is played out and how national citizenship is invoked and used in this process. This agenda is particularly relevant in relation to issues of sexuality and reproduction, which are performed in the domestic sphere; the role of the state is limited to legal regulation. Das and Addlakha use three examples from Delhi of disabled women whose marital and reproductive lives were spun between natal and conjugal families, and at sites that included a psychiatric ward and a civil registry office. They show how the parents of Mandira, a young woman with a disfiguring birthmark on her face, managed to help her get a husband despite the disapproval of the wider kinship group, a public that voiced itself in gossip and rumors. Mandira's parents made use of her rights as a state citizen to have a civil marriage, and they paid a price in terms of their position in their kin group. Two other cases concerned married women who suffered long-term mental illness. In the psychiatric ward, a site associated with the state, they talked about their families, and especially about their husbands. Yet their diagnoses meant that their voices were discounted as mad, and their husbands made use of this in their playing out of relations in the domestic sphere. We see how family and community complement and articulate with state citizenship.

This articulation is also in focus in the Israeli situation described by Weiss. In her book (2002:137) and in her chapter in this volume, she posits a "cultural script" underlying Israeli glorification of the healthy body and its devaluation of the disabled one. Eugenic practices include wide use of prenatal screening and selective abortion, and donor insemination choices that emphasize certain desired traits. Newborns are carefully scrutinized; Weiss gives disturbing examples of failure to bond with a newborn who has a visible impairment, even one with a good prognosis such as cleft lip. About 50 percent of babies born with impairments were abandoned at the hospital; Weiss claims that Israel is number one in the world in the rate of rejection of impaired children. The proportion was much higher for those with visible defects than for those with internal problems. Even those who were "adopted" (accepted) by their own parents, sometimes after a liminal period in which cosmetic surgery was done, were often treated as anomalies. The story of Pazit, a child born with both facial and internal impairments, and grudgingly accepted by her parents, is a haunting account of rejection and seclusion in a darkened corridor, "a ghetto for monsters." Weiss considers the suggestion of Das and Addlakha that the Israeli case exemplifies a denial of domestic citizenship; visibly impaired children are protected only by their state citizenship. However, she has reservations because she finds that the focus on domestic citizenship distracts from examining the cultural construction of the state itself, which legitimizes "a particular culture of eugenics." Nor did domestic citizenship insure care and support for those children who were taken home. The alignment of state and domestic spheres is striking. Whereas Das and Addlakha are interested in how belonging is performed in relation to issues of sexuality and reproduction, Weiss draws attention to an underlying cultural script that pervades all spheres of life but is clearly illustrated by parents' responses to the body image of their newborns.

At the other end of the lifecourse are disabled elderly people whose lives are played out in various configurations of state and domestic spheres. With its increased longevity and high proportion of elders, Japan is an opportune setting in which to examine the interweaving of state policy, family responsibility, and moral obligations. Traphagan worked in Tohoku, the northern part of the main island of Honshu, a partly agricultural area where multigenerational households are still common (although these are declining overall in Japan). In his chapter, he describes a moral world in which care of the elderly is the duty of a daughter-in-law or a daughter. At the same time, disabilities of old age can be construed as antisocial: they make one a burden on family members, requiring constant care, and render one unable to reciprocate. The ideal of continual effort at self-actualization and social engagement becomes a basis for assessing elderly people: Are they doing everything possible to avoid the unfortunate situation of dependence? Failing to remain sufficiently active carries a moral stigma. Traphagan shows how such basic assumptions about morality are woven together with public and private programs of care that are only acceptable as safety nets. Recently the Japanese state instituted a long-term-care insurance program similar to one that had been put in place in Germany. Costs to national and local governments are considerable, and this is the context in which Traphagan places the ambivalent rhetoric that both explains the program and encourages people not to use it. The moral discourse on individual effort and pursuit of socially shared interests in order to postpone the inevitable disabilities of age is mobilized by government officials and forms part of older people's presentations of themselves.

CONNECTING POSITIONS

The chapters to follow position people. They take perspectives—sometimes of disabled people, sometimes of others—and show how points of view relate to one another. They do not pretend to "speak for disabled people," although they often provide such a lifelike description of a situation that they awaken empathy and understanding. The task is rather to show what connections are important to actors and what connections the researcher finds useful for comprehending the situation. The accounts are of relations between actors in local worlds, to institutions, and to policies, classifications, technologies, and discourses that are taken as "global." At the same time they illustrate how disconnections are experienced and even facilitated.

It is striking that in the local worlds described here, disability is not a condition of individuals alone but a matter that is shared by relatives. The relevance of domestic and kinship relationships as a primary context for understanding disability is so clear in the ethnography, and so often overlooked in discourses about technology, policy, and human rights. Dombá's shaman brother-in-law in the form of a bird tapping his beak at the hospital window in São Paulo, Thandi's siblings in Botswana pushing her to school in a wheelbarrow: the descriptions of everyday lives with disability depict connections with family members. The metaphor of weaving together is enacted on the bodies of Somali women in Somalia in that the stitching closed of women's genitals realizes the binding ties of agnation; the very word for sewing also refers to agnatic kinship.

It is not that connections to relatives are necessarily supportive and enduring. One of the important contributions of the ethnographers is to show how family relations are enhanced and transformed, as in the case of the Ugandan tricyclists, or severed, as when Israeli parents abandon disfigured newborns at the hospital. Das and Addlakha's focus on domestic citizenship draws attention to just this use of state institutions by family members who are trying to live their lives, deal with other kin, and care for a disabled person.

The relevance of social and biomedical technology is a matter for empirical exploration. It does seem that new ways of attending to differences of the body and the person are emerging in many settings as new discourses and new "solutions" appear. But the connections to programs and treatment that can be made by some are out of reach for others, as the case of new reproductive technologies in developing countries so sharply illustrates. The divide is not only between countries in the North and the South, but within them.

The theme of local and global worlds draws attention to the ways in which people living in a world are touched by or reach out for programs, visions, and technologies that seem to open broader horizons. It is our argument that the energizing potential of human-rights declarations, progressive policies, and national statements of intent toward disabled citizens has to be measured in the context of local worlds. For that is where people are acting to make things work, and where the potentials may (or may not) be effected and effective as they were intended to be. Sacred occasions, like the two-week celebration of deaf culture in Rome, are transformative periods for those who attend and a source of inspiration for many others. But what also matter are the follow-up links and the relevance of the vision for the everyday worlds to which people return.

For anthropology, the study of disability helps to bring home a realization of our own positioning in the world. Each of us undertakes studies not only about a world, but in a world or worlds. The connections we have woven here, our descriptions and arguments about disabilities and contexts, can have effects. They can raise questions, and they can be questioned. That is our goal with this collection.

NOTES

1. Bauman distinguishes between universalizing and being globalized, pointing to the vision of making a new and better order on a global scale that has seemingly been replaced by a sense of being caught up in processes without a center and beyond anyone's control: Universalization "declared the intention to make similar the life conditions of everyone and everywhere, and so everybody's life chances; perhaps even make them equal" (1998:59). Our approach to both these concepts is different in that we wish to trace the specific connections that he skips over in his attempt to paint a broad picture.

2. Discussions about technology and disability tend to focus on the consequences of new technology, a pattern that we also fall into here. But we should not forget that the implementation of "old technology" has had far-reaching effects in developing countries. There is no doubt, for example, that vaccination programs against polio and measles have prevented many people from becoming disabled. In developing countries with well-functioning health-care systems it is rare to see polio victims under 20 or 30 years of age, and brain damage from encephalitis following measles is also less frequent.

3. A similar position is taken by people who oppose cochlear implantation on the ground that it denies the dignity and normality of life as a deaf person and inhibits socialization into the signing community. By facilitating normalization, technology is seen as denying the value of difference.

REFERENCES

Ablon, J. 1984. *Little People in America: The Social Dimensions of Dwarfism.* New York: Praeger.
Albrecht, G. L., K. D. Seelman, and M. Bury, eds. 2001. *Handbook of Disability Studies.* Thousand Oaks: Sage.

Albrecht, G. L., and L. M. Verbrugge. 2000. The global emergence of disability. In *Handbook of Social Studies in Health and Medicine*, ed. G. L. Albrecht, R. Fitzpatrick, and S. C. Scrimshaw, 293–307. London: Sage.

Anspach, R. 1979. From stigma to identity politics: Political activism among the physically disabled and former mental patients. *Social Science and Medicine* 13A: 765–73.

Asch, A. 2001. Disability, bioethics, and human rights. In *Handbook of Disability Studies*, ed. G. L. Albrecht, K. D. Seelman, and M. Bury, 297–326. Thousand Oaks: Sage.

Barnes, C., G. Mercer, and T. Shakespeare. 1999. *Exploring Disability: A Sociological Introduction*. Cambridge: Polity.

Barnes, C., M. Oliver, and L. Barton, eds. 2002. *Disability Studies Today*. Cambridge: Polity.

———. 2002. Introduction. In *Disability Studies Today*, ed. C. Barnes, M. Oliver, and L. Barton, 1–17. Cambridge: Polity.

Bauman, Z. 1998. *Globalization: The Human Consequences*. New York: Columbia University Press.

Becker, H. 1963. *Outsiders: Studies in the Sociology of Deviance*. New York: Free Press.

Bickenbach, J. E. 2001. Disability human rights, law, and policy. In *Handbook of Disability Studies*, ed. G. L. Albrecht, K. D. Seelman, and M. Bury, 565–84. Thousand Oaks: Sage.

Bickenbach, J. E., S. Chatterji, E. M. Badley, and T. B. Üstün. 1999. Models of disablement, universalism and the international classification of impairments, disabilities and handicaps. *Social Science and Medicine* 48: 1173–87.

Biehl, J. 2004. Global pharmaceuticals, AIDS, and citizenship in Brazil. *Social Text* 22: 105–32.

Braddock, D. L., and S. L. Parish. 2001. An institutional history of disability. In *Handbook of Disability Studies*, ed. G. L. Albrecht, K. D. Seelman, and M. Bury, 11–68. Thousand Oaks: Sage.

Breckenridge, C. A., and C. Vogler, eds. 2001. *The Critical Limits of Embodiment: Reflections on Disability Criticism*. Public Culture 13(3). Durham: Duke University Press.

Breitenbach, N. 2001. Aging with intellectual disabilities; discovering disability with old age: same or different? In *Disability and the Life Course: Global Perspectives*, 231–39. Cambridge: Cambridge University Press.

Breivik, J.-K. 2001. Deaf identities in the making: Metaphors and narrations in translocal lives. Doctoral thesis, University of Oslo.

Cohen, L. 1998. *No Aging in India: Alzheimer's, the Bad Family, and Other Modern Things*. Berkeley and Los Angeles: University of California Press.

Cooper, C. 1997. Can a fat woman call herself disabled? *Disability and Society* 12: 31–41.

Coreil, J., G. Mayard, and D. Addiss. 2003. *Support Groups for Women with Lymphatic Filariasis in Haiti*. Social, Economic and Behavioural Report Series 2. Geneva: WHO/TDR.

Corker, M., and T. Shakespeare, eds. 2002. *Disability/Postmodernity: Embodying Disability Theory*. London: Continuum.

Disability Awareness in Action [DAA]. 2004. United Nations Convention Protecting the Rights and Dignity of Disabled Persons. *Disability Tribune*, June/July 2004: 5–8.

Davis, J. M. 2000. Disability studies as ethnographic research and text: Research strategies and roles for promoting social change? *Disability and Society* 15: 191–206.

Davis, L. J. ed. 1997. *The Disability Studies Reader*. New York: Routledge.

———. 2001. Identity politics, disability, and culture. In *Handbook of Disability Studies*, ed. G. L. Albrecht, K. D. Seelman, and M. Bury, 535–45. Thousand Oaks: Sage.

Dilley, R. 1999. Introduction: The problem of context. In *The Problem of Context*, ed. R. Dilley, 1–46. Oxford: Berghan.

Francis, L. P., and A. Silvers, eds. 2000. *Americans with Disabilities: Exploring Implications of the Law for Individuals and Institutions*. New York: Routledge.

Frank, G. 2000. *Venus on Wheels: Two Decades of Dialogue on Disability, Biography, and Being Female in America*. Berkeley and Los Angeles: University of California Press.

———. 2001. Anthropology/disability studies: Toward reflection and dialogue. Paper presented to the annual meeting of the American Anthropological Association, Washington D.C.

Geertz, C. 1966. Religion as a cultural system. In *Anthropological Approaches to the Study of Religion*, ed. M. Banton, 1–46. London: Tavistock.

———. 2000. *Available Light: Anthropological Reflections on Philosophical Topics*. Princeton: Princeton University Press.

Goffman, E. 1961. *Asylums: Essays on the Social Situation of Mental Patients and Other Inmates*. Garden City: Anchor.

Holzer, B., A. Vreede, and G. Weigt, eds. 1999. *Disability in Different Cultures: Reflections on Local Concepts*. Bielefeld: transcript Verlag.

Ingstad, B. 1997. *Community-Based Rehabilitation in Botswana: The Myth of the Hidden Disabled*. Lewiston: Edwin Mellen.

———. 2001. Disability in the developing world. In *Handbook of Disability Studies*, ed. G. L. Albrecht, K. D. Seelman, and M. Bury, 772–92. London: Sage.

Ingstad, B., and S. R. Whyte, eds. 1995. *Disability and Culture*. Berkeley and Los Angeles: University of California Press.

Inhorn, M. C. 2004. Foreword. *Medical Anthropology Quarterly* 18: 129–38.

Jackson, M. 2002. *The Politics of Storytelling: Violence, Transgression and Intersubjectivity*. Copenhagen: Museum Tusculanum.

Jenkins, R., ed. 1998. *Questions of Competence: Culture, Classification and Intellectual Disability*. Cambridge: Cambridge University Press.

Kasnitz, D., and R. P. Shuttleworth. 1999. Engaging anthropology in disability studies. *Position Papers in Disability Policy Studies* 1: 1–35.

Kohrman, M. 2005. *Bodies of Difference: Experiences of Disability and Institutional Advocacy in the Making of Modern China*. Berkeley and Los Angeles: University of California Press.

Lollar, D. J. 2002. Public health and disability: Emerging opportunities. *Public Health Reports*, Mar.–Apr., 117(2):131–36.

Mattingly, C. 1998. *Healing Dramas and Clinical Plots*. Cambridge: Cambridge University Press.

Mendis, P. 2004. CBR and research: Perspectives from the South. Paper presented to the Research Symposium on Disabilities in a Framework of Development, Poverty and Human Rights, University of Oslo, 7–8 December 2004.

Michalko, R. 1998. *The Mystery of the Eye and the Shadow of Blindness*. Toronto: University of Toronto Press.

———. 1999. *The Two in One: Walking with Smokie, Walking with Blindness*. Philadelphia: Temple University Press.

———. 2002. *The Difference That Disability Makes*. Philadelphia: Temple University Press.

Nguyen, V.-K.2005. Antiretroviral globalism, biopolitics, and therapeutic citizenship. In *Global Assemblages: Technology, Politics, and Ethics as Anthropological Problems*, ed. A. Ong and S. J. Collier, 124–44. Malden: Blackwell.

Petryna, A. 2002. *Life Exposed: Biological Citizens after Chernobyl*. Princeton: Princeton University Press.

Pfeiffer, D. 1998. The ICIDH and the need for its revision. *Disability and Society* 13(4): 503–23.

———. 2001. A bit of history. *Disability Studies Quarterly* 21: 1–2.

Priestley, M. 1995. Commonality and difference in the movement: An 'association of blind Asians' in Leeds. *Disability and Society* 10: 157–69.

———, ed. 2001a. *Disability and the Life Course: Global Perspectives*. Cambridge: Cambridge University Press.

———. 2001b. Introduction: The global context of disability. In *Disability and the Life Course: Global Perspectives*, ed. M. Priestley, 3–14. Cambridge: Cambridge University Press.

Rabinow, P. 1996. Artificiality and enlightenment: From sociobiology to biosociality. In *Essays on the Anthropology of Reason*, 91–111. Princeton: Princeton University Press.

Rapp, R. 1999. *Testing Women, Testing the Fetus: The Social Impact of Amniocentesis in America*. New York: Routledge.

Rapp, R., D. Heath, and K.-S. Taussig. 2001. Genealogical dis-ease: Where hereditary abnormality, biomedical explanation, and family responsibility meet. In *Relative Values: Reconfiguring Kinship Studies*, ed. S. Franklin and S. McKinnon, 384–409. Durham: Duke University Press.

Rose, N., and C. Novas. 2005. Biological citizenship. In *Global Assemblages: Technology, Politics and Ethics as Anthropological Problems*, ed. A. Ong and S. J. Collier, 439–63. London: Blackwell.

Scott, R. 1970. *The Making of Blind Men.* New York: Russell Sage.

Shakespeare, T. 1998. Choices and rights: Eugenics, genetics and disability equality. *Disability and Society* 13: 665–81.

Shakespeare, T., and N. Watson. 2001. Making the difference: Disability, politics, and recognition. In *Handbook of Disability Studies,* ed. G. L. Albrecht, K. D. Seelman, and M. Bury, 546–64. Thousand Oaks: Sage.

Shuttleworth, R. P., and D. Kasnitz. 2004. Stigma, community, ethnography: Joan Ablon's contribution to the anthropology of impairment-disability. *Medical Anthropology Quarterly* 18: 139–61.

Silla, E. 1998. *People Are Not the Same: Leprosy and Identity in Twentieth-Century Mali.* Portsmouth: Heinemann.

Stiker, H.-J. 1999. *A History of Disability.* Trans. W. Sayers. Ann Arbor: University of Michigan Press.

Strathern, M. 1995a. The nice thing about culture is that everyone has it. In *Shifting Contexts: Transformations in Anthropological Knowledge,* ed. M. Strathern, 153–76. London: Routledge.

———. 1995b. Afterword: Relocations. In *Shifting Contexts: Transformations in Anthropological Knowledge,* ed. M. Strathern, 177–85. London: Routledge.

Tsing, A. 2000. The global situation. *Cultural Anthropology* 15: 327–60.

Üstün, T. B., S. Chatterji, J. E. Birkenbach, R. T. Trotter II, R. Room, J. Rehm, and S. Saxena, eds. 2001. *Disability and Culture: Universalism and Diversity.* Seattle: Hogrefe and Huber/World Health Organization.

Van den Bergh, G. 1995. "Difference and sameness: A sociocultural approach to disability in western Tanzania." Candidatus Politices thesis, Department of Social Anthropology, University of Bergen.

Weiss, M. 2002. *The Chosen Body: The Politics of the Body in Israeli Society.* Stanford: Stanford University Press.

Whyte, S. R. 2004. Disability: Global languages and local lives. In *Companion to Psychological Anthropology: Modernity and Psychocultural Change,* ed. C. Casey and R. Edgerton, 168–81. London: Blackwell.

Williams, G., and H. Busby. 2000. The politics of 'disabled' bodies. In *Health, Medicine and Society: Key Theories, Future Agendas,* ed. S. J. Williams, J. Gabe, and M. Calnan, 169–85. London: Routledge.

Wolbring, G. 2001. Where do we draw the line? Surviving eugenics in a technological world. In *Disability and the Life Course: Global Perspectives,* ed. M. Priestley, 38–49. Cambridge: Cambridge University Press.

World Health Organization [WHO]. 1980. *International Classification of Impairments, Disabilities and Handicaps.* [ICIDH.] Geneva: World Health Organization.

———. 2001. *International Classification of Functioning, Disability and Health.* [ICF.] Geneva: World Health Organization.

PART I

Locating Embodied Identities

1   The Two-Week Village

The Significance of Sacred Occasions for the Deaf Community

HILDE HAUALAND

Attempts to describe Deaf culture and society have often been forced into a frame based on single nationality and territorial anchorage. Breivik (2001) showed that these frames for understanding Deaf culture are insufficient, and that there is a need to go beyond national and territorial borders to grasp what Deaf culture, society, and identity are about. The Deaf community is characterized by its scattered translocality; members may live at considerable geographical distance from one another. Many do not share an everyday life and only meet occasionally. There is no obvious *place* for the lives of Deaf people. Traditional anthropological concepts of belonging and proximity ignore one of the basic features of the Deaf culture: its meeting places are transitory and temporary. The community of sign language users exists for Deaf people despite, not because of, the fact that they have a geographical place they call home most of the time.

The research project "Transnational Connections in Deaf Worlds" has focused on transnational activity and bonding among Deaf people. In the period 2001–3, the research team (consisting of two anthropologists and one sociologist—one Deaf and two hearing) has followed international key events in the Deaf world, like the Deaflympics, Deaf Way, and the World Federation of the Deaf World Congress, as well as several regional events in the Deaf world, to learn more about the dynamics and processes of Deaf transnational activities.[1]

Through intensive fieldwork certain common traits of these events have been identified. The events clearly have the properties of ritual. The participants come together to celebrate the Deaf community, and the events are arenas for developing and reinforcing social relationships, testing and playing out personal roles, and constructing, discussing, and challenging various ways to live as Deaf. The temporary space analyzed in this text is part of a transnational tradition in the Deaf world that has been evolving for centuries (Ladd 2003; Mottez 1993). Because Deaf communities must be understood as translocal and increasingly transnational (Breivik 2001, 2002a), there is a need to explore the occasions and gathering spots that function as strong centers of gravity in the Deaf world. Their significance for Deaf people challenges profound anthropological assumptions of durable physical locations as the prime site for identification and belonging.

DEAF RITUALS

This article describes some of the people, processes, and transformations encountered during the two weeks of the Deaf World Games held in Rome in 2001. Analyzing the event in terms of liminality and tourism, with inspiration from Turner's analysis of pilgrimages as social processes (1974:166–230), reveals the import of sacred occasions in the Deaf world. The main focus will be on the Deaf tourists and their plurality of experiences during the antistructural communitas of the Deaf World Games. In portraying the event as it unfolded—its dramaturgy, its interaction with and impact on Rome—I show the significance(s) of the games for the participants, as well as for the transnational Deaf community. Like other transnational gatherings, the Deaf World Games in Rome were a site for negotiating and identifying core values in the Deaf community. During such events Deaf culture is constructed and sometimes reformed.

Traditional long-term anthropological fieldwork, based on the unremarked common sense that "a culture" is naturally the property of a localized people and that the way to study such a culture is to go "there"— "among the so-and-so" (Gupta and Ferguson 1997:3)—was not an option in the project "Transnational Connections in Deaf Worlds." Like the other transnational events in the Deaf world, the Deaf World Games in Rome lasted only a very short time. In order to fulfill the Malinowskian principle that each phenomenon must be studied through its broadest possible manifestations in many different contexts in order to reveal underpinning values and principles (Breivik 2002b), the fieldwork was short and intense, like the events themselves. The research team engaged in the same concentrated social life as everyone else. Three fieldworkers were able to be several places at once and generously shared field notes with one another. Sometimes all attended the same events but made different observations of the same incidents. This multiplicity of perspectives was experienced as one of the strongest qualities of the research team. It yielded a thicker description of the Deaf World Games than any solo fieldworker could have produced. Each of the researchers could draw on three pairs of eyes and three sets of field notes from the Deaf World Games. All the observations and descriptions of places and people in this chapter are based on incidents experienced, observations made, and/or interviews done by one or more of the researchers, and have been discussed with the other team members.

I use two short extracts from my own fieldwork notes about entering and leaving the space of the Two-Week Village. Being an insider in the Deaf world and a frequent attendant at similar events, I found that doing anthropological fieldwork at the 2001 Deaf World Games was not only about finding a context in which to apply theoretical and conceptual categories. It was also about using analytical categories to rename and reframe what was already known (Narayan 1993). Through writing detailed fieldnotes, the unconscious was reformed into conscious knowledge, and thus provided a valuable source of insight for the entire research team.

TIME, PLACE, AND SPACE OF THE DEAF WORLD GAMES

Most Deaf gatherings take place at a new spot every time. The consistent change of locality has several consequences. First of all, it renders possible attendance by a relatively large group of locals who could not afford to travel to distant places. Second, it contributes to a sense of flux, as local spatial, social, and cultural qualities frame each event and leave their mark on the total impression of each particular happening. Third, a temporary "[re]production of the locality" (Appadurai 1997) occurs, as the heavy increase in the number of signing people changes the visual impression of the place for a short time. This last feature means that the physical place and the temporary Deaf space cannot be studied as entirely separate phenomena. It is a challenge to the anthropologist doing multi-sited fieldwork "to examine the circulation of cultural meanings, objects, and identities in diffuse time-space" (Marcus 1995:96). Although this chapter focuses on the significance of temporary spaces as sacred occasions in the Deaf world, it will also point to some aspects of interaction between time, space, and place in transnational contexts.

The history of organized Deaf sports goes back more than a hundred years. The games in Rome were the nineteenth celebration of the Deaf World Games since their founding in France in 1924. The Paralympics, where Deaf athletes do not participate unless they have a movement or visual impairment, were established much later. The International Olympic Committee (IOC) recognizes that Deaf people have their own games.[2] The International Committee on Deaf Sports (CISS) explains:

The Deaf athlete is physically able-bodied and able to compete without significant restrictions, with the exception of communication barriers. In team sports and some individual events, hearing loss can be limiting. However, these restrictions disappear in the Deaf Games. . . . World Games for the Deaf and other Deaf sports competitions serve as strong vehicles for socialization among Deaf persons. These aspects of Deaf sports cannot be merged within the organizational framework provided by the Paralympics. (http://www.ciss.org)

Over the years, the Deaf World Games have steadily increased in size, and records have been broken game by game. The first games, in 1924, attracted 145 athletes from nine countries. At the games in Copenhagen (1997), 2,078 athletes from 57 countries attended, while about 4,500 athletes from more than 70 countries participated in the 2001 games in Rome. The number of spectators and tourists has increased steadily, too. It is estimated that more than 10,000 people (both tourists and athletes) attended the games in Rome. Today, the Deaf World Games function as a biennial celebration of Deaf athletes as well as an appreciation of the Deaf community.

ARRIVING IN ROME (FROM THE AUTHOR'S FIELDNOTES)

As always when entering spaces that draw large numbers of Deaf individuals, my mind was immediately set on finding other sign language using people. I was instantly searching for quickly moving hands in the crowds of people, a very effective way to catch other Deaf persons thanks to the visibility of sign languages. But this time, I was bound up, holding one child tightly in each hand to make sure they would not be lost in the swarms of travellers and natives in Rome. I was unable to spontaneously wave my hands and ask, "Deaf?" when I saw people communicating in sign language. Arriving in Rome and staying there one night with my family before the games opened gave a golden opportunity to just observe all the people I otherwise might have encountered right away. Except for their signing hands and sharp, trained eyes, the Deaf tourists were not much different from other tourists, with their uniforms of shorts, sturdy sneakers, T-shirts, maps and—at the central station Termini—their big suitcases and backpacks. The first signed conversation of which I got a glimpse was between a man who seemed to be a local and two women with a little child, their suitcases and bags piled on an over-loaded baggage cart. With very clear international signs, the local explained the location of a place where, as far as I understood, one could get more information about the games. This was the day before the official opening of the games, and the density of signers was still relatively low. Not before reaching the Spanish Steps, did I get a glimpse of more Deaf persons. A couple in their 50s were talking together; they appeared to be Americans as far as I could see from their signs. I watched her signing to him, "Okay, now we have seen the steps, now let's go somewhere else," and they soon disappeared in the dense mass of tourists thronging the Spanish Steps. Later the same night I saw a group of Deaf athletes at the crowded Piazza Navona, but I was not able to see where they came from. After waving my family good bye the next morning, I was ready to be a part of the society that I witnessed beginning to unfold the previous night—and which flourished in Rome over the next two weeks.

ESTABLISHING A DEAF SPACE

To observe signing people by chance three times in a few hours is not a normal occurrence in the everyday life of most Deaf or hearing people. But the three instances described above were nothing compared to what was to come. Within a few days, signing people could be seen everywhere all the time, and a process similar to the one outlined by Breivik (2001) took place. He describes how, on his journey from Norway to the World Congress of the Deaf in Brisbane in July 1999, he witnessed the frequency and density of sign language users increasing at every flight transfer point on the way to Australia. As more and more spectators arrived for the Deaf World Games, they also increasingly made their mark on Rome. There were Deaf people in the trams, piazzas, and streets, in all the different parts of the city where the sports arenas were located, and at all the cafés for which Rome is so famous. The city not only got a different visible feature; the density of Deaf people could soon be noticed in the way the waiters at the cafés and *ristoranti* treated their Deaf guests. A reproduction of Rome occurred, and a distinct but elusive Deaf space evolved.

The first few days, most waiters just looked somewhat confused and puzzled as they attempted to communicate with their Deaf customers. They understood their Deaf guests' attempts to ask for the price or the bill with gestures or signs, but did not respond in a way that was comprehensible. The waiters continued to answer by shouting out numbers or questions in Italian or English. But within a few days, many waiters had noticeably improved their visual communication skills. Rather than barking out the prices in *lire*, they now showed the prices in fingers, and quickly produced a pen and paper if gestures were not enough.

The mayor of Rome, Valter Veltroni, suggested in his greetings to the participants in the official Guide to the Silent Games that the very presence of those "physically disadvantaged" in Rome was an "occasion for all of us to enrich our moral luggage" (Handbook 2001:13). But one must question whether the acts of excellent service from the numerous waiters in Rome really were symptoms of their high morals. Since Deaf tourists paid for food, drinks, and tips at dining establishments, it stands to reason that increased awareness of how to communicate with Deaf patrons was encouraged by commercial interests. Deaf people are not disabled when it comes to drinking cappuccino, sipping a glass of red wine, or eating pizza; they would not come back if they received less than good service. They were there as tourists—the ultimate consumers. Seeking and gathering sensations, Bauman (1998:81–83) points out, is the first goal of a consumer in a freewheeling postmodern world where material resources and things are too tangible to give the thrill that a sensation or a mere desire can offer. Experiencing Rome and the countless myths and sagas of the Eternal City included visits to the famous piazzas and the cafés, and the waiters were there to serve the visiting consumers, whether Deaf or hearing.

Rome was partly and temporarily transformed into a Deaf village, where Deaf people were visible and numerous enough to gain rights and services they often cannot claim or experience at home without being viewed as demanding or "difficult." The density of people communicating in sign language made it impossible for the hearing surroundings to ignore this visual mode of communication, and they eventually had to adapt to the Deaf ways of communicating. Most of the time, Deaf people experience that they have to adjust themselves to the hearing, auditive ways of communicating, because they are too few to make any significant weight against the pervasiveness of sound-based communication.

Events like the Deaf World Games allow the participants, often unconsciously, to participate in a "play world" (Holland et al. 1998) of Deaf people, where it is possible to pretend that the product is ("as if") authentic even if, or maybe just because, the agents know that this play or its product is of limited durability. Had the play world of a Deaf village that emerges during the games been of extended duration, or a stable state, the symbolic effect and emotional involvement would have been of a quite different quality.[3] It is as if the games are a center or goal for a journey, which is "invested with too much potency to survive prolonged familiarity: the contemporary pilgrim . . . gathers strength and illumination from the experience, and moves on elsewhere" (Brown 1996:40). But as Holland and colleagues point out, the art of play "has a spectrum of effects: new genres are created and recorded in the durable media, old ones are refigured, and new worlds and new identities are created" (Holland et al. 1998:238). Even though distant and liminal, an event like the Deaf World Games may provide the delegates with fuel for further identity agency and negotiation. The connections and friendship bonds that were forged, revived, and strengthened during those two weeks were certainly a crucial part of the strong sense of transnationality that permeated the games. But this transnationality was not evident from the beginning, as the symbolic rhetoric of the opening ceremony shows.

THE OPENING CEREMONY

If transnationality implies that countries, nations, states, regions, or places of origin are of secondary importance in social interaction, "transnational" is not the right concept to describe the opening ceremony. After a delay of several hours due to technical problems, the spectators could finally witness the athletes filing into the huge Stadio Olimpico. Following the Olympic tradition—with a Deaf twist—France was first in line, because they hosted the first Deaf World Games in 1924. Other countries followed, one by one in alphabetical order, with the host nation, Italy, entering the stadium last. To much chagrin and despair on behalf of the local organizing committee, the commentary on the entrance parade was not made accessible to the Deaf public, nor to the Deaf athletes. The international interpreters,[4] who were displayed on large screens at both sides of the stadium, stood for long periods unable to hear anything going on in the stadium. If they by chance were able to hear something, little could be translated, because the screens did not work properly. Large black dots covered crucial parts of the interpreters' hands and faces. The program seemed to be best suited for hearing Italians. An ultimate transgression of the values of visual communication celebrated at the games occurred when one of the Deaf organizers from Italy used his voice rather than signing his part of the opening ceremony.

Partly because of all the technical difficulties and problems getting some intelligible information from the formal ceremony, the spectators started to get to know each other, which for many probably was one of the primary reasons for their trip to Rome. The national groupings among the public reflected how the athletes entered the stadium, compatriots seated together, with the national colors very visible. Clusters of flags and placards from all over the world peppered the huge stadium, but some were more visible than others. A row of about 20 young Norwegians sat next to a large Greek contingent with their flags. A very spirited supporting team from Sweden was continuously cheering and waving a few rows down, and the Danes were not far away either, with their characteristic red-and-white outfits. Several crowds of Americans could also be seen, wearing and waving the Stars and

Stripes; the Dutch orange sparkled from another corner of the stands. As the athletes' delegates passed by, different groups among the audience rose and cheered the delegation from their own country. When the official part of the opening ceremony ended with intense symbols like white doves, balloons in the Olympic colors, and a Deaf athlete lighting the Olympic fire, the international spirit was vibrant, despite the problems in grasping the messages the local organizing committee had tried to give. The inaugural rite united the colors of the world for the purpose of peace and unity between the attending countries during the games. At the same time, it initiated a state of temporary geographical concentration of the otherwise scattered Deaf world.

The games were a chance for making the imagined Deaf community into a temporarily very visible one. They provided an opportunity to articulate imagined cultural differences between Deaf and hearing/nonsigning people. This in turn allowed the members of this community to establish a space "in between" their own imagined community and the people *beyond* this imagined community—in this case,—hearing Romans. This "in between" space of meeting and interaction became "terrain for elaborating strategies of selfhood—singular or communal—that initiate new signs of identity, and innovative sites of collaboration, and contestation, in the act of defining the idea of society itself" (Bhabha 1994:1–2). During the games the members of the Deaf community were able to collectively spell out the figured differences between themselves and nonsigning people, since for once they existed in numbers that could not be ignored or erased by a nonsigning majority. Hearing people continuously encountered the numerous "Deaf ways" of life and communication. A complementary relationship emerged between the Deaf athletes and spectators and the nonsigning inhabitants and visitors in Rome. The way the waiters eventually changed their services for their Deaf customers was just one example of acknowledging in public the distinct communication mode of sign language users. Another effect was how the hearing cohabitants at the research institute where the research team stayed took advantage of the presence of all the signers as an occasion to ask about Deaf people and sign language in general. They were, like the waiters, given a brief—and perhaps instructive—insight into the Deaf community and some of its characteristics.

THE DRIVE FOR VISUAL SPACES

The drastic increase in signers, who were there to meet each other and at the same time make their commonality visible, and the strict temporality of this increase challenge two profound premises about the anthropological field. The first anthropological "truth"—that 'home' is a place of cultural sameness" (Gupta and Ferguson 1997:32) is called into question by the presence of all the signers who have left their everyday homes to seek the experience of commonality with other Deaf people. At home they are surrounded by hearing people, who mostly do not know sign language and are ignorant about the communication prerequisites of Deaf people:

> Everyday life in a hard-to-sign (hearing) environment where many Deaf subjects are "settled," raised and positioned (most of the time)— [does] not contain the key constituting elements of belonging. Identification and belonging are thus more connected to projecting, longing for, planning and performing Deaf communal life beyond this—at temporary occasions. . . . Conscious efforts in making such occasions appear, through active involvement and planning, is thus becoming central. The sense of belonging is thus connected to the places and occasions where visual communication is practiced. (Breivik 2002a:13)

This sense of belonging is well exemplified by gold medalist and swimming star Terrence Parkin from South Africa. Very few of the athletes at the Deaf World Games compete in international hearing sports championships. Parkin is a rare exception. He is a silver medalist from the Olympic Games in Sydney in 2000, and his participation in the games in Rome added prestige to the Deaf World Games. To visible approval Parkin stated that being in Rome was like "being with my family." Going to Rome meant not going to see the *other*, but going to meet those like *us*. Being away from home—or being in quest of the *other*—is considered a characteristic feature of tourists, but in this case one can question who was the *other* and who *we* were.

Another anthropological "truth" being put under trial is the notion of the geographical place as the site of origin for the features that are of anthropological interest during fieldwork. It is impossible to grasp the underlying social processes during the games by referring to Rome as such, or to the culture or history of Rome and Italy. The field in question here is not Rome as a place, but the "cluster of *embodied* dispositions and practices" (Clifford 1997:199) that happened to be in Rome for just those two weeks in July 2001. The city—the traditions, history, and culture of Rome— certainly had its impact on the experiences of those attending the games, but must still be understood as a backdrop for the presentation and negotiation of the Deaf selves that took place during this temporary gathering. The Deaf community could be perceived as a global city, which "is not a place, but a process. A process by which centers of production and consumption . . . are connected in a global network, while simultaneously downplaying the linkages with their hinterlands, on the basis of information flows" (Castells 1996:417). The centers of this community move constantly because of the ever shifting locations of the large transnational events like the biennial Deaf World Games and the quadrennial WFD World Congress.

The significance of these moving centers has changed in the past few decades. The traditional spaces for construction and maintenance of Deaf communities and Deaf ways of life have been the Deaf schools and the Deaf clubs. But there is a general observation in the Deaf world that the numbers of pupils in Deaf schools are decreasing, and there are signs that Deaf clubs are being closed down on a large scale in Europe and North America. The trend toward integration has essentially led more Deaf and hard of hearing people to receive at least part of their education in regular, hearing schools. At the same time, the gradual decline of membership in the traditionally working-class-dominated Deaf clubs has presumably coincided with the rise of a Deaf middle class. With the development of new technological devices like text telephones, electronic information technology, and now mobile communication devices, Deaf people are increasingly able to organize their meetings and social gatherings outside the Deaf clubs. The same technologies that ease the planning of large gatherings may partly explain why attendance records have been broken steadily at the translocal and transnational Deaf gatherings. The Deaf Way II festival in Washington, D.C., in July 2002 was the largest transnational Deaf event ever, attended by well over the 10,000 who officially registered. It has been asked if these large translocal events are the final breath of communities that were once joined by Deaf schools, or if they are the wave of the future, as mainstreaming perhaps will produce a greater need for these temporary events.[5] The diverse backgrounds of those attending the games could indicate that the desire to be in a place where visual communication dominates remains strong, independent of personal education history or connectedness to formal Deaf networks (like associations or clubs) at home.

THE TOURISTS—A GLOBAL ELITE?

People traveled to Rome in numerous ways, and with a variety of motivations beyond the desire to meet other signers from all parts of the world, and perhaps to take in the sights of Rome. Many of the young people made a prolonged stay in Rome during an Interrail trip that was to continue after the games. Some were even making a stop in Rome on their once-in-a-lifetime trip around the world. Two British buddies drove an empty trailer all the way from England via Dover-Calais, through Paris to Milan, and on to Rome. Some comrades from Lithuania and Russia had stuffed themselves into a Lada, and some of their mates from Eastern Europe could be observed trying to cover expenses in Rome by selling their own paintings and other knickknacks. Hordes of North Americans and Europeans came on regular or chartered airplanes and buses, either on individual itineraries or tours organized by Deaf associations, Deaf travel agencies,[6] and private persons. People were accommodated in everything from tents at a campsite on the outskirts of Rome and five-star hotels to a bunk bed in the home of a more or less familiar acquaintance. The numerous modes of travel and accommodation reflected the variety in age, country of origin, and socioeconomic status of the tourists. Different as they were, they constituted a minority who in one way or another are able to travel—in contrast to the majority of the world, who are stuck in the locality where they live (Bauman 1998).

The games in Rome broke records for the number of participating nations, and it was mostly an increase in athletes from developing countries that expanded the number of officially participating countries. However, the delegations from many of these countries consisted of only one or two persons—an athlete and a manager or a coach, who also participated in the CISS general assembly that took place prior to the games. Rarely did supporters from their own country accompany them. The games have been, and to a large degree still are, an event drawing people with money, time, and resources to attend. Remarkable about the contingent from the United States was the high proportion of African-American athletes and the almost complete absence of African-American tourists. The Deaf world, despite its strong traditions of transnational activities, shares the worldwide patterns of ethnic and socioeconomic inequality. The majority of the attendants were from developed countries, and enjoy living conditions and rights Deaf people in the Third World are not even close to. The people who attend the events are members of an elite, who are characterized by their high *"degree of mobility*—their freedom to choose where to be"* (Bauman 1998:86). Mobility freedom is definitely not available to the majority of Deaf people in the world.

PLAYERS OFF THE EVERYDAY TRACK

The games did not last long enough to get a deeper knowledge of every person encountered, met, or talked with, either for the fieldworking anthropologists or for most of the participants. However, this does not negate the validity of our observations and arguments. Viewing the games as a liminal stage or a play world for innovative and experimental strategies of selfhood and society, I will not claim that the roles played by the actors during the games should be taken to represent their personalities or identities as such. The journey to the games strongly resembles a rite of pilgrimage, which "liberates the individual from the obligatory everyday constraints of status and role. . . . He is no longer involved in that combination of historical and social structural time which constitutes the social process in his rural or urban home community" (Turner 1974:207). Rather, the roles and the types we met can be taken to represent and symbolize the variety and diversity among the attendants of the games. Like Turner (1974:208), I view the tourists—or pilgrims—as "symbols of totality." The participants not only came from all over the world; they also had a variety of reasons for coming and chose various strategies in their journey through the social space of the games. In sum, they are seen as constituting the "communitas" that emerged during the games, in which social structure is not completely eliminated, just radically simplified (ibid.:196).

One group of attendants were the classic *tourists*. The American couple I saw on the first night by the Spanish Steps were "collecting" sights in Rome. They could be seen as engaging in a search for "authenticity" that drives the tourist to continuously seek new places; "his brochure provides a ceremonial agenda, which he follows more or less 'religiously'" (Brown 1996:37).

Perhaps not as determined in their quest for sights as the American tourists, but still in Rome also for the sake of the city itself, was the *group of friends* in their 30s who rented an apartment in a northern part of town. They were anxious to see the Colosseo, Forum Romanum, the Vatican, and other famous attractions. In their rented apartment, they were able to dish up homemade Italian food, and living close to the city center they were also able to enjoy a café or a glass of red wine at a piazza. At the same time, they were spirited supporters for the athletes representing their country and had brought flags and apparel in their national colors. Their activity shifted from exploring ancient Rome and traditional Italian food to being patriots of their home country. But also importantly, they were frequent and eager visitors to the main area for nighttime social activity during the games, the Foro close to Stadio Olimpico. Their purposes for going to Rome and the games were clearly multivalent, and this is a feature they indeed shared with most of the participants. However, different weight was given to the different activities, as we can see in the behavior of yet other delegates.

Another kind of player on the stage of the games in Rome was the *cosmopolitan*. A cool Danish dude made a very hip impression with his High Street brand-name sunglasses and well-trimmed pointed beard. Even though often surrounded by good-looking girls, he appeared to be very little affected by their presence. He seemed to be living at the edge of the games, never showing up at any social event until the atmosphere was at the peak. He was only occasionally seen with his compatriots during the competitions, and we never saw him wearing or carrying any colors that suggested national patriotism. He lived at a friend's place in Trastevere—the hottest *rioni* (city quarter) in Rome—along with some other equally laid-back people from several countries. These cosmopolitan friends had in common extensive experience traveling and living in other countries (some had been studying at Gallaudet University)[7] and had become acquainted as a consequence of this mobility. They all knew several sign languages (at least, all knew American Sign Language [ASL]),[8] and most were excellent international signers too.

A couple of American *backpackers* even utilized the games as a springboard for their round-the-world trip. The games were their marketplace for acquiring names and addresses of people who could put them up on the remainder of their tour. (This resembles the network of Esperanto speakers, albeit being less formal.) It seems that for the cosmopolitans and the backpackers, Rome and the international competitions were of less interest than the social life, which had its peak at the Foro every night.

All the people mentioned here belonged to a global elite with the resources to travel. The CISS and FIS *volunteers*,[9] who did everything from computer-punching results and selling tickets to making video reportages, also seemed to be of this elite. Their distinctive nonnational outfit fit with another cosmopolitanist feature, the urge not to be too readily identifiable (i.e., as supporters) within a crowd of participants (Hannerz 1996). Cosmopolitanism is a matter of competence (ibid.), and the Trastevere clique, the volunteers, and the backpackers possessed the linguistic and cultural knowledge needed to move effortlessly within the transnational Deaf network without being locked to a certain nationality or one specific sign language.

The games had their spirited national *supporters* too. Some of the countries with the largest contingents of athletes also brought official supporter leaders. The size of the supporter teams varied immensely both in numbers and visibility. However, during the competitions, they highlighted the nationalities represented in the competitions and left no doubt about the games being an *inter*national event. While most of the supporters, like the group of friends in the rented apartment, put away their flags and national colors after the competitions, a few Vikings with horned helmets, Bavarians, and high-spirited Yankees could still be seen wearing highly visible national colors and flag cloaks even at night in the Foro. What several of these had in common were their entertaining talents, to the great amusement and pleasure of others. Like the cosmopolitans, these explicit supporters were also excellent international signers. They were giving the Foro an international flavor by clearly showing which country they lived in, but at the same time they were among the most active in seeking contact and building relations across both national and social borders.

This contrasted somewhat to a couple of *hard-of-signing* friends from England, who both were rookies in this arena. Neither had received education in sign language, and their mastery in both English and British Sign Language was poor.[10] Despite being very hard-of-signing, their drive to meet and interact with other signers appeared to be strong. One of them systematically picked up new signs and tried to get in touch with the people they encountered. They eventually seemed to succeed in making new acquaintances, but they were much more restricted in their attempts to meet other people than the cosmopolitans. For such newcomers, an event like the Deaf World Games offers an opportunity to learn more about the Deaf community and how visual communication works.

SIGN LANGUAGE AND TRANSNATIONAL COMPETENCE

All the types attending the games were keen on communicating with other "pilgrims," but not all were equally competent to do so. Ability to use sign language is crucial in such transnational spaces. A survey conducted among Deaf and hard of hearing young people in Norway in the fall of 2001 showed a gap in degree of international interaction among those who had received education in sign language and in spoken languages. Among the sign language educated youths, 68 percent reported that they had traveled abroad in order to meet other Deaf people, while less than 7 percent of the youths educated exclusively in Norwegian reported the same (Haualand et al. 2003). Further investigation is needed to find out how national education and welfare policies influence opportunities to participate in the increasingly important global arenas. It seems that Deaf (and perhaps also disabled) people are especially vulnerable to education decisions made on their behalf early in life.

An emphasis on teaching a Deaf or hard of hearing child to speak (the philosophy also called *oralism*) rests upon an assumption that the child must find its primary social contacts in the community or neighborhood into which it is born. Many never learn to speak, and some of these are allowed to enter a community of Deaf signers a few years later, but only when all other options have "failed." Yet others learn to master a spoken language quite well and may be able to communicate in a spoken language, with or without hearing aids. Many become fair lip-readers and communicate, more or less easily, with other people who share their mother tongue. However, lipreading a foreign language is significantly more difficult than lipreading a first language. People with a profound hearing loss generally have more problems communicating verbally in foreign spoken languages, even if they are familiar with the other language in written forms.

Signed languages are more easily adapted to a form of international sign communication. Learning one sign language makes it easy to learn other sign languages as well. One may therefore assume that knowledge of a sign language increases the possibilities for transnational activities for people with a hearing loss, regardless of the person's hearing status. Knowledge of one or more sign languages enhances mobility and freedom to choose where to be. Oralism carries the risk of tying Deaf and hard of hearing people to one nation or one language. This could be a serious handicap in a world where the demand for, and importance of, transnational communicative competence is on the rise. Multilingualism is an important resource in managing the accelerating globalizing processes. A meeting place like the Deaf World Games offers an opportunity for outsiders to take part in a transnational network of Deaf people, and they may eventually join this network even if they have not been given the opportunity to interact with other sign language users earlier in life.

A DEAF PLAY WORLD

For Deaf people attending the games, leaving their geographical homes behind for a while permitted them to meet other people like themselves and did not automatically lead to a sense of being "away." But what was at stake nonetheless was the authenticity of own experiences (the senses) and the surrounding—the world that is "as if," the play world. The traveler or tourist "is after both authentic social relations and sociability (which would certainly include an authentically 'good time') as well as some sort of knowledge about the nature and society of the chosen destination"[11] (Selwyn 1996:8). If the games provide an innovative terrain for elaborating the self and identity as Deaf—or represent a liminal stage—the social relations and sociability during the games will perhaps be of a more experimental kind than at one's geographical home.

At the same time, some rules for social behavior are highlighted or intensified, in order to strengthen and underline the myth of the Deaf community. The strong reaction against the Deaf Italian who greeted the athletes and spectators during the opening ceremony using his own monotone voice is one sign of the higher expectations of visual communication during the games. Penalizing an entire team because of one single hearing aid demonstrates the stricter rules that come into function during such a mythical event. During a soccer game between Iran and the United States, the ball hit the ear of one of the Iranian players, and the referee discovered that he was wearing his hearing aid during the match. The Iranian team was immediately expelled for the rest of the match, and the U.S. team was given a walkover victory (Breivik 2002a).

Participation in the Deaf World Games is restricted to persons who have a hearing loss of at least 55 dB in the better ear (http://www.ciss.org). It is not allowed to wear hearing aids during the competitions. The participants may be asked to undergo hearing tests in addition to the regular doping tests during the games, and will be taken out of competition immediately if failing hearing tests (meaning hearing better than 55 dB in the better ear) or doping tests. This might be explained from a fair-play perspective (Solvang et al. 2005) but can also be seen as a definite boundary against the world that is left behind during the rite of the games. Wearing hearing aids or hearing better than 55 dB becomes a taboo for the athletes at the games, a rule that cannot be broken without fateful consequences: being excluded from the games or deprived of medals already won. Here we see the duality of the *play world:* "its freedom is as contained as its discipline. Both depend upon the authority and power which establish the possibility that is also the boundary, the space of possibilities, that holds play apart from ordinary life" (Holland et al. 1998:239).

The play world contributes to a slight change of concepts used both during the liminal stage and in the everyday life that sequels the event. The tourist experience is here a close parallel. While the play world reinvents and recreates practices, places attracting tourists are renamed and reinscribed in order to make them attractive for more travelers. The myth of the Eternal City is an example of the production of Rome as a place of authenticity, as well as a commodification of the past, making it a potential place to visit (Coleman and Crang 2002).

During the Deaf World Games, the main meeting places and competition arenas were quickly given new name signs. Even the sign for Rome was transformed into a sign with direct reference to a common experience of many of the attendants. Due to the ill-planned organization of the games, the numerous cancellations and misguided information in the handbook along with the usual chaos of Rome, the previous sign for Rome was changed into one reflecting an idea of "chaos" or "mess." Rome was thus given a new meaning in many sign languages.[12] Perhaps one could say that a slightly prolonged reproduction of the locality occurred. The visibility of signed languages vanished the day all the tourists went home and the waiters probably stopped using their fingers and notebooks to communicate, but a changed representation of Rome in various sign languages could be witnessed worldwide for months afterwards. In the aftermath of the games, the CHAOS sign for Rome was observed in Texas as well as Tanzania and even on the afternoon news in Sign Language on Norwegian TV. Many of those using the sign had not even been in Rome, much less attended the games. The narrative of Rome has seemingly been given a slightly new content or representation among Deaf people worldwide. The new sign for Rome reinscribes the local by adding the experience of the attendants at the Deaf World Games to the construction of Rome. The duality of the play world, or the liminal stage, is again evident. Its innovative force both rests upon and reinvents everyday representations.

THE OLYMPIC IDEAL AND THE DEAF FAMILY

Since most of the athletes were restricted by curfews, they were not able to socialize much with the tourists, certainly not at the beginning when few had finished their competitions. Comments from athletes indicated that there is an invisible divide between the athletes and the tourists at the games. They differed not only in their degree of freedom or scheduling, but also slightly in their goal for going to the games. Both certainly wanted to meet new friends and socialize with Deaf people from all over the world, but they had different arenas and times for these activities. It could thus seem like there were two different worlds at the games, with the athletes and official delegates in one, and the spectators and tourists in the other. The tourists met in the stands, at the cafés, and at the nightclub at the Foro, while the athletes met at the hotels, before and after the specific competitions on the sports fields. But as more and more athletes finished their competitions, they too joined the growing crowd at the prime nighttime meeting place, the Foro.

The two worlds gradually became one. The statement from the Olympic swimming champion Terrence Parkin elegantly united the Olympic ideal of *citius-fortius-altius* and the joy of meeting and making friends with Deaf people from all over the world. When Parkin announced that he had

chosen to attend the Deaf World Games rather than a World Cup swimming contest elsewhere because being in Rome was like *being with my
family*, he made a link between athletic achievements and the sense of
belonging to the Deaf community. Being a world-class swimmer, he broke
several records during the games in Rome. Being both an outstanding athlete with a radiant personality and a "true" Deaf person (by announcing
his membership in the Deaf family in fluent international signs), he per-
sonalized the vibrant sense of communitas (Turner 1974) that could be
sensed throughout the games. Moreover, he used symbolic language with
parallels to the Olympic Truce, which underlines *the spirit of brotherhood*
that shall be prevailing among groups and individuals all over the world
during the period of the Olympic Games.[13] When Parkin asserted that he
was part of the worldwide Deaf family, and at the same time had made outstanding achievements at the regular hearing Olympic Games, the entire
Deaf world (his *family*) was lifted to higher levels too. The empowerment
perspective is one angle (Fosshaug 2002), but Parkin stood for a broader
community. The Deaf World Games, like the Olympic Games, are informed
by "the hyperbolic expectation to exceed all limits, break all boundaries
and burst all formats, to reconfirm bi-annually that the human condition is
to transcend its own condition" (Berkaak 1999a:51). By his very presence
and his former achievements, Parkin for a short time contributed to the
transcendence of his entire *family*, the Deaf community.

CLOSING THE GAMES—RETURNING TO CYBERSPACE

Not only because of Parkin's statement, but also because of the intensified
social interaction with other signers, it was a transcendent community that
met again at the enormous Stadio Olimpico on the last day. The Nineteenth
Deaf World Games terminated with a closing ceremony that recalled the
opening one in organizational chaos. But the processes and the social min-
gling of the games had made an impact on life in the stands. Two weeks earlier, most spectators were seated by nationality during the opening
ceremony. This time people were mixed across national boundaries. Most
used international signs; some were strongly influenced by ASL. Many
had already exchanged mobile-telephone numbers during the games, as
short text messages were highly useful in light of the continuous cancellations and changed schedules. Now others exchanged contact information
so they could stay in touch.

The impact of the revolution in information technology was obvious.
The Internet, e-mail, web cams, messenger freeware, mobile-telephone

text messages, and pagers have eased communication across national and geographical distances in the Deaf world too. As one scholar states: "The media ecology may even change the organization of society, and the leverage of any entity within it. Virtual communities appear to be playing a key role in this move to a more dynamic, complex social system" (Uncapher 1999:277). Virtual networks can be utilized for planning immediate ad-hoc meetings of considerable size (Klein 2000). Those holding the resources to communicate in cyberspace will eventually also have the power to fill the elusive but still physical Deaf transnational gatherings with their own content and people. And they will also be able to stay in contact afterwards.[14]

As at the opening, the spectators spent more time talking with one another than watching the closing ceremony. But only a glance was necessary to see that the neat national order of procession that had characterized the opening ceremony had been replaced by a disorder of nations and delegates mirroring the transnational mix that had taken over in the stands. The athletes just walked onto the field in one large crowd, and everything was completely out of control. But no one seemed to care, and all were eagerly waiting for the ceremony to end so the closing party at the Foro could start.

The party was a grand finale of the intense social life of the past two weeks. On the last night, the Foro was filled with athletes, tourists, interpreters, professionals, official representatives, the cosmopolitans, the nerds, the supporters, and everyone else who had been attending the games. The tension was magic: everyone talked with each other, and all seemed to have a great time. What had opened as an international event, in order to celebrate both outstanding sportsmanship and the *spirit of brotherhood*, had been fused into a transnational family, where neither class, age, nor nation had significance. The party reflected the promise of a visual community that for the moment was in a clustered state, but could continue in cyberspace after dispersal.

LEAVING ROME (FROM THE AUTHOR'S FIELDNOTES)

As the establishment of a Deaf village could be witnessed the day before the games opened, the journey home gave an equally strong feeling that the same village was vanishing. The final morning I encountered quite a few signers on my last minute souvenir shopping, before I stuffed my clothes back into my suitcase and headed for the train to Fiumicino Airport. Some sign language users sat on the train, and I was happy to see some friends from Norway at the airport. However, they were booked on another flight, so I was to travel home alone. At the gate lounge, a couple of young Deaf Britons were also waiting, but I was too tired to make a reasonable conversation, so I did not reveal to them that I was Deaf. I slept most of the time on the plane from Rome to Heathrow, and never saw the Deaf co-travelers again. At Heathrow, waiting for the plane to Oslo, I was all of a sudden surrounded by hearings only. There were no communicating hands visible, and all were just a crowd of real strangers. I felt dissolved, and it was like the sign language community in Rome just vanished as suddenly as it had unfolded two weeks earlier.

The egalitarian and existential relationships that had been developed and maintained during the games were replaced with the too-well-known structure of everyday life upon arrival in London. The structure that "holds people apart, defines their differences, and constrains their action" (Turner 1974:274) was once again dominant, and the "web" of power of the (mostly unconscious) hearing majority was for a moment unpleasantly crisp and clear. But I had experienced an alternative reality.

A parallel to Turner's pilgrimage is close. If attending events like the Deaf World Games can be viewed as participation in a kind of "sacred existence, with the aim of achieving a step toward holiness and wholeness in oneself" (1974:208), it is not inconceivable that this "formation" desired by the pilgrims eventually leads to a "more intense realization" (ibid.) of Deaf culture and its core values with its emphasis on visual communication through sign languages. The actual time span of the games, which gives the participants a very definite and restricted period in which to gather new friends, acquaintances, and experiences, makes it a very intensive event, somewhat disconnected from the everyday rules for social behavior that apply at home. The Deaf World Games can be viewed as a ritual that contains both aspects of liminality and potent symbols. The potential for sacredness as well as myth making connected to the games is evident. Powerful symbols include the Olympic inaugural and closing ceremonies, assertions by a prestigious participant that being at the Deaf World Games is like being with the family, and the intensified visibility and encounters of sign languages.

The liminality and the separation of home/away experience moves the "tourist into a sacred world, where s/he is transformed or renewed and then turns him or her back to normality. . . . The normal rules are in abeyance . . . and replaced by Turner's close and egalitarian 'communitas'" (Brown 1996:35). The Deaf World Games can be viewed as a play world that gives the attendants an opportunity to emphasize visual communication and to act *as if* sign language users were in a majority. By revealing alternative and positive ways of living as a Deaf person, the ritual of the Deaf World Games has consequences for the members of the Deaf community far beyond the actual time span of the games themselves.

NOTES

1. The other members of the research team, Jan-Kåre Breivik and Per Solvang, have contributed significantly to the content of this article. I take the opportunity here to offer them my deepest thanks.

2. The IOC has now approved the name "Deaflympics" for the Deaf World Games. The new name was officially used for the first time at the Deaf World Winter Games in Sundsvall, Sweden, in 2003.

3. This perspective first of all applies to Deaf people who do not live in or near extended Deaf communities such as Gallaudet University. (See n. 8 below.) The impact of seeing and meeting so many other sign language users may not be so dramatic for Deaf people who meet other sign language users on a broad and everyday basis.

4. Sign languages are not international. However, many signs are more easily adapted into a mode of communication that can be understood across linguistic borders. Signers might therefore more easily communicate with each other internationally than people who only know spoken language(s). International interpreters are often hired at large occasions like this, and convey messages using a selection of more or less standardized signs and grammar.

5. Carol Padden, personal communication.

6. Travel agencies making special advertisements directed toward Deaf people or arranging travels/tours exclusively for Deaf people exist in many countries, including Denmark, Norway, the United States, Turkey, Italy, Costa Rica, and Germany.

7. Gallaudet University in Washington, D.C., is the only liberal-arts university in the world designed exclusively for Deaf and hard of hearing students.

8. American Sign Language (ASL) has increasingly been assuming the role of a lingua franca of the Deaf world.

9. The Italian Deaf Sports Association.

10. The goal of teaching Deaf children to speak, following a gross underestimation of the efficiency of using sign language as a language of instruction in schools, has deprived many Deaf and hard of hearing children of an adequate education. In the tradition of oral education (centered around speech acquisition), focus has (unintentionally?) been on form rather than content, and ability to pronounce sentences has been confused with knowledge. This may have the consequence that the children grow up without access to any language they are able to use and understand spontaneously. As adults, many will have great difficulties in communicating fluently in both spoken and signed languages, like the Britons mentioned here.

11. I here primarily view the games themselves and the social life surrounding these as "the destination," not Rome as such.

12. This process recalls the way sports arenas in Lillehammer were renamed during the 1994 Winter Olympic Games. New social and cultural connotations were actually created for the competition localities, and the natives did not have much influence on these processes. The downhill-skiing arena at Kvitfjell ("White Mountain") outside Lillehammer had belonged to nearby farms for centuries, and the various landmarks had names connected to daily farm work. But when an Olympic site was established there, the same landmarks were given names that made sense to the television public, not necessarily to the natives at Kvitfjell (Berkaak 1999b). In the aftermath of the Winter Olympic Games, the new names represent Kvitfjell, not the names that had existed for centuries.

13. http://www.olympic.org/ioc/e/facts/truce/.

14. The impact of information technology in the Deaf community is another theme for the research project "Transnational Connections in Deaf Worlds." These topics are only superficially touched upon in this article, as our analysis is in a purely initial stage at the time of this writing.

REFERENCES

Appadurai, Arjun. 1997. Fieldwork in the era of globalization. *Anthropology and Humanism* 22(1):115–18.

Bauman, Zygmunt. 1998. *Globalization: The Human Consequences.* Cambridge: Polity.

Berkaak, Odd-Are. 1999a. A place in the sun. In *Olympic Games as Performance and Public Event,* ed. Arne M. Klausen, 137–720. New York: Berghahn.

———. 1999b. "In the heart of the volcano": The Olympic Games as a megadrama. In *Olympic Games as Performance and Public Event,* ed. Arne M. Klausen, 49–74. New York: Berghahn.

Bhabha, Homi K. 1994. *The Location of Culture.* London: Routledge.

Breivik, Jan-Kåre. 2001. Deaf identities in the making: Metaphors and narrations in translocal lives. Doctoral thesis, University of Oslo.

———. 2002a. Doing transnational fieldwork: Methodological challenges. In Jan-Kåre Breivik, Hilde Haualand, and Per Solvang, *Rome—A Temporary Deaf City,* 7–18. Rokkan Working Paper 2. Bergen: Rokkansenteret.

———. 2002b. Deaflympics and the social role of deaf sports. In Jan-Kåre Breivik, Hilde Haualand, and Per Solvang, *Rome—A Temporary Deaf City,* 39–59. Rokkan Working Paper 2. Bergen: Rokkansenteret.

Brown, David. 1996. Genuine fakes. In *The Tourist Image: Myths and Myth Making in Tourism,* ed. Tom Selwyn, 33–47. Chichester: Wiley.

Castells, Manuel. 1996. *The Information Age: Economy, Society and Culture.* Oxford: Blackwell.

Clifford, James. 1997. Spatial practices: Fieldwork, travel and the disciplining of anthropology. In *Boundaries and Grounds of a Field Science,* ed. Akhil Gupta and James Ferguson, 185–222. Berkeley and Los Angeles: University of California Press.

Coleman, Simon, and Mike Crang. 2002. Grounded tourists, travelling theory. In *Tourism: Between Place and Performance,* ed. S. Coleman and M. Crang, 1–20. New York: Berghahn.

Fosshaug, Siv. 2002. Døveidrett i et empowermentperspektiv [Deaf sports in an empowerment perspective]. Master's thesis, Norwegian State College of Physical Education and Sport, Oslo.

Gupta, Akhil, and James Ferguson, eds. 1997. *Boundaries and Grounds of a Field Science.* Berkeley and Los Angeles: University of California Press.

Handbook 2001. *Guida for the Nineteenth Deaflympics Games, Rome, 22 July–1 August.*

Hannerz, Ulf. 1996. *Transnational Connections.* London: Routledge.

Haualand, Hilde, Arne Grønningsæter, and Inger Lise Skog Hansen. 2003. Uniting divided worlds. *Disability Studies Quarterly* 23(2):76–87.

Holland, Dorothy, Debra Skinner, William Lachicotte, Jr., and Carole Cain. 1998. *Identity and Agency in Cultural Worlds.* Cambridge, Mass.: Harvard University Press.

Klein, Naomi. 2000. *No Logo.* London: Flamingo.

Ladd, Paddy. 2003. *Understanding Deaf Culture: In Search of Deafhood.* Clevedon: Multilingual Matters.

Marcus, George. 1995. Ethnography in/of the world system: The emergence of multi-sited ethnography. *Annual Review of Anthropology* 24: 95–117.

Mottez, B. 1993. The deaf-mute banquets and the birth of the deaf movement. In *Looking Back,* ed. R. Fischer and H. Lane, 143–56. Hamburg: Signum.

Narayan, Kirin. 1993. How native is a "native anthropologist"? *American Anthropologist* 95(3): 671–86.

Selwyn, Tom, ed. 1996. *The Tourist Image: Myths and Myth Making in Tourism.* Chichester: Wiley.

Solvang, Per, Jan-Kåre Breivik, and Hilde Haualand. 2005. Minority politics and disability discourse at global deaf events. In *Resistance, Reflection and Change: Disability and the Role of Research,* ed. Anders Gustavsson, Jan Tøssebro, Johans Sandvin, and Rannveig Traustadottir, 177–89. Lund: Studentlitteratur.

Turner, Victor. 1974. *Dramas, Fields and Metaphors: Symbolic Action in Human Society.* Ithaca: Cornell University Press.

Uncapher, Willard. 1999. Electronic homesteading on the rural frontier: Big Sky Telegraph and its community. In *Communities in Cyberspace,* ed. Marc Smith and Peter Kollock, 264–89. London: Routledge.

2   From "Complete" to "Impaired" Body

*Female Circumcision
in Somalia and London*

AUD TALLE

THE RELATIVITY OF IMPAIRMENT

In the introduction to the volume *Disability and Culture,* the editors ask if and how impairments affect one's value as a human being and one's position as a social person: "Are persons with impairments impaired persons?" (Whyte and Ingstad 1995:24). The question opens a discussion of the relativity of impairment in the sense that what counts as a disabling condition—a "specific category of difference" (Whyte 1995:269)—does not follow automatically from the impairment as such, but must be culturally and socially mediated. This is of course a familiar anthropological position in cross-cultural studies, but the question has nevertheless spurred me to write this chapter about female circumcision in exile, which concerns Somali refugee women in London. In the contemporary Western setting, circumcised African women constitute a bodily anomaly—an unthinkable creature in a modern era. Their cut genitals are living examples of an "evil past" from which Europe has struggled to free itself. The sudden presence of Somalis in our home territories is existentially troubling; we are confronted with a reality that must and should be shrouded in "history."

Female circumcision (also called female genital mutilation, FGM) is a cultural and ritual practice that in most cases implies excision of vital physical organs (the clitoris, labia minora, and parts of the labia majora). The practice is particularly widespread in northeastern Africa, but is also common in West Africa and in parts of East Africa (Shell-Duncan and Hernlund 2000; Talle 2001). In the world today, it is estimated that perhaps as many as 130 million women are circumcised. According to circumcision type and the context of the operation, the surgery has varying consequences for women's health and sexual functioning. As to the latter, there

56

are many opposing views, and reliable data on the topic is scarce (Ahmadu 2000; Chalmers and Hashi 2000; Shell-Duncan and Hernlund 2000). The excision is nonetheless radical in the sense that it marks the woman's body for the rest of her life.

With reference to an anthropological discussion of disability, female circumcision is not a disability in the ordinary sense, as the condition of impairment is neither a consequence of "misfortune" nor a congenital difference nor a condition caused by disease. On the contrary, it has been intentionally inflicted by close family members in order to create a culturally "beautiful" and moral woman. Thus to include a chapter on female circumcision—an ethnic body mark—in a book on disability may compromise the potency of the disability concept itself and in the worst case risk weakening it. On the other hand, recognizing that the definition of disability is negotiated contextually, culturally, and historically, as well as within arenas of power, the reterritorialization of a local practice such as female circumcision in a global setting of a human-rights discourse may help us theorize "disability" one step further. What lies at the heart of my discussion here is the interface between local "cultures" and global power structures, in this case mediated through female bodies. The relocation of circumcised bodies to London places women as actors in shifting contexts of meaning and hegemonic power that are of profound consequence for Somali female identity and perception of self.

My analysis in this chapter rests on a combination of "discourse analysis" of female circumcision in the universal global debate (what language and whose voice is heard, following Foucault 1999) and of people's practical experience of being different or devalued. In the concluding chapter of *Disability and Culture*, Susan Whyte (1995) insightfully advocates a combination of these two levels of methodological approach in future comparative research on disability. I find her analytical position useful also for my account in this chapter.

BACKGROUND

On and off during the 1980s, I carried out anthropological fieldwork in Somalia, both among women in the capital, Mogadishu, and among camel nomads in central Somalia close to the Ethiopian border. In addition to my own research project on comparative gender systems among pastoral peoples in East Africa, I was also involved in a Somali-Swedish collaborative anthropological and medical-research and intervention project on female circumcision. For that project, we conducted in-depth interviews with some hundred women, men, circumcision practitioners, and religious leaders. During the 1980s, the political situation in the country became increasingly repressive, and people fled the country in large numbers. My last trip to Somalia was in 1989. One and a half years later a fierce civil war broke out and in fact still lingers on in many parts of the country.

Once the war had begun, it was impossible to return to Somalia. Furthermore, my collaborators had left for different parts of the world, mainly Europe and North America. I decided to continue my involvement with Somali studies through research on female circumcision in the exile. My experience and knowledge of this cultural practice in the Somali context spurred me to hypothesize that a study of circumcision in the exile situation would produce meaningful knowledge on this anthropologically difficult and somewhat enigmatic cultural and social reality. Without being quite certain as to what I would find beyond the Somali scene, my decision was an "imaginative investment" (Hastrup 1995:67) into an unknown landscape via the detour of the known. The fact that my friends and research collaborators were forced into exile generated an opportune moment for continued and novel research on a familiar theme.

The movement of hundreds of thousands of Somalis at this point in history can be regarded as a displacement—an unwilled flow resulting from forces distant to their lives. It is estimated that some 800,000 Somalis were displaced as a consequence of the civil war of the 1990s. Some 200,000 of these have been repatriated, but hundreds of thousands of Somalis continue to live as refugees outside their home country, both within and outside Africa (USCR 2002). In London alone there are approximately 34,000 Somalis, a majority of whom have come as refugees (Office for National Statistics 2004).[1]

The refugee predicament is global in the sense that wide-ranging political systems of power uproot people from their lands, drive them to unknown territories—often across vast expanses—and join them in new cultural and social formations and power relations. With reference to refugees in particular, globalization is a process that not only connects the world but also creates new boundaries and inequalities. In a recent study on failed expectations of modernity and economic progress in Africa, James Ferguson refers to globalization as a force that produces "new forms of disconnection" and in the process bypasses and ignores places (Ferguson 1999:243). I also argue that as refugees, Somali women in London, although residing in the midst of a world metropolis, constitute one such "bypassed" location. It is within this context of locational estrangement that we must understand the argument of this chapter.

Diaspora and displacement of populations are embodied processes: people move with their live bodies, and in the case of Somali refugees we are witnessing a translocal flow of circumcised female bodies. In other words, the uprootedness of the Somali population—often under traumatic circumstances—is a displacement, or dislocation, of bodies as well as of persons. I am referring not to a "natural setting" problematic in the sense that people belong naturally to a particular place, but to the fact that when Somali women arrive in London the body is the "first and most natural instrument" (following Mauss 1979) through which they perceive and experience themselves as positioned subjects and relational selves. The body is also the medium through which others to a great extent define and relate to them.

IN ANOTHER PLACE

One of my collaborators in Somalia, Khadiya, who is a trained gynecologist, became a refugee in Britain. My first meeting with Khadiya was a rather bright but chilly morning at the end of October 1999. We had decided to meet at her workplace, a health center in north-central London. As I entered the premises, I was asked by the receptionist to sit down and wait. After a short while, Khadiya walked across the floor. She was dressed in a floor-length skirt, long-sleeved woolen sweater, thick socks, boots, and a scarf tightly wrapped around her head. Her appearance was unfamiliar, but I recognized her upright way of walking and, at a closer distance, her smile.

Memories flashed back to Mogadishu, where I oftentimes had visited Khadiya where she worked, at the Benaadir Gynecological and Obstetric Hospital, where so many pregnant women and young girls had arrived in agony as a consequence of a severe circumcision. There, in the tropical climate of a coastal town, Khadiya always wore the transparent, loose female dress known as the *dirie*—hers often a blend of gray and white colors—and the unicolored matching *garba saar* draped lightly over her head and shoulders. The architecture of Benaadir Hospital allowed the maximum of breeze to enter the premises (they had no air conditioning in the hospital), giving the women an elflike look as the gentle wind moved their gauzy light clothes.

My heart sank at my very first sight of Khadiya in London; the enchantment of "the field" had disappeared. The figure in front of me was of a less sophisticated European woman, not the attractive Somali woman I used to know. Khadiya had taken onto her body the dreariness of the place she lived in. The cold, misty climate of Britain surely required warm clothes.

But there was more meaning to her clothing, which I learned about only later, and to which I will return shortly.

Khadiya in London was different not only in terms of her clothes. The trauma of her flight, the brutal assassination of a close colleague (in addition to the murder of many others), and the rape of her young cousin (whom she had to examine and stitch afterwards) were experiences that now inhabited her. Her status as a refugee in Britain, her unemployed economist husband, and her lack of license to practice as a medical doctor added distress to a disrupted lifeworld. There was in fact nothing "ordinary" (Malkki 1997) or everyday about her life any longer, not in the way both she and I used to know it before the war. Even the place she lived in upon her arrival in London, a ramshackle high-rise building, housed rapists and drug abusers. Many other Somali refugee women in London underwent similar extraordinary and extreme life experiences, which they had to incorporate into their lives. For Khadiya, as for so many other Somali women, the transfer from Somalia to London had meant a social degradation and a dramatic and sudden repositioning of body-self.

A "COMPLETE" BODY

Before I continue to describe and analyze Somali women in the exile situation, I will provide a brief account of the context and meaning of female circumcision in Somalia. This is important in order to understand the particular feeling of bodily "loss" and general disorientation many Somali women experience and have to deal with when they arrive in London. (See also Duale 1999.)

The Somalis practice the infibulation form of circumcision (*gudniin*, also called Pharaonic circumcision), which in surgical terms is considered the most severe intervention of its kind. The outer genitals are pared away and the sides of the vulva stitched together, forming a flattened surface and a tiny opening—an outlet for urine and menstrual blood—at the lower end of the pudenda. It is a risky and painful undertaking and often implies considerable medical and health consequences for those who sustain the operation (El Dareer 1982; Shell-Duncan and Hernlund 2000). The Somalis are meticulously preoccupied with the form of the infibulation scar: it should be without unnecessary scar tissue—forming a straight line—and the opening as small as possible. An attractive female body should bear smooth and nicely sewn genitals (Talle 1993). One may be tempted to speculate that an ugly scar evokes the memory of an "ugly" event, and thus instills uneasiness and doubt in the beholder.

Those parts of the female body that are cut away are culturally labeled "childish" (*kinterleey,* from *kintir,* "clitoris") and are sometimes compared to the hump of the camel or the cock's comb (because they "stand up"). They have to be removed in order to humanize and feminize the woman and to secure her moral uprightness and bodily beauty. The girls are operated upon when they are still young, between six and ten years, and they remain closed until they get married some ten or fifteen years later. A tight opening is a sign of distinction for a Somali woman. It elevates her body to an aesthetic ideal, and only as a "sewn girl" (*gabar tolan*) may she represent her family later in life at marriage (Talle 1993). The verb *tol,* which means to "sew" or "bind" together, also signifies agnation, which in fact is the structural backbone of Somali sociality and political organization. When used in the context of patrilineality, the term indicates that kin related on the male side are considered to be as close as if they were sewn together. The sewing metaphor evokes images of intimacy, cohesiveness, and permanence in clan relations. The word *tol,* used as a reference to agnatic kinship and also applied to an infibulated girl, links the social ("culture") and the individual body ("nature"). Inspired among others by Mary Douglas's (1996) analysis of the body as a metaphor for "society," I have written elsewhere about female circumcision in Somalia, particularly about the relationship between the individual female body and the patrilineal group as a social body (Talle 1993).

There is, however, more to the relationship between the individual and the social bodies than metaphors and collective representations of the "natural and cultural." The relationship is also about power and control (Scheper-Hughes and Lock 1987:23). The Somali female body is a political body, of immense importance for male dignity, strength, and alliances between lineages. It is quite common to hear Somali women and men claim that if a girl's infibulation ("virginity") is broken before marriage, her parents will not receive a proper bridewealth for her, which above all means lack of respect for them.

The untimely defloration of a girl represents a transgression of the unity of agnates: such a girl cannot stand up for her natal group in marriage and be reciprocated with another nubile girl. It is the privilege of the husband of the girl to open her and "make her into a woman" (*naag,* "wife," "nonvirgin"). Defibulation is the inversion of infibulation: instead of "sewing" and "closing," the symbolic and bodily themes of this act are those of "separating" and "opening."

During the various stages of the process of infibulation and defibulation (or reinfibulation after giving birth, or remarriage after divorce), a woman endures a large amount of physical force and pain. At every occasion, however, when interventions are performed on her genitals, it is impressed upon her that her pudenda have a tremendous worth far beyond the boundaries of her physical self. The manipulation of the female body is of primary concern to another "body"—her agnatic group and that of her husband. Infibulation encloses a woman within the agnatic group but in an inferior position; defibulation separates her from the same group. Many women we interviewed in Somalia experienced penetration by the husband as a more violent act than the closing. The closing, although recognized to be extremely painful (cf. Chalmers and Hashi 2000), is experienced as a "positive" event willed by many young girls and performed within the circle of close female relatives. The pain is meaningfully subordinated to higher goals in life—that of becoming a full and complete member of a social group.

A GLOBAL CONCERN

Female circumcision became a politicized issue during the feminist wave of the 1970s on many fronts: in academia, in political discourse, in the media, and generally among the public in the Western world. At the 1980 World Conference of the United Nations Decade for Women, in Copenhagen, the issue was brought to widespread international attention. Opponents of the practice asserted that female circumcision was a severe abuse of women's and children's rights and demanded legislation against it. It was proposed that the relativistic term "female circumcision" be replaced by "female genital mutilation" (FGM). This was done in order to draw attention to the medical severity of the intervention on the bodies of girls and women as compared to the less harmful circumcision of men (Hosken 1982; Toubia 1995). Although it has received widespread acclaim in the worldwide discourse on the issue, FGM is still a contested term, because it holds the implicit assumption that parents and kin deliberately intend to harm and mistreat their children. (Cf. Walley 1997.) In many places recently FGM has been replaced by the more neutral term "female genital cutting" (FGC: Shell-Duncan and Hernlund 2000; James and Robertson 2002).

Legislation against female genital mutilation is on the agenda of international organizations such as Save the Children, Amnesty International, WHO, UNICEF, UNFPA, and other UN and human rights agencies. The recent influx of Somali refugees to the West has sharpened the debate and added urgency to political actions against the practice. In order to prevent the spread of such "medieval" surgeries in their countries, European governments are passing laws criminalizing all forms of genital mutilation on female subjects—for citizens and residents alike. This applies to operations done inside as well as outside the country of residence. Many African countries, among them Egypt, Sudan, Kenya, Tanzania, Ghana, Senegal, Togo, Burkina Faso, and Côte d'Ivoire, have followed suit and passed legislation against the practice as well.

In February 2003, the Inter-African Committee on Traditional Practices Affecting the Health of Women (an umbrella organization of 26 African countries abbreviated as Inter-African Committee/IAC) held its annual conference in Addis Ababa entitled "Zero-tolerance to FGM." The speakers called for a renewed effort to combat the tradition of circumcising girls. In spite of more than 20 years of intervention work, progress in eliminating the practice was still modest, they claimed. Several of the papers at the conference asked for further systematic coordination among activist organizations and more carefully formulated plans of action. UNICEF declared a political objective to abolish the practice by the year 2010.

Within this discourse, female circumcision is seen as a "primitive" and "uncivilized" cultural practice and a "barbaric" abuse of the bodily and personal integrity of girls and women. We are all acquainted with the discourse on female circumcision through Western tabloid media where the Somalis and others who perform such operations are considered less than human (Robertson 2002; Talle 2003). This master narrative of an "inhuman" practice is echoed far beyond the confines of the tabloid media, and has found its way into serious and powerful organizations whose voices have great effect on the shaping of world politics. A case in point is the recently released international action plan against FGM issued by the Norwegian Foreign Ministry (Utenriksdepartementet 2003), whose preface is entitled "En bestialsk skikk" (A bestial custom).

The contemporary dominant discursive context of female circumcision is one of "human rights," where women's rights also are human rights and "freedom from FGM" is one of them (Amnesty 1997; Nussbaum 1999:129). Violence and injustice toward women and children are potent arguments in a worldwide effort to eliminate the tradition of genital surgeries.

AN AWKWARD PRACTICE

In London, female circumcision is an awkward practice, raising questions, causing embarrassment, and evoking anger and pity. The infibulated women are subjects of great concern and negative attention, a situation the women I met detested. "We do not like all the fuss about our circumcision," they despaired. Many of them recounted stories of humiliating and embarrassing experiences, especially in hospitals and at consultations with general practitioners (GPs). Somali women on the whole suffer from perpetual gynecological problems (real and imagined), and their relationship to health authorities in Britain, as in Somalia, is frequent and intense. Women in exile also have a high fertility rate (at least compared to the host communities), and this brings them into continual interaction with the health system.

It was visits to the GPs in particular (many of them of Asian origin, women emphasized) that caused frustrations and uneasiness according to informants. First of all, the women thought that their problems, which were chiefly related to gynecological illnesses of different kinds, needed specialist treatment. Second, the women complained that many of the GPs revealed an arrogant and insensitive attitude toward them as persons and toward their "culture." There are practicing doctors in London who are still unaware of the existence of female circumcision and do not fail to show their disgust or surprise when they encounter patients with cut genitals. Stories about unhappy encounters with "rude" and "ignorant" doctors are told and retold among the exiled women in London. Some of these stories are certainly exaggerated, but they do make refugee women apprehensive toward health personnel. My impression was that many women just felt uncomfortable and uneasy in their relationship to health workers, even if they personally had not experienced an offending clinical situation or a rude doctor. A few had not even been to a doctor but could still anticipate the sense of abashment when presenting their bodies for medical examination carried out by uninformed practitioners. A survey of 432 Somali women in Toronto showed that as many as 40 percent had experienced what they regarded as offending and hurtful treatment by medical staff (Chalmers and Hashi 2000).

Due to their severe circumcision type, women from Somalia and other infibulation-practicing areas are recognized by the British health system as requiring special treatment and attention during pregnancy and delivery. The primary focus of the medical intervention is the closed vulva. Though the infibulated woman has become pregnant, the vaginal entrance, particularly in primiparas, is often considered too narrow (upon clinical examination) for a safe delivery, particularly should an emergency situation occur. Therefore, in anticipation of the birth, the vulva must be opened to a "normal"-sized vagina. The routine in London is that the woman is "opened" in the twentieth week of pregnancy. The timing of the opening is carefully planned so as to occur well ahead of scheduled delivery (in case of premature birth), but late enough in pregnancy to avoid the risk of a spontaneous abortion. Should a woman happen to have a miscarriage after she has been opened by hospital staff, she is likely to blame her misfortune on the medical intervention. A case of spontaneous abortion would compromise medics' and activists' professional position that this procedure is a warranted and necessary medical intervention. Though imposed by health authorities, the women themselves, are sometimes skeptical about the usefulness of opening their infibulation scar ahead of delivery. The study from Toronto quoted above found on the whole a large discrepancy between women's wishes and clinical procedures followed: for instance, while only 1 percent of the women interviewed in this study wished to deliver by a cesarean section, over 50 percent of the women had in fact experienced such an intervention (Chalmers and Hashi 2000).

The rules and regulations surrounding medical treatment and the encounters with health personnel contribute to establishing a feeling of powerlessness in the women. Khadiya, who worked part-time as an assistant and interpreter at a health clinic for Somali women, recounted how tense their bodies were when she and the British nurse examined them. This was never the case when they came to her clinic in Mogadishu, she assured me. The only explanation she could give for this bodily disquietude was "the whole situation." What she meant was that as refugees, Somali women experience considerable apprehension and insecurity from living in what they consider a basically "hostile" environment. (For similar findings, see also El-Sohl 1993; Tiilikainen 1998.)

AFRICAN WELL WOMEN'S CLINIC

In 2000, an African Well Women's Clinic was established in the fieldwork area in northeast London to meet a recognized health need of women who have experienced cutting of their genitals. As stated in a report from the clinic, "health personnel has not known how to treat a woman with female circumcision" (Bourne and Edmans 2000:10). There are a few similar clinics in other parts of London (some of which are located in hospitals). Since the year 2000, the issue of female genital mutilation has been receiving national attention within the health system (Bourne and Edmans 2000). The African Well Women's Clinic is open to any woman who has experienced female genital operations; a majority are Somalis. The clinic advocates a holistic approach in health care and a "culturally sensitive service for women affected by FGM" (Bourne and Edmans 2000:4).

The clinic is open once a week and attracts women from all over London, but a large number of the patients come from the surrounding suburban areas. The women seek treatment and consultation for various problems and afflictions, many of which, but not all, can be related to their circumcision operation. According to the clinic's staff, a typical Somali patient presents multiple problems; that is, they seek therapy for several illness conditions simultaneously. Among 105 women visiting the clinic in one year, one-third came for fertility-related problems, one-fourth for vaginal or urinary infections, and one-fourth for cervical smears. Other afflictions observed to be widespread among exiled Somali refugee women in Europe are obesity, high blood pressure, hypertension, and nervousness (Tiilikainen 1998). Furthermore, many young Somali women suffer from a tight infibulation, which causes menstrual and urinary disorders and frequently conjugal problems for those who are married. About 12 percent of the patients at the African Well Women's clinic came for treatment of such conditions. The best and often only remedy for this kind of suffering is a surgical defibulation: that is, to open and remove scar tissue. In London, these operations are called "reversals": that is, to cut or bring the women back to how they were before they were "sewn." (Opening at pregnancy is also categorized as "reversal.")

The women wishing to have reversals are referred to one of the two hospitals known to perform such operations in London. I do not have precise data on the number of reversals being performed, but I have a strong feeling that reversals have become an issue among the women in exile to quite another extent than they were back home in Somalia. This opinion was confirmed by the clinic staff. Not only married and pregnant women come for such surgeries, but occasionally also young unmarried women, and this is a new situation. Surgical opening of the infibulation scar has always been widespread in north Somalia, but less so in the south. Northern Somalis have a reputation for sewing their girls extra tightly, making it difficult for the husband to penetrate by his own force. In the southern parts of the country, where the sewing is said to be looser, there has been little tradition for opening the bride surgically. On the contrary, penetration of the wife's infibulation by the husband is taken as a sign of his virility (*raginamo*, "to become a man" [Talle 1993]). To call upon assistance to perform this task is seen as an outright failure of manliness.

The growing demand for reversals in London has a practical explanation: the operation is quick, painless, easy to obtain, and free of charge. The clinic staff phones the hospital, and the woman usually receives an appointment within a week or so. However, because of an increasing number of patients, the waiting lists have become longer, and more hospitals in minority-dense areas now plan for such surgeries in order to cope with the demand. The operation is performed in the day-surgery unit under local anesthesia, and the patient normally leaves the hospital the same day.

Surgeons in London performing these operations on Somali women have publicly stated that many of the women still have the whole clitoris or remnants of it intact under the infibulation scar. One surgeon estimated that perhaps as many as 50 percent of the women she operated had their clitoris (personal communication), and she emphatically added that the women themselves were visibly eager to hear whether their clitoris had been cut or not. "One woman was so happy when I told her that she still had her clitoris that she flung herself around my neck," said the surgeon, obviously content with her results. The surgeons' findings correspond to what women, especially those from northern Somalia, often say, namely that it has always been regarded as extremely dangerous to cut too deep around the clitoris for fear of excessive hemorrhage. Instead of cutting the whole clitoris, they pare away the skin around it and stitch the raw parts together. Thus for some, the doctor's findings do not come as a surprise, but rather confirm local knowledge. For others however, it leads to a rethinking and a reexperiencing of the bodily self.

At the clinic one day, a woman phoned from the other side of town and told Khadiya that she could not "find her part" (by "her part" she meant the clitoris). The woman had had a reversal some time back, and the doctor had told her that she still had parts of her clitoris in spite of the fact that she was infibulated. Now she wanted Khadiya to confirm the doctor's findings. Khadiya was a well-known gynecologist in Somalia, and many Somali refugee women in London come to her for a second opinion. This woman was not a regular patient at the clinic as she lived too far away, but she had an urgent concern that day. Now that she had refound her clitoris, she obviously did not want to lose it.

After an hour she arrived at the clinic. I noted that she was young and pretty, but grossly overweight. Khadiya took her behind the screen and examined her. The surgeon was right: her clitoris was there. The woman, being content with the answer, did not make any further comments. The reason she could not find her clitoris, Khadiya told her, was that she had grown too fat recently. The location of the clitoris was not knowledge this woman embodied, but had to be consciously sought. Upon the confirmation from a physician she trusted, the woman was relieved, and the two of them continued to talk about her obesity, a growing problem among Somali women in exile. Although the woman listened carefully to

Khadija's admonitions about the usefulness of a fat-free diet and of exercising to achieve a slimmer and healthier body, it seemed she did not take a complete interest in what she was being told. Her reason for visiting the clinic that day had been something other than her obesity; she had come in search of a lost body part, a crucial marker of "humanity" in the place she now resided.

The fact that the presence of a clitoris has been officially declared by medical professionals directs attention to the female circumcised body in quite novel ways. This case, like others that I have come across in my fieldwork in London, testifies that the clitoris has become a matter of concern in the exile community, which according to my knowledge was not the case in the women's home country. Not that the clitoris was unimportant in Somalia—quite the contrary—but there the clitoris is defined as an unclean part of the female body, and when "excised" and enclosed at young age it is removed from thought as well as speech (Talle 1993). The "absent" clitoris is in fact incorporated as a body "habitus" of adult Somali women. However, the increasing medicalization of the circumcised body in London (as part of a global, universalizing discourse) has brought the clitoris "back" to the women (and to the health personnel) and to a more general discursive level among Somali refugees. There are, for instance, the occasional Somali men in London today who make a point of not marrying traditionally infibulated women because of their "defective" genitals. And young men sometimes favor Somali girls who are brought up in London because they are less likely to have undergone extensive genital cutting.

WOMEN IN DISTRESS

The general uncertainty of Somali refugee women in exile, and their acute and often painful awakening to being "different," is embodied in many ways: for example, in clothing, diffuse illness conditions, tense limbs, and aching hearts (Tiilikainen 1998). There is also a great amount of shame and stigma associated with the outsider position—the shame of being inferior. One telling episode of a close affinity between feelings of difference and shame among women in my field area is a woman who consulted her GP for a reversal referral, which she herself took to be a straightforward request in the context of a medical consultation. Instead of responding directly to her request, however, the doctor posed a counterquestion, wondering why her opening was not sufficient for her husband. The question was not necessarily meant to be intimidating, but the woman took it as severe invasion of her (and her husband's) bodily and personal intimacy.

Everyday encounters such as this one, and many others women tell about among themselves, aggravate their experience of exile life as difficult and unpredictable.

Somali women in Finland compare themselves to "disabled persons" (*curyaan*, people who are unable to walk but have to crawl), because often as single mothers with broken marriages or absent or diseased husbands they are not only overburdened with work and worries but also suffer from loneliness and isolation. They are imprisoned in their own homes with their young children, unable to efficiently familiarize themselves with their new surroundings and life beyond a small flat. The fact that a great majority of them have a poor command of the national language is an added burden in Finland as in Britain (Tiilikainen 1998; Bulman and McCourt 2002). The lack of language proficiency is perhaps the single most important factor for the women's coping and well-being in the exile context. When racial remarks are thrown at them in the streets, which quite often is reported in Finland, they are unable to understand, or respond, which intimidates them even further. Although grateful for being in a safe place (Finland as compared to war-torn Somalia), they nevertheless feel a stark sense of loss of autonomy inherent in their restricted freedom of movement and reduced decision-making power (Tiilikainen 1998).

In his chapter in *Disability and Culture,* our late colleague Bernhard Helander describes the concept of disability (*naafo*) among the Hubeer clan of Somalia (and among the vast majority of Somalis) as a social and cultural process where illness (*cudur*) is eventually seen as a disabling condition if not healed over time (Helander 1995). The Hubeer see prolonged immobility as a sign of severe illness: "inactivity [in physical terms] signals that something is wrong" (ibid.:89). In this worldview there is no sharp line between conditions of disease and of disability; it is rather a gradual transition. Somalis in general, also those in exile, identify themselves as a "nomadic" people, and within that identity construction, movement or travel is a social and cultural value of great importance (Griffiths 1997; Rousseau et al. 1998) Refugee women who find themselves immobilized in their homes (a sign of "disease") seek extensive therapy lest illnesses become prolonged, and thus eventually disabling. The loss of autonomy then experienced by exiled women has a deeper existential meaning, that of having lost power over one's own life.

Somali refugees are latecomers as immigrants in Europe and North America, and it is often claimed that the authorities and the local communities have not learned how to deal properly with this immigrant group. Health employees, who most often have intimate contact with refugees, suffer from considerable uncertainty in how best to approach and treat the increasingly high number of infibulated women they see as patients. Also, they have to handle an unfamiliar encounter, and although many are mindful of the situation, frequently Somali women in Britain and beyond experience lack of knowledge, effort, and interest, and sometimes even cruelty, on the part of medical staff (Chalmers and Hashi 2000; Bulman and McCourt 2002). The language barrier, coupled with inadequate interpreter services, makes encounters difficult for both the women and their helpers. A study from west London found that lack of language competence in the maternity wards often led to unsatisfactory treatment during pregnancy and labor. Treatment failures concerned the clinical management of circumcision in particular (Bulman and McCourt 2002:369). In Britain as well as in other countries, standard guidelines are now being worked out by health authorities in order to optimize clinical treatment of circumcised women.

A PAINFUL DIFFERENCE

The displaced circumcised bodies in exile are bodies in pain. The presentation of multiple problems at the African Well Women's Clinic in London is but one indication of a troubled and pining life. Likewise, the most common complaint in Marja Tiilikainen's study of the state of health among Somali refugee women in Finland was pain. Their whole body was aching—"the neck, knees, stomach, back, muscles, ears and heart" (Tiilikainen 1998:314.). Another study, from Oslo, reveals how anticipation of pain debilitates women in labor and childbirth (Johansen 2002).

The public "noise" (a global debate) encompassing circumcision in London and elsewhere in exile is painful, intimidating cut women and drawing boundaries between "healthy" and "diseased" people. For individual Somali women in London, the experience of bodily difference and the outsider position as refugees is terribly concrete and tormenting. A predominant theme in their circumcision discourse in exile is precisely pain, both the pain they experienced during and immediately after the operation and the pain of fleeing a beloved homeland and of meeting with the British health authorities. They relate the pain in different ways, by word of mouth, in texts, but primarily through an incorporated body practice of ailment and indisposition. (Cf. Connerton 1989.) Traces of the pain that occurred in their bodies a long time ago at the circumcision operation and later at marriage and childbirth (Talle 1993) appear to surface through the gazes of others—on the streets, at the health centers, in the media. Some of the women see the widespread obesity among themselves as pathology of their body. "Perhaps we are fat because we are infibulated," said one. When I doubted her observation, she asked rhetorically: "But why then would we be so fat [compared to others]?" There must be an explanation, she ventured. She found the explanation in a Somali cultural tradition that, when they resettled in London, had marked them as anomalous people. The "abnormality" of circumcised bodies as defined in intersubjective encounters in exile tends to generate a negative identity in cut women. The initial pain earlier in life lingers on and emerges in women's reflections and representations of their circumcision experience.

"They walk with it," was the comment of one of my informants in London when I tried to reason with her that after all some women live with the circumcision experience without too many adverse effects on the body and soul. Being infibulated herself, she did not believe that it was possible to go through this experience unmarked. She was right, of course; the purpose of the surgical intervention is exactly to "mark" the woman as a social and cultural being. What she was referring to was the submerged effect circumcision has on the female self. The inscription of a cultural sign, the sewn "virginity," has been embodied as pain and resistance. In London, Somali women have begun to personify the "gaze" of others on their own bodies, not by reproducing others' views and commentaries (Foucault 1999) uncritically, but by transforming them into heightened reflections and enforced opinions.

The increasing use of the veil (*hijab*) among Somali women in diaspora (also in Somalia recently) can be considered a protection against views from the outside and against looking toward far-reaching horizons. Their clothing must be taken as a reemphasis on their identity as "true" Somalis, where the link between religious and ethnic identity is hardly distinguishable (El-Sohl 1993). The veil is not necessarily a sign of subjugation in the contemporary life of Somali women in London; it is an indication of female agency and action. Somali women told me that they have become more truly religious in exile and, most significantly, they have begun to read the Quran more actively than they ever used to do. "We could leave circumcision, but not the *hijab*," claimed two elderly women I met at a refugee center engaged in reciting verses of the Quran to each other. I found no reason to argue. The way they put their words convinced me that they spoke the truth. "Decent" dressing in Muslim style has in the multicultural context of London become more socially appropriate than the cutting of their genitals. It is worth noting that orthodox Islam does not prescribe female circumcision, at least not the severe form traditionally practiced by the Somalis. On the contrary, many Muslim groups in Europe disparage African Muslims for such nonreligious practices. (The cutting of female genitals existed in this part of the world long before the spread of Islam [Mackie 1996].) The reworking of the Somali female identity in diaspora and in shifting contexts of self/other relations suggests a new area of meaning and representation where female circumcision is a contested element (Moore 1994; Griffiths 1997:19). During my fieldwork in London, I have noted widespread verbal opposition to the practice among both women and men. These observations correspond with findings in other exile areas (Chalmers and Hashi 2000; Johnsdotter 2002).

THE "IMPAIRED" BODY

Sagal, an attractive mother of four, attended an information course for immigrants. During one of the lectures, she heard two African men whispering behind her back: "You see this woman there [referring to Sagal]: she is very beautiful, but she is from Somalia, and Somali women do not have vaginas." Being a brave woman and secure in the knowledge that she had after all given birth to four children, Sagal turned to them and laughed at their comment. Whereupon they, according to her account, felt ashamed and apologized for their indiscrete remark. Sagal told the anecdote in order to show how life may present itself for exiled Somali women. They have to "fight" all the time, she said, not only for existence and survival, but also against prejudices, misunderstandings, and far-fetched fantasies and delusions about their bodies.

The growing popularity of reversals among young Somali women in London may be interpreted as a way of "normalizing" the body by bringing it back to its "natural" condition and thus up to standards of the encompassing community. The fact that the clitoris is sometimes found under the scar tissue is a bonus, so to speak, that women get from the medical intervention. The clitoris would probably not have been "discovered" by the woman herself, nor by medical health personnel, were it not for these rehabilitative interventions. In strictly medical terms, rehabilitation is mainly to transform the closed genitals into a normal vulva by removing the scar tissue. These surgical interventions enable women to function normally and with less pain. Many women who have had a reversal give accounts of great relief and added comfort in their sexual life and in general. Rehabilitation as health authorities envision it also involves counseling of women and girls who need support to cope with traumatic pain experiences and to renounce the tradition of circumcision and stand up against relatives and friends. The rehabilitation concept as it is put forward in governmental action plans has even spurred some young women to ask for surgical operations to reconstruct their genitals (personal communication). This is by all accounts an unintended but logical consequence of governmental welfare policies coupled with advanced technologies.

In the Western discourses of disability, rehabilitation is a political and social tool for correcting or modifying an impairment or injury that hinders "normal functioning" in the person. The underlying assumption is that although impairments can never be cured, people with impairments can be rehabilitated and in that sense brought to cultural and social normalcy (Ingstad 1995). Rehabilitation of circumcised Somali refugee women through reversals and regular maternity intervention is a way of normalizing and integrating them into their host community and its institutions of medical surveillance. Such "normalizing" processes, certainly intended for the benefit of impaired people, nevertheless draw attention to "difference" (that which has to be intervened upon) by bringing it to a conscious level of discourse through measures of laws and regulations, institutional procedures, and everyday practices.

The situated lives of Somali refugee women in London make them acutely aware of their bodily difference as compared to mainstream society, not only to British society, but also to other Muslims in the British capital. The scar of circumcision, a sign of distinction inscribed on their bodies when they were still very young, has become a mark of difference and deficiency—of inferior worth in a global world. In this case, difference means *less*. By being infibulated or sewn, Somali women are marked and marginalized as "incomplete" women. For the women themselves, it is hard to ignore these gazes on their genitals, which tend to reduce their personhood to their closed vulva. Sagal is one example of a woman rejecting such a blunt reduction of her person to a single (and ironically "missing") body part.

Throughout this chapter we have seen that exiled Somali women in various ways react to this ascription of negative identity. During the years I did research in Somalia, I learned that there was considerable doubt and ambivalence toward the practice, even where its stronghold was most unyielding. I believe this doubt stems from a deep-seated experience of extreme suffering and violence. Many women carried memories of overpowering pain from the time of operation and later at marriage. The "pain of circumcision," however, was commonsense knowledge and seldom articulated. In the shifting context of London the opposition to the practice may be articulated much more directly. In the words of one woman: "There is nobody who really believes that infibulation is beneficial to women." She meant that women in Somalia know of its harm, but there they could not act otherwise. As long as infibulation remains a "social convention" (Mackie 1996) they have to perform the surgeries, she concluded. Even those parents who might have been against the practice had slim chances of escaping the social and cultural pressure to circumcise their daughters.

Nevertheless, in the early 1980s in Somalia many women began to voice their views against the practice, mainly through governmental organizations, but also privately. In her capacity as a medical doctor, Khadiya, for example, worked actively against circumcision at sensitization meetings with women's groups in the capital as well as through her private clinic. In spite of verbal opposition to the practice, however, the number of girls avoiding the operation remained modest. As refugees in London, many educated women have continued to protest against the practice. They form welfare associations and organize meetings where they sensitize themselves and others to the negative consequences of female circumcision for women's lives (Summerfield 1993). Whenever the issue of circumcision (referred to as "FGM" when English is spoken) was raised in such meetings, it was integrated into a larger discourse on women's health and reproductive functions. It was rarely represented as a matter of "male" dominance or "cultural" oppression—or of human-rights abuses, for that matter. Circumcised women in exile mostly do not represent themselves as "victims," in spite of their cut genitals. That, together with the fact that circumcision falls within the spheres of "private" life that people are reluctant to disclose, may be a reason why they have not begun to form interest or support groups on the basis of circumcision as a "disability."

For the Somali women in London, infibulation is a term on the cognitive map, but the terrain has changed beyond recognition. The medical gazes on their genitals, the surgical reversals of infibulation, and requirements from health authorities for special arrangements in pregnancy and labor transform their bodies into "special" cases for clinical scrutiny. Their "cases," however, are heard far beyond the medical setting. The mark of infibulation has become a sign of a "deficiency"—a being not fully human. Opinion makers in Somalia who wanted to eradicate circumcision defined the tradition as damage to the female body, an injury harmful to women's and girl's health and well-being (and they have continued to argue so). The shifting context of exile locates the circumcised body within a universalizing discourse of "mutilation," thus transforming a harmful injury into a personal "lack." This is an "othering" process where circumcised women are set aside and devalued as human beings. In that very process the "impaired" bodies of Somali women have become powerful images of a worldwide moral discourse on "good" and "bad" cultural practices. They have become signs in a story they have not written themselves.

NOTES

I want to acknowledge the two editors for seeing the value of the case of "female circumcision in exile" to the overall topic of the volume. My thanks to Benedicte Ingstad for pushing me to write this chapter and to Susan Reynolds Whyte for sound and constructive comments on its argument. I also wish to acknowledge useful comments from the two anonymous reviewers. Furthermore, I extend my deeply felt thanks to my Somali collaborators in London.

1. The first Somali immigrants to Great Britain began to arrive some hundred years ago (El-Sohl 1993; Summerfield 1993). These immigrants were sailors employed by the British Merchant Navy and mostly hailed from the British protectorate of Somaliland and the seaport of Aden in Yemen, which was under British control until 1967. Many of the Somali sailors were married, but lived singly in Britain or took white women as second wives. Political uprisings in Aden in the mid-1960s forced many ethnic Somalis to leave the city. The first female Somali immigrants came as refugees from Aden to join their husbands living in Britain.

REFERENCES

Ahmadu, F. 2000. Rites and wrongs: An insider/outsider reflects on power and excision. In *Female "Circumcision" in Africa: Culture, Controversy, and Change*, ed. B. Shell-Duncan and Y. Hernlund, 283–312. Boulder: Rienner.

Amnesty. 1997. *Female Genital Mutilation and International Human Rights Standards*. AI Index Act 77/14/97. London: Amnesty International.

Bourne, J., and T. Edmans. 2000. Feminine sorrows: African Women's Health Clinic, Waltham Forest. Unpublished report.

Bulman, K. H., and C. McCourt. 2002. Somali refugee women's experiences of maternity care in west London: A case study. *Critical Public Health* 14(4): 365–80.

Chalmers, B., and K. Omer Hashi. 2000. Somali women's birth experiences in Canada after earlier female genital mutilation. *Birth* 27(4): 227–34.

Connerton, P. 1989. *How Societies Remember*. Cambridge: Cambridge University Press.

Douglas, M. 1996 [1970]. *Natural Symbols: Explorations in Cosmology*. London: Routledge.

Duale, A. K. 1999. Somali women in London. A study of the adaptation patterns in a new environment. Unpublished manuscript.

El Dareer, A. 1983. Epidemiology of female circumcision in the Sudan. *Tropical Doctor* 13: 41–45.

El-Sohl, C. F. 1993. "Be true to your culture": Gender tensions among Somali Muslims in Britain. *Immigrants and Minorities* 12(1): 21–46.

Ferguson, J. 1999. *Expectations of Modernity: Myths and Meanings of Urban Life on the Zambian Copperbelt.* Berkeley and Los Angeles: University of California Press.

Foucault, M. 1999. *Diskursens orden* [L'ordre du discours (1971)]. Oslo: Spartacus.

Griffiths, D. 1997. Somali refugees in Tower hamlets: Clanship and new identities. *New Community* 23(1): 5–24.

Hastrup, K. 1995. *A Passage to Anthropology. Between Experience and Theory.* London: Routledge.

Helander, B. 1995. Disability as incurable illness: Health, process, and personhood in southern Somalia. In *Disability and Culture*, ed. B. Ingstad and S. R. Whyte, 73–93. Berkeley and Los Angeles: University of California Press.

Hosken, J. P. 1982. *The Hosken Report: Genital and Social Mutilation of Females.* Lexington: Women's International News Network.

Ingstad, B. 1995. Public discourses on rehabilitation: From Norway to Botswana. In *Disability and Culture*, ed. B. Ingstad and S. R. Whyte, 174–95. Berkeley and Los Angeles: University of California Press.

James, S. M., and C. C. Robertson. 2002. Introduction: Reimaging transnational sisterhood. In *Genital Cutting and Transnational Sisterhood*, ed. S. M. James and C. C. Robertson, 5–15. Urbana: University of Illinois Press.

Johansen, R. E. B. 2002. Pain as a counterpoint to culture: Toward an analysis of pain associated with infibulation among Somali immigrants in Norway. *Medical Anthropology Quarterly* 16(3): 312–40.

Johnsdotter, S. 2002. *Created by God: How Somalis in Swedish Exile Reassess the Practice of Female Circumcision.* Lund Monographs in Social Anthropology 10. Lund: Lund University Press.

Mackie, G. 1996. Ending footbinding and infibulation: A convention account. *American Sociological Review* 61(6): 999–1017.

Malkki, L. H. 1997. News and culture: Transitory phenomena and the fieldwork tradition. In *Anthropological Locations: Boundaries and Grounds of a Field Science*, ed. A. Gupta and J. Ferguson, 86–101. Berkeley and Los Angeles: University of California Press.

Mauss, M. 1979 [1950]. *Sociology and Psychology: Essays.* Trans. Ben Brewster. London: Routledge & Kegan Paul.

Moore, H. 1994. *A Passion for Difference.* Cambridge: Polity.

Nussbaum, M. 1999. *Sex and Social Justice.* New York: Oxford University Press.

Office for National Statistics. 2004. 2001 census data. www.statistics.gov.uk/tc.asp.

Robertson, C. C. 2002. Getting beyond the EW! factor: Rethinking U.S. approaches to African female genital cutting. In *Genital Cutting and Transnational Sisterhood*, ed. S. M. James and C. C. Robertson, 54–86. Urbana: University of Illinois Press.

Rousseau, C., M. S. Taher, M.-J. Gagne, and G. Bibeau. 1998. Between myth and madness: The premigration dream of leaving among young Somali refugees. *Culture, Medicine and Psychiatry* 22: 385–411.

Scheper-Hughes, N., and M. Lock. 1987. The mindful body: A prolegomenon to future work in medical anthropology. *Medical Anthropology Quarterly* 1(1): 6–41.

Shell-Duncan, B., and Y. Hernlund. 2000. Female "circumcision" in Africa: Dimensions of the practice and the debates. In *Female "Circumcision" in Africa: Culture, Controversy, and Change*, ed. B. Shell-Duncan and Y. Hernlund, 1–40. Boulder: Rienner.

Summerfield, H. 1993. Patterns of adaptation: Somali and Bangladeshi women in Britain. In *Migrant Women: Crossing Boundaries and Changing Identities*, ed. Gina Buijs, 83–98. Oxford: Berg.

Talle, A. 1993. Transforming women into "pure" agnates: Aspects of female infibulation in Somalia. In *Carved Flesh/Cast Selves: Gendered Symbols and Social Practice* ed. V. Broch-Due, I. Rudie, and T. Bleie, 83–106. Oxford: Berg.

———. 2001. "But it *is* mutilation"—Antropologi og vanskelige temaer. *Norsk antropologisk tidsskrift* 12(1–2): 25–33.

———. 2003. *Kvinneleg Omskjering: Debatt og Erfaring* [Female circumcision: Debate and experience]. Oslo: Norske Samlaget.

Tiilikainen, M. 1998. Suffering and symptoms: Aspects of everyday life of Somali refugee women. In *Variations on the Theme of Somaliness*, ed. M. S. Lilius, 309–17. Proceedings of the EASS/SSIA International Congress on Somali Studies 1998, Turku: Centre for Continuing Education, Åbo Akademi University.

Toubia, N. 1995. *Female Genital Mutilation: A Call for Global Action*. New York: Women, Inc.

U.S. Committee for Refugees [USCR]. 2002. *World Refugee Survey 2002*. Washington, D.C.: USCR.

Utenriksdepartementet. 2003. Plan for regjeringens internasjonale arbeid mot kjønnslemlestelse av jenter, 2003 [Norwegian Foreign Ministry: International action plan against genital mutilation of girls]. Oslo: Utenriksdepartementet.

Walley, C. J. 1997. Searching for "voices": Feminism, anthropology, and the global debate over female genital operations. *Cultural Anthropology* 12(3): 405–38

Whyte, S. R. 1995. Disability between discourse and experience. In *Disability and Culture*, ed. B. Ingstad and S. R. Whyte, 267–91. Berkeley and Los Angeles: University of California Press.

Whyte, S. R., and B. Ingstad. 1995. Disability and culture: An overview. In *Disability and Culture*, ed. B. Ingstad and S. R. Whyte, 3–32. Berkeley and Los Angeles: University of California Press.

World Health Organization. 1998. *Female Genital Mutilation: An Overview*. Geneva: WHO.

3   Reproductively Disabled Lives

Infertility, Stigma, and Suffering in Egypt and India

MARCIA C. INHORN

ADITYA BHARADWAJ

In 1994, the International Conference on Population and Development (ICPD) was held in Cairo, effectively initiating a broad new approach to women's health in the non-Euro-American world. The Cairo initiative, dubbed "Reproductive Health," placed reproductive impairment on the population and global health agenda for the very first time. Infertility, or the inability to conceive a desired child, was officially recognized as an impediment to family planning, in the true sense of that term, and was also deemed an important cause of social suffering, especially for the world's women.

The placing of infertility on the global reproductive-health agenda has been a true boon to the scholarly community, which has subsequently received increased research funding to study infertility in non-Euro-American contexts. But the question remains: Has such global recognition improved the lives of those suffering from infertility on the local level? The answer to this question is much less clear. To begin with, despite the broad definition of reproductive health put forward at the Cairo conference, the Reproductive Health initiative still remains focused on population reduction through family planning. Indeed, some critics argue that the term "reproductive health" has simply replaced the term "family planning" in population and international-health discourses (Hartmann 2002), resulting in little substantive change at the level of actual programs for either fertile or infertile women. Furthermore, although the ability to conceive a desired child may now be conceptualized as a fundamental "reproductive right" following the Cairo conference, such reproductive-rights discourse is based on Eurocentric liberal-bourgeois notions of reproductive "choice" that may not be applicable or operationalizable in many non-Euro-American societies around the world. For the infertile in particular, reproductive choices are limited by both biology and by the severe constraints on access to appropriate infertility treatments—constraints that the Reproductive Health initiative has done little to overcome. Even more fundamentally, becoming a parent is rarely a choice for most men and women in non-Euro-American societies, where reproduction, both biological and social, is a cultural imperative, and where parenthood, for both women and men, is an integral aspect of adult personhood (Inhorn and Van Balen 2002). Because reproductive-health discourses are still predicated on Western-generated notions of the right to choose (be it contraception, abortion, infertility treatments, or parenthood itself), they do not necessarily accord very well with the lives of infertile women and men around the world, whose reproductive choices may be very limited indeed.

This Euro-American liberal notion of rights is similarly manifested in the disability-rights movement, which is beginning to gain momentum internationally (Ingstad 1995; Whyte and Ingstad 1995). Perhaps unfortunately, infertility has never been officially defined, either before or after the Cairo conference, as a disability-rights issue, despite its profoundly disabling social consequences. Nor has it been conceptualized, theorized, or politicized as a form of bodily disablement. As a consequence, infertility has failed to capture the imagination of the disability-rights community as a platform for political struggle. Indeed, Euro-American-generated disability-rights discourse, like the reproductive-rights discourse described above, assumes at some rudimentary level a body of autonomous individuals who are free to make choices and who can come together in a concerted way to vocalize their resistance as political agents. Yet, in many non-Euro-American societies, individual agency is often subsumed within larger collectivities such as the family, and thus strategies of everyday resistance are not openly political within cultural constraints framing and offering differing opportunities for action and expression. As a result, the infertility-patient-led support groups that are now a political fixture in many Euro-American societies—where they press for additional research and governmental recognition while monitoring the excesses of the medical and pharmaceutical industries (Becker 2000; Van Balen 2002)—are rarely, if ever,[1] found in the non-Euro-American world. There, such patient-led political mobilization may violate numerous cultural norms, including the need for patient confidentiality (Inhorn 2003a), and may even be seen as personally dangerous among infertile individuals who fear participation in larger political collectivities. Thus, in the non-Euro-American world, infertility has not been part of either patient-rights or disability-rights activism, in which reproductively disabled people act together as a coherent minority group, demanding an end to discrimination and injustice. Even in Euro-America, where disability-rights activism has gained considerable momentum following the political victory of the passage of the Americans with Disabilities Act in 1990 (Davis 1997), infertility is seldom included as a disability-rights issue.

This omission of infertility *as disability* is rather surprising when one considers this basic fact: The social ramifications of infertility in both Euro-American and other societies around the world accord quite well with both the United Nations and the World Health Organization definition of "handicap," troubled as that definition may be (Wendell 1997).[2] According to the UN and WHO, a handicap is "a disadvantage for a given individual, resulting from an impairment or disability, that limits or prevents the fulfillment of a role that is normal, depending on age, sex, social and cultural factors, for that individual" (WHO 1980; UN 1983). Infertility is an inherently socially handicapping condition, which disrupts the ability of individuals to fulfill normative social roles as mothers and fathers. As such, it is a profoundly disabling condition for both men and women, and especially the latter. In the non-Euro-American world, the stigma and social ostracism that may redound from infertility and childlessness are often so acute that they lead to social disablement in the multiple realms of marriage, family, friendship, and community life. Particularly for women, who often experience infertility as a disabling "master status" (Greil 1991a), the social oppression accompanying infertility may include reproductive blame even in the face of male reproductive impairment; emotional and physical abuse perpetrated by husbands, in-laws, and community members; and divorce and abandonment, with perilous consequences for infertile women who are economically dependent upon men (Inhorn 1994, 1996; Bharadwaj 2001; Boerma and Mgalla 2001; Inhorn and Van Balen 2002).

If infertility leads to social oppression, as we would argue here, then infertility should certainly be viewed as a form of disability. Recent definitions of disability foreground the notion of "oppression" as the key variable linking all disabled people together. As noted by Wendell (1997:264): "Disabled people share forms of social oppression, and the most important measures to relieve that oppression have been initiated by disabled people themselves. Social oppression may be the only thing the disabled have in common; our struggles with our bodies are extremely diverse."

Indeed, in virtually every society in which infertility has been described, infertile individuals struggle with their barren bodies, attempting to make themselves fertile producers of progeny. Efforts to identify a cause for this particular misfortune often take the infertile, particularly women, on quests to both ethnomedical and biomedical specialists (Inhorn 1994; Gerrits 2002; Jenkins et al. 2002; Riessman 2002; Sundby 2002). In the world of biomedicine, individuals often learn of the numerous potential biological impediments to fertility in both men and women—a list that grows longer each year as various failures of fertilization and implantation are ferreted out in in-vitro fertilization and reproductive biology laboratories around the world (Bentley 2000; Bittles and Matson 2000; Fishel et al. 2000). Such failures of biology—or the failure of one's reproductive body to cooperate with the reproductive body of another—are experienced by most infertile individuals as tremendous *social failures.* Indeed, as described in the recent monograph *Infertility in the Modern World: Present and Future Prospects* (Bentley and Mascie-Taylor 2000), infertility is an inherently biosocial problem, with the biological problem of infertility impinging in a profound manner upon the social lives of its sufferers. Infertility and its treatment are similar to other disabilities in the social realm: infertility places a fundamental restriction on social life and growth, in that children are central to the extension of sociality. Furthermore, these social ramifications and restrictions are usually much more pronounced in the non-Euro-American world. To wit:

> [Infertility] often has social and economic consequences in developing nations that far outweigh the consequences for infertile couples in most industrialized nations. In addition the social luxury of choosing to remain childless is simply not an option for many women and men where having children provides security for old age, social rank, and a source of labour for household activities and subsistence. Above all who can quantify the indescribable source of emotion, pleasurable and otherwise, that most children engender in their biological and social parents? It is perhaps this, above all else, that drives individuals to take extreme measures to achieve . . . parenting in the modern world.
> (Bentley and Mascie-Taylor 2000:12–13)

It is our task in this chapter to describe some of these social effects in two of the most populous (and hence pronatalist) countries of the developing world. These countries are Egypt and India, where the authors have undertaken ethnographic research. There, the biological impediments to successful fertility become inevitable preconditions for social disability and oppression. Infertility in Egypt and India marginalizes those who live with this problem—a problem that is often incurable.[3] For women in particular in both of these societies, infertility exerts a form of institutionalized biological determinism, whereby a woman's cultural persona is characterized by her biological inability to conceive and deliver. As an engulfing master status, infertility becomes the basis of her social identity, whereby she is seen as an inauspicious, polluted, even dangerous, barren woman. Thus, infertility imputes severe impairments on gendered personhood in Egypt and India, leading to marital duress as well as desperate medical measures to overcome the social stigmatization and ostracism. These desperate medical measures, furthermore, are highly class-specific and gender-specific. Like other technologies for disability, the assisted reproductive technologies (ARTs) to overcome infertility are differentially distributed and appropriated globally. Thus, poor infertile women are barred access to ARTs in places like Egypt and India, while affluent women also face a number of negative and highly gendered social consequences emerging from the recent globalization of ARTs to their local societies. Furthermore, this emergence of ARTs as a global solution to the problem of infertility gives infertility *as a disability* some special characteristics. Namely, both the impairment of infertility and its rehabilitation through ARTs are tightly enmeshed in local politics of social personhood. As we will see for both Egypt and India, ARTs challenge deeply held convictions about the nature of human life and of disability itself, perhaps more radically than do responses to many other disabilities.[4]

Following a brief description of the study sites and methodology, we will examine some of the disabling consequences of infertility and its treatment for both women and men in India and Egypt, comparing these two non-Euro-American societies with each other and with Euro-America. Specifically, we will compare and contrast our own non-Euro-American data with those found in Arthur L. Greil's (1991a) "A secret stigma: The analogy between infertility and chronic illness and disability," the only piece of Euro-American research that explicitly examines infertility *as disability* in the U.S. setting. We will argue that, despite many cross-cultural similarities in all three sites, the socially disabling impacts of infertility in the realms of personhood and marriage are much more profound in non-Euro-American settings, leading infertile Egyptians and Indians on often morally contentious quests for conception in highly medicalized infertility-treatment settings.

THE RESEARCH

This chapter is based on medical anthropological research undertaken independently by the authors in Egypt and India. The Egyptian data are drawn from two distinct periods of research during the late 1980s and mid-1990s. In the first period (1988–89), Marcia Inhorn conducted 15 months of anthropological fieldwork on the general problem of infertility in Egypt, basing her research in Alexandria, Egypt's second largest city. Working through the University of Alexandria's large public OB-GYN teaching hospital, popularly known as Shatby, she conducted in-depth semistructured interviews with 100 infertile women and 90 fertile ones. Eventually, she made her way into the communities and homes of these women, where she conducted less formal interviewing and participant observation. With few exceptions, these women were poor, uneducated, illiterate, or only semiliterate housewives who were not employed in wage labor and were economically dependent upon their unskilled laboring husbands. Many of these poor urban women were seeking treatment at Shatby Hospital not only because the infertility services there were free, but specifically because of the hospital's widely publicized claims to a free government-sponsored in-vitro fertilization (IVF) program.

The second period of research occurred in 1996, in the midst of the "IVF boom period" in Egypt. By that time, Egypt was in the midst of massive reproductive-technology transfer, with new urban IVF centers cropping up in private hospitals and clinics on a regular basis. In the midst of this IVF explosion, the author spent the summer of 1996 in Cairo conducting in-depth semistructured interviews with 66 mostly middle-class and upper-class women and their husbands; most of them were undergoing IVF or related technologies at two of the major IVF centers in this city of nearly 20 million inhabitants. The patients presenting to these IVF clinics were generally well educated, professional, comparatively affluent women who were often accompanied by their husbands. Indeed, in 40 percent of the interviews conducted in these IVF clinics, husbands were present and participated in discussions, often enthusiastically. Moreover, whereas interviews in the first study were conducted entirely in the Egyptian colloquial dialect of Arabic, many of the women and men who participated in the second study spoke fluent, even flawless, English as a result of their advanced educations, and they chose to conduct the interview in their second language. Thus, the Egyptian research incorporates both a diachronic and a class-based comparison of infertile women seeking treatment in the two largest cities of Egypt.

The ethnographic data from India are drawn from a multisited research project undertaken by Aditya Bharadwaj to examine the day-to-day working of infertility clinics, as well as the views of infertility-treatment seekers and infertility experts in five Indian cities (Bharadwaj 2001). His research was carried out over a period of 15 months in 1997–98. Bharadwaj conducted 45 in-depth semistructured but open-ended interviews with both individuals and couples attending three IVF clinics in the cities of

Delhi, Jaipur (Rajasthan), and Mumbai. Nineteen of these interviews were conducted in English and the rest in Hindi, with later translation and transcription of tape recordings. In 46 percent of these interviews, couples were interviewed together, while 28 percent of husbands and 21 percent of wives were interviewed without their partners. An additional 5 percent of informants were interviewed with an accompanying family member present. No conscious effort was made to interview individuals either separately or as couples. In most cases, due to the sensitive nature of the research or problems of access (e.g., husbands at work, wives undergoing an IVF procedure), it was not always possible to interview couples together.

As with the Egyptian IVF study, this Indian study is also clinic-based. In both studies, the possibility of follow-up interviews and participant observation outside the clinics was minimal, due to the sensitive nature of material, informants' desires for secrecy, and inaccessibility of some individuals who were coming to these IVF centers over great distances. Because undergoing IVF in both of these societies is accompanied by considerable personal difficulties (financial, familial, physical, etc.), as well as profound social stigma (Bharadwaj 2001; Inhorn 2003a), infertile individuals were often willing to be interviewed—or even seen with the researcher—only within the safe confines of the clinic. In India, infertile IVF seekers were often so reluctant to share personal information with the researcher that the most basic demographic data, including subjects' names, class/caste background, and employment/income profile, could not be easily obtained. Fourteen individuals who did openly share information on their class and economic backgrounds were either very affluent, or at least middle-class professionals, working and living in major metropolitan areas. The remainder of the respondents were putting themselves through some degree of financial hardship in order to fund their IVF trials. The same was true in Egypt, where even upper-middle-class IVF seekers experienced financial pressures.

It is also significant that all respondents in the Indian study were Hindus, compared with the predominantly Muslim study population in Egypt. As we shall see in this chapter, religiously based moral systems are significant in the realm of infertility, affecting both the forms of social oppression surrounding this condition and acceptable measures to overcome it as well.

INFERTILITY AND PERSONHOOD

In both Egypt and India, infertility is a deeply disabling social handicap. Whereas the notion of "disability" bespeaks the consequences of reproductive incapacity on the physical body, the idea of "handicap" actualizes and locates infertility within the social body (Scheper-Hughes and Lock 1987), where the infertile must "live" their reproductive impairment within the midst of society at large. Taken together, these linked notions of disability and handicap embody and interpenetrate the private and public realms of stigma, suffering, and social injustice, which are the common experiences of infertility for both women and men in these two countries.

In both Egypt and India, infertility is an inherently stigmatizing condition, particularly for women, who bear the physical evidence of the failure to conceive. In his seminal essay *Stigma: Notes on the Management of Spoiled Identity*, Goffman (1963:3) defined a stigma as:

> An attribute that makes [her] different from others in the category of persons available for [her] to be, and of a less desirable kind—in the extreme, a person who is quite thoroughly bad, or dangerous, or weak. [She] is thus reduced in our minds from a whole and usual person to a tainted, discounted one. Such an attribute is a stigma, especially when its discrediting effect is very extensive.

A stigma, then, is an attribute of a person that is deeply discrediting to social identity. How soon a stigma discredits one's very personhood depends upon its visibility. Thus, Goffman describes the various "abominations of the body" (e.g., physical deformities) that are quite visible and make disabled persons immediately discredited, versus those "blemishes of individual character" and "tribal stigmas" that are less easy to perceive. Following Goffman, Greil (1991a:22) describes infertility as a "secret stigma" for women and men in the United States, for a variety of reasons:

> Unlike paraplegics or the blind, but like diabetics and epileptics, the infertile possess a *secret stigma* in that they display no obvious stigmatizing features and that it is relatively easy for them to pass as normal. In addition, for most of the infertile, there are no *physically imposed* mobility barriers to full participation in one's normal round of life. Finally, the infertile have a condition that is neither visibly discrediting or obviously discreditable. Unlike those with epilepsy, for example, who must be concerned that an inopportune seizure might reveal their stigmatizing condition to others, the infertile are relatively free to keep their stigma secret.

On the contrary, in Egypt and India, a woman's infertility is never a secret. From the moment she marries, she is scrutinized by other female members of her own and her husband's family for the first signs of pregnancy. This form of bodily monitoring and surveillance begins almost immediately upon marriage but continues throughout the reproductive life of an infertile woman. As long as she does not show the visible signs of pregnancy—manifest most dramatically in the pregnant belly—she remains discredited within her social world. Similarly, for men, infertility makes visible the double failures of masculinity. Namely, men whose wives are not obviously pregnant may be discredited as lacking fertile sperm or as lacking erect phalluses capable of impregnating a woman. Among men, then, infertility bespeaks the emasculating possibilities of both male infertility and impotency (Inhorn 2002, 2003b, 2004). Ultimately, then, in both Egypt and India, human conception and sexuality are made visibly public through pregnancy and childbirth, which are both expected within marriage and closely monitored. The corresponding absence of offspring in a marriage is a highly visible reminder of an unacceptable failure in these dual realms, both of which are seen as central to the reproduction of social life (Inhorn 2002, 2003b, 2004; Bharadwaj 2003).

Whether it is the man or woman who is infertile in any given couple,[5] it is women who generally bear the brunt of social scrutiny, intimidation, and ostracism. In patriarchal pronatalist societies such as Egypt and India, women are expected to become mothers within marriage, with little choice to pursue other avenues such as satisfying professional careers apart from motherhood. Thus, the achievement of adult personhood for women rests on their attainment of motherhood. Without motherhood, infertile Egyptian and Indian women fail to uphold the "identity norms" or "norms of being" (Goffman 1963) that are deeply felt and socially shared by almost all members of society. Although fatherhood is also a cultural mandate for men in both societies, fatherhood is less central to the lives of adult men. On the one hand, most men pursue other avenues of adult fulfillment, including employment, peer networks, religious participation, and the like. In addition, although many men in Egypt and India are loving, devoted, and openly affectionate fathers, the major day-to-day tasks of childrearing and nurturance are primarily women's responsibilities.

In both Egypt and India, women who cannot achieve the role of mother are literally defined by this failure. An infertile woman's biological impairment becomes her "master status," the overarching feature of her social identity. In the United States, Greil (1991a:27) describes infertility as a master status for American women as well, noting that among the women he studied "infertility came to permeate every aspect of their lives." But Greil is also careful to point out that the "spoiled identity" of infertile American women emerges largely through a process of "self-labelling," or "the inability to live up to one's own expectations of self" (Greil 1991a:34). Outright discrimination and negative attributions toward the infertile made by others are relatively rare, and may consist of insensitive comments made by fertile women who did not realize that an infertile woman was in their midst. In other words, in the United States, infertile women may *feel* the "loss of self" (Charmaz 1983) and diminutions of personhood that are characteristic of stigmatization, but much of this stigmatization is internally rather than externally generated.

In Egypt and India, on the other hand, infertile women are stigmatized by others, who may openly remind the infertile woman that she is less than other women, neither a full adult, a full woman, nor a full human being. In India, infertile women are often viewed by others as inauspiciously polluted and may be avoided as a result. In Egypt, infertile women are seen as potentially dangerous, for they may harm other people's children through their uncontrollable envy (and the subsequent casting of the evil eye). Indeed, in both Egypt and India, of all the types of persons that one could be, there are very few less desirable social identities than that of the infertile woman, giving this particular identity all of the classic features of a stigma.

Not surprisingly, infertile Egyptian and Indian women may be taunted about their barren, inauspicious status. In Egypt, fertile women of the lower classes often hurl unkind epithets at infertile women in their families or neighborhoods (e.g., calling them *dhakar*, "male"). As one woman with seven children explained: "Some people talk and say, 'Two men are living together. She's the same as he is. She's like barren land.'" Another fertile woman added: "People hurt her. They tell her, 'You don't have children. You are like the rooster that does not break the hen and doesn't have children. You are a homosexual rooster.' Lots of people say these things." Even among upper-class Egyptians, infertile women are reminded by others of their childless status. One wealthy infertile woman, Amira,[6] explained how her neighbor subtly insulted her:

> Just now, before I came here [to the IVF center], I met a neighbor. "What's this? You didn't go to Alex on vacation?" I said, "My husband doesn't have vacation." She said, "What vacation! You can go any time, because you don't have children. *I* have to go now [while her children are out of school]." Sometimes I meet her in the market, and I say, "I don't know what I'm going to cook today," and she says, "Cook anything! You are only two. You can go to MacDonald's if you want to."

Similarly, the experience of an Indian couple named Arvind and Parul, who were interviewed together in a Rajasthani IVF clinic, is telling of the social discrimination and harassment experienced by infertile Indian women within their husbands' families and communities:

ADITYA BHARADWAJ (AB): What was the problem?

ARVIND: Nothing happened and then you have to listen to things because of society.

AB: What do you mean by "because of society"?

ARVIND: You know a woman's position is as good as nothing. Like other women interfere, like you don't have a child, you are barren [*banj*].

AB: Who are these women who talk like this?

PARUL: In the family [*Ghar ghrihasti mai*], relatives, near ones, even neighbors.

AB: What do they say?

PARUL: They say he will leave you, you don't have children, why aren't you having any?

Men, on the other hand, often escape such virulent social scrutiny and condemnation by grafting their own infertility onto the bodies of their fertile wives. In both societies, women are usually blamed for infertility, whether or not they are the infertile partner. But a common pattern in both Egypt and India (and a number of other societies, including some in the West) is for perfectly fertile, healthy wives to knowingly assume the blame for their husbands' infertility in order to protect these men from the assumed public humiliation of this emasculating condition. Among both lower-class and upper-class women in the Egyptian study, wives typically reported that they "covered" for their husbands in this way (Inhorn 1996, 2002, 2003b). Similarly, in India, most infertile husbands condemned their wives to carry the social burden of male infertility by failing to confess this condition to others (Bharadwaj 1999). This cross-cultural pattern of social misrecognition in the case of male infertility may be linked in large part to the common, although incorrect,[7] conflation of male infertility and impotency, the latter being perhaps even more stigmatizing than the former.

INFERTILITY AND MARRIAGE

In childless Egyptian and Indian marriages where the husband is fertile but the wife is not, men may receive tremendous social pressure, within their own families and among their social peers, to abandon an infertile wife through informal repudiation or formal divorce or, in the case of Muslim men, to take a second wife through polygynous remarriage. Although marital duress among infertile couples has also been reported by Greil and others in Euro-American settings (Daniluk 1988; Greil et al. 1989; Abby et al. 1991; Nachtigall et al. 1992; Van Balen and Trimbos-Kemper 1995; Greil 1997), female infertility resulting in male-initiated divorce is not a common occurrence and has rarely been reported in the Euro-American infertility literature.

In contrast, in many non-Euro-American societies around the world, including Egypt and India, men with infertile wives are literally expected to divorce them. Family interference, particularly on the part of husbands' relatives, is an enduring feature of the marriages of many childless couples in these societies. For example, in Egypt, many infertile women consider their mothers-in-law the bane of their existence. Not only do they pressure their sons to remarry—thereby providing offspring to strengthen the patrilineal extended family—but they also torment their infertile daughters-in-law, routinely chastising them for failing to "produce" for the husband and his family.

The threat of marital abandonment, coming from in-laws or even directly from husbands, is a fear that underscores the lives of many infertile women in Egypt and India, who are trapped in infertile bodies and marriages beyond their control. In Egypt, where a wife's infertility is deemed under Islamic personal-status laws to be a major ground for divorce (Inhorn 1996), Muslim women, especially of the lower classes, literally live in fear that their marriages will "collapse," as men succumb to such social pressure and pursue their desires for children with a new wife. Although women, too, may remarry if a husband is proven to be infertile, the enduring stigmatization of a female-initiated divorce means that few Egyptian women will ask for divorce unless their marriages are truly unbearable. Thus, Muslim women see themselves as maritally vulnerable,[8] as revealed in the following comments made by two lower-class infertile women in Egypt:

> If infertility is from the wife, 100 percent he will go and marry and leave her. If it's from him, the wife always has to support him because there's nothing she can do.
>
> Most men don't accept the fact of not having children, which is why they get married one or two or three times to have children and build a family. The husband always has the power; it's in his hand if he wants to marry or remarry, because sometimes a woman asks for a divorce and still the husband doesn't divorce her. So the woman is always the loser, because he has the power.

Similarly, in India a woman's infertility is deemed a justifiable reason for a husband to abandon his wife and return her to her natal family. For example, Jeffery and Jeffery's (1989:87) study of women and childbearing in northern India describes how failure to bear children is often "just cause for a man to return his wife to her parents and several women in

Dharmnagri and Jakri (who ultimately bore children) recall worrying about times when their husbands were pestered to replace them."

In the present study of IVF-clinic patients in India, one infertile woman, who worked as a nutrition consultant for a nongovernmental organization, recounted how it was assumed by women in the villages she visited that she would be cast out of her marital home and ultimately be in need of her own father's protection:

> I meet people in the villages, like, in fact I take this problem of not having a child very philosophically and can laugh about it, discuss it . . . even at the grassroots level. I met a, you know, like I was talking to village women and one of them was a traditional birth attendant. She asked me "Are you married?" I said yes. "How long?" I said five years. She said, "Do you have any children?" No! The second question she asks me—she didn't ask me about my husband or something—she says "Do you have your father alive?" Yes, my father is very much there. You know, those kind of things, like, in her own way, it wasn't judgmental, she wasn't looking down on me, but she was empathizing with my situation. She said "Where will this girl go?" So I laughed it off and all that.

The traditional-birth attendant described in this story was voicing an all-too-familiar fear that also permeates the lives of infertile Indian women. The force of community disapproval can, in fact, irretrievably disable the lives of infertile couples, whose only desire is to be left alone. A highly educated doctor named Rajkumar, interviewed in a Mumbai infertility clinic, spoke of the torment he and his wife were enduring at the time:

> It is a *majboori* [compulsion, to seek treatment]—what can you do?! I am a doctor, my wife is a doctor. We don't have any problem, but the society always interferes in your life. The need to ask—"You don't have children; why?"—is always there. Even the patients said, "O! the *doctrni* [lady doctor] is barren!" So you do feel. The patients who come say, "This doctor is barren, what treatment can she possibly offer us? I don't want to be delivered by her." . . . I [as a result] don't stay for more than two years in a place. I ask for a transfer; before someone says anything it is better to go to a new place, so that nobody should say that the doctor doesn't have any children. In the past, whenever my wife went for deliveries, she was told, "Don't let this woman touch you, she is a *banjh* [barren woman]." She feels it [*sic*]. So we had to get a transfer because people found out that this *doctrni* is unable to produce children, that she is barren.

The stigma of infertility and the force of social ostracism can penetrate and even subvert otherwise fixed social hierarchies in India. Social markers of class and caste, as well as elite professional boundaries, are no safeguards against social stigma and disablement, as seen in the case of Rajkumar and his infertile physician wife. The oppressive cultural expectations of fertility, therefore, make ideas such as "reproductive rights," "agency," "privacy," and "choice" deeply problematic in contemporary India, even among the upper class. In a cultural context where a continuing absence of children in a marriage becomes sufficient grounds for social interference, "selective disclosure" of one's infertility in an attempt to manage one's "spoiled identity" is simply untenable. Riessman, in fact, has quite rightly argued that Goffman's model of stigma "management" does not work well in non-Euro-American contexts such as India, given its presumption of "a self-determining, autonomous individual with choices and a mass society that allows for privacy" (Riessman 2000:113).

Faced with such culturally entrenched stigma and socially debilitating community ostracism, it is not uncommon for Indian couples to withdraw into a world of their own. Unable to bear the continuing torment of social disparagement, a couple from Gujarat, Ram and Sujata, had stopped going to social functions, a highly unusual state of affairs for an Indian couple:

> RAM: Sometimes it makes us very sad. People ask things like, "When will you have a baby?" We get very depressed but still we have got a hope, that's why we are here and we are taking every care, rest is up to Almighty.
>
> AB [TO RAM'S WIFE, SUJATA]: What has your experience been like?
>
> RAM: We avoid people.
>
> AB: Has it affected your social life?
>
> RAM: It has. We will not go . . . we will not mix in social functions.
>
> SUJATA: Unnecessary talk all the time.
>
> RAM: Sometimes all people are not equal, some may talk in polished language, some might talk in a rough way. People will not understand that this is also a kind of disease, but this particular disease they will take it some other way. People are having cancers, people are having TB, people are having kidney problems, people are having brain hemorrhage, so many things, but this particular they will take the other way.
>
> AB: Why do you feel that is the case?
>
> RAM: That we felt sometimes. That is why we generally will not go to social functions. We have cordial relations with everyone otherwise. Not that we are not friendly relations [*sic*], I am also very social man. We will not go to meet people often.

Similarly, in Egypt, relative withdrawal from community life was a common response of infertile women and couples in the study, who simply found it less draining to resist this form of social oppression through avoidance than to attempt "assimilation" into the community of "normals" (e.g., by befriending fertile couples with children and working hard to normalize their social relationships with them). Egyptian husbands were often very supportive and protective of their infertile wives in this regard, as is seen also in the Indian cases described above. Indeed, one of the major findings of the Egyptian research was the significant degree to which Egyptian men do, in fact, resist family and community pressure to replace their infertile wives through polygyny or divorce (Inhorn 1996, 2003a). Infertile marriages in Egypt, among both lower and upper social classes, are often characterized by a remarkable degree of "conjugal connectivity"—or a sense of marital enmeshment that comes from the intimacy of shared suffering and longing. Furthermore, when children are not forthcoming in a marriage, marital partners have more time to focus on each other and may, in fact, pamper an infertile spouse (particularly an infertile husband) as if he/she were the missing child in the marriage. Among both poor and elite couples in Egypt, many childless marriages could be described as highly companionate, defying the cultural expectations of marital demise that are thought to follow upon a medical diagnosis of infertility (especially of the wife). This does not mean that all childless marriages in Egypt or India survive; indeed, some do not.[9] Moreover, new forms of medical treatment, especially for male infertility, may paradoxically *increase* the risks of male-initiated divorce, for reasons that will become painfully clear in the following section.

INFERTILITY AND MEDICALIZATION

The social stigmatization of infertility and the accompanying threats of this disabling condition to both personhood and marriage are what drive most infertile women, and sometimes infertile men, on a "quest for conception" (Inhorn 1994) that may be relentless and ultimately unfruitful. In most non-Euro-American societies where this therapeutic quest has been described, infertile women typically avail themselves of numerous remedies for infertility, based in both natural and supernatural systems of belief and healing (Inhorn and Van Balen 2002). In Egypt, where an elaborate armamentarium of ethnogynecological therapies for infertility dates back literally 5,000 years, poor infertile women continue to avail themselves of such traditional therapies, which have been described in some detail elsewhere (Inhorn 1994). Increasingly, however, poor women in both Egypt and India rely on the infertility services provided by biomedical practitioners, some of whom may be specialized in infertility and reproductive medicine. Indeed, in both countries today, infertility is "big business" for biomedical specialists, who may offer the newest high-tech forms of assisted conception to affluent clients in urban areas (Bharadwaj 2001a; Inhorn 2003a). As these clinics are private affairs, generally lacking any form of state subsidy, patients presenting to them tend to be elites, who can afford expensive assisted reproductive technologies (ARTs)such as in-vitro fertilization (IVF).[10] Nonetheless, even elite infertile couples who turn to assisted conception in the hope of being assisted out of their long, protracted battles with infertility struggle financially, physically, and emotionally during the typically draining periods in which they are undertaking an IVF cycle. In the hope of salvaging their fertility through biomedical interventions, infertile couples in both Egypt and India may prolong the agony of their social suffering by resorting to biomedically desperate measures that may or may not secure an end to their socially disabling handicap.

In this respect, infertile Egyptian and Indian couples are similar to Euro-American couples who look to medicine, and particularly assisted conception, as a solution to their suffering. As reported by a number of ethnographers working in Euro-American settings (Greil 1991b; Sandelowski 1991; Franklin 1997; Becker 2000; Thompson 2005), infertility has become increasingly medicalized, particularly with the advent of ARTs such as IVF (Sandelowski and de Lacey 2002). However, in Euro-American societies, couples may pursue other options, including "child-free living" or adoption, once they come to accept the fact that their infertility cannot be solved through medical means. In both Egypt and India—and probably in many other pronatalist societies in the non-Euro-American world—there are no other truly viable options for infertile couples, given that couples are *never* expected to live "child-free," nor are they culturally condoned to adopt abandoned or orphaned children.[11] Indeed, for Muslims in both Egypt and India—as well as for most Hindus and Christians in those countries— adoption is decidedly *not* an option, given the Islamic scriptural prohibitions against this practice, as well as rather profound cultural proscriptions against adoption in both countries (Inhorn 1996, 2003a; Bharadwaj 2003). In India, children given up for adoption are predominantly conceived in premarital or extramarital relationships (Bharat 1993) and hence seen as "bastard children." To absorb such socially disabled children in infertile marriages is even more debilitating for stigmatized couples. While "child-free" living is not an option, many choose the stigma of barrenness or infertility over exposing an adoptee to a life of ostracism, jibes, and ridicule. Many others either adopt or foster children from within the wider family.

In Egypt, similarly, most infertile couples would prefer to remain in a stigmatized state of childlessness than to parent an orphan. Although the Islamic scriptures encourage kind treatment of orphans, legal adoption as it is known in the West is formally prohibited by Islam (Sonbol 1995). Furthermore, most orphans are assumed to be the products of premarital or extramarital adultery, *ibn haram,* literally "son of sin." Orphans, whether physically healthy or disabled, are considered of "bad blood," illegitimate, and even evil beings (ibid.). Hence, few Egyptians, poor or elite, are willing to consider bringing such "strangers" into their families.

Given this situation, infertile Egyptian and Indian couples—isolated, forlorn, and bereft of any possible social futures for alternative family-building—often seek to remedy intractable infertility by actively seeking medical help. Couples like Ram and Sujata, whose case was described above, see the medicalization of their infertility as the only tenable option in the face of growing social opposition to their childlessness. Society's inability to see infertility as a "disease," "disability," or "handicap"— comparable to the common and socially acceptable conditions of cancer, tuberculosis, kidney problems, or strokes in India—is particularly disconcerting for Ram. He obliquely hints at how (in)fertility and sexual dysfunction are often conflated, when he states, "this [infertility] they [society] will take the other way." In Ram's case, he had undergone corrective surgery for impotency, which apparently cured his sexual dysfunction. But throughout the interview, he remained tight-lipped about his own experience of social ridicule. Even though the truth of his impotency was not common knowledge in his family or community, his sensitivity toward his own past sexual disability compounded the anxiety of social disapproval, as his wife's inability to achieve pregnancy had implicated his manhood yet again.

This perhaps explains why some Indian men, like some Egyptian men (Inhorn 2002, 2003a, 2003b), abandon their barren wives and remarry in order to escape the cultural conflation between their own sexuality and fertility. This may also explain why many infertile Indian men of Hindu or Christian background—*unlike* Indian or Egyptian Muslim men—accept the use of donor sperm in assisted conception. Such desperate measures as "accepting any sperm" (as one Indian clinician put it) become a way of escaping "public disability," only to reinstate it within the private conjugal realm. Reluctantly accepting donor sperm is the closest that some Indian men can come to acknowledging, in the private clinical encounter, that they are the cause of the couple's infertility and social disability. A sense of anxiety in "owning up" to the IVF status of their offspring also compounds the "taboo on speech" (Das 1995) that couples, and in some cases their family members, come to observe when seeking IVF, especially with donated gametes (Bharadwaj 2003). Dr. Shanta, an IVF practitioner based in Delhi, described the secretive world of such couples, who, in bringing new life into the world, typically misrecognize the circumstances leading up to the child's birth:

> Fifty percent of the patients don't tell after the baby is born that it was an IVF baby at any social gathering, in front of another lady, never. Even when they talk to someone in private, they make sure they tell that person not to tell anybody that this is an IVF baby. They think there is stigma attached to the baby. . . . Our society is still not so liberated that they accept adoption. They [couples] accept taking donor oocyte, they accept artificial insemination by donor semen, anything. But they want to deliver the baby so the whole world can see that she has delivered a baby. So many men have got very near normal sperm but out of sheer frustration they say, "Oh, use any sperm you want. I want a baby." They just don't care! They just want to prove their fertility, that is all . . . a woman at some stage in the family wants to prove it . . . the man just wants to prove to the world that his wife has produced a child, that he is capable of fathering a child.

There is some truth to Dr. Shanta's assertions about the use of donor gametes. In the Indian study, a great majority of couples, when asked to share their views on donor-gamete conception, felt it was acceptable as long as it was kept quiet. On the issue of the donor himself/herself, the unanimous response of these couples was that they were happy to let the doctor source a suitable donor, and they claimed that they had no personal preferences in the matter. These couples were very much less concerned about the sourcing of eggs and sperm for inducing conception than about the eventual birth of a child.[12] An open acceptance of the "other" in the reproduction of the "self," however, was a gradual process in the lives of most of these couples, as a Mumbai-based IVF practitioner, Dr. Sachin, clarifies:

> The basic idea is that somebody is violating your marital relationship, a third party. That feeling itself is not very easy to accept. If I put myself in a patient's place I understand how they would feel. Here the marriage is considered as the ultimate bond and to have a child with donated gametes does upset a lot of couples. But then again once they reach the age of 35–36, they know they've no other option besides adoption. In adoption they get a child whose background is not known. Here, okay, at least egg or the sperm, at least one of the gametes is their own, plus the woman has the satisfaction of delivery. Donated gamete

is acceptable as long as it remains confidential and the husband and wife are very sure of each other. They understand what they are going in for without any cheating—that is, one person is not told and it's done. You know, things like that should not be done.

In Egypt, on the other hand, the situation surrounding third-party donation is completely different, underlining the importance of understanding the "local moral worlds" (Kleinman 1995) in which infertile and otherwise disabled individuals make sense of new medical technologies that come their way. As described at length in *Local Babies, Global Science: Gender, Religion, and in-Vitro Fertilization in Egypt* (Inhorn 2003a), Islamic religious authorities in Egypt and in other parts of the Sunni Muslim world (Meirow and Schenker 1997) have declared that IVF and similar therapies are an acceptable line of treatment—as long as they are carried out by medical experts *with sperm from a husband and ova from a wife* with "no mixing with other cells from other couples or other species, and that the conceptus [the embryo] is implanted in the uterus of the same wife from whom the ova were taken" (Aboulghar et al. 1990:266). In other words, Sunni Muslim religious scholars have clearly spelled out which individuals undergoing reproductive therapies have the right to claim the status of "mother" and "father"—namely, only the *biological* mother and father, who thereby maintain "blood ties" to their IVF offspring. Sperm, ova, and embryo donation, as well as surrogacy, are strictly prohibited.[13]

In Egyptian IVF centers, most patients are relative experts on the local religious opinion regarding IVF. Stating that the religious aspect of IVF is its "most important" element, Egyptian IVF patients in the study explained that sperm, egg, or embryo donation leads to a "mixture of relations." Such mixing severs blood ties between parents and their offspring; confuses issues of paternity, descent, and inheritance; and potentially leads to incestuous marriages of the children of unknown egg or sperm donors. Thus, the thought of using donor sperm from a bank was simply reprehensible and was tantamount in their minds to committing *zina,* adultery. For many Egyptian elites, this was one of the main reasons preventing them from traveling abroad to seek IVF and other assisted reproductive technologies. As one wealthy woman explained:

If I go abroad, and I have something wrong [infertility], they take my eggs and his sperm and put [them] in another woman, the "carrier." And they have "the bank of the sperms"—if you want him yellow [blonde], fair, black, dark hair. What is this? Nonsense! No way! For Muslims, this is wrong, and for Christians everywhere, too. But everyone does it there in the U.S. and Europe. I have no idea why, because the punishment of this is horrible. It's like when someone makes love to a woman without marriage. It's *zina*, adultery. It's not his son. Maybe these mistakes are made abroad, but not *here*. Here, no way! Because all the doctors are Muslims, and it will be *their* punishment. So they are religious, too. "There can be no halves for God." [I.e., everything must be done wholly right, not halfway.]

Indeed, in Egypt, much of this righteous moral discourse about IVF is now constructed in relation to discourses about the moral corruption occurring in the Christian West. In Egypt, news stories and television movies imported from America and Europe show women who "rent their wombs" only to struggle over the custody over the children they bear, or infertility doctors who impregnate hundreds of women with their own sperm only to be sent to prison, or IVF mothers who bear black and white twins by two fathers because of careless sperm admixtures in "Western" IVF laboratories. Proclaiming that this would never happen in Egypt—where patients can trust that their IVF doctors are good, religious Muslims—patients in Egyptian IVF centers described these stories, all of which happen to be true, with a kind of righteous incredulity. They concluded, often apologizing to the American anthropologist researcher, that "each society has its own traditions and customs." Indeed, the fact that the Egyptian case is so different from the Indian case described above—as well as from the Euro-American societies where these forms of third-party donation (and negligence [Reame 2000; Robertson 1996]) do happen—bespeaks this basic truth: that the assisted reproductive technologies are, in fact, subject to the traditions and customs of each society, and particularly to the prevailing social norms governing each local moral world.

However, from a Euro-American perspective, there may be a down side to the restrictive moral code governing the use of assisted reproductive technologies in the Muslim world—one that affects Sunni Muslim women in particular. On the one hand, Islam glorifies motherhood and all it entails (Schleifer 1986), insisting that women are endowed with a "natural maternal instinct" and that children are the "decorations of worldly life." Yet, infertile women who attempt to achieve glorious motherhood through resort to reproductive technologies are quite narrowly limited in their technological options by virtue of a religious code that prohibits third-party donation and surrogacy. Moreover, these constraints on achieving motherhood seem even greater when one considers two other important factors: namely, the Islamic prohibitions on adoption and the gender ramifications of the "newest" new reproductive technology designed to overcome male infertility.

With regard to this last point, over the past decade, intracytoplasmic sperm injection (ICSI) has revolutionized the treatment of male infertility by allowing even the most infertile men to father biological children. As long as one viable spermatozoon can be retrieved from the male body— even through painful testicular biopsies or aspirations—this spermatozoon can be injected directly into the ovum under a high-powered microscope in an IVF laboratory. In Egypt, this newest variant of IVF has been available since 1994 and has led to the virtual flooding of Egyptian IVF clinics with long-term cases of intractable male infertility. Unfortunately, many of the wives of these Egyptian men, who have "stood by" their infertile husbands for years, even decades in some cases, have grown too old to produce viable ova for the ICSI procedure. Because Islamic religious mandates in Egypt forbid any kind of egg donation or surrogacy, couples with a reproductively elderly wife face four difficult options: to remain together permanently without children, to permanently foster an orphan, to partake in a polygynous union with a younger, more fertile woman,[14] or to divorce outright so that the husband can remarry such a woman. Unfortunately, more and more highly educated upper-class men are choosing the last option—believing that their own reproductive destinies may lie with younger "replacement" wives who are allowed to men under Islam's personal-status laws. Certainly, these laws—coupled with the Islamic position on the need for biological parenthood in the practice of IVF and ICSI—place infertile Egyptian women and the old wives of infertile Egyptian men in an extremely precarious position vis-à-vis their reproductive and marital futures.

Thus, in some senses, the introduction of a revolutionary new infertility technology in Egypt and other parts of the Muslim world has introduced a sad new twist to gender and marital politics, suggesting that these medical technologies are anything but morally neutral and value-free. The need to critically assess the social effects of these technologies seems abundantly clear, particularly as these new reproductive technologies spread around the globe to places like India and Egypt, where their implications for the reproductive—and social—health of reproductively impaired men and women are truly profound.

CONCLUSION

We began this chapter by asking what the post-Cairo Reproductive Health initiative had done for infertile people, and particularly infertile women, around the globe. Coming full circle, we would like to end our discussion of infertility *as* disability by asking the same question: What can be done?

In our view as medical anthropologists who have studied infertility and the assisted reproductive technologies in two non-Euro-American "developing" societies, the most salient and clear-cut need is for the Reproductive Health initiative to tackle the prevention of the many *preventable* causes of infertility—in Egypt, India, and many other parts of the non-Euro-American world. Indeed, primary prevention of infertility—particularly early and effective treatment of reproductive-tract infections that lead to tubal infertility in women (Sciarra 1994)—is clearly the key to avoiding most of the serious social sequelae of infertility, including the gendered suffering, relentless treatment-seeking, and very problematic resort to ARTs described in this chapter. This means that the Reproductive Health initiative must target *men* as well as women, for men are often the ones who carry sterilizing sexually transmitted diseases to their wives, even rendering them infertile on their wedding nights.

Nonetheless, because not all infertility can be prevented—and this is particularly true of male infertility, which contributes to more than half of all infertility cases around the world (Irvine 1998)—there will always be a demand for the latest, most modern reproductive technologies to overcome this problem, even in resource-poor locations of the non-Euro-American world such as Egypt and India. At the present time, the assisted reproductive technologies are the only viable medical solution for the millions of cases of tubal and male infertility worldwide. Thus, a broadened Reproductive Health initiative might assume some form of responsibility for monitoring the global development and transfer of these technologies, making them more affordable and equitable in terms of their distribution to the millions of infertile sufferers in the developing world. Although these technologies are clearly *not* a panacea for overcoming infertility—because of their relatively low success rates and their substantial risks to women's bodies (as pointed out by generations of feminist scholars in the West [Thompson 2002])—they are currently the only solution for infertility in many parts of the world where adoption is disallowed and parenthood culturally mandated. Indeed, in the sweet, wrinkled faces of test-tube babies in both Egypt and India, one sees the success of these technologies in bringing an end to the misery that *is* the lived experience of infertility.

Furthermore, the very presence of these technologies in non-Euro-American societies—and the media glorification that surrounds the birth of test-tube "miracle babies" in places like Egypt and India—has, to some degree, introduced the problem of infertility and its high-tech treatment to the public, providing new national discourses on the problem of infertility, creating sympathy for its sufferers, and leading to a process of gradual normalization for both infertility and ART treatment-seeking (Bharadwaj 2000, 2002; Inhorn 2003a). The very fact that the parents of both Egypt's and India's first test-tube babies have "gone public" via the national media suggests that the very presence of these new technologies, coupled with media fascination over them, may lead to more tolerant attitudes toward both infertility and ARTs over time. In this way, new reproductive technologies have gone beyond solving individual problems of infertility by leading to new public awareness of infertility in both societies. That this process has also happened with other therapeutic and rehabilitative technologies in many other societies suggests that a broader social process of technology-driven public awareness of disability is clearly at work.[15]

Having said this, it is important to point out that media representations of infertility in both Egypt and India are quite centrally entrenched in the biomedical disease model of the condition. Media reports in these countries help to perpetuate the public perception that impediments to fertility can be medically corrected by ARTs, such that no woman or man need be childless any more! Such uncritical glorification in the media is, in fact, based on an erasure of the disability model of infertility, which, if popularized, could well open the way to alternatives like adoption or fostering, or at least create new public dialogues on the subject. However, because the media "hard sell" in both Egypt and India is about high-tech baby making and the promotion of particular IVF clinics and their doctors (Bharadwaj 2000, 2002; Inhorn 2003a), it serves to entrench, rather than unseat, the disease model of infertility, thereby blocking creative alternatives, such as disability-rights activism, infertility self-help groups, fosterage and adoption, and even child-free living.

In other words, without romanticizing the power of either the media or technology to influence public perceptions, it is nonetheless important to point out that the emergence of NRTs and their media glorification in Egypt and India have perhaps undermined more creative cultural responses to the biosocial problem of infertility. In neither society at the current time are public debates emerging to promote alternatives to ARTs, particularly adoption or child-free living. Even if these debates were to emerge, they would likely be restricted to urban elites—most notably, the so-called progressive intelligentsia in India, or educated cosmopolitan, secular Muslims in Egypt. Thus, in both societies, efforts to critically grapple with the infertility problem are currently being made only by the biomedical communities, who more and more are offering ARTs as the only real solution to infertility.

However, because ARTs do not work for most of those who suffer from infertility, and because ARTs are inaccessible to the vast majority of infertile couples who might benefit from them, ARTs are clearly not the answer to infertility in resource-poor societies such as Egypt and India. In our view as infertility scholars, it is time for both the reproductive-health and international disability-rights movements to take a bold stand by prioritizing infertility on their political platforms, asking what can be done to help the infertile people of the world. By *not* doing so, they effectively condemn millions of infertile citizens, including men but particularly women, to lives of pointless pain and suffering. For, as we have seen in this chapter, infertility is no trivial matter for most men and women in the pronatalist societies of the Third World. Infertility may ruin reputations, marriages, livelihoods, physical health, and long-term security in ways that are truly disastrous. In short, infertility is a particularly pernicious form of social disability—one that engulfs whole lives in endless circles of treatment-seeking, social stigmatization, and human suffering, and one that needs to be duly acknowledged as we enter the new millennium.

NOTES

1. To our knowledge, there are no patient-led infertility self-help groups of this kind in any country outside of Euro-America.

2. As noted by Wendell (1997:263), the UN/WHO definition makes a "shaky" distinction between the physical and social aspects of disability and does not contextualize the notion of "normality," which "depends upon the society in which standards of normality are generated."

3. Most cases of infertility are, in fact, incurable, in that the actual biological impairments causing failures of conception cannot be repaired. Thus, today, most of the treatments for infertility do not truly cure this condition; rather, they solve it by bypassing the physiological impediments to conception, such as blocked fallopian tubes.

4. This was pointed out to us by Susan Reynolds Whyte, who suggested that the debate over cochlear implants to restore hearing in the deaf might be the only comparable example.

5. Male infertility contributes to more than half of all cases of infertility in the world and is the sole cause of reproductive dysfunction in at least 30 percent of all cases (Irvine 1998).

6. All names used in this chapter are pseudonyms.

7. Although male infertility and impotency (erectile dysfunction) are commonly conflated in the popular imagination, most cases of male infertility are *not* caused by male sexual dysfunction. Rather, male infertility is usually related to various defects of sperm (i.e., in count, motility, and morphology), the etiology of which remains unclear (Irvine 1998).

8. The minority Coptic Christian community in Egypt, comprising approximately 5–10 percent of the Egyptian population, is religiously disallowed

from divorcing. Thus, Egyptian Copts are often active infertility-treatment seekers, given that divorce is "no way out" of their reproductive problems.

9. During the summer of 1996, Marcia Inhorn's infertile research assistant was callously divorced by her husband of ten years once he learned with certainty that his wife would never be able to bear his children.

10. In Egypt, the cost of an average cycle of IVF in 1996 was $2,500–$3,000, in a country where per-capita income was only $1,200 (Population Reference Bureau 1999). In India, an average cycle of IVF in 1997–98 was $850–$1,000, in a country where per-capita income in 2000 was only $450 (World Bank 2000).

11. In some parts of sub-Saharan Africa and Oceania, child fosterage within the family is a common cultural pattern and helps infertile couples to achieve their parenting desires. Even so, infertile couples who are foster parents within such societies may still pursue costly medical remedies in the hopes of conceiving their own biological children.

12. Compare this to an Indian interviewee in Hirsch's southeastern England study (1999:121) who insisted that the possibility of anonymous genetic material would be unthinkable in Indian culture: "Now they want to know, if it's an anonymous sperm, will you know which caste it comes from? So it's completely out of the question, they will never accept it. Never accept it, even if they are given 100 per cent verity it's a high caste, they still won't accept it."

13. By the end of the 1990s, religious authorities of the minority Shi'a sect of Islam approved the use of donor gametes, particularly donor egg. Thus, donor egg and embryo programs can be found in the Shi'a-majority countries of Lebanon and Iran, although acceptance of donor sperm remains more problematic (Inhorn 2004).

14. Very few Egyptian women today will accept being a cowife in a polygynous marriage. Even among poor women, most say they would rather be divorced than to "share" their husband with a cowife.

15. This was also pointed out to us by Susan Reynolds Whyte.

REFERENCES

Abbey, Antonia, Frank M. Andrews, and L. Jill Halman. 1991. Gender's role in responses to infertility. *Psychology of Women Quarterly* 15(2):295–316.

Aboulghar, M. A., G. I. Aboul Serour, and R. Mansour. 1990. Some ethical and legal aspects of medically assisted reproduction in Egypt. *International Journal of Bioethics* 1:265–68.

Becker, Gay. 2000. *The Elusive Embryo: How Men and Women Approach New Reproductive Technologies.* Berkeley and Los Angeles: University of California Press.

Bentley, G. R. 2000. Environmental pollutants and fertility. In *Infertility in the Modern World: Present and Future Prospects,* ed. G. R. Bentley and C. G. Nicholas Mascie-Taylor, 85–152. Cambridge: Cambridge University Press.

Bentley, G. R., and C. G. Nicholas Mascie-Taylor, eds. 2000. *Infertility in the Modern World: Present and Future Prospects.* Cambridge, United Kingdom: Cambridge University Press.

Bharadwaj, Aditya. 1999. Barren wives and sterile husbands: Infertility and assisted conception in India. Paper presented at the conference "Gender, health, and healing: Reflections on the public and private divide," University of Warwick, April 23–24.

———. 2000. How some Indian baby makers are made: Media narratives and assisted conception in India. *Anthropology and Medicine* 7:63–78.

———. 2001. Conceptions: An exploration of infertility and assisted conception in India. PhD thesis, University of Bristol.

———. 2002. Conception politics: Medical egos, media spotlights, and the contest over test-tube firsts in India. In *Infertility around the Globe: New Thinking on Childlessness, Gender, and Reproductive Technologies,* ed. M. C. Inhorn and F. van Balen, 315–33. Berkeley and Los Angeles: University of California Press.

———. 2003. Why adoption is not an option in India: The visibility of infertility, the secrecy of donor insemination, and other cultural complexities. *Social Science and Medicine* 56:1867–80.

Bharat, S. 1993. *Child Adoption in India—Trends and Emerging Issues: A Study of Adoption Agencies.* Bombay: Tata Institute of Social Sciences.

Bittles, A. H., and P. L. Matson. 2000. Genetic influences on human infertility. In *Infertility in the Modern World: Present and Future Prospects,* ed. G. R. Bentley and C. G. Nicholas Mascie-Taylor, 46–81. Cambridge: Cambridge University Press.

Boerma, J. Ties, and Zaida Mgalla, eds. 2001. *Women and Infertility in Sub-Saharan Africa: A Multi-disciplinary Perspective.* Amsterdam: Royal Tropical Institute.

Charmaz, K. 1983. Loss of self: A fundamental form of suffering in the chronically ill. *Sociology of Health and Illness* 5:168–95.

Daniluk, Judith C. 1988. Infertility: Intrapersonal and interpersonal impact. *Fertility and Sterility* 49:982–90.

Das, Veena. 1995. National honor and practical kinship: Unwanted women and children. In *Conceiving the New World Order: The Global Politics of Reproduction,* ed. F. D. Ginsburg and R. Rapp, 212–33. Berkeley and Los Angeles: University of California Press.

Davis, L. J. 1997. Introduction. In *The Disability Studies Reader,* ed. L. J. Davis, 1–6. New York: Routledge.

Fishel, S., K. Dowell, and S. Thornton. 2000. Reproductive possibilities for infertile couples: Present and future. In *Infertility in the Modern World: Present and Future Prospects,* ed. G. R. Bentley and C. G. Nicholas Mascie-Taylor, 17–45. Cambridge: Cambridge University Press.

Franklin, Sarah. 1997. *Embodied Progress: A Cultural Account of Assisted Conception.* London: Routledge.

Gerrits, Trudie. 2002. Infertility and matrilineality: The exceptional case of the Macua of Mozambique. In *Infertility around the Globe: New Thinking on Childlessness, Gender, and Reproductive Technologies*, ed. M. C. Inhorn and F. van Balen, 233–46. Berkeley and Los Angeles: University of California Press.

Goffman, Erving. 1963. *Stigma: Notes on the Management of Spoiled Identity*. Englewood Cliffs: Prentice-Hall.

Greil, Arthur L. 1991a. A secret stigma: The analogy between infertility and chronic illness and disability. *Advances in Medical Sociology* 2:17–38.

———. 1991b. *Not Yet Pregnant: Infertile Couples in Contemporary America*. New Brunswick: Rutgers University Press.

———. 1997. Infertility and psychological distress: A critical review of the literature. *Social Science and Medicine* 45:1679–1704.

Greil, Arthur L., Thomas A. Leitko, and Karen L. Porter. 1989. Infertility: His and hers. *Gender and Society* 2:172–99.

Hartmann, Betsy. 2002. Charting a path ahead: Who defines women's health and how? Paper presented at the conference "Defining women's health: An interdisciplinary dialogue," Harvard University, May 4, 2002.

Hirsch, Eric. 1999. Negotiating limits: Interviews in south-east England. In *Technologies of Procreation: Kinship in the Age of Assisted Conception*, 2nd ed., ed. J. Edwards, S. Franklin, E. Hirsch, F. Price, and M. Strathern, 91–121. London: Routledge.

Ingstad, Benedicte. 1995. Mpho ya modimo—A gift from God: Perspectives on "attitudes" toward disabled persons. In *Disability and Culture*, ed. B. Ingstad and S. R. Whyte, 246–63. Berkeley and Los Angeles: University of California Press.

Inhorn, M. C. 1994. *Quest for Conception: Gender, Infertility, and Egyptian Medical Traditions*. Philadelphia: University of Pennsylvania Press.

———. 1996. *Infertility and Patriarchy: The Cultural Politics of Gender and Family Life in Egypt*. Philadelphia: University of Pennsylvania Press.

———. 2002. Sexuality, masculinity, and infertility in Egypt: Potent troubles in the marital and medical encounters. *Journal of Men's Studies* 10:343–59.

———. 2003a. *Local Babies, Global Science: Gender, Religion, and in-Vitro Fertilization in Egypt*. New York: Routledge.

———. 2003b. "The worms are weak": Male infertility and patriarchal paradoxes in Egypt. *Men and Masculinities* 5:236–56.

———. 2004. Middle Eastern masculinities in the age of new reproductive technologies: Male infertility and stigma in Egypt and Lebanon. *Medical Anthropology Quarterly* 18:162–82.

Inhorn, M. C., and F. Van Balen, eds. 2002. *Infertility around the Globe: New Thinking on Childlessness, Gender, and Reproductive Technologies*. Berkeley and Los Angeles: University of California Press.

Irvine, D. S. 1998. Epidemiology and aetiology of male infertility. *Human Reproduction* 13 (Supplement):33–44.

Jeffery, Roger, and Patricia Jeffery. 1989. *Labour Pains and Labour Power: Women and Childbearing in India*. London: Zed Books.

Jenkins, Gwynne L., with Silvia Vargas Obando and Jose Badilla Navas. 2002. Childlessness, adoption, and *milagros de Dios* in Costa Rica. In *Infertility around the Globe: New Thinking on Childlessness, Gender, and Reproductive Technologies*, ed. M. C. Inhorn and F. van Balen, 171–89. Berkeley and Los Angeles: University of California Press.

Kleinman, Arthur. 1995. *Writing at the Margin: Discourse between Anthropology and Medicine*. Berkeley and Los Angeles: University of California Press.

Meirow, D., and J. G. Schenker. 1996. The current status of sperm donation in assisted reproduction technology: Ethical and legal considerations. *Journal of Assisted Reproduction and Genetics* 14:133–38.

Nachtigall, Robert D., Gay Becker, and Mark Wozny. 1992. The effects of gender-specific diagnosis on men's and women's response to infertility. *Fertility and Sterility* 54:113–21.

Population Reference Bureau. 1999. World population data sheet: Demographic data and estimates for the countries and regions of the world. Washington, D.C.: Population Reference Bureau.

Reame, Nancy King. 2000. Making babies in the twenty-first century: New strategies, old dilemmas. *Women's Health Issues* 10:152–59.

Riessman, Catherine Kohler. 2000. Stigma and everyday resistance practices: Childless women in south India. *Gender and Society* 14(1):111–35.

———. 2002. Positioning gender identity in narratives of infertility: South Indian women's lives in context. In *Infertility around the Globe: New Thinking on Childlessness, Gender, and Reproductive Technologies*, ed. M. C. Inhorn and F. van Balen, 152–70. Berkeley and Los Angeles: University of California Press.

Robertson, John A. 1996. Legal troublespots in assisted reproduction. *Fertility and Sterility* 65:11–12.

Sandelowski, Margarete. 1991. *With Child in Mind: Studies of the Personal Encounter with Infertility*. Philadelphia: University of Pennsylvania Press.

Sandelowski, Margarete, and Sheryl de Lacey. 2002. The uses of a "disease": Infertility as rhetorical vehicle. In *Infertility around the Globe: New Thinking on Childlessness, Gender, and Reproductive Technologies*, ed. M. C. Inhorn and F. van Balen, 33–51. Berkeley and Los Angeles: University of California Press.

Scheper-Hughes, Nancy, and Margaret Lock. 1987. The mindful body: A prolegomenon to future work in medical anthropology. *Medical Anthropology Quarterly*, n.s., 1:6–41.

Schleifer, Aliah. 1986. *Motherhood in Islam*. Cambridge: Islamic Academy.

Sciarra, J. 1994. Infertility: An international health problem. *International Journal of Gynecology and Obstetrics* 46:155–63.

Sonbol, Amira al-Azhary. 1995. Adoption in Islamic society: A historical survey. In *Childhood in the Muslim Middle East*, ed. E. W. Fernea, 45–67. Austin: University of Texas Press.

Sundby, Johanne. 2002. Infertility and health care in countries with less resources: Case studies from sub-Saharan Africa. In *Infertility around the Globe: New Thinking on Childlessness, Gender, and Reproductive Technologies,* ed. M. C. Inhorn and F. van Balen, 247–60. Berkeley and Los Angeles: University of California Press.

Thompson, Charis M. 2002. Fertile ground: Feminists theorize infertility. In *Infertility around the Globe: New Thinking on Childlessness, Gender, and Reproductive Technologies,* ed. M. C. Inhorn and F. van Balen, 52–78. Berkeley and Los Angeles: University of California Press.

———. 2005. *Making Parents: The Ontological Choreography of Reproductive Technologies.* Cambridge, Mass.: MIT Press.

United Nations [UN]. 1983. *World Programme of Action Concerning Disabled Persons.* New York: United Nations.

Van Balen, F. 2002. The psychologization of infertility. In *Infertility around the Globe: New Thinking on Childlessness, Gender, and Reproductive Technologies,* ed. M. C. Inhorn and F. Van Balen, 79–98. Berkeley and Los Angeles: University of California Press.

Van Balen, F., and T. C. M. Trimbos-Kemper. 1998. Involuntary childless couples: Their desire to have children and their motives. *Journal of Psychosomatic Obstetrics* 16:137–44.

Wendell, Susan. 1997. Toward a feminist theory of disability. In *The Disability Studies Reader,* ed. L. J. Davis, 260–78. New York: Routledge.

Whyte, S. R., and B. Ingstad. 1995. Disability and culture: An overview. In *Disability and Culture,* ed. B. Ingstad and S. R. Whyte, 3–32. Berkeley and Los Angeles: University of California Press.

World Bank. 2000. *World Bank Report.* www.worldbank.org.

World Health Organization [WHO]. 1980. *International Classification of Impairments, Disabilities, and Handicaps.* Geneva: World Health Organization.

4   The Chosen Body and the Rejection of Disability in Israeli Society

MEIRA WEISS

The Zionist revolution that aimed to create a new people for a new land had a unique bodily aspect. For central Zionist thinkers at the beginning of the twentieth century, returning to the land of Israel and becoming involved in agriculture was supposed to restore the health of Jewish bodies. Agriculture, land, territory, and military power were seen as antidotes to what was perceived as the passivity and "spirituality" of Jews and Judaism in the diaspora. In Max Nordau's term, coined as early as 1898, Zionism was to be "Judaism with muscles."[1] This glorification of the physical body has had implications for the devaluation of the disabled body. In this chapter I extend my reading of the body in Israeli society to include disability issues.

My focus on the body as a mirror of social paradigms and a performative cultural script reflects socioanthropological insights that have emerged in the second half of the twentieth century (Martin 1990, 1994). Traditionally, "the body" has been treated by social scientists as a universal biological entity that "falls naturally into the domain of the basic sciences and is therefore beyond the purview of social and cultural anthropology" (Lock 1993:134). Since the late 1970s, as Lock (1993) argues in her review of the body in anthropology, the universalistic perspective of the body has been shifted. Bodily practices and knowledge were put under the sociological gaze.[2] As Berthelot (1986) has remarked in regard to socioanthropological literature, "the body would now appear to be everywhere." My anthropological take on the body follows the work of Foucault (1971, 1973, 1977, 1980), who placed the body in a political context and within processes of knowledge and power. This critical view was also developed by sociologists working in the Marxist and feminist traditions, who stressed the role of the body as a window to class and gender hierarchies. "Writing the body"

(Game 1991) has now become a feminist ideological platform signifying an alternative mode of "embodied thought" and a deconstruction of the male logocentric master narrative of rationality (Braidoti 1994). Writing the body hence becomes a subversive strategy, capable of "undoing" the social. This motivation is also behind the present study, which sets out to undo the taken-for-granted devaluation of disability in Israeli society.

The social construction of the "chosen body" within Zionism followed a gendered, utopian, and collectivist pattern characteristic of nineteenth-century European nationalistic movements. Several researchers have already probed into the connection between bodybuilding and nation building (Levy-Schreiber and Ben-Ari 2000). Anita Shapira (1989:28), for example, wrote that Zionism sought to "replace the *Yeshiva* [religious high-school] student with a healthy youngster, daring and ready for battle." Michael Gluzman (1977:147) emphasized the gendered aspect of that conversion. In his words, the Zionist body is Jewish, Ashkenazi, and masculine: "Maccabi reincarnated." This trope appears, for example, in canonical Zionist texts such as Herzl's *Alteneuland* (German for "Old New Land," meaning Zion; Gluzman 1997:149). Gluzman and others have stressed the gendered aspects of the Jewish pioneer and the Sabra, yet ignored another, no less important physical characteristic: the idealization of health, power, and physical perfection. I call this masculine, Jewish, European-born (Ashkenazi), perfect, and wholesome trope, for short, "the chosen body." This trope is an ideal type by which concrete Israeli bodies are screened and molded from gestation to death.

Since its pre-state Zionist era and following its inception in 1948, the Israeli collectivity has been regulating bodies as part of the ongoing construction of its identity. Israel's continuing involvement in an armed conflict with its Arab neighbors has created a society deeply concerned with territorial borders as well as bodily boundaries. Building on my book *The Chosen Body* (Weiss 2002), this chapter focuses on the relation between the Israeli nationalistic ethos of the perfectible body and disability issues. I track the footprints of the "chosen body" in disability-related fields such as prenatal screening and the rejection of appearance-impaired children by their families.

DISABILITY IN ISRAELI SOCIETY

How does Israeli society generally treat people with disabilities? According to the Report of the Public Committee on Legislation Concerning People with Disabilities (1997), approximately 10 percent of the Israeli population have disabilities. It is a "minority group that suffers discrimination, segregation, and stigmatization" (Report of the Public Committee 1997:12). The report paints a bleak picture in which people with disabilities are ignored by most of the systems in Israel. According to it, only far-reaching legislation regarding the rights of people with disabilities could correct the existing situation.[3] Many public buildings in Israel are inaccessible to handicapped people. Most of the persons with developmental disabilities live in institutions (approximately 80%). There is no national agenda for sponsoring or budgeting of leisure activities for persons with disabilities.

Sagit Mor (2005) shows that people with disabilities are marginalized and excluded. In particular, she examines Israel's social welfare law and concludes that efforts to compensate for disability manifest not acceptance of disability but rather its rejection and denial. In her words, "welfare laws and policies have also had a significant role in developing, furthering and reinforcing the power hierarchies to which people with disabilities are subjected. . . . hierarchies of welfare benefits reflect national values and collective imageries but at the same time reinforce and reconstitute those values and modes of imagination. . . . these patterns eventually render [all disabled people] inferior and of a lesser value than the nondisabled" (Mor 2005:63–64).

In 2005, a governmental committee published its report on how to improve the situation of people with disabilities in Israel and to help them return to work; representatives of Israeli organizations for and of people with disabilities protested that the report did not do enough to improve the situation and that it is a bad idea to establish a kind of "Wisconsin Program," in which private agencies would be responsible for allocating work to people with disabilities (Edri 2005). Finally, in a recent survey it was found that a relatively large proportion of Israeli society—as many as 17 percent—reported that in their view people with disabilities were an obstacle for society (Sinay 2006).

Persons with disabilities caused by war constitute a significant issue in Israeli society, not only because of their relatively large number but since they have given part of their bodies for the country. In a manner similar to fallen soldiers, handicapped veterans should have received as much symbolic acceptance and gratitude. Yet, according to the Report of the Public Committee (1997), this is not the case. Although handicapped veterans receive ample financial support from the Ministry of Defense through its Department of Rehabilitation, in practice they are segregated. Israeli society, as a whole, is inaccessible—physically and culturally—to persons with disabilities. Public buildings that are usually inaccessible include hospitals, kindergartens, schools, colleges, museums, clubs, swimming pools, cinemas, and so on. Public transportation is not equipped for persons with disabilities. Handicapped veterans are thus entitled to receive a specially equipped car from the Ministry of Defense. Symbolically, however, the specially equipped car is also a mechanism of seclusion. "We [Israeli society] are practically showing our backs to them [namely ignoring persons with disabilities]. You are a handicapped? Don't go to a restaurant—eat a sandwich at home" (letter cited in the Report of the Public Committee 1997:42).

In Mor's words (2005:65):

> People with disabilities in Israel are subjected to two interrelated systems of power, which mutually inform one another and together contribute to the overall marginalization and exclusion of *all* people with disabilities. One concerns the construction of difference between disabled and nondisabled people; the second is the division and fragmentation among three main categories of people with disabilities: disabled veterans, the work-injured, and the general population of people with disabilities. I argue that even veterans' disability is eventually understood as inferiority, and efforts to compensate for disability do not manifest acceptance of disability but rather its rejection and denial.

In his testimony before the Public Committee on Legislation Concerning People with Disabilities, Doron Yehuda, chairman of the Coalition of the Disabled in Israel, an organization representing more than half a million people, leveled similar accusations. "We can't get jobs because we can't get into most buildings," he said. "If I do find a job, I can't use the toilets, because they're unsuitable" (Report of the Public Committee 1997). The symbolic exclusion and segregation of persons with disabilities—and particularly of handicapped veterans—is also a harsh testimony of the cultural hegemony of the discourse of the "chosen body."

PRENATAL GENETIC TESTING, DISABILITY
RIGHTS, AND THE CHOSEN BODY

In 1928, the house physician of the first Hebrew school in Tel Aviv wrote in his diary: "Zionism was accepted only by compatible men and women who were whole-bodied and physically fit. . . . Our people are currently experiencing a natural process of screening." It has taken about 70 years until prenatal genetic testing has made this process of screening ever more contrived and scientific. Prenatal genetic testing evokes a spectrum of responses. At one end, some question whether parents should allow a genetically diseased infant to be born; at the other, some attack the morality of elective abortion (Rothman 1986). An intermediate position, allowing or encouraging abortions for some kinds of genetic diseases but not others, raises difficult questions of drawing lines in regard to relative "severity" and "mildness." If society offers prenatal testing for genetic diseases, who defines "disease"? The definition of disease, as well as of handicap and disability, inevitably involves social values and cultural construction (Shakespeare 1995; Parens and Asch 2000).

In recent years, genetic testing has become big business in Israel. Tay-Sachs screening is now recommended to the entire Jewish population and is state-subsidized (Zlotogora and Leventhal 2000). The number of prenatal genetic tests being offered is constantly increasing, and so is the proportion of women using them. It was found by Sher et al. (2003) that 61 percent of Israeli Jewish women performed the triple test (as opposed to only 7% of the ultrareligious women), and 94 percent of the secular women older than 35 years performed amniocentesis (in contrast to 36% of the religious, and none of the ultrareligious). Being secular, having a higher income, supplementary medical insurance, and fewer children, and being of Ashkenazi origin were found to be significant factors in determining performance of genetic tests (Sher et al. 2003). The popularity of genetic testing and counseling among secular Israelis is arguably influenced by a national ideology combining pronatalism and veneration of the body (Kahn 2000), as well as by a medical establishment that, generally speaking, legitimizes directivity (Shuval and Anson 2000). For example, 68 percent of Israeli geneticists agreed that giving birth to a child with a serious impairment is socially wrong. In contrast, geneticists around the world usually regard such a decision as primarily personal. Fourteen per cent of the Israeli geneticists agreed with the claim that "the role of genetics is to purify the human genetic pool" (Wertz 1998).

The Israeli case highlights the contradiction between genetic testing and disability rights. While genetic counselors are trained to be nondirective and avoid value judgments in their communication with counselees, they are often perceived as moral advisers. Genetic testing and counseling, in Israel and elsewhere, are "premised on the desire for normalcy and fear of unknown abnormalities" (Rapp and Ginsburg 2001:538). This is the reason why genetic counseling is conceived as neo-eugenic by a growing number of scholars in anthropology, sociology, bioethics, and even medicine. (See Lock, this volume.) As Parens and Asch (2000, 2003) forcefully argue, selective abortion following genetic testing for traits considered disabling is morally problematic, because it expresses discrimination. In addition, it is driven by misinformation, because parents and counselors often have little understanding of what life with disability is like for children with disabilities and their families. For example, Down syndrome is characterized by a spectrum of phenotypic expression ranging from severe to mild, yet genetic testing cannot provide exact information about this, and parents are usually not provided with detailed information regarding the complex variation of expression and the multiple methods that exist for care. Rapp and Ginsburg (2001:538) speak in this context about the "cultural segregation" of disability: "When it comes to information about the forms of medical and community support that might be available to the family of a child with a stigmatized difference, the access of prospective parents is limited. They are often unaware of the social fund of knowledge that would help them make a more knowledgeable choice."

Selective abortion in Israel requires an approval of a special committee of social workers and physicians. The Israeli law of abortion enables pregnancy termination on the basis of fetal defects as well as other factors. (See Amir and Navon 1989; Shenkar 1996.) When young unmarried women (under 17) approach the committee requesting pregnancy termination, they are usually reproached for "not using proper contraception" and warned "to take responsibility next time" (Amir and Binyamini 1992a, 1992b). In cases of fetal defects, however, there is no moral preaching involved, probably since in this case the application is perceived by the committee members to be in line with the normative order and the reproductive requirements of the collectivity.

Most important for our purposes, there has never been in Israel an ethical-medical-religious discussion on the definition of "fetal defects" and why a child with a certain defect cannot be part of Israeli society. There is no public list of fetal defects that can be used to justify early or late (after 23 weeks of gestation) abortions. Until April 1999 the committee forms for pregnancy termination did not even contain a place for describing the defect. Parents and doctors in Israel tend to select abortion in cases that would generate hesitation in many Western countries, such as an easy case of Gaucher disease, spina bifida, or even a cleft lip (Prof. Gideon Bach, head of the genetics department, Hadassah Hospital, Jerusalem; personal interview, 11/7/00).

In Israel Zionist eugenics turned into a selective pronatal policy backed by state-of-the-art genetic technology. According to Tzipi Ivry (1999), the worldview of Israeli gynecologists who are involved in legitimate abortions is based on military terminology. Physicians who regard themselves as "commando fighters" will justify abortions, since military thinking sees killing as a necessary means for attaining its goals. In most Western countries, late abortion is legally prohibited. In Israel, the law permits late abortions and is used by many parents as a basis for malpractice suits against hospitals that allegedly "failed" to warn the parents about fetal defects.

The Israeli Ministry of Health also complains against parents for not conducting late abortion on a defective child that now costs the state a lot of money. (See also Ivry 2004; Hashiloni-Dolev, forthcoming.)

Donor insemination is yet another reproductive technology whose social usage in Israel is influenced by the script of the "chosen body." Israeli sperm banks (currently 16) do not enable voluntary trait screening; however, they employ other practices of screening. Since 1998, donor insemination (DI) recipients are offered, by one Israeli sperm bank, a list of donors' profiles from which to choose.[4] Many recipients are, however, unaware of the option and consult other, secretive clinics. All sperm banks guarantee a thorough medical screening of potential donors' health. Birenbaum-Carmeli and Carmeli (2002) found that when asked about their preferences regarding a DI baby, men were more "loyal" to their features in comparison with women, who were more willing to compromise the "natural family" model in favor of an appearance considered more attractive in terms of Israeli Ashkenazi hegemony (e.g., tall and white, with blue eyes and light-colored hair).[5] Their analysis of this observation is quite pertinent to the idea of the "chosen body" (ibid.:374; see also Carmeli et al. 2001):

> Although presently containing different ethnic, class and national groups—to a much higher degree than that which characterized Israeli society when it started developing—Israel's political culture does not include an ethos of pluralism. Groups and sectors struggle not only for participation but also for control over the symbolic (as well as the economic and political) center. Although veteran Ashkenazi Israeli carriers of the white Western image of the *Sabra* have lost much of their power, original images set up by this group are apparently still hegemonic. Furthermore, the politics of appearance and beauty have to do with the 'naturalization' of hegemony, in our case that of the dominant *Ashkenazi* man.

The "chosen body," I argue, provides a common cultural background underlying the various phenomena just described, such as prenatal genetic screening, selective abortion, and donor insemination. I now turn from these pregnancy-related technologies to the rejection of disability after the child had been born.

CONDITIONS OF BONDING:
ISRAELI PARENTS AND THEIR NEWBORNS

My Ph.D. research project focused on parents' reactions toward their appearance-impaired children.[6] What caught my attention in these reactions was a pattern of rejection—alternatively consisting of leaving the child in the hospital and of various forms of abuse at home. About 50 percent of the impaired children were rejected. About 80 percent of the impaired children who were taken home were nevertheless secluded within the home (Weiss 1994). Israel has been number one in the world in its rate of child rejection due to impairments.[7] My observations indicated a list of external attributes that, once spotted, could result in the child's rejection by its parents. This list included blue skin color, an opening along the spine, a cleft lip, lack of proportion in the facial features, medical apparatus attached to the body, or openings made in the body. Moreover, I found that parents were bothered more by external, openly visible impairments than by internal or disguised defects.

According to Kantor and Jacqualyn (2003:10): "It is estimated that 1.1 million [American] children are severely limited by chronic diseases, 150,000 of which are unable to engage in any major childhood activities. Half of these 150,000 children receive care in the home while the remaining half (6.8%) receive care in institutional settings. Mental disabilities are the most frequent causes of institutionalization among this population group." Although the population groups are different by definition, it is interesting to note that the reported percentage (6.8%) of institutionalized disabled children in the United States is the same as the percentage (7%) of Israeli children with an internal impairment who are institutionalized. It is in the context of *visible* impairment that the percentage of abandonment peaks (to 68.4%) in Israel. This finding fits the thesis that Israelis pay special attention to bodily *appearance* since the "chosen body" reflects and prescribes a particular *image* of the body.

Although openly condemned in Western societies, practices of rejecting children with impairments are frequent in Israel. Sadly enough, this has been part of human history in general.[8] Child rejection and neglect, however, was supposed to have been corrected by the advent of technological progress and the welfare society. In contemporary Western society, we find that stigmatization of impaired appearance often persists, although practices of infanticide and mortal neglect have been replaced by hospitalization and social denigration. The issue of impaired appearance of American children was studied by Beuf (1990), who found that such mainly aesthetic disorders as vitiligo, psoriasis, cleft palate, obesity, and myopia are often deeply stigmatized.[9] The stigma persists in spite of economic and technological progress. However, although the rejection and stigmatization of appearance-impaired people is a worldwide phenomenon, Israel is still prominent in the proportions of excluding appearance-impaired children.

In accounting for child rejection, anthropologists have traditionally invoked either religion (usually in the case of "simple" African societies) or material hardships (as in Third World countries such as Brazil). In modern Israel, these two factors presumably do not play a major role, and child rejection must therefore be linked to other cultural scripts. I relate the stigmatization of impaired appearance to the culture of the "chosen body" after presenting the following examples. Taken out of the overall data, these cases are representative of the entire study population that I observed.

"IS EVERYTHING IN PLACE?"— MOTHERS' FIRST REACTIONS TO THEIR NEWBORN

I begin with a description of the behavior exhibited by Israeli mothers immediately upon giving birth to a normal child. The following amalgamated pattern of reactions is a "prototype," manifested whether the newborn is normal or impaired; however, it is in the former case, not in the latter, that the queries are positively answered and the potential dilemma is resolved.

The mothers' remarks generally follow a similar pattern. The moment the child is born, the mother expresses interest in the newborn's sex on the basis of external sex organs. At this point some mothers request to see their babies' sex organs in order to confirm the midwife's proclamation regarding the child's sex, which generally elicits a response either of delight or of disappointment. It seems that sex is indeed the primary component of external appearance in establishing relations.

The next reaction is the same for both sexes. At this stage, when a connection between external form and normalcy is already established, mothers begin to examine their babies visually. They check the body limb by limb, comment on the coloring, size, weight, perfection, and proportion. Consider the following remarks of new mothers from different ethnic and educational backgrounds: "Is he O.K.?" "What a cute girl! She's really big . . . and pink." "Is he all right? Not missing anything?" "Everything in place?" "Why are her fingers so small and blue?" "Why is his head so big? Is that normal?" "Why is she so bald?"

If the baby passes this external examination, it is called "sweetie" and other names of endearment, and its acceptance into the family is indicated by references to some external similarity between the child and another member of the family. However, if the newborn does not pass the test of appearance or, worse, invalidates its measures as a result of some impairment, patterns of rejection might come into play.

Case 1: The Child with a Tail

The Meshulams' son was born with spina bifida. Mrs. Meshulam, a 21-year-old native Israeli of Yemenite extraction, is a housewife with ten years of schooling. She and her husband identify themselves as religious and have another son. The midwife noticed the serious defect the moment the child was born, since part of the membranes of the spinal cord were exposed and protruding:

> MOTHER: Wonderful! Is it a boy, or a girl?
> MIDWIFE: A boy.
> MOTHER: Oh, I'm so happy! I so much wanted a boy. Let me see him.
> ANOTHER MIDWIFE: Yes, but he seems to have something on his spine.
> MOTHER: Is it serious? Is it crooked? Are they going to operate on him in order to remove the crookedness?

The doctor, who was summoned immediately, brought the father into the delivery room and explained the situation to the parents, saying that "the child has no chance of surviving for more than a few months. We cannot repair such a defect. My advice is that you sever contact with the child."

Heavyhearted, the parents remained silent. Then they whispered to each other and finally came to a decision:

> MOTHER (EMPHATICALLY): We want to see the child.
> DOCTOR: I don't think you should. It will be hard for you.
> FATHER: We insist.

The nurse brought in the child, who was already dressed and looked very cute:

> MOTHER: What a doll! You look so cute.
> FATHER: Really beautiful.
> MOTHER: He is such a lovely child. Your saying that he has a defect and is going to die just doesn't make any sense. I certainly won't cut off contact with him.
> FATHER: Exactly. We're going to take him home.
> NURSE: OK, give him to me now so I can diaper him.
> MOTHER (DISTRUSTFUL, SUSPICIOUS THAT HE WOULD BE TAKEN AWAY FROM HER): First we want to see just what it is our son has on his back.
> NURSE: Maybe tomorrow?
> MOTHER: No, right now.

The mother kissed and hugged the baby, then grudgingly handed him over to the nurse. The nurse undressed him and showed the parents his deformity. The parents immediately recoiled as if they had received an electric shock:

> MOTHER: Get him out of here. Take him away [motioning away with her hand]. What an ugly thing.

For two days the mother did not go to see her baby. She told a nurse whom she had befriended in the ward that she had given birth to a "baby with a tail" and that she was not going to let "such an ugly thing" into her house. The mother was discharged from the hospital; her child remained there, and she never returned to see him.

Like other mothers whom I observed, the first thing this woman was interested in was the sex of her child. She was happy to hear that she had had a boy. The common greeting, uttered by midwives and nurses in such cases, is: "Hopefully he will grow up to become a fine soldier." Next, the mother's interest shifted to his external appearance. She cast a rapid, superficial glance at her child (because he was speedily whisked out of the room), enough to see his body, hands, and feet. The parents' momentary decision not to sever contact with the child reflected their perception that the child's external appearance was more important than what the doctor said. But the rapid reversal in their decision was also founded on the same perception; they were repulsed by the child the moment they saw his deformity as it was, bare and undisguised.

Case 2: A Cosmetic Repair

Gabi suffered from spina bifida; but in his case the defect was very slight and curable. In a manner parallel to other studies of appearance-impaired children who underwent cosmetic surgery (see Beuf 1990), the case of Gabi serves to illustrate the change in attitude toward the child before and after the operation. On first encountering Gabi and his physical deformity, the parents—nonreligious and of European extraction—reacted with complete rejection and disclaimed any responsibility for him, saying, "He is dead for us." This reaction was not altered by the favorable prognosis given by a senior physician. Only after the external deformity was removed did the parents consider "readopting" their child—not, however, before cautiously examining his looks so as to assure themselves of the repair's success.

In this full transformation from abandonment to acceptance, the "cosmetic repair" operates as a rite of passage, involving even the ceremonial act of renaming: as the father announced after the operation: "We have decided to change his name to Samuel. If a new son has been born to us, . . . he should have a new name, as well."

Miriam, another child born with spina bifida, which in her case resulted also in a paralysis, was abandoned at birth. She had an operation that removed the physical deformity but left her paralyzed and with a very poor prognosis for recovery. The mother was informed that the physical deformity was removed, and thus she arrived, after months of neglect, checked her daughter's naked body, and thereafter remained at her bedside and nursed her. Unlike Gabi's case, in which the cosmetic "repair" removed all the symptoms, Miriam was left paralyzed. Yet the similar changes of heart demonstrated by the parents attest to the overarching significance they attached to the external deformity.

Furthermore, I observed many "normal" children born with a cleft lip or lack of proportion in their facial features who were abandoned at the hospital even though the prognosis for cure was excellent. It thus appears that the rejection by parents is due not to the severity of the disease but to the visibility of the deformity. In addition, acceptance of formerly appearance-impaired children was seen to take place after the deformity had been removed, irrespective of the severity of their disease as established by the doctors.

The following case is different from the others in that it deals with an appearance-impaired child who was taken home by her parents (although not so willingly). It illustrates that although acceptance into the family (i.e., parents' consent to take the child home) may indeed take place, the actual rejection does not stop there but takes many shapes within the supposedly safe environment of the home.

Case 3: The Monster's Ghetto

Pazit's parents reside in a town in the central region of Israel. They are Jews, 30 years old. They have elementary education. The mother is a housewife, considered to be warm and caring toward both her healthy sons, aged five and six. The family resides in a small apartment.

Pazit was born with external deformation—asymmetry of the facial organs—and internal organic deficiency of the heart and kidneys. Her chromosome formation was normal, and there was no indication of mental retardation. Two days after delivery, Pazit's parents requested her transfer to an institution. They maintained this position even when after several weeks all tests confirmed that the baby was mentally normal. The mother explained: "It's difficult for us . . . we are good parents . . . but this girl we do not want at home . . . because she's sick and looks like a monster . . . she is blue [due to a heart defect], each ear is different, she has a large nose. . . . everyone who sees her is appalled [the mother bursts out crying]. . . . It's impossible to accept her condition and her appearance. . . . We don't want this girl." The mother concludes: "We can't bring this girl home. I'm willing to visit her at the hospital, but not to take her home. Where will we put her?

We have a small home. . . . We can't isolate her so that no one will see her. No one will want her in his room. We don't have a balcony to put her on, and if we put her in the corridor everyone will have to see her . . . we are not taking her home."

The parents' refusal to take Pazit home persisted for a few months. Over this period they shut themselves up at home, drew the shutters and refused to admit strangers, fearing that Pazit might unexpectedly be brought home. Once a week the mother visited Pazit, accompanied by the local social worker.

When Pazit was eight months old, the hospital authorities filed a complaint of child desertion and demanded police intervention. Two days later Pazit's parents received a cable informing them that the girl would be brought home the following day. Early the next morning, a hospital nurse, accompanied by a policeman, brought Pazit to her parents' home. The father, together with me, opened three parts of the closed shutter, looking at the ambulance bringing the policeman and the nurse. When their ringing at the door remained unanswered, the policeman put Pazit, well wrapped, at the door. He stood waiting. Very shortly afterwards the door opened, and Pazit was hastily taken in. I had arrived at their home about an hour earlier and observed the parents' behavior.

> FATHER (VERY QUIETLY PICKING PAZIT UP): Where will we put her?
> MOTHER: In the living room?
> FATHER: That's a problem. How will we watch television?
> MOTHER: Maybe we should put her in the kitchen?
> FATHER: Impossible. We eat there.
> MOTHER: So, we'll put her in the corridor. There is no other way. The children will play in their room or in the living room.

And so, Pazit was put in the corridor. The father removed the light bulb, leaving the corridor in total darkness so that Pazit could not be seen. "It's a ghetto for monsters," said the parents. The mother tended to Pazit reasonably well. She was kept clean and had no wounds. Yet, about every two weeks she was hospitalized. During these periods the corridor was lit again, and the house was opened to visitors. "We have to breathe once in a while," said the father. The mother also "tried to rest" when Pazit was in the hospital. Pazit passed away when she was one year and three days old.[10]

BODY IMAGE AND PARENTHOOD

Although difficult to accept, the behavior just described represents a common pattern. Most of the children suffering external defects (68.4%) were abandoned by their families, even though most of them did not suffer life-threatening illnesses and in certain cases the defect was severe only aesthetically (e.g., a cleft palate). In contrast, most of the children suffering internal diseases were not abandoned even in cases of serious illness where the chance of recovery was slim. These findings cast profound doubts on the "natural" and "regular" process of parent-child attachment called "bonding." Nancy Scheper-Hughes (1992), who found similar types of child neglect among Brazilian mothers, related it to the "struggle of survival" taking place under conditions of high mortality and high fertility in poor urban suburbs. This kind of materialist explanation, however, is not relevant to the conditions of life in Israel. Alternatively, several possible explanations suggest themselves.

First, one may suggest that we are dealing here with an ethnically based, specific sociocultural phenomenon, whose reasons are to be located in the traditional culture of Israeli immigrants. Indeed, other anthropological studies have explored parts of Israeli society as traditional social groups undergoing accelerated processes of modernization; when confronted with modern medical technology, members of these groups reacted with apprehension and refusal. "Bonding," then, must have, as Badinter (1981) and Scheper-Hughes (1992) both have argued, "sufficient conditions" (namely the bourgeois nuclear family) in order to be successfully employed as a reproductive strategy.

Notwithstanding the possible validity of such a critique of the myth of bonding, such ethnically based cultural explanations would have to be ruled out, since the observed phenomenon cut across ethnic, economic, and educational categories. The overwhelming frequency of the observed phenomenon could be readily explained according to sociobiology as an evolutionary mechanism functional to the survival of the fittest. However, this general explanation does not account for the rejection of newborns with only slight external deformities. Following Douglas (1973), one may hypothesize that a society deeply concerned with external borders is also deeply concerned with body boundaries.

The disturbing findings on parents' rejection of their appearance-impaired children led me to a seductive yet elusive concept: body image. Body image is uniquely significant in the very first stages of bonding, since no other information concerning the newborn really exists. The image of the body is therefore regarded as being also, one might say, the image of the "soul." This assertion is strengthened by many traditional beliefs that connect an appearance-impaired body with some "sin" committed by the person (possibly in previous life). It is this extreme significance of appearance in the case of the newborn that can account for the finding that

68.4 percent of appearance-impaired newborns were abandoned, whereas 93 percent of newborns suffering from internal defects were "adopted." The congenitally deformed infant challenges the tentative and fragile symbolic boundaries between human and nonhuman, natural and supernatural, normal and abominable. Such infants may fall out of category, and they can be viewed with caution or with revulsion as a source of pollution, disorder, and danger. This can result in the stigmatization of the appearance-impaired child as a "nonperson" and lead to its rejection.

CONCLUSION: THE DOMESTIC AND THE PUBLIC IN DISABILITY STUDIES

This study joins many other studies that focus on the juxtaposition of disability and culture in order to examine the dialectic of the "disabled" and the "temporarily abled" (Ingstad and Whyte 1995). The ideas and practices of the "chosen body" may be uniquely expressed in Israel, but they are also one case among many in the universal dialectic of "normalcy" and "abnormality." By questioning the construction of normalcy and problematizing it within specific sociocultural contexts (such as the Israeli context), the issue of abnormality and disability is also questioned and problematized. The general lesson is that "abnormality" and "disability" are not universal biological essences but rather culturally constructed and demarcated social phenomena.

The conditional character of "bonding," or the parental acceptance of fetuses and newborns, is highlighted in this chapter through the case of children with disabilities or impairments, even when the anomalies at issue are not functional disabilities but rather aesthetic defects. Veena Das and Renu Addlakha (this volume) suggest in a review of my work: "It seems that the tyranny of the norms of appearance threw these children out of domestic citizenship into the domain of the state as the only sphere in which their rights, including the right to life, could be claimed." The idea of "domestic citizenship," an oxymoron at first sight, is interesting, because it blends two opposite realms together: the private and emotional realm of the home and the public and bureaucratic realm of citizenship. In my eyes, this concept captures the conditional character of bonding and, indeed, the cultural tyranny of the norms of appearance prescribed by the "chosen body." If the parental acceptance of children is conditioned upon cultural prescriptions, then Das and Addlakha correctly suggest that a universal and detached concept of "bonding" is often worthless. They suggest replacing it with "citizenship" in order to shelter the rights of children, especially those with impaired appearance.

However, my findings show that such a suggestion probably leads to a dead end, for at least two major reasons. First, while the concept of "citizenship" assumes a rational system of rights and obligations connecting the state and the individual, this system is evidently also culturally constructed. In Israel, the state subsidizes various new technologies of reproduction, including artificial insemination and prenatal testing, as part of its historical pronatal policy underlined by the quest for the chosen body. The Israeli law of abortion, while prohibiting (for religious reasons) the termination of pregnancy for socioeconomic reasons, allows it in virtually all cases of fetal abnormality. Israeli geneticists are directively promoting the use of genetic testing. The result of all this is a particular culture of eugenics that derives its legitimacy from the involvement of state authorities.

Second, while the concept of "domestic citizenship" assumes that emotional bonding can be replaced by a rational commitment to rights, my findings show otherwise. Indeed, the fate of many of those appearance-impaired children who were taken home (even for short periods) was not necessarily better than the fate of those who were left at the hospital or institutionalized. Many of the children who were taken home were neglected, abused, or hidden in dark areas of the house. Perhaps this is indeed unique to Israel. Rayna Rapp (1999), for example, found that in New York, parents of children born with Down syndrome formed associational communities and support groups in order to better support their children and influence the public institutions of state and science. I did not find such strategies of negotiation among Israeli parents. However, let us not forget that in New York state and many other places, the mother of a newborn diagnosed in the hospital is always offered fosterage or adoption placement (Rapp and Ginsburg 2001).

It therefore appears that—as perhaps with everything human—the rejection of disability has biological (functional, universal) and sociocultural (particular) aspects that are inextricably mixed. The case of disability in Israel, when compared to the United States or Europe, presents a particularly difficult mix of the functional as well as cultural rejection of disability. The culture of the chosen body has supported the creation of ideologies and practices that devalue and segregate people with disabilities. If there is a lesson in the Israeli case, it is that advocacy of disability rights should be attuned to as many aspects of disability as possible. The rejection of "disability" should be viewed as a systematic construction whose institutional, cultural, ideological, and practical sources and implications can and should be confronted.

NOTES

1. To fully discuss the history of Zionism is of course beyond my scope here. For discussions on the emergence of Zionism see Laqueur 1972; Vital 1975; and Avineri 1981.

2. The sociological agenda concerning the body comprises, for example, reproduction, sexuality, and gender (Foucault 1980; Laqueur 1990; Martin 1990, 1994), the emotions (Lutz 1988), illness (Zola 1992; Martin 1994; Turner 1994), and postmodern consumer culture (Glassner 1988, 1989).

3. The situation of people with disabilities in Israel should not be compared to other countries only on legal terms. It should be noted that the whole public discourse on disability rights, so characteristic of American social life, is much less present in Israel. (For a description of the U.S. discourse, see Frank 2000.)

4. The phenomenon of selective DI sperm banks is not unique to Israel, of course. Some banks allow recipients to select the donor themselves; others offer a "personal donor" program (e.g., the Xytex Corporation in Georgia, the Berkeley Sperm Bank in California). These new policies bestow on DI recipients an unprecedented ability to modify the procreative process.

5. It is important to note that the preferences found (through questionnaires) are hypothetical, as in Israel no choice was offered and donor matching is performed exclusively by doctors.

6. My research (1978–85) was conducted by means of observations, combined with interviews with parents of children hospitalized in nine wards of three Israeli hospitals. Most of the observations were conducted in the hospitals themselves, while some 200 were conducted in the subjects' homes. The children observed (newborns, toddlers, and older children) suffered from internal and external deformities and various sorts of diseases. Altogether, I observed 100 mothers who gave birth to normal children and 350 parents of impaired (appearance or otherwise) children. These 350 newborns comprised all the impaired children born in the three hospitals during my period of observation; 250 of them suffered from impaired appearance (e.g., spina bifida, cleft lip, bone malformations, etc.), and 100 suffered from internal abnormalities (e.g., heart or kidney diseases). To keep all parties involved anonymous, as promised, all names, details, and other identifying characteristics have been disguised.

7. Personal communication with managing administrators of medical centers for people with impairments in Oakland, California, and New York, New York, USA.

8. Rejection, abandonment, killing, and abuse of such children have been widely reported on since the time of the Greek polis Sparta. (For historical accounts, see de Mause 1976; Pollock 1983.) In European folklore, the handicapped child was perceived of as a "changeling," a creature laid in the cradle by fairies who stole the mother's (real) child. Irish changelings were often "helped" to return to the spirit world whence they came, in some cases by burning them in the family hearth (Scheper-Hughes 1992:375). In almost all cases of handicap, mental retardation, and impaired appearance in infants, there

is a powerful stigmatization at play. Examples abound not only in Western history but also cross-culturally. The African Nuer studied by Evans-Pritchard (1956) referred to the physically deformed infant as a "crocodile" child, and presumably submerged it in water. Another similar attitude toward "witch children" (characterized by such physical anomalies as breech presentation, congenital deformity, and facial or dental abnormality) was practiced until very recently among the West African Bariba. (See Scheper-Hughes 1992:376.) Such physical abnormalities are also counted among the "signs" that tell Brazilian shantytown mothers that their child is "taboo," which leads to his or her mortal neglect. (See Scheper-Hughes 1992:376, where a more elaborated cross-cultural list of such practices can also be found.).

9. This was also shown in studies of handicapped children, infants with facial deformities (Barden et al. 1987), and amputee children.

10. For an analysis of the personal as well as territorial stigmatization of appearance-impaired children in the home, see Weiss 1994.

REFERENCES

Amir, Delila, and Orly Benjamin. 1992a. Abortion approval as ritual of symbolic control. In *The Criminalization of Women's Body*, ed. Clarice Feinman, 5–25. New York: Harrington Park Press.
———. 1992b. The abortion committees: Educating and controlling women. *Journal of Women and Criminal Justice* 3: 5–25.
Amir, Delila, and David Navon. 1989. *The Politics of Abortion in Israel.* Sapir Center, University of Tel Aviv. [In Hebrew.]
Avineri, Shlomo. 1981. *The Making of Modern Zionism: The Intellectual Origins of the Jewish State.* New York: Basic Books.
Badinter, Elizabeth. 1981. *The Myth of Motherhood.* London: Souvenir.
———. 1995. *On Masculine Identity.* New York: Columbia University Press.
Barden, R. C., A. G. Jensen, and M. Rogers-Salyer. 1987. Effects of facial deformities and physical attractiveness on mother-infant bonding. In *Craniofacial Surgery: Proceedings of the First International Congress of the International Society of Cranio-Maxillo-Facial Surgery, Cannes–La Napoule, 1985*, ed. Daniel Marchac. Berlin: Springer.
Berthelot, James Matthew. 1986. Sociological discourse and the body. *Theory, Culture and Society* 3: 155–64.
Beuf, Ann Hill. 1990. *Beauty Is the Beast: Appearance-Impaired Children in America.* Philadelphia: University of Pennsylvania Press.
Birenbaum-Carmeli, Daphna, and Yoram S. Carmeli. 2002. Physiognomy, familism and consumerism: Preferences among Jewish Israeli recipients of donor insemination. *Social Science and Medicine* 54(3): 363–76.
Boswell, J. 1988. *The Kindness of Strangers: The Abandonment of Children in Western Europe from Late Antiquity to the Renaissance.* New York: Pantheon.

Braidoti, Rosi. 1994. *Nomadic Subjects: Embodiment and Sexual Difference in Contemporary Feminist Theory.* New York: Columbia University Press.

Carmeli, Yoram S., Daphna Birenbaum-Carmeli, Igael Madgar, and Ruth Weissenberg. 2001. Donor insemination in Israel: Recipients' choices of donors. *Journal of Reproductive Medicine* 46(8): 757–63.

Douglas, M. 1973. *Natural Symbols.* New York: Pantheon.

Edri, Yitzchak. 2005. People with disability fighting for their future. *Ha'oketz* 5/18/2005. http://cgibin/getmsg/htm6. [In Hebrew.]

Evans-Pritchard, Edward. 1956. *Nuer Religion.* Oxford: Clarendon Press.

Foucault, Michel. 1971. *Madness and Civilization: A History of Insanity in the Age of Reason.* London: Tavistock.

———. 1973. *The Birth of the Clinic: An Archeology of Medical Perception.* New York: Vintage.

———. 1977. *Discipline and Punish: The Birth of the Prison.* New York: Pantheon.

———. 1980. *Power/Knowledge.* Brighton: Harvester.

Frank, A. 1989. Bringing bodies back in: A decade review. *Theory, Culture and Society* 7: 131–62

Frank, G. 2000. *Venus on Wheels.* Berkeley and Los Angeles: University of California Press.

Fuchs, R. 1984. *Abandoned Children: Foundlings and Child Welfare in Nineteenth-Century France.* Albany: SUNY Press.

Game, Anne. 1991. *Undoing the Social: Towards a Deconstructive Sociology.* New York: Open University Press.

Glassner, Barney. 1988. *Bodies: Why We Look the Way We Do and How We Feel about It.* New York: G. P. Putnam's Sons.

———. 1989. Fitness and the postmodern self. *Journal of Health and Social Behavior* 30:180–91.

Gluzman, Michael. 1997. The yearning for heterosexuality: Zionism and sexuality in Alteneuland. *Teoria UBikoret* 11: 145–60. [In Hebrew.]

Hashiloni-Dolev. Forthcoming. *What Is a Life (Un)Worthy of Living? Reproductive Genetics in Israel and Germany.* International Library of Ethics, Law, and the New Medicine, ed. David N. Weisstub. Dordrecht: Springer-Kluwer.

Ingstad, Benedicte, and Susan R. Whyte, eds. 1995. *Disability and Culture.* Berkeley and Los Angeles: University of California Press.

Ivry, Tzipi. 1999. Reproduction as Martial Art. Paper presented at the International Institute of Sociology annual conference, Tel-Aviv, July 12–15. [Part of a Ph.D. dissertation entitled "Pregnant with meaning: Conceptions of pregnancy in Japan and Israel," Dept. of Sociology and Anthropology, Hebrew University of Jerusalem.]

———. 2004. Pregnant with meaning: Conceptions of pregnancy in Japan and Israel. Ph.D. dissertation, Department of Sociology and Anthropology, Hebrew University of Jerusalem.

Kahn, Susan M. 2000. *Reproducing Jews: A Cultural Account of Assisted Conception*. Durham: Duke University Press.

Kantor, Bonnie, and Martin Jacqualyn. 2003. From a constellation to a continuum: Policy and management implications for long-term care. *Frontiers of Health Services Management* 5(2): 3–35.

Laqueur, Walter. 1972. *A History of Zionism*. New York: Basic Books.

———. 1990. *Making Sex, Body and Gender from the Greeks to Freud*. Cambridge, Mass.: Harvard University Press.

Levy-Schreiber, Edna, and Eyal Ben-Ari. 2000. Body-building, character-building and nation-building: Gender and military service in Israel. *Studies in Contemporary Judaism* 16: 171–90.

Lock, Margaret. 1993. Cultivating the body: Anthropology and the epistemologies of bodily practice and knowledge. *Annual Review of Anthropology* 22: 133–55.

Lutz, Catherine. 1988. *Unnatural Emotions*. Chicago: University of Chicago Press.

Martin, Emily. 1990. The end of the body? *American Ethnologist* 18: 121–38.

———. 1994. *Flexible Bodies: The Role of Immunity in American Culture from the Days of Polio to the Age of AIDS*. Boston: Beacon.

Marx, Tzvi. 1993. *Halakha and Handicap: Jewish Law and Ethics on Disability*. Jerusalem: all rights reserved to the author.

de Mause, L., ed. 1976. *The History of Childhood*. London: Souvenir.

Mor, Sagit. 2005. Between charity, welfare, and warfare: A disability legal studies analysis of privilege and neglect in Israeli disability policy. Yale Journal of Law and the Humanities 18(2): 63–136. [Available at SSRN: http://ssrn.com/abstract=930163.]

Parens, E., and A. Asch, eds. 2000. *Prenatal Testing and Disability Rights*. Washington, D.C.: Georgetown University Press.

———. 2003. Disability rights critique of prenatal genetic testing. *Mental Retardation and Developmental Disabilities Research Reviews* 9(1): 40–47.

Pollock, L. 1983. *Forgotten Children: Parent-Child Relations from 1500 to 1900*. Cambridge: Cambridge University Press.

Rapp, Rayna. 1999. *Testing Women, Testing the Fetus: The Social Impact of Amniocentesis in America*. New York: Routledge.

Rapp, Rayna, and Faye Ginsburg. 2001. Enabling disability: Rewriting kinship, reimagining citizenship. *Public Culture* 13(3): 533–56. (Special issue, *Reflections on Disability Criticism*.)

Report of the Public Committee on Legislation Concerning People with Disabilities in Israel. 1997. State Ministry of Israel, Ministry of Social Affairs, Ministry of Justice.

Rothman, Barbara. 1986. *Tentative Pregnancy: Prenatal Diagnosis and the Future of Motherhood*. New York: Norton.

Schaffer, H. Rudolph, ed. 1977. *Studies in Mother-Infant Interaction*. London: Academic.

Scheper-Hughes, Nancy. 1992. *Death without Weeping: The Violence of Everyday Life in Brazil.* Berkeley and Los Angeles: University of California Press.

Scheper-Hughes, Nancy, and Margaret Lock. 1987. The mindful body: A prolegomenon to future work in medical anthropology. *Medical Anthropology Quarterly* 1(1):6–42

Scrimshaw, Susan C. 1984. Infanticide in human populations. In *Infanticide: Comparative and Evolutionary Perspectives,* ed. Glenn Hausfater and Sarah Blaffer Hrdy, 463–86. New York: Aldine.

Shakespeare, T. 1995. Disabled people and the new genetics. *GenEthics News* 5: 8–11.

Shapira, Anita. 1989. *Walking on the Horizon.* Tel Aviv: Am Over, Ofakim. [In Hebrew.]

Shenkar, Y. 1996 Is it justified to kill a fetus for medical reasons? *Medicine* 131(c–d): 101–3. [In Hebrew.]

Sher, C., O. Romano-Zelekha, M. S. Green, and T. Shohat. 2003. Factors affecting performance of prenatal genetic testing by Israeli Jewish women. *American Journal of Medical Genetics,* July 30, 120(3): 418–22.

Shuval, J., and O. Anson. 2000. *Social Structure and Health in Israel.* Jerusalem: Magnes Press, The Hebrew University. [In Hebrew.]

Sinay, Ruti. 2006. Seventeen percent think people with disabilities are an obstacle. *Ha'aretz,* 8/28/2006. [In Hebrew.]

Turner, Bryan S. 1994. *Regulating Bodies: Essays in Medical Sociology.* London: Routledge.

Vital, David. 1975. *The Origins of Zionism.* Oxford: Oxford University Press.

Weiss, Meira. 1994. *Conditional Love.* New York: Bergin and Garvey.

———. 2002. *The Chosen Body: The Politics of the Body in Israeli Society.* Stanford: Stanford University Press.

Wertz, D. 1998. Eugenics is alive and well: A survey of genetic professionals around the world. *Science in Context* 3–4: 493–510.

Wertz, D., and J. Fletcher. 1989. *Ethics and Human Genetics: A Cross-Cultural Perspective.* Heidelberg: Springer.

Zlotogora, J., and A. Leventhal. 2000. Screening for genetic disorders among Jews: How should the Tay-Sachs screening program be continued? *Israel Medical Association Journal* 2: 665–67. [In Hebrew.]

Zola, Irvin Kenneth, ed. 1992. *Disability Studies Quarterly* 12(2): special issue, *The Body.*

5   Disability and Domestic Citizenship

Voice, Gender, and the
Making of the Subject

VEENA DAS
RENU ADDLAKHA

The figures of the diseased and the disabled have been at the center of analysis in conceptualizing certain postmodern forms of sociality. Paul Rabinow (1996) formulated the concept of *biosociality* to suggest the emergence of associational communities around particular biological conditions. Many others (e.g., Ginsburg 1989; Rapp 1999) have theorized that major transformations in biotechnology have led to new forms of community in which people with disability or impairment have formed associational relationships in order to act in civil society and to influence, on the one hand, the decisions of the state, and on the other, the course of scientific research. But while such political mobilizations are extremely important in changing the environment of the disabled, they locate the subject positions of the disabled firmly within a liberal political regime. Issues of sexuality and reproduction can be addressed in such a framework only in terms of the legal rights guaranteed by the state to its community of citizens. As Anne Finger (1992:9) states the issue: "It is easier for us to talk about—and formulate—strategies of discrimination in employment, education, and housing, than talk about our exclusion from sexuality and reproduction."

In this essay, we propose to analyze notions of impairment and disability through a reconfiguration of the domestic sphere, offering ethnographic vignettes from the fieldwork we have conducted in different kinds of locations in Delhi. We hope to show that the domestic, once displaced from its conventionally assumed reference to the private, becomes a sphere in which a different kind of citizenship may be enacted—a citizenship based not on the formation of associational communities, but on notions of *publics* constituted through *voice*. The domestic sphere we present, then, is always on the verge of becoming the political. A focus on kinship not as the extension of familial relations into community, but as the sphere in which the family has to confront ways of disciplining and containing contagion and stigma, yields startling revelations about disability and impairment as located not in (or only in) individual bodies, but rather as "off" the body of the individual and within a network of social and kin relationships.

Finally, by pairing the notion of the domestic with that of citizenship, we will also suggest that *community* as imagined by the modern liberal state in India makes state and citizenship complicated entities, and that claims to membership and belonging within the state may be enacted in everyday life in all kinds of dispersed sites. We identify the hospital as one such site, at which the domestic is instantiated performatively in relation to both state-bounded and kinship-bounded figurations of community. Our ethnographic examples are drawn from a study of Punjabi kinship in which Veena Das was engaged with varying intensity from 1974 through 1994, and from a study of hospitalized female psychiatric patients in Delhi conducted by Renu Addlakha from 1990 to 1992.

VISUAL MARKING: THE IMPORTANCE OF FACE

According to the editors of a recent volume entitled *"Defects"* (Deutsch and Nussbaum 2000), studies on disability have only recently begun to show an interest in the genealogies of earlier periods. Scholars have begun to take up diverse matters—femininity as monstrosity, ugliness as aesthetic category, deafness and sign language, the exotic deformed in the early modern and Enlightenment periods—in order to explore the historical connections between the imagining of community and the construction of normalcy. The category of gender is particularly important for such discussions within disability studies, demonstrating how contingent discursive inscriptions of "defect" could imperil the life projects of female subjects, even in the absence of any functional disability or impairment of the senses. Eighteenth-century European women whose smallpox-scarred faces were rendered "damaged" are one example of defective subjects produced at the intersection of norms of femininity and normalcy (Campbell 2000). Indeed, the importance of the face in defining norms of masculinity and femininity provides a cross-cultural point of entry into this range of issues and shows how defect may produce serious social disability. The example we highlight comes from contemporary Israel.

In surveying the recent literature on disability, we found striking evidence of the conditional character of the parental acceptance of newborn infants with disabilities or impairments, even when the anomalies at issue are not functional disabilities but rather aesthetic defects that mark the child as "ugly." Meira Weiss (1998:149) refers to such children as "appearance-impaired." She explains that this "awkward term refers to children born with facial and other external, visible, deformities which mark the child as 'blemished' and/or 'ugly.'" In her sample of 200 Israeli families, such conditions as spina bifida, cleft palate, bone malformations, and Down syndrome affected the perceived attractiveness of the newborn child. At the time of her study, 50.8 percent of all children born in Israeli hospitals who manifested a major physical or medical defect were abandoned at the hospital; of these, 68.4 percent were appearance-impaired. Her interviews reveal that the parents of such infants were convinced that the sight of the infant would be disturbing to their other, "normal" children or their social acquaintances. In some cases in which the hospital staff compelled parents to take their babies home for at least short periods (e.g., weekends) in the hope that some bonding would occur, the babies were hidden in dark areas of the house. It would not be an exaggeration to say that parents felt that their lives were thrown into peril because the sight of their impaired infants posed danger to their social relations. What was remarkable in these accounts was not that such feelings were present, but that other feelings, such as sorrow, regret, or hope, were rarely expressed. It seems that the tyranny of the norms of appearance threw these children out of domestic citizenship into the domain of the state as the only sphere in which their rights, including the right to life, could be claimed.

It cannot be claimed that what Weiss describes is representative of the ways in which parents treat infants with disabilities or impairments in Israeli families, since her study does not offer a comparative account of families who are bringing up such children. The statistics she cites show that the abandonment of disabled children is not a problem that is considered exceptional. But we would argue that the interview techniques she follows reveal more about the way that the family is positioned in relation to the state in Israel than about forms of belonging in family and community. By contrast with Weiss's example, Rayna Rapp's (1999) work on parents of children born with Down syndrome illustrates a variety of ways in which caregivers and families not only negotiate norms, but also form associational communities such as support groups to learn, provide support, and influence the public institutions of state and science. However, our claim is that the methodologies of data collection of both authors—namely, interviews with parents or with medical personnel—themselves construct disability as an object; and they do so through a great reliance on enunciative statements to track the course of disability. In other words, the modalities of talk in which conversation is oriented to an interviewer interested in information are quite different from, let us say, modalities of talk in which disability is being tracked through rumor, gossip, or other networks of talk that place the family within other forms of sociality.

In the methods we have followed in this essay, we try to elicit notions of domestic citizenship from the *performance* of kinship—we observe how domesticity and kinship are *enacted* in relation to disability and impairment. Further, we track networks of rumors and gossip, exploring how disability and impairment are constituted as objects within these kinds of discursive formations. The particular feature of rumor—namely, its lack of signature and its infective quality—creates a public, as inflected by voice; since speech acts in this mode of talking cannot be tethered to particular persons, they come to be heard as the voice of an overarching, overseeing, hostile collectivity. Within this constructed public, disability and impairment come to be defined as particular kinds of objects that slide into notions of defect that mark other social categories, such as that of gender. Our effort is animated not by a simple advocacy of the *reading* of biological anomalies, with the implication that these are differently constructed in different social contexts—a banal statement—but by the premise that a methodological emphasis on performances and on networks of talk shows these objects in a completely different light. Let us now turn to our first ethnographic case, as narrated by Veena Das.

Mandira was born into a lower-middle-class Punjabi family displaced from their home in Lahore by the 1947 Partition of India. A birthmark covered nearly half her face, but she was considered normal in all other respects. At the time of my fieldwork among this network of families, Mandira had been recently married and had borne a child. On account of the long period over which I maintained my connection with the families in this network, I was able to follow the course of her marriage and motherhood, and the untimely death of her husband. As with other life histories I have documented, particularly those I undertook with the purpose of describing how the violence of Partition was folded into the lives of women, Mandira's history was constructed not through formal interviews, but through the gathering of testimony offered in the context of other activities of everyday life. (See Das 2000a, 2000b.)

For the purpose of this essay, I have strung together the observations, performances, rumors, and fragments of narratives offered on different occasions by different people to tell Mandira's story. However, the linearity of the narrative in this case is an ethnographic device; a tension among various voices is retained, but there is also an attempt to braid them together.

In the two other cases, offered by Renu Addlakha, the story is told through a series of interactions in which the failure of the domestic is enacted through the voice of "madness." There, we do not attempt to present any linearity; a tension between different ways of interpreting madness is registered without efforts at resolution. This is because in the setting of the psychiatric ward in a hospital, the patient's story is told in part through enactments with the doctors and other medical staff and in part through stories that circulate among relatives and other caregivers who have gathered around the patient. Also, once the patient is released from the hospital, her family members rarely encourage further interactions with the anthropologist because of the fear of inquisitive neighbors or other kin in the community. This puts strict limits on what can be tracked through networks in the case of such an impairment.

To return to the case at hand: Mandira had two older brothers and one younger sister. The aspect of her impairment that caused her parents the most anxiety was its impact on her marriage prospects. Indeed, within the wider kinship network, Mandira's birthmark was seen as a major misfortune for her parents, since most of their relatives considered it extremely unlikely that a suitable husband could be found for her. Elsewhere, I have described the predicaments of young North Indian Hindu women who are thrown into a life of dependency on their brothers: despite the recognition of traditional rights of maintenance that a woman may claim from her natal kin, such rights are normally invoked only under the direst of circumstances—a failed marriage or widowhood. (See especially Das 2000b.) Though Mandira received an adequate education, it was not considered honorable among upper-caste Punjabi families in the 1950s and early 1960s, when she was growing up, to allow girls to work outside the home, and despite the relative poverty the family faced as a result of their displacement from Pakistan, these norms governing women's work were still rigidly observed. The parents' whole effort in providing for Mandira, then, was geared toward trying to find her a suitable marriage partner.

As Mandira was growing up, some proposals of marriage did come in, but these were either from the families of men who were marked by some kind of disability or, in one case, from an elderly widower who was interested in finding someone who could look after him in his old age. Such conjugal arrangements for girls who were considered defective in one way or another because of biological or social circumstances were and are not at all uncommon. The social circumstances in question could include a variety of conditions ranging from extreme poverty to rumors of sexual violation or "defects in character." Such a range of factors makes for slippery concepts of defect and may account for experimentation with normality in Punjabi families. For example, norms regarding honor and shame were bent in arrangement of marriages in order to deal with the misfortunes brought about by the Partition. Mandira, however, was a much-beloved daughter. Though the wider kinship network pressed her parents to settle for such a match—which would, in their eyes, solve the problem of her impairment by the promise of some kind of normal married life and also insure that the honor of the wider kinship group was not compromised—the parents resisted this pressure. Meanwhile, the family was finding itself more and more isolated from the kinship network as a result of rumors circulating to the effect that young men (primarily the older brother's friends) were being encouraged to come to their house because the parents hoped to entice one of them to marry her.

When Mandira was about 30 years old—far above the age at which a girl is considered marriageable—it was heard that she had been secretly married. The young man in question was a friend of her brother who worked as a white-collar employee in a reputable firm but was from a different caste and region. It appeared that he was a frequent visitor to the house and had a promising career ahead of him, but no one knew anything about his parents. Instead of hosting any celebrations, Mandira's parents simply sent boxes of sweets to the closest relatives with the announcement that the groom's family was not in a position to come to Delhi for the wedding, and he preferred to have a civil marriage instead of a religious ceremony.

After this event, rumors began to circulate with great intensity. Some relatives whispered that Mandira's parents had visited the pilgrimage center of Hardwar, where they had contracted with a *tantrik* for the performance of dangerous magical rites to ensure that the boy would propose marriage to Mandira. The *tantrik's* magic was supposed to have worked, but the relatives feared that the family would have to pay a terrible price for it. It was also rumored that the boy had fancied Mandira's younger sister, but that, as a result of the magical rites the parents had participated in, his affections were deflected to Mandira. Still others hinted that she had managed to get herself pregnant by him and that the parents had obviously connived at this arrangement, for how else could the couple have found the privacy to engage in sex in the small, two-room apartment in which the family, with its five members, lived? As these rumors mounted, the family became more and more isolated from the rest of the kinship group. It was not that anyone confronted them with such allegations, but the typical feature of rumor—its lack of signature—created an atmosphere of humiliation for them. Over the years of my fieldwork, I witnessed how they were made marginal to the affairs of the *biradari*, the network of cognatic kin. Their visits to relatives became confined strictly to ritual occasions.

Mandira had always been sensitive to participation in large events such as weddings, where she felt people would stare at her or comment on her appearance; now she became reluctant to move out of her house. The situation was further complicated by the fact that she soon became visibly pregnant and gave birth to a baby boy seven months after her marriage. The parents told everyone that the birth was premature, but there were many jokes and innuendos about her pregnancy. For instance, when I asked one of her aunts if she had gone to greet the mother and child, she stated in the midst of laughter that she did so only after nine months were over. Nevertheless, the marriage was observed with great interest to see if it would survive. Meanwhile, it also became evident that with the plunging reputation of the family, it would not be easy for the parents to find a match for the younger daughter, and in fact she went on to college and to an independent career as a schoolteacher.

Whatever the truth of the rumors, it turned out that the marriage was successful, both by the standards of the community and for the couple. Perhaps for the first time in her life, Mandira told me, she was free of always feeling apologetic about her existence. Yes, she expressed regret that her parents were cut off from the relatives, that her father had lost something of his position in the wider kinship network—he was not consulted on issues relating to the affairs of the *biradari*. But then, they knew that their relatives had always considered it impossible for her to have a future as anything other than a dependent relative in her brothers' home, or else as the marriage partner of a person marked as defective in some way or another. Mandira felt that it was envy that was behind her relatives' rumors about her, because her marriage had confounded their expectations.

Tragically, five years after her marriage, her husband suddenly died of a myocardial infarction. I remember going to her house to mourn and feeling that Mandira had turned to stone. As I was leaving, I hugged her, as is the custom, and she did not respond—she just let herself be hugged. When she stood up to see me to the door, I asked her to please sit back down. She responded with a sigh and said:[1] *Yes, I am sitting.* But to the idea of sitting she conveyed the sense of having lost everything—all movement, all life.

For many of the relatives, there was almost a sense of satisfaction that she had received her just deserts. Her parents had played with the sacred in a clandestine manner—brought her happiness against what was written in her fate—and now she and her family were paying the price. But there was one relative, a cousin's wife, who interpreted the intervention of the *tantrik* in a different way. She said that perhaps the *tantrik* had not cast a veil over the husband's capacity to see and judge, as alleged by others—perhaps he had *lifted* a veil and allowed Mandira's husband to see her *as she truly was,* penetrating the surface appearance, as it were. This was the one occasion on which I found a complex citation of cosmological ideas about beauty and ugliness that mediated the way in which the social norms were articulated. Hindu mythology and iconography are replete with examples in which the capacity to behold beauty truly, to overcome feelings of repulsion and terror at the sight of what to the uninitiated is ugly and terrifying, is the sign of a true devotee.

Mandira's life took a different turn after her widowhood. She was invited by her deceased husband's mother, who had been earlier estranged from her son, to come to Hyderabad, where the grandson could, in time, claim the rights to his ancestral property. Her parents did not want her to leave Delhi, but she felt that as a widow her rightful place was with her lamented husband's mother. I did not ever meet her again, but I learned that she had taken a job and was bringing up her son. She might have faced hardships in her conjugal home as a widow, but the labor of her parents had created a version of a normal trajectory for her life. Her natal family did not, however, ever regain the symbolic capital they had lost. They became quite isolated from the rest of the kinship group. In creating a life as close to normalcy as possible for the child with impairment, they had played with other norms in a most dangerous way, but were willing to pay the price.

In analyzing this case, we wondered how much the parents' ability to defy the traditional norms of marriage and kinship—as instantiated in the strategies they deployed in getting a suitable husband for their daughter— was due to the fact that Partition had, in their case, already put the normative family and kinship into question. The upheaval had brutally exposed the fragility of the overall social order within which such normativities were inscribed. In the public sphere, the preservation of kinship norms required the articulation of narratives of family honor that enjoined on men the brutal killing of sisters, wives, and daughters to save them from dishonor, and on women a voluntary embrace of death by suicide. (See Das 1995.) Of the large numbers of women who were abducted or raped during the massive communal violence of this period, many were said to have killed themselves. However, several recent studies have shown that although such normativity did govern the lives and deaths of many men and women, the tactical recourse to alternative ways of dealing with the catastrophe meant that individual stories did not always correspond to this societal emplotment (Butalia 1998; Menon and Bhasin 1998).

It appears that the complex relation between narratives disseminated in the public sphere and experimentation with norms in the domestic sphere might have pried open the domestic space so that new definitions of domestic citizenship emerged for girls like Mandira. Her physical impairment became assimilated with social defect—as exemplified in the figuration of "dishonor" that cast its shadow in this period over theretofore hegemonic norms of life trajectories, opening new avenues for women. Thus, it was the option of contracting a civil marriage, rather than a religious ceremony, that allowed Mandira and her parents to resist the pressures of the *biradari* and, by a strange twist of fate, for her marriage to be acknowledged as legitimate by her deceased husband's mother.

Nicholas Watson (1998:15) has observed: "The experiences of impairment and disability are both public and intimate. It is only through people's stories and biographies that the understanding that unites the public and the private into a coherent entity can come into being." The case of Mandira, on the other hand, leads us to question the idea of the public and the private as unified, coherent entities whose unity can be instantiated through narrative. Our framing of kinship not as an extension of naturalized family relations, but rather as the domain in which a "polityzation" of the domestic is enacted, identifies the way in which Mandira's place within her own domestic space is actually brought into confrontation with her family's place within the set of wider kinship relations. In other words, rather than stable conceptualizations of space, we contend that it is performances of kinship that separate the spheres of the domestic and the public—the public is constituted and inflected with certain ways of deploying voice.

As we saw, the use of utterances that have perlocutionary force, such as rumor, innuendo, and gossip, enacted kinship norms as "public" norms through which pressure was generated on Mandira's immediate family to make her life projects consistent with the societal emplotment of the destiny of women with "defects." Working around this effort to ensure a "normal" trajectory for Mandira, a labor of love was performed by her parents that put the domestic dimension of kinship in a confrontational relation with its public dimension. Thus, in place of the spatialized distinction between the public as constituted by various forms of civility among strangers and the domestic as relations of particularity based on primordial loyalties, we propose that the split between the public and the domestic is negotiated performatively within the domain of kinship relations. It is in this split that we locate the productive tension that can lead to the recasting of social norms. Furthermore, it is the manner in which voice is deployed, rather than forms of spatiality, that demarcates the public sphere within the domain of kinship. We shall see in the next case how the dialectic between the emergence of voice and its denial may define other kinds of publics within which, as a disabled subject, one may or may not have the resources to author his or her own story.

If human anomaly troubles the rhetoric of liberal individualism with its fetishizing of autonomy and agency, the domain of kinship provides an important critical site at which the connections between body-selves can be examined. Since hereditary defects are positioned in the uncanny moment when the familial becomes strange, the public sphere of kinship, in the case of Mandira, was invoked to constrain and domesticate this strangeness. Subtle pressure was generated such that Mandira should either accept the position of a dependent relative (leading to an erasure of her sexuality and her reproductive desires) or be married to a man with a disability or impairment—thus sequestering what was seen as a blemish on the kinship group itself. In this way, the group sought to preserve the normalcy of its other constituent body-selves. The sexual politics of disability in this case—in particular, the anxious concern to deflect the prospect of Mandira's reproduction—was animated not only by strategies to increase symbolic capital, but also by an interest to contain the stigma of disability within an individual body.

In counterpoint, Mandira's parents' recognition of their daughter's full membership in human society, as they knew it, was defined in terms of their vision of a normal sexual and reproductive future for her. Significantly, in pressing their acknowledgment of her as a sexual and reproductive being, they could mobilize Mandira's claim as a citizen of the state to contract the civil marriage that enacted their successful defiance of kinship norms. The performative success of this act points to interesting ways in which the state in India is poised in a contradictory relation to norms of family and kinship. On the one hand, the state grants the concept of *community* a valorized place in the constitution itself; on the other hand, it also provides alternative ways in which membership of the state can override belongingness to the family. Thus the constitution guarantees the right to follow community norms in marriage and divorce as in the recognition of personal law, but it also provides several provisions in civil law for individuals to exercise their own choices in these matters.

Finally, we can see that disability and impairment are treated in the domain of Punjabi kinship as a matter of connected body-selves, rather than simply as a matter of individual agency or autonomy. In this context, the story of Mandira's sister is particularly suggestive, for in her case the parents felt that, having lost their symbolic capital in the wider kinship group, they had to allow a different life trajectory to emerge for this younger daughter. It is this break with the *biradari* that led to the recourse of the family to the emergent norms—novel within their social milieu—of female education and employment. There is thus an intricate relationship between changes in the definition of public space in the 1960s in Indian cities such as Delhi, in which female education expanded, and the way in which Mandira's parents were able to stake a claim in these new public structures once they had lost the symbolic capital that would have enabled them to find their younger daughter a groom through more traditional *biradari*-centered patterns of marriage arrangement.

MADNESS AND BELONGING

We now turn to our second case, in which the voice of the "defective" woman emerges framed by a diagnosis of madness—an uncanny illustration of a failure to live up to norms of femininity being glossed as defect. In a hospital psychiatric ward, claims over both the domestic sphere and the state are enacted, but here, in contrast with the case of Mandira, we encounter the failure of voice. This is to say not that Pushpa, the protagonist of Renu Addlakha's (and her) story, is deprived of *words*, but rather that she is unable to make her voice count. If the lethal quality of voice was evident in the region of rumor and gossip in the case of Mandira, it is the failure of Pushpa to be counted *even as a subject of rumor* that constitutes the dramatic denial of her citizenship within the domestic.

Pushpa was admitted to the Lady Harding Medical College Psychiatry Ward with a diagnosis of "chronic schizophrenia, undifferentiated type." The space of the psychiatric ward in a state-subsidized general hospital in India is not easy to characterize. The hospital wards are structured not on the principle of patient privacy, but as spaces in which family members and the medical establishment are expected to cooperate in nurturing the patient toward a state of recovery sufficient to be discharged from the hospital. This strategy is dictated, in part, by the shortage in public hospitals of qualified staff and other resources. Lady Harding Medical Hospital has a policy that no female patient can be admitted unless accompanied by a female attendant. (See Addlakha 1998.) Since no female attendant was available in the case of Pushpa, the hospital requirement was met by hiring an *ayah*, a private maid. Such practices augment the ward's character as a public space, and patients and their relatives can often develop a spontaneous sociality over the duration of an illness. It is also one of the important spaces in which the state enters the everyday life of poor and low-income families. In conversations in the corridors and wards of public hospitals, one can often hear patients and relatives making claims over the state by invoking their citizenship. (See Chatterji et al. 1998.) If denied admission or medical attention in the hospital, the common refrain of those seeking treatment is: "Why? Am I not a citizen of this country?"

After admission and observation, a differential diagnosis of schizoaffective disorder was made in the case of Pushpa, based on her excessive talking, singing, and evidence of grandiosity. Presenting symptoms listed in the medical dossier were "not doing housework" and "not observing personal hygiene for the last six years." I interviewed Pushpa and her husband during her admission and was also present during an interview with the attending physician. In a few other cases I was monitoring I was able to follow up on patients' subsequent lives in domestic settings, but this proved to be impossible in the case of Pushpa.

At the time of her admission to Lady Harding, Pushpa was 34 years old and had been living with her husband and her widowed mother-in-law. She had been married for 12 years but was childless. Both her parents were dead, and her only sibling, a brother, lived with his wife in a nearby small town. When Pushpa was brought to the hospital for admission, she was reported to have torn her husband's clothes, thrown household articles into the street, and to have once left the house without informing anyone. On the day prior to her arrival at the hospital she had been unable to sleep.

When Pushpa was brought to the Outpatient Department (OPD), there was a postgraduate examination scheduled for the day. She was chosen for the "long case"—used for pedagogical purposes—primarily because of her florid psychopathology. As exhibited, she presented an ambiguous persona with regard to gender. She was dressed in a gray-colored men's *kurta pajama*, beneath which could be glimpsed a sari blouse. Her pale face was framed by an unevenly cropped crew cut of graying locks, and on her upper lip and chin was a thin but distinct growth of gray hair. To complement this striking appearance were a high-pitched voice and an incessant stream of commentary delivered in a forceful, abrasive manner that drew the attention of all within hearing. While Pushpa was the center of attention, her husband and brother cowered in a corner.

After making a cursory tour of the ward while waiting to be seen by the doctors, she returned to the OPD and announced in a loud voice:

> The sisters in this hospital are the worst. In Holy Family hospital the sisters are very good. My mother was admitted there. They made no difference between patients. "Work is worship."

Pushpa's brusque manner, the sharp tone of her voice, and her lack of deference as well as her appearance were in sharp contrast to the demeanor of unobtrusiveness and self-effacement expected of a woman in public spaces. From the outset, Pushpa was the center of attention in the ward because of her open defiance of her husband. When he visited her the morning after her admission, she pointed to him and informed the other ward occupants loudly:

> He is married to Miss Mona Sharma. He married three years ago without my "permission." Miss Mona Sharma is a widow with two children—Gita and Sakshi. There is a murder charge against him. He wants to kill me. He has "ego sperm."

When I asked her what ego sperm was, she replied:

> That is an illness if one has "sexual relations" in childhood.

Then, switching over to English and addressing her husband, she said:

> "You are not my husband, Mr. Rajinder Suri. I am your ex-wife. Get out of my room."

The following exchange took place during a subsequent examination by a doctor making his rounds:

> PUSHPA: Yes, yes, I have hair on my face. My "gynecological tests" have been done at St. Stephen's Hospital, and "testosterone" has been done.
> DOCTOR: What is "testosterone"?
> PUSHPA: It is the man's "sperm," which are weak. There is nothing wrong with me. "I am 100 percent medically fit." His "sperm count" is less. My mother-in-law beats me. She wants me to get "raped." My husband wants to prove me mad. He wants to remarry.

Pushpa's exposure of the family's private life and her pointed aspersions on her husband's sexual prowess and his infidelities challenged the norm of female subservience in a space configured as public by the combination of the practices in the hospital, which allow relatives of patients to stay in the wards or in the corridors, and the manner in which the voice of the patient or her relatives is articulated within it. Yet her condition of madness also allowed others to disregard her allegations. In fact, it was because her proclamations on the private life of the family could not be managed within the domestic space—drawing relatives and neighbors into allegations that they would have preferred to ignore—that Pushpa was brought to the hospital. The medical diagnosis helped to bracket her speech for purposes of maintaining the normativity of the family. The more she transgressed, the more easily her words could be completely denied. I cite a small extract from an interview with her husband, in which he said:

> Then, six years ago, her mind started going in a different direction. She became suspicious, saying that I was meeting other women outside the house. In front of my colleagues' wives, she started saying that their husbands were not good. Then she stopped looking after herself. She didn't wear proper clothes. She would dress the way she was dressed when she was brought here. She also began spending on useless items.

In sharp contrast was Pushpa's own rendering of her life in her conjugal family. Here is one extract from her interview:

> In depression [*dapreson mem*], I was afraid of water. I felt I shouldn't eat. I would hug and kiss my mother-in-law, Mrs. Rajrani Suri. She would say to me, You are inauspicious. You are a *hijda* [eunuch]. No woman has hair on her face. My husband says it is because I have "gents' *ki* qualities" [malelike qualities]. Anyone can have hair on the face. They beat me. They are mad. He tore up my poems. Then I told him, I would have no relations with him. He is too "sexy." Girls came to the house. My mother-in-law would say, Go make food for those harlots. They would hold hands and kiss. He would say to me: You are of olden times; these are "modern" times. My mother died. My brother was alone. Then he [the husband] became "modern."

At one time during the course of the interviews, the brother tried to tell the doctor that Pushpa's husband abused her. Her husband turned to him and said angrily:

> And how long have you kept her? How long did your wife treat her properly? When she came back, she said: My brother and sister-in-law hit me with a broom. They threw my bag out and told me to leave.

Pushpa's lament that her brother did not grant her a daughter's traditional entitlement of access to the parental home constituted the backdrop of the tragic family drama that was being enacted in the hospital space. In the absence of any support from her brother, Pushpa had no choice but to submit and, in her own words, to "adjust" to life in her conjugal family. Consequently, after one or two weeks in the ward, perhaps after some quieting of her symptoms, she began to present herself in a manner that would signal her readiness to return home. She began to pay attention to her appearance, discarding her husband's clothes and wearing the more gender-appropriate *salvar qamiz* outfits. She begged her husband to bring saris from home, borrowed a cosmetic *bindi* mark, and started to apply the married woman's vermilion to her hair parting. She also became more constrained in her physical movements. Most significantly, she began to voice desires and aspirations that would signal her readiness to resume her social role as a wife, although her statements carried a tinge of alienation from these roles. Consider these statements made to the doctor:

> I am not mad. I will adjust in that house. I will go home, "maintain" myself, cook good food. I must get my husband's love. I love him. I want to stay with him. His habits are not good. I don't want him to drink and beat me. He'll realize his mistakes, and then he will give me respect.
>   I will get "adjusted." I even told him that he could remarry. "Honesty is the best policy! Examinations are not a test of ability! I'll regain my health."

And then in an interview with me:

> I and Mona Sharma are both mad, because of our love for him. I have decided that he will marry her. She will come and live on the second floor. I will live on the first floor. Our mother-in-law will live on the top floor. He will control both of us by being in the middle. In return, I will get the two girls, Gita and Sakshi. Let's not talk about it anymore. The matter is settled. When the husband and wife are in agreement, what can the priest do [*miyam bibi razi to kya karega qazi*]?

Pushpa's speech marks an irony toward the female roles she is expected to perform, such as quiet acceptance of her husband's infidelity and of the physical abuse to which she was subjected. She tried to shift the blame for her childless status toward her husband and his condition of "ego sperm." The voice of madness here identifies categories such as that of being "modern" (*my husband became* "modern") as the disabling conditions that drove her to madness. Her speech is ironic in the way in which it cites pithy sayings and proverbs. ("Work is worship." "If the husband and wife are in agreement, what can the priest do?") And this irony defines her relationship to her own madness. Although Pushpa was able to use the public space of the hospital to project her own voice temporarily, in the absence of any support from her natal kin, she lacked the resources to make her story stick. Her brother tried to intervene once, affirming her husband's abuse to the doctor; he was silenced by the husband's reprimand. (*And how long have you kept her?*)

Unfortunately, I was not permitted to follow Pushpa's case in the setting of her family, because her husband felt that it would be painful and would make the neighbors suspicious about the condition of his wife. Nevertheless, on a recent visit to the neighborhood, Veena Das and I learned that the husband had divorced Pushpa and remarried and that they both had moved out of the neighborhood. From the stance of the neighbors, it was clear that it was Pushpa who was considered to be "mental" (a word that has replaced the more derogatory *pagal*, "mad"). However, some neighbors referred us to a nearby shopping center where they thought the husband had started a pharmacy. Our efforts to trace Pushpa and her husband were not successful, but one person in the neighborhood shopping complex offered the information that Pushpa had started a small beauty salon. I recalled that before Pushpa got married she had worked in a salon. It was not possible for us to trace this story over a longer period of time, because Pushpa's story died, in a way, within the spheres of sociality in which her conjugal family was placed. Indeed, Pushpa's erasure reminds us of the way in which women whose lives did not conform to the social scripts of honor disseminated during the riots of Partition were obliterated in the narratives of family and kinship.

We suggested earlier that citizenship is performed as a form of belonging with regard to both the state and the domestic sphere. In Mandira's case, the family was able to align itself with the state, at important moments, in defiance of the wider kinship community. We also posited the centrality of voice in the production and maintenance of publics. The position of the public hospital as a site that both embodies the state in the lives of low-income families and enables a dialectic relation between the maintenance of gender norms and their limited transgression comes out with stark clarity in Pushpa's case. Pushpa failed to comport herself in accordance with gender norms, even in the public spaces configured by her domestic life—the overflow of her behavior beyond the domestic bounds was a threat to the honor of the family—which is how she came to be brought to the hospital. Her speech in the hospital was much freer than Mandira's ever was, but it was this very transgressive freedom that allowed her voice to be erased from her story.

In a sense, we can read the contrast between the cases of Mandira and Pushpa as stemming from the success or failure of natality for women. In the former, membership within the state could be used effectively by Mandira's parents to strengthen her claim to normalcy in the sphere of sexuality and reproduction, while in the latter the institutions of the state (hospitalization, legal divorce on the grounds of madness) were used by

Pushpa's husband to push her out of normalcy. But the relationship between natality and conjugality turns out to be more complex with regard to claims of belongingness in both the state and the domestic spheres, as the following example shows.

CONNECTED BODY-SELVES

Psychiatric disability, as encountered in the space of the hospital, brings to the fore the problematic of disability's location off the body of the patient and within networks of connected kin. It can also demonstrate, conversely, how interested social actors may seek to localize and isolate disability within the body of one person. Vinita's case, which Renu Addlakha briefly describes here, further illustrates the complex articulation between the space of the hospital and the space of the domestic in defining citizenship.

I met Vinita in the psychiatric ward during the course of her two hospitalizations in 1991 and 1992 and also made several home visits between the periods of her hospitalization. Vinita's medical history revealed a disease trajectory of 15 years. The antecedents of her illness were not clear, but the symptoms were reported to have surfaced after she and one of her daughters suffered a road accident in which both of them were mildly injured. Vinita had been a regular patient in the psychiatric department at Lady Harding Hospital since 1982. She had been on psychotropic medication, interspersed with electroconvulsive therapy (ECT) at regular intervals. As is well known, ECT is used in public hospitals in India with far greater frequency than elsewhere (Desjarlais et al. 1995). However, Vinita suffered cardiac arrest after being administered ECT during her admission in 1989 and thereafter had been treated with medicines on both an inpatient and an outpatient basis.

A core element of Vinita's psychopathology, according to hospital records, was her persistent delusions of her husband's infidelity. She accused him of having not only extramarital relations, but also incestuous relations with their daughters. She explained to me:

> This is why he sends me to the hospital. Before, he used to send me to my mother's house, and now he sends me to hospital. That is why the hospital is my natal family [*pihar*].

She also accused him of throwing her into prostitution, saying:

> He sends me to the hospital for prostitution [*randipesha*].

The hospital, in this case, embodies dangers and hopeful possibilities alike presented in the alliance of medicine and state. Vinita's life was endangered by the ECT administered to her, but the vocabulary she used in speaking about the hospital was shot through with images of kinship and sexuality. Visits to the hospital were, in her rendition, like visits to her natal family, which for a married woman is a traditional place of rest and respite from the tribulations of existence in the conjugal family. Yet even this space of respite was marked by the suspicion that her husband was removing her from her rightful place as wife to indulge in extramarital and incestuous relations. Hospital stays, in Vinita's suspicions, were also fraught with the possibility that she would be pushed into prostitution—a fear expressed often by women who have been unable to maintain norms of femininity within the domestic space of their conjugal families.

On one occasion, Vinita's elder daughter voiced the changed nature of their domesticity in this way:

> Our father has put up with her for so many years, and who knows how long it will last? In the ward, most of the women have been left by their husbands after they became ill, but he did not leave her. He does not talk to us [the daughters] much either, because then she grows more suspicious and violent. We have to always be careful, lest she speak her evil thoughts in front of visitors.

In contrast with Pushpa's story, the case of Vinita shows that a simple opposition between natality and conjugality cannot be posited in the modeling of domestic citizenship. Clearly, different kinds of belonging were at issue, but it was not the case that impairment or disability automatically led to an expulsion from the conjugal family. In Vinita's case, the family had to close in on itself to manage its reputation, and the hospital became an important site through which new and more attenuated norms of relatedness and domesticity could be developed; the hospital emphasized the avoidance and distance that the family had to cultivate instead of intimacy and closeness—in order to maintain their reputation. While the accusations of infidelity and incest could be bracketed as the voice of madness within the space of the hospital, they could not be so easily sidelined within the space of the domestic. As Lawrence Cohen (1998:175) has observed in his ethnographic study of old age in the North Indian city of Banaras: "Old people in several of the neighborhoods were said to speak uselessly or to *bakbak*. . . ." The voice was heard not only as hot but as prolific—the bodies of the old are seen to be weak, but their voices are projected as strong and as disruptive to the social fictions of family and kinship solidarity.

A comparison of these cases brings to light the important ways in which issues of sexuality and reproduction are addressed in relation to disability and impairment. In contrast with the readiness with which the literature on disability speaks of rights and of associational communities, there seems to be a relegation of the discussion of sexuality and reproduction to the sphere of the private and the intimate. In proposing the (admittedly awkward) notion of domestic citizenship, we tried to capture the variability of the familial norms, capacities, and resources that interact to create the life trajectories of family members with disabilities or impairments. But equally, we wanted to displace questions of sexuality and reproduction from their confinement within the private and the intimate. Our complicating of various kinds of belonging also represents an effort to speak about the complexity of the nation-state in India, which is variously in alliance and in competition with the family at various sites in the construction and management of disability.

We saw how idealized norms of feminine appearance and feminine behavior slide into the idiom of "defect," with individual body-selves becoming inscribed as more or less defective through speech acts and other performative acts negotiating the demarcation of the domestic and different kinds of publics. Thus, the notion of domestic citizenship creates, we hope, a productive disturbance within an established discussion of disability and impairment that remains dependent on the fetishized autonomous subject of liberal political discourse. When complemented by the concept of different publics as constituted through the articulation of voice, rather than through distinctions of spatiality or modes of sociality, domestic citizenship also brings to light different kinds of sites on which issues of intimacy, sexuality, and reproduction can be analyzed in relation to disability.

The formulation of voice that emerges is not necessarily benign—indeed, voice can have a lethal quality, as in its strict monitoring of norms instituted through rumor and gossip, or when a woman like Pushpa takes on the voice of madness but is unable to author her story. It is this braiding of voices, traversing the domestic and the publics, that shows how the inner and the outer are simultaneously created and read—as, for instance, when changes in Pushpa's outward appearance are seen as signs of her changing inner states. Thus, instead of mythic tropes of universal parental love, on the one hand, and the ever rational state, on the other, we see, through narrative and performance, a variability in the ways that domestic citizenship can empower or fail the disabled and the impaired. Notions of legally defined rights or social entitlements have traditionally informed the analysis of differential allocations within the household. But neither category appeared to us to offer a satisfactory way to theorize the forging in the spheres of the domestic and its various publics of the relationships through which defect, disability, and impairment are embodied, performed, projected, and narrativized, to create the delicate work of the creation as well as separation of different body-selves through which the subject is made and remade.

Is what we have described peculiar to the case of India, whose constitution recognizes and lists communities for several purposes, such as marriage, divorce, and inheritance, even as it bestows rights on individuals? Is it specific to forms of family in which the woman is seen as "belonging" to her husband's house? We hope that the space we have opened up will allow matters to be framed cross-culturally in relation to disability and impairment. After all, imagining the particular forms of family and community that complement the state is part of the repertoire of the construction of citizenship in all state formations. We need ethnographies of performance, tracking disability through utterances that have perlocutionary force, such as rumor and gossip, to evaluate whether biosociality is to be understood primarily in terms of affiliative, associative communities, or whether postmodern forms of sociality demand a reimagining of filiative community (Das 1995) as well. We believe that the twofold project of displacing citizenship from its conventional association with publics defined through civility and displacing domesticity from its conventional place in private, particularistic loyalties offers a productive way of engaging with and responding to issues and provocations raised by a critical disability studies.

NOTES

It is a pleasure to acknowledge the stimulating comments made by Carol A. Breckenridge and Candace Vogler on an initial draft of this essay that helped both to clarify our thoughts and to carry some of them further. The editorial board of *Public Culture* provided a close reading of this chapter that is deeply appreciated. We also want to thank Roma Chatterji and Deepak Mehta for many conversations on the issues discussed in this essay.

1. Translations from Hindi here and in other quoted passages by Renu Addlakha. Quotation marks indicate words originally spoken in English.

REFERENCES

Addlakha, Renu. 1998. Aspects of psychopathology and society. Ph.D. dissertation, University of Delhi.

Butalia, Urvashi. 1998. *The Other Side of Silence: Voices from the Partition of India*. New Delhi: Penguin.

Campbell, Jill. 2000. Lady Mary Wortley Montagu and the "glass revers'd" of female old age. In *"Defects": Engendering the Modern Body*, ed. Helen Deutsch and Felicity Nussbaum, 213–52. Ann Arbor: University of Michigan Press.

Chatterji, Roma, Sangeeta Chattoo, and Veena Das. 1998. The death of the clinic? Normality and pathology in recrafting old bodies. In *Vital signs: Feminist Reconfigurations of the Biological Body*, ed. Margaret Shildrick and Janet Price, 83–97. Edinburgh: Edinburgh University Press.

Cohen, Lawrence. 1998. *No Aging in India: Alzheimer's, the Bad Family, and Other Modern Things*. Berkeley and Los Angeles: University of California Press.

Das, Veena. 1995. *Critical Events: An Anthropological Perspective on Contemporary India*. Delhi: Oxford University Press.

———. 2000a. Violence and the work of time. In *Signifying Identities*, ed. Anthony Cohen, 59–75. London: Routledge.

———. 2000b. The act of witnessing: Violence, poisonous knowledge and subjectivity. In *Violence and Subjectivity*, ed. Veena Das, Arthur Kleinman, and Mamphela Ramphele, 205–26. Berkeley and Los Angeles: University of California Press.

Desjarlais, Robert, Leon Eisenberg, Byron Good, and Arthur Kleinman. 1995. *World Mental Health: Problems and Priorities in Low-Income Countries*. New York: Oxford University Press.

Deutsch, Helen, and Felicity Nussbaum. 2000. Introduction. In *"Defects": Engendering the Modern Body*, ed. Helen Deutsch and Felicity Nussbaum, 1–31. Ann Arbor: University of Michigan Press.

Finger, Anne. 1992. *Past Due: A Story of Disability, Pregnancy, and Birth*. Seattle: Seal.

Ginsburg, Faye D. 1989. *Contested Lives: The Abortion Debate in an American Community*. Berkeley and Los Angeles: University of California Press.

Menon, Ritu, and Kamla Bhasin. 1998. *Borders and Boundaries: Women in India's Partition*. London: Routledge.

Rabinow, Paul. 1996. *Making PCR: A Story of Biotechnology*. Chicago: University of Chicago Press.

Rapp, Rayna. 1999. *Testing Women, Testing the Fetus: The Social Impact of Amniocentesis in America*. New York: Routledge.

Shakespeare, Tom, Kath Gillespie Sells, and Dominic Davies. 1996. *The Sexual Politics of Disability: Untold Desires*. London: Cassell.

Watson, Nicholas. 1998. Enabling identity: Disability, self and citizenship. In *The Disability Reader: Social Science Aspects*, ed. Tom Shakespeare, 147–62. London: Cassell.

Weiss, Meira. 1998. Ethical reflections: Taking a walk on the wild side. In *Small Wars: The Cultural Politics of Childhood*, ed. Nancy Scheper-Hughes and Carolyn Sargent, 149–63. Berkeley and Los Angeles: University of California Press.

6   Dombá's Spirit Kidney

Transplant Medicine and Suyá Indian Cosmology

NANCY SCHEPER-HUGHES

MARIANA LEAL FERREIRA

Until recently, kidney transplant was an expensive and technologically complex medical procedure that was out of the reach of all but affluent patients living in large cities in the industrialized West. But what were once experimental procedures performed in a few advanced medical centers (most of them connected to academic institutions) have now become commonplace surgeries throughout the world. Today, kidney transplantation is commonplace throughout North and South America, Europe, the Middle East, and Asia, and in parts of Africa. Survival rates for kidney transplant have increased markedly over the past decade, although these still vary by country, region, the quality and type of organ (living donor or cadaver), and access to immunosuppressants such as the powerful and expensive antirejection drug cyclosporin.

In parts of the Third World where morbidity rates from infection and hepatitis are high, there is a strong preference for a living donor whose health status can be documented before the transplant operation. In Brazil today, for example, there is considerable resistance in the general population to accepting a "public" organ from an "anonymous" cadaver that may not have been properly screened. In the aftermaths of the HIV pandemic and a hepatitis-C epidemic, the search for living donors has become ever more acute. Even so, the queues for cadaver organs are long, and the waiting lists are often subject to manipulations and *jeitos* (little corruptions) by influential surgeons who manage to secure the needed organs for their *private* paying patients.

Meanwhile, the transplant units at public hospitals are often empty and vastly underutilized. Transplant surgeons, who normally work in both public and private-sector hospitals often refuse to perform transplants for "public" patients who are insured under the Brazilian national health-care system (SUS), which pays what surgeons feel is a mere pittance. (See Coelho 2000; Scheper-Hughes and Biehl 2000.)

Consequently, dialysis clinics (often privately owned), the alternative to kidney transplant, are a lucrative business in Brazil, a veritable "cash cow" that many nephrologists and other medical professionals depend on for their livelihoods. But dialysis is not beloved by kidney patients, for whom "the machine" is often viewed ambivalently at best, and at worst as a kind of penance ("time on the cross"). Three-times-weekly dialysis sessions prevent death from acute and chronic kidney failure, but a life attached to and dependent on dialysis is increasingly viewed by patients as substandard medical care and even as an "unnatural" (that is, a crudely mechanized) solution to kidney failure.[1] Transplant is today the preferred option— though one, for reasons described above, that remains out of the reach of many, especially those without sufficient financial resources.

Unfortunately, however, unlike heart disease and some forms of cancer, kidney disease is extremely "democratic," affecting all classes, ethnic groups, and ages. The most common causes of chronic renal insufficiency are diabetes, hypertension, glomerulonephritis (inflammation of the kidney's filtering units), and polycystic kidney disease (an inherited disorder). In poor and Third World communities undiagnosed or untreated infections often result in damage to the kidneys. Under the best of circumstances, kidney failure can be difficult to diagnose until the disease is already well advanced. In developing nations, the lack of available resources to diagnose and treat end-stage renal disease results in untold human suffering and an inevitable death sentence. In all countries, racial and ethnic minorities and/or indigenous peoples bear a disproportionate burden of kidney failure. (See McDonald et al. 2002.)

Among the most common symptoms of kidney failure are swelling of the body and increased frequency of urination. The afflicted individual may also suffer from severe anemia, fatigue, weakness, headaches, and loss of appetite. Renal insufficiency occurs in children as well as adults. As the disease progresses other symptoms such as nausea, vomiting, and itchy skin can develop as toxic metabolites, normally filtered out of the blood by the kidneys, build up to harmful levels. Patients with chronic renal insufficiency may live with this irreversible condition for a decade or two before it develops into end-stage renal disease, or kidney failure. At this point the patient has only two options for survival: weekly dialysis or kidney transplant.

The spread of advanced medical technologies worldwide has made transplant an attractive option for patients living almost anywhere in the world, from the deserts of Oman to the forests of central Brazil. Transplant promises if not exactly a new lease on life, a seemingly "miraculous" extension of what Giorgio Agamben (1998) refers to as "bios"—*basic* or naked life. Throughout the recent history of organ transplantation, concerns have focused on risk and quality of life for the recipients because, although organ transplantation often saves and prolongs lives, it never restores the patient to full health. The struggle against organ rejection and the side effects of immunosuppressive drugs are lifelong. In other words, organ transplant substitutes one form of chronic disease for another, less immediately life-threatening disease. To most transplant patients, however, the constant risk of organ rejection and the noxious side effects of immunosuppression drugs are accepted as risks and dangers worth taking.[2]

As kidney transplant has universalized and become a common, almost routine procedure, we are inclined to forget that not so very long ago, transplantation was viewed as a bizarre, radical, ethically problematic procedure. To begin with, transplantation required a redefinition of death itself as "brain death," a kind of Copernican revolution in the popular consciousness that was resisted by many individuals, world religions, and societies.[3] Medical anthropologists can recapture some of the initial "strangeness" of transplant technologies by observing their effects in new and very different social settings. Wherever they migrate, transplant technologies transform the human communities with which they interact in profoundly intimate ways. Transplantation introduces new and often alien conceptions of the body (body/corpse/cadaver) and its parts (integral vs. divisible bodies), and new definitions of the person/nonperson. (See Scheper-Hughes and Lock 1987.) Transplant challenges previous meanings of life, death, and transcendence, often "troubling" cultural and religious conceptions of reality, including the ontological status of the real/unreal, seen/unseen, and matter/spirit, not to mention beliefs and practices toward sickness, disability, and human suffering.

TRANSPLANTATION AND THE SOCIAL BODY

Transplantation is the most social of all medical/surgical practices. Traditionally, it relied on the good will of (deceased) strangers and of living kin who agree to share organs altruistically. More recently, kidney transplant has become dependent on strangers who can be recruited or persuaded to part with a part of themselves for cash or other material benefits.[4] Consequently, the "commodified kidney" has emerged as an economic mainstay in some poor and marginalized villages and shantytowns in

South India, the Philippines, Moldova, and Romania. (See Cohen 1999, 2002; Scheper-Hughes 2000, 2004b; Jimenez and Scheper-Hughes 2002a, 2002b.)

In the interior of northeastern Brazil, where Nancy has been conducting ethnographic research for over a quarter of a century, she observed a radical change in the way poor people there view the body and its parts in response to the spread of transplant and the increasing demand for the sharing of organs. In 1997 she interviewed a middle-aged schoolteacher in the Pernambucan market town of "Bom Jesus da Mata" who had donated a kidney to a distant male relation in exchange for a small gratuity. Despite the payment for her body part "Rosalva" insisted that she had freely donated her kidney "from the heart" and out of a true sense of compassion and moral obligation. "Wouldn't *you* feel obligated to share something of which you had two and the other had none?" she challenged Nancy.

It was not so long ago in this same rural town that the anthropologist had accompanied a small procession of mourners to the municipal graveyard for the ceremonial burial of an amputated foot. No one thought the burial of that foot in its tiny coffin anything out of the ordinary. The severed foot was still emotionally and spiritually attached to its owner, and it was to be placed in the site where the rest of the body would eventually come to join it. The body and all its parts were understood as indivisible and unalienable, and the integrity of the body derived from its moral charter as a sacred "temple of the Holy Spirit." Rosalva's view, less than two decades later, of her body as a handy reservoir of duplicate and "spare" (mechanical) parts represented a radical shift in the corporeal imaginary. Examples like these lead one to consider whether the radical materialism involved in surgically transferring organs from one body to another *necessarily* produces a secular, reductionist, commodified view of the body, organs, and tissues, health, disease, and healing.

In posttransplant societies new concepts of divisible bodies depose earlier and more holistic notions of body/soul/person integrity. The sense of one's body as continuous with one's self (which in most places is a decidedly embodied self) is replaced (as in Rosalva's statement, above) by a perception of the body and its parts as "owned" by, and therefore separate and distinct from, "the self," making the circulation of internal organs seem a plausible proposition. But in those places where organ donation is still a unique and new medical technology, popular understandings of organ and tissue "compatibility," "matching," and "rejection" often reflect popular social conceptions and representations of gender, sex, age, race, and class.

In earlier decades, the idea of organ transplant was accompanied by the diffuse anxiety that a transplanted organ would transmit to the recipient some defining personal characteristics of the donor. A Mexican-American doctor who worked at a pediatric cardiology clinic in southern Texas told Nancy that he frequently encountered resistance to transplant among recent Mexican immigrants, who feared that their child would be in a sense "unrecognizable" following a heart transplant. Given their perception of the centrality of the human heart as almost indistinguishable from the "soul," spirit, animus of the person, a new heart signified the death of the child they once knew. David Rothman (personal communication) found something similar in his encounter with a tearful little Puerto Rican boy at a New York medical center who adamantly refused transplant surgery. Finally, he articulated his fears to Rothman, who was not a surgeon: "Will my new heart still love Jesus?"

In South Africa during apartheid, white transplant patients at Groote-Schurr Hospital in Cape Town often feared receiving black South Africans' hearts. Christiaan Barnard and his transplant team often suppressed information about the primary source of transplantable organs—black South Africans (Johan Brink, personal communication). In 1999, Scheper-Hughes interviewed in a suburb of Cape Town an elderly heart-transplant patient, a retired member of South Africa's Security Forces under apartheid, who, upon learning inadvertently that the donor of his heart was a young mixed race ("colored") nurse, demanded that the "inferior woman's" heart be surgically removed and a "proper" white man's heart be given to him instead. On being told that this would be impossible, the man raged and banged his fist against the wall of his recovery room. Later, the general repented his foolishness and tried to contact the parents of the donor to express his gratitude for the new lease on life their daughter's heart had given him, only to be rebuffed by them in turn. The family was not pleased to learn the identity of the man who was the recipient of their largesse. "To think that such a heartless man should get our sweet child's heart," a relative of the donor said.

SUPPRESSION OF DIFFERENCE AND
NEW FORMS OF BIOSOCIALITY

Before the discovery of powerful antirejection immunosuppressive drugs, the constant threat of organ rejection required close surveillance and HLA cross-matching.[5] The issues of "difference" and "rejection" loomed large in the social imaginary. Living donors whose altruistically given kidney was "rejected" by a sibling or another relative suffered from qualms about identity and physical compatibility. (Am I really related to my brother? If not, who was my real father?) Thus, transplant patients in Brazil sometimes experience organ rejection from a living related donor as a sign of personal and psychological rejection (Vasconcelos 1995), an idea shared by some medical doctors. Surgeons in Iraq, for example, encourage kidney recipients and their paid living donors (usually total strangers) to "bond" with each other before surgery so as to minimize the risk of organ rejection.[6]

With the development of powerful antirejection drugs that made receiving organs (primarily kidneys) from living strangers possible, the HLA tests once used to identify and to recognize potentially destructive "differences" were replaced by a chemical technology capable of "suppressing" differences. (See Cohen 2002:9–14; UNOS 2002.) Technically speaking, the powerful antirejection drugs have obliterated significant biological differences and created a world in which almost anyone can become a "kidney kin" to another. Outlaw transplant surgeons, operating in covert private clinics in Turkey where they take kidneys from paid living donors (Christian, Eastern Orthodox, and Muslim) from impoverished rural zones and put them inside affluent Turks and Israelis, often describe the stranger donor as "like [or as good as] a brother," although the pair might meet each other, like ships passing in the night, only as they are wheeled in or out of their adjoining operating rooms. Meanwhile, paid living donors frequently make claims on the recipients of their kidneys in kinship terms. "I hope that one day we will see each other again, *now that we are one*," a poor Brazilian slum dweller wrote to the presumed wealthy North American recipient of his purloined kidney following their double operation, which took place in Durban, South Africa in 2002, arranged by international organ brokers in Israel (Scheper-Hughes 2004a). Differences of race, language, culture, nationality, or religion posed no obstacles to these global operations.

The following narrative, while echoing many of these same transformative dimensions of transplant, tells a slightly different story, one in which the potentially alienating experience of transplant is accepted and ultimately made sense of and "domesticated" through the powerful sacred cosmology of an indigenous Suyá Indian man and his shamans from the Xingu Indigenous Park in the central Brazilian state of Mato Grosso. While the idea of "organs swapping" (as Dombá referred to it) was certainly alien to the Suyá community, with the help of spirit-protected shamans the transplant process was gradually incorporated into the fluid and open-ended Suyá conceptions of reality, nature, human/animal, and self/other relations.

The experience of kidney failure itself must be understood as a medical disability imbued with powerful local meanings and equally powerful local treatments.

DOMBÁ'S ILLNESS

Following several years of increasing disability from an inherited kidney abnormality, terminating finally in end-stage renal disease, Dombá, by then a mature married man of 41, was advised by his Brazilian physician, "Dr. George," who made occasional medical calls by helicopter into a health clinic at the Diauarum Indigenous Post in Xingu, to leave his community for a period of testing and evaluation at a major urban Brazilian medical center. In 1996, Dombá agreed to be flown from his village in Xingu Park to the megacity of São Paulo, where he submitted to a six-month course of hemodialysis, which was followed by transplant surgery with a kidney taken from a young white man who had been killed in a car accident. Dombá went through these events with calmness and determination, despite the initially strong resistance of his wife and his father, Romdó, the oldest living Suyá and headman of the Suyá village in Xingu.

The remarkable narrative of Dombá and his spirit kidney was told to us in several installments: to Mariana Ferreira in the Xingu Park and in São Paulo and to Ferreira and Nancy Scheper-Hughes at the Hospital São Paulo. This primary narrative is presented in conjunction with fragments of the at times contrasting accounts given by Dombá's wife, his primary shaman, Intoni, and his personal physician and surgeon. Dombá's narrative illustrates an aspect of transplant surgery that has been previously overlooked by medical anthropologists—the mimesis between the biomedical transmigration of organs and the shamanic transmigration of souls and spirit matter.

In posing our opening question—How did Dombá, a traditional forest Indian from central Brazil, make sense of his kidney transplant?—we found ourselves immersed in a gripping tale of cosmic voyage in which *our* assumptions of reality—real/unreal, seen/unseen, visible/invisible—were constantly challenged while the biomedical reality of transplant was readily incorporated into Dombá's Suyá cosmology. The narrative is a sobering reminder of the extent to which scientific categories obliterate other truths and perceptions of nature and the world, while shamanic categories can expand to include new truths and alternating perceptions. So, in a sense, this story should be taken as a subtle critique of biomedical/scientific fundamentalisms. There is no doubt that Dombá's recovery from a traumatic surgery was the result, as he and Intoni (his shaman) readily understand,

FIGURE 6.1. Suyá village men, Xingu National Park, Brazil.
(Photo: Mariana L. Ferreira)

of collaborations between hardworking white doctors and equally hard-working cosmic and visionary shamans.

Nancy first met Dombá in July 1997, several months after his kidney transplant and in the course of her multisited ethnographic study of the globalization of transplants. (See Scheper-Hughes 2000, 2002a, 2002b.) Dombá had just returned from Xingu Park to the Hospital São Paulo for a series of follow-up clinical exams only to learn that he was suddenly and unexpectedly facing an incipient organ-rejection crisis. Despite this latest crisis, Dombá was calm and relaxed as he welcomed us into his semiprivate hospital room on the tenth floor of one of Brazil's largest and most famous public hospitals. As Dombá himself noted: "Everyone wants to go to Hospital São Paulo!" Dressed in a bright turquoise T-shirt and multicolored swimming trunks, his normally long, thick black hair cut short in a more urban style, Dombá seemed to be on vacation, and rather enjoying his hospital stay. During our taped conversation his attention was at times divided between his visitors and a *telenovela* (Brazilian soap opera) playing on the color TV above his bed.

In the bed next to Dombá was a middle-aged Brazilian businessman nervously awaiting his own kidney transplant, an event that filled the patient with dread of the unknown. Would he live or die? Would his body

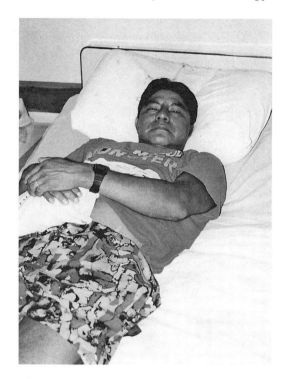

FIGURE 6.2. Dombá recovering after kidney transplant
at Hospital São Paulo. (Photo: Nancy Scheper-Hughes)

accept or reject the stranger's organ? Would he remember anything of the
trauma of the surgery? Later, Dombá remarked that his "roommate" was
not facing his surgery in the right way: "He should strive to be calm and
happy; he must not entertain disturbing thoughts. It is too bad he cannot
call on spirit helpers to protect him." But most white people, Dombá realized, did not *really* believe in spirits, not even Catholics. In Dombá's case,
his shaman and their spirit helpers had brought him successfully through
his operation, and they were continuing to protect him even now as we
were talking during the latest crisis. "They are always tapping on the
window of my room asking to be let inside," said Dombá.

A BRIEF SUYÁ HISTORY AND COSMOLOGY

Dombá is a member of the Suyá people, a Gê-speaking indigenous nation
who call themselves the Mekin Seji, the "People of the Great Round
Villages," and who have inhabited northern Mato Grosso for at least

200 years (Seeger 1985, 1987; Ferreira 1994, 2001). Since the beginning of the twentieth century, the Suyá have been in periodic contact with Brazilian government agencies. The first agency for Indian Affairs, the SPI (Service of Indian Protection), active during the years 1910–61, was dominated by adventure-seeking white jungle dwellers, fur hunters, and gold prospectors interested in the riches of the country's deep interior rain forests. Exploratory expeditions into central Brazil led by the famous Villas-Bôas brothers in the late 1940s fed the popular imagination with images of pristine primitive groups still untouched by civilization, an example of what Renato Rosaldo (1989) would later refer to as "imperialist nostalgia." Postcards of naked Indians, their bodies covered in the red *urucu* (*Bixa orellana*) and black *genipapo* (*Genipapa americana*) dyes, sometimes displaying bows and arrows, sometimes dancing, made their way to faraway lands. Global leaders throughout the world soon "elected" the Xingu Indigenous Park as a kind of universal sanctuary and shrine honoring prehistoric life (Ferreira 1996, 1997, 1998a).

Although the Villas-Bôas brothers held broadly "protectionist" attitudes toward the Indians of the Xingu area, they believed, along with the Brazilian government, that the best plan for Brazil's indigenous peoples was a gradual acculturation into Brazilian society. However, they also jealously guarded the Suyá as a last remnant of "savagery" in Brazil, and they prevented Christian missionaries, teachers, anthropologists (with few exceptions), and the Summer Institute of Linguistics, among other groups, from having contact with "their" tribe. During the military dictatorship period (1964–85), the Xingu Park became an exotic tourist resort, and Brazil's elite military air force (Força Aérea Brasileira [FAB]) flew illustrious guests to monthly, sometimes weekly, gastronomic feasts among savages (Ferreira 1998b). In July 1965, Scheper-Hughes and another Peace Corps volunteer were invited by an air-force general "to survey" the Xingu Park and other smaller reserves (Parecis, Tapayuna, Aripuana) from the air in a single engine FAB plane.

When the Xingu National Park was created in 1961, the Suyá found themselves encapsulated within the reservation, only to see their traditional territory eventually excluded from the boundaries of the park. In 1970, a former Brazilian intelligence officer, General Oscar Jerónimo Bandeira de Mello, was named president of the Fundação Nacional do Índio (FUNAI), the new Brazilian National Indian Foundation that replaced SPI. General de Mello created a special government fund from the sale of Indian products and the leasing of Indian lands. The money was to be put into various "development" projects designed to bring Indian peoples into the twentieth century. (See Davis 1977:57–58.) As a result, Suyá ancestral lands were illegally opened up for homesteading and land-grabbing by cattle raisers and gold prospectors.[7] In 1998, after a series of heavy conflicts in the area, the severely reduced 212 remaining Suyá were finally granted the right to reoccupy a small portion of their ancestral lands, an area of approximately 370,000 acres (Ferreira 1998a).

Lured by FUNAI's promises of "much food and medical assistance," the Suyá moved closer to the recently founded Diauarum Indigenous Post,[8] where Dombá has lived and worked as a handyman and a boat pilot since 1968. This was the year Dombá first came into contact with a team of physicians led by Dr. Roberto Baruzzi, from the Department of Preventive Health at the Escola Paulista de Medicina (now called Universidade Federal de São Paulo [UNIFESP]), who became officially in charge of the health of all 17 indigenous peoples of the Xingu Park in 1965. Dr. Baruzzi's Xingu Project supplied the small brick-walled, tin-roofed dispensaries built by the Villas-Bôas brothers at indigenous posts alongside the Xingu River with airplane loads of pharmaceuticals to combat further outbreaks of malaria, measles, tuberculosis, whooping cough, and pneumonia, diseases largely responsible for the extermination of 90 percent of the country's indigenous peoples since colonial times.

Dombá remembers being fascinated in his early teens, as he scrubbed the Diauarum dispensary's cement floor, by stacks of boxes and bottles inscribed with undecipherable symbols, filled with colorful pills, fragrant lotion, and translucent powder, which most individuals like him from far-away villages were eager to try out. As he grew older, Dombá's favorite "medicine" soon became *injeção* or *cutuc*—the indigenous version of the Portuguese verb *cutucar*, "to poke," in reference to the act of piercing the skin with a needle. The injection's "pain" helps increase the symbolic efficacy of the *remédio do branco* or white man's medicine, as Xingu peoples in general feel they are somehow "paying for it," in lieu of time-consuming therapeutic practices, such as the enactment of Suyá dream omens and curing chants (*sangere*). *Sangere* sung by shamans draw on the charisma and power of an animal that has an attribute the sick individual needs. For example, an individual stricken by malaria will desire the cayman's ability to stay still and cool under water, which will counteract the high temperature and shivering caused by the disease. Suyá paint their bodies with red *urucu* and black *genipapo* in order to mimic the ornamental patterns of the skins of animals such as the spotted jaguar, whose strength they admire and wish to draw on.[9] Tapping into the energy carried by fierce animals like the anaconda and the jaguar helps Suyá and other Gê-speaking peoples

FIGURE 6.3. Romdó, Dombá's father, painted as a spotted jaguar and dressed to heal. (Photo: Mariana L. Ferreira)

deal with non-Indians and with threatening events such as serious illnesses (Seeger 1985; Ferreira 1994, 1998a).

In addition, *cutuc* is popular because pharmaceutical substances injected into Suyá bodies provide a powerful means for incorporating the *white man's power*. Acquiring features of the "white man's power" (*força do caraíba*) can be achieved through the exchange of bodily fluids or other essential substances (such as antibiotics), thus providing the basis for membership in a common "substance group" shared with *caraíbas*. Being a part of the "white man's" substance group and still remaining a "real Suyá" is empowering, a rationale informing the decision of Dombá's close kin to allow him to undergo dialysis sessions, the transplant surgery itself, biopsies of his brand-new kidney, and the lifelong medication he was on to curtail the possibility of a rejection.

The relative ease with which Dombá accepted transplant surgery is thus explained in part by the protection afforded him through his indigenous knowledge, and in part by recent Suyá history—especially the tribe's intense contact with 16 indigenous nations in the Xingu Indigenous Park, and with the surrounding cattle ranchers, rubber tappers, gold miners, visiting government officials, Christian missionaries, and health professionals. These prolonged contacts encouraged the development of a hybrid and polysemic conception of the body and the nature of reality among this Gê-speaking population. But to be sure, the original Suyá conception of the world was never a closed, singular one that demanded a unitary interpretation of reality. The Suyá world is implicitly multiple and fluid, a world in which human and animal, spirit and matter, lived and dreamed realities bleed into each other (Seeger 1985, 1987).

Dombá's experience of diagnosis and removal from the Xingu Park for treatment in Brasília, the country's capital, or in São Paulo, where the headquarters of the Xingu Project and the Hospital São Paulo are located, is not uncommon—but avoided by the Suyá whenever possible. Contrary to FUNAI's argument that "Indians like to get free plane rides to go shopping," the Suyá fear coming back to the Xingu Park after unsuccessful biomedical encounters "flying in a coffin," a common occurrence, especially for young children. Thus, the Suyá prefer to rely on their own curing chants and dream omens to prevent and treat various kinds of ailments, independent of the source or type of illness.

In 1998, Romdó suggested that the real reason his son Dombá had become ill with a *doença de branco* [white man's sickness] was precisely because he had assumed a *caraíba* identity in refusing to pierce his lip and to wear a lip disk "like every true Suyá being does."[10] And, conversely, the success of Dombá's kidney transplant was attributed to the fact that Dombá accepted the assistance of the same shamans who had tried to convince him to wear the Suyá-signifying lip disk. At that time, says Romdó, Dombá resisted the lip piercing because he did not believe Suyá ritual and medicine could be "stronger" than *caraíba* culture and medicine. Afterwards, Dombá finally understood the power of shamanism, without which he could not have survived his surgery in Hospital São Paulo.

Over the last 30 years there has been an intensification of shamanic knowledge and power in the Xingu Indigenous Park following several historic events: the emergence of indigenous social movements in the 1970s and 1980s, new respect and legal grounding for cultural rights found in Brazil's 1989 Constitution, and the unanticipated effects of schooling in the 1980s and 1990s. The seemingly paradoxical and defensive growth of shamanism in situations of colonial domination, especially within the larger global economic system, has been well documented in Brazil and in other South American countries (Gruzinski 1988; Wright and Hill 1992; Vainfas 1995; Hugh-Jones 1996; Ferreira 2001).

In contrast, biomedicine is regarded by numerous indigenous peoples as nothing more than a complement to shamanic practices, as the Suyá interpretation of Dombá's transplant surgery clearly indicates. But even when the

Suyá finally resort to biomedicine, either by asking for a *cutuc* at local dispensaries or by sending chronic or terminally sick individuals to Brasília or São Paulo, successes or failures are invariably attributed to the power (or lack thereof) of shamans and other supernatural creatures of the Suyá cosmos.

In the early 1980s, Dombá was allowed by his father, Romdó—a celebrated Suyá ritual leader (as well as village headman)—to study at the Diauarum indigenous school in Xingu Park where Mariana was then a teacher of literacy and mathematics (1980–84). Already manifesting some of the signs and symptoms of his inherited kidney disability, Dombá was unable to keep up with the strenuous tasks he was hired for by FUNAI: chopping wood, clearing gardens, cleaning houses, hauling water, and fixing engines at the Diauarum Indigenous Post. And while his classmates, including Dombá's future brother-in-law, the young shaman Intoni, took part in vigorous hunting and fishing expeditions, Dombá stayed alone at the post, dedicating himself to mastering mathematics and learning how to read and write in both Portuguese and Suyá.

After becoming an anthropologist, Mariana returned as a consultant to several different indigenous groups, including the Suyá, assisting them, most notably in a court case concerning land tenure in 1998–99 (Ferreira 1998a, 2001). During this period, Dombá became one of Ferreira's key informants, as well as her boat pilot and guide during her trips in the Xingu Park in the 1990s. By the mid-1990s Dombá's health had deteriorated and Mariana, who was then teaching at the University of São Paulo, was able to follow closely some of Dombá's dialysis sessions, as well as his initial recovery from transplant surgery.

Dombá's narrative almost seamlessly weaves together accounts of his dialysis sessions, his conversations with his doctors, curing chants of his relatives, dream omens, and cosmic flights of magical shamans. It was never immediately clear during these narrative sessions just when Dombá was describing a "real" physical occurrence, and when he was referring to a dream or to a "vision." Neither was it immediately evident when Dombá recounted the many times that his spirit helpers, the Suyá shamans, were summoned from the forest of Mato Grosso to the hospital, whether the "call" was made (as it often was) through the hospital's short-wave radio or whether the summons was made telepathically or through a dream (as it often was). All these events—natural or supernatural—were treated in the same understated, evenhanded way, representing a reality in which the seen/unseen, visible/invisible comfortably coexisted.

During his hospital stay Dombá was often "visited" by his father, Romdó, and by his brother-in-law, Intoni, from Xingu Indigenous Park.

Metamorphosed into small magical birds (*xexéu: Cacius celli*),[11] the two powerful shamans flew many times from the dense forest of Mato Grosso to the heart of São Paulo in order to accompany and oversee various phases of Dombá's surgery and his recovery. The shaman-*xexéu* "appeared" in the operating room, where they looked over the shoulders of the surgeons, and they often tap-tapped with their hard, pointed beaks on the window panes of Dombá's hospital room,[12] later appearing by his bedside in their human form, decorated with ear plugs and painted bodies, and carrying plugs of vulture tobacco that they used to diagnose any problems standing in the way of Dombá's speedy recovery.

Prior to, during, and after his surgery, Dombá's wife, Kokowá, who stayed close by Dombá in the hospital, frequently contacted the villagers and shaman of their Suyá *aldeia* (village) in Xingu using the hospital's short-wave radio. She would post almost daily reports on Dombá's condition and make explicit requests for shamanic visits whenever necessary. The shamans always complied, chanting the healing songs that released their souls into magical flights that Dombá, even under the knife and the influence of anesthesia, could sense as a strong physical presence that calmed his nerves and allowed him to face the surgery and its aftermath with equanimity. As he grew stronger, Dombá began to use the hospital's short-wave radio himself in order to contact the Suyá people in Xingu directly rather than relying on the messages that were brought in and sent out by the flying shamans.

After Dombá returned to the Xingu Park in 1998, he continued to rely on his two powerful relatives, his father, Romdó, and Intoni, his brother-in-law, whose shamanic skills were instrumental not only in Dombá's survival and recovery from the transplant operation itself but also in renegotiating Dombá's new status within his original substance (kin) group, now that he possessed a white man's organ—making him a part-white person.

THE NARRATIVE

Here we present Dombá's narrative as he told it to us in Hospital São Paulo and to Mariana Ferreira in the Xingu Park, at her home, and in the Casa do Índio in São Paulo. We begin, as Dombá did, with his surgery and from there work back in time, rather than in a more straightforward chronological order.

DOMBÁ'S SURGERY

I was lying in my hospital bed, high up on the tenth floor, half awake, half asleep, the night after my surgery when I heard a tap-tapping on the window. Spirit birds were asking to be let into the room. It was midnight, and I was still weak from the operation. I knew that I should not be scared, but my legs were shaking, and I was still dizzy in my head from the anesthetic. But I managed to pull myself out of bed and open the window. Now the birds flew in as people with cigars in their mouths and decorated with ear plugs and painted bodies.

The two *pajés* [shamans] wanted to have a closer look at the operation, to probe the hole where my sick kidney was taken out that afternoon, and to blow tobacco smoke into the place where the new kidney was put inside me. A new kidney! The doctors said that I was a lucky man, because they chose a really good one for me, a strong kidney from a young guy who died in a car crash.

Well, the *pajés* kept talking into me through the hole in my belly and blowing smoke onto this new kidney that I had gotten from a white man. My protectors wanted to make sure that it was a real human's kidney and not an animal's kidney. And they were trying to see if any malignant beings were trying to get hold of me through the opening in my flesh, because, you know, when you are open like that anything can happen.

Well, they prayed and chanted for a long time. And I soon stopped shaking, because they used the white cayman's[13] curing chant.[14] The white cayman is the maker/creator of still waters—yes, he is. He spreads his hands out; he plants his legs firmly on the bottom of the river, calm, so calm. He does not shake! So I, too, stopped shivering. But when I woke up the next morning I was so cold again. It was as if a strong gust of wind had blown over my body. Then I knew for certain that the *pajés* had been there with the white cayman song for me. Because that cayman's body is cool, cool like the shallow waters that flow in the rivers of Xingu Park.

In the morning I told my wife about it. Kokowá said, "I know, the *pajés* are always tapping on the window. When you were in the operating room, they came to you to make sure that the doctors did not hurt you, and I let them in." They are always there at the window. They are here right now in the hospital room. Sometimes I see my brother-in-law, and sometimes I see another man. [Perhaps Dombá is not allowed to mention his father's name.] I always see them as people, never as animals. So I know that these are healing shamans. They are not witches. I never dream of big, ugly animals either. Whenever big animals appear in a dream, you are in for trouble, and only a *pajé* can cure you, because they can see who is causing the harm. When the *pajés* don't see anything, then it's probably a white man's disease, something they can't cure. That's how it was with this kidney of mine. It's not a Suyá illness; otherwise the *pajés* would have cured me a long time ago. When the *pajés* came to me they asked: "Any ugly animals in your dreams?" I said no. And that is why I am doing so well. No ugly, smelly animals like catfish or jaguars or tapirs in my dreams or in my body.[15]

Dombá had been flown to São Paulo from the Xingu Indigenous Park a year before his kidney transplant (1995) for his first extensive biomedical exams and a biopsy. It was at a time when the man could no longer bear the intense suffering caused by his malfunctioning kidneys.

DOMBÁ'S SUFFERING

I felt so much pain in my body [*araksö*]—my body hurt so much! I could no longer work. All I could do was a little bit of fishing. It was so embarrassing! At the Diaurum Post my job is to do many things— to plant manioc and rice, to hunt and to fish, to build and clean houses, to repair the boats. But now I couldn't do anything, I was in such pain. The white doctors who came to the post said that I needed a "real" doctor. I knew what they meant—stop seeing your weird witch doctors!

The truth is I *was* being treated by our own doctor, my brother-in-law, Intoni, who is a *pajé*, and by my father and by many *pajés* from other indigenous groups here in Xingu. But they weren't able to help me, not because they are "witches" but because this thing that I have is a white man's disease, not something our *pajés* can cure. Anyway, witches don't cure anybody; they just cause people harm. The white doctors just don't understand the difference.

So I came straight to São Paulo in November 1995, after a few weeks in Brasília. I was glad to get out of Brasília, because it's a place you only go to if you want to die. The doctors there only pretend they are taking care of you. They do have to pretend, though, because Brasília is their government's headquarters. But our Suyá people have noticed that once you are treated in Brasília, you only come back flying in a coffin.[16] And sometimes they shut the coffins so tight that our spirits have a hard time setting themselves free. No one wants to die and spend the rest of their lives stuck in a coffin under the earth!

At the Hospital São Paulo they treat Indian people much better. Indians don't die there as much, and when they do their coffins are easy enough to open. So we much prefer being hospitalized there. The bad thing is that you have to wait your turn, because obviously everyone wants to use the Hospital São Paulo! I had to spend a whole year at the Casa do Índio [a kind of halfway house for indigenous people visiting São Paulo] facing hunger and all these wretched skin diseases that you catch in that place, but I stuck it out because I really needed to see a white doctor.[17]

My turn finally came, and I went through all these exams, lots of x-rays. Then they put me on the blood-sucking machines [dialysis]. White doctors need all kinds of machines to see through our bodies, while our *pajés* don't need any of that. Well, the white doctors did find something wrong with my kidneys, my *iturutö*. I was born with a sick *iturutö*, and the doctors said that now I needed a new one.

"A new one?" my father asked me. "How can you get a new body and be the same person? You *are* your body, you *are* your heart, your liver, your stomach, and your throat. A new body is not my son; a new kidney is not my son, and I want my own son, not someone else's son." That is what my father said.

So I had to explain what the doctors had told me, that I would get a new kidney from a young, strong man who died in a car accident. The kidney would be nice and fresh, the doctors said, the best one that they could find. They promised me that it wouldn't be an animal's kidney. I was sure of that. But my father still wasn't convinced.

"If you change your body, and if you take inside yourself a white man's kidney, your spirit will never be the same. You will share the other person's blood; you will share his feelings. And do you even know who this person is? His relatives will be your relatives. You will be part of his family. Oh, you are going to face big problems later on in life."

So I explained again and again what the doctors told me, that it really didn't matter whose kidney I got. But that was very hard because while to them it doesn't matter, to us it matters a whole lot! One doctor even said that it wouldn't matter if I got a woman's kidney! Now that, I told the doctors, I would *never* accept. I didn't dare tell this part to my father. Can you imagine me, Dombá, with an *iturutö* from a woman! [He laughs at the absurdity.] So the doctors finally promised me that the kidney would come from a man, and I was greatly relieved.

I told my father that my own kidney is just no good and that it was always that way. I was not sick because of a *waiãga's* [witch's] spell. A *waiãga* can do something to kill you, and you feel weak and dizzy. But then you can ask a *pajé* for help, and he sees the *waiãga* in his dreams. But my father and my brother-in-law searched and searched in their dreams, and they never found anyone trying to harm me. And I believe that, because I have always been so generous to everyone! Since I earn money working at the Post, I buy all the kinds of things that people envy, like watches, a radio, new clothes, and I am always having to give it all away so that nobody will give me the evil eye.

That's what happened to Nhidjoco [Dombá's friend and agemate who went to the Diauarum school with him]. Nhidjoco went out collecting honey, and when he came back he didn't give it to anyone in the village. That night he dreamed that the honey was eating up his liver. He started screaming, and then he woke himself up. Every night it was the same thing, Nhidjoco dreamed of a kind of hornet that we call *mbet* stinging the inside of his belly. Nhidjoco had a big fever, and we called my brother-in-law. He prayed and prayed, but the spell was just too power-ful. An evil witch had put a spell on him because Nhidjoco had not been generous, had not shared the honey all around. The next morning Nhidjoco was vomiting blood from all the stinging inside him. So they radioed an airplane to take him away to Brasília, where he died that same night. When he died his belly was filled with blood. Two days later the plane came back with Nhidjoco in a coffin, and he was only 35 years old.

So we know pretty well when a *waiãga* casts a spell on someone, and my father knew that no *waiãga* had bewitched me. We called on different *pajés*, too, from all over Xingu Park, and I had to pay them a lot for their work—aluminum pans, hammocks, and blankets. I asked them, "Can you see anything like an *ituru, iturutö, irokenkut* [urethra, kidney, kidney disease]?" And they wouldn't say anything. All they could see was a large catfish [*pirarara*] disturbing the still waters, but that was about something that happened a long time ago, when I ate catfish and got ill. "Catfish don't like you," the *pajés* would say, "but they are not bothering you right now." So it really had to be some white man's disease. Because this is how we proceed: first we try our own medicine, our *pajés*. If that doesn't work, then and only then we will look for the white man's medicine.

So I asked the white doctors what it could be. They thought that the problem was with my *ituru*, the tube where my urine passes through. Some things these white guys can cure, but this idea of giving me a new kidney didn't seem right at all. My wife didn't like it either. She said that it would be like her having another husband, a white husband, and that she would *never* have sex with a white man! I told her that she would have to think differently this time, since what I had was a disease and not a spell. "Look," I said, "do you think that a *pajé* could replace my kidney?" My father finally had to agree at this point because I was very sick, too sick to sit up and talk for a long time. His *sangere* [healing chants] had stopped working, and my temperature was up in the sky. "Go ahead,' my father finally said; "go ahead and do it. We will be at your side the whole time."

DOMBÁ'S EXPERIENCE WITH DIALYSIS AND TRANSPLANT SURGERY

First they brought me into the little house where they plug you into a machine. The most incredible thing, something you would never expect, and there it is—a machine to suck up and clean your blood so that you can actually see it leave your body and go up into the tubes and into the machine. The *pajés* went crazy the first night I was in dialysis: in their dreams they saw my soul leaving my body. As the blood was sucked up into the machine, so was my soul. My brother-in-law happened to be in Goiânia [capital of the state of Goiás] on that day, and he called my wife in São Paulo to ask if I was OK because he said he had seen [i.e., had had a vision of] my soul going up into a machine. Kokowá said, "The machine is just cleaning his blood."

Two or three times a week I was plugged into the machine while I waited for a young man to have a car accident! It was way too much suffering. Sometimes I did feel like my soul was leaving my body to get away from all the pain, and just leave me behind. Then, I would pull myself together and think, "No, I have to endure. I can't wish for a young man's death just to get his kidney!" That would be like turning into a witch myself. Then, after about six months, a young man offered his kidney to me, and I decided to take it.

It was hard, but my father sent me medicine to take before the operation. We call it *hwintuktö* or *hwintuktire*.[18] It is a root that you soak in water and spread all over your body. My wife spread it all over me so that I would not fear the operation. Boy, did I feel better after that! That night I had bad dreams that the doctors were stirring up my insides with a big knife, and there was blood pouring out of my belly. When I woke up, my heart was pounding fast, *tum-tum-tum.* My body ached, and I began to panic. I told my wife, "Quick, send a radio message to Xingu right away, call my brother-in-law."

Around midnight, he knocked on the window and I let him in. "I dreamed that they stuck a knife inside me," I cried, and the *pajé* asked me if there were any big fish in my dreams. "No: no fish," I said; "just men in white messing up my insides with a knife." "Good, I have come to pray over you." So he lit up a cigar and looked all around the room. He searched and searched, and he didn't find anything, no spells against me.

So I was calm when the time came for the operation and there were doctors and nurses coming in and out of my room. My wife sat by my side and whispered to me: "They are here with you, your father and your brother-in-law." I looked around and could not see them. I felt pain; the nurses were sticking needles in my body, and I had to hold very still. I closed my eyes, and then I saw my father. He was humming the white cayman's song for me. I lay still, still on the sand bed at the bottom of the river, and I felt the coolness of the water on my skin. The nurses took my blood pressure: "The pressure of an Indian is strong!" they said. Another nurse checked my *irontö* [heart] and said, "Yes, the Indian's heartbeat is very strong!" It was like that. When I got to the ICU [Intensive Care Unit], they checked me again. "You are certainly very brave!" they said. I only saw their faces through a cayman's eyes, and they looked to me like big, white, fleshly nurses that I could just swallow in a single big gulp! Then I went to sleep with the sound of the white cayman's song, my father's *sangere*, my father's own curing song for me.

When I woke up it was five o'clock in the afternoon. I felt weak, so I went to sleep again. Only the next morning did I feel all right. The nurses told me to bathe myself. "But should I really?" "Yes, you should," they replied, so I got up and bathed. My wife looked at the cut, and she began to cry when she saw that big huge opening all stitched up while the nurse cleaned me there. I couldn't say anything, I just stared at my body. Kokowá saw my father was standing in the corner of the room. She said that she explained the operation to him, and my father became wild with anger to learn that his son's body had been cut into. And then she told him, "Your son has a part of a white man inside his body, but it's inside, inside!" My wife was so afraid that the new kidney would be hanging out, and so was I. But it was all neatly stitched in inside! These white doctors really know their stuff!

DOMBÁ'S RECOVERY

After two days I got stronger, and the nurses said to me, "Wow! You are peeing very well, much better than others do." But the anesthesia was wearing off now, and I began to suffer with strong pains for several hours. I asked for help, and then I felt a gush of wind, and I looked up and stared into my brother-in-law's [Intoni's] eyes. He had just come flying over to see me, as a bird, and he flew right into the open window. He smiled at me, and then I knew I would be all right. The pains subsided, and I could sleep.

Now I thought of the poor white woman lying next to me on the other bed, who had received the other kidney from the dead fellow. She didn't look good at all; she looked pale, and my brother-in-law told me when I saw him later back at Xingu that he actually saw her soul rising from her body the moment he flew into the room. There was no one praying for her before the operation, no *sangere*, and she only had bad dreams, I know. She was nervous before the operation, and I could just feel the presence of all these wild animals roaming around her body. Like vultures circling around dead meat. I felt so sorry for the woman. Didn't anyone care for her? Did she know they were putting a *man's* kidney into her? In the end, she didn't make it, the doctors said, and her body rejected the kidney. Well, that was probably a good thing.

After that, my doctor came in and took hold of my arm: "This Indian has a lot of courage!" But I just closed my eyes and began to dream of ["with"][19] my people in the Suyá village. They all wanted to know how I was doing. I felt my body warming up, my new *iturutö* [kidney] coming back to life. But here was the problem: now I am white, too! In my dream I was walking among my people, and they didn't recognize me. They were all walking around me, staring at me, staring at my belly, amazed. They wanted to find out who was *in* that body, because it was so confusing! Was it a Suyá or a *caraíba*, a white man?

I woke up and told my wife, "You must send a radio message to Xingu right away, because the people there no longer know who I am. Tell them I am really myself, I am still myself!" So Kokowá sent a radio message and told everyone that I was really fine. They were so happy! She told my kids, my son-in-law, my father, and they were all very excited! "We will have the *djuni* [hummingbird] ceremony! The women will prepare the *yamurikumá* [a special ceremony in which they reiterate their power to the men]!" My kids shouted, "My father is cured! He will come back to Xingu!" My oldest son was so glad that he shouted, "Come home to us!"

Everyone gathered around the radio shack in the village to find out exactly what happened. They had many questions. "What was the operation like?" they asked. Kokowá answered, "I myself did not see it. First they took Dombá away to the ICU and then to the operating room. But I didn't see how they put the new *iturutö* inside. I am so happy that it is inside his body, because I thought that it would be sticking out, hanging outside him. But his body is just like ours." This is what she told the people.

Kokowá couldn't stop staring at me. She looked through my eyes, through my skin, into my body, searching for my soul, trying to get to know me better. She smelled me all over, and then, finally, she accepted that I was pretty much the same as before, and she felt very good. After that, everyone began to like the transplantation. My wife told them, "It worked! The doctors worked hard on him; the *pajés* worked hard on him, and it worked." Even my father-in-law and my son-in-law were convinced.

I went to sleep, and my heart was pounding very fast. I had another dream about the operation. It is a dream I now have often. I am on my way to the hospital where all these doctors in white want to swap my body parts. But I know that I will be all right, because I see my brother-in-law [as a magical bird] perched on the doctor's shoulders, looking down at me. And I know that *Kakwaik-wapama*, our Creator God, is overlooking us all. So why should I be afraid?

DISABILITY AND THE SUYÁ CORPOREAL IMAGINARY

Dombá's disability—inherited kidney insufficiency—connotes far more than a simple organic dysfunction. It is rather lucky for Dombá that his kidney disease did not manifest itself very early in life and that it did not mar or alter his physical appearance. The Suyá, like other Amazonian tribes, practice neonaticide (postpartum abortion) of newborns who manifest at birth severe physical disability, especially an anomalous physical appearance. Thomas Gregor (1988) reported that infanticide was still being practiced, though covertly, by the Mehinaku Indians of the Brazilian Amazon in the case of twins (seen as a birth anomaly), some illegitimate births, and in the case of birth defects. The birth of a physically deformed infant is referred to by the Mehinaku as a *kanupa*, a forbidden or a tabooed thing, and is a source of great shame to its parents. At birth, each infant is carefully examined by the parents and other members of the kin group: "We look at its face, at its eyes, its nose, and at its genitals, its rectum, its ears, its toes and fingers. If there is anything wrong, then the baby is forbidden. It is disgusting to us. And so it is buried" (ibid.:4). Moreover, the

Mehinaku Indians contrasted their wisdom to the irrational behavior of white people who allowed their physically challenged babies to live: "The white people have many worthless, disgusting individuals among them. There are people we have seen without eyes, noses, without ears. In São Paulo there was even a man with two rectums. If such a child were born here, it would be buried in the ground immediately. Not nearby, no, but over there, far away! That is why we are so beautiful!" (ibid.).

The Suyá also practice infanticide, and Mariana witnessed a child with a harelip buried alive immediately after birth.[20] On another occasion, she saw the killing of an infant with what was probably spinal bifida. But these postnatal decisions take place, like abortion in the industrialized world, before the child has acquired a human status. Disabilities that are not immediately visible at birth or do not manifest themselves until later—such as blindness, deafness, lameness, mental slowness, and epilepsy—are treated kindly by the Suyá. And while infants that suffer convulsions may be killed (as witches), an older child or an adult with epilepsy is accorded a special, protected status. Not infrequently, Suyá children suffer an accident in the course of growing up in the forest zone. Children who lose an eye resulting from a stray arrow, or who become lame (*manco*), "dragging a paralyzed leg" behind them after stepping on a poisonous stingray, are treated as "special" children and are given positive nicknames.

Indeed, the ability to survive a severe illness or accident is often the sign of special powers and favors that can be marshaled and used to heal others. Powerful shamans explain their skills in terms of their having overcome adversity. For example, Intoni derives his status as a man of great spiritual power and insight from his having survived a deadly encounter with an anaconda (as well as other misfortunes). Any powerful illness that suggests a near-death experience from which the patient recovers is seen as the sign of personal charisma, and the survivors represent an elect population—those who have proved themselves stronger than the most powerful animal or witch adversaries. Among adult Suyá are found many individuals with the scars, twisted bones, and various "missing pieces" of an active hunting, fishing, and gathering population. Even the most poorly healed wounds can signify strength (not weakness) to the Suyá.

Dombá's particular disability is more complex, however, for the kidney occupies a special status in Suyá body imagery, kinship reckoning, and cosmology. Kidney disease signifies a major physical and social disability. Suyá social self-identity and kinship derive from an elaborate corporeal imaginary based on the production and exchange of bodily substances. The Suyá reckon kinship not around lineages but around the sharing of intimate bodily substances, including milk, blood, urine, sweat, feces, vaginal secretions, spit, pus, and semen. A substance group is a kind of extended family based on birth, marriage, affiliation, alliance, and proximity. The Suyá individual is formed from the accumulated semen of *every* man with whom the mother has had sexual relations.

Those who "rub shoulders" with each other, who eat together, who share food, drink, sleep under the same roof, who bathe, swim, urinate, and defecate together, constitute a basic "substance group." Thus, from conception onwards one may become "kin" to a great many people with whom one shares ties of neither blood nor marriage. Substance groups have little depth, rarely extending beyond two generations, but a lot of breadth, readily including concentric circles of socially extended kinship.

A substance group shares body parts (in sex and through birth), bodily secretions, and embodied emotions, feelings, thoughts, and dreams. What affects one individual in a substance group affects the others. They are socially, physically, and emotionally bound to each other. One cries; the other weeps. One speaks to parrots; the other befriends parakeets. Dombá believes, for example, that red peppers offend his new kidney (producing a painful urination), and so no one in his substance group may eat red peppers.

Most significantly, when Dombá accepted the offer of a strange white man's kidney, he (and his entire substance group) accepted into their bodies and into their selves a new social and psychological persona. They all became "part white," an identity filled with ambivalence and fraught with unseen danger as well as with potential power. And so Romdó warned his son: "The person with another man's kidney will encounter many problems later on."

The transplant surgeons did not then, and still do not today, understand the severity of Dombá's dilemma, and they repeat to Dombá and to his wife like a mantra the biomedical platitude that "it makes no difference whose kidney you have." For a Suyá the statement is nonsensical. Dombá understands that the white doctors *believe* this to be true, but "for us," Dombá says, "it makes *every* difference in the world."

DR. MEDINA, CHIEF SURGEON AT HOSPITAL SÃO PAULO

Dr. Medina, Dombá's surgeon, considered the transplant of a Brazilian Indian a real medical coup and triumph. He was looking forward to a trip he planned making to the Xingu Park in order to visit with Dombá and his shamans. He said he wanted to learn something about the plants the *pajés* used to cure and to meet with them "shaman-to-shaman." Although we encountered Dr. Medina as he rushed through the wards and corridors of

Hospital São Paulo, it was time enough to see that he had a good and caring relationship with Dombá.

But while Dr. Medina admired Dombá's strength of character, the surgeon could not resist correcting the Indian from time to time in the midst of Dombá's narrative. When, for example, Dombá spoke of seeing shamanic birds in the operating room, Medina chuckled and said dismissively: "Well, yes, but that was just a predictable effect of the anesthesia." Or when Dombá referred to the magically protective salve that his wife put on his abdomen just before surgery, Medina said: "Oh, but our nurses would have washed that off, as we have to maintain a sterile field."

The surgeon said that he really loved handling this case, which was the first kidney (or any) transplant of an Indian from Xingu Park, and possibly the first indigenous person in all of Brazil to be transplanted. Because of Dombá's special status as a "wild" Indian and the cultural capital that he accrued from that status, Dombá was treated specially. Dr. Medina admitted, for example, that he gave the Indian more personal attention than he gave to the "ordinary" transplant patient. He defended this special treatment by saying: "Our [Brazilian] Indians have suffered so much, I did my best to make sure that Dombá got as quickly as possible to the head of the waiting list and that he got a very good kidney." Medina had (he said) personally gone through the medical files and had "hand-picked" the best candidate he could find: a 22-year-old man who had died in a car crash.[21]

When asked what had most moved him about Dombá, the surgeon replied that it was how calm and tranquil the Suyá Indian was compared to his other patients. Dombá never complained, he said, except to say that he could not tolerate the hospital meals, which the Indian described as "such a mixed-up mess" that they made him lose his appetite. Dombá missed "real" food—hunted meats, fresh fish, manioc cakes. Medina was also impressed with Dombá's reply to his question about what he missed most in being away from his home in the Xingu Park. Dombá had replied: "It makes my heart sad that I can't see very far outside my hospital room window. I look and look, and all I can see are other buildings." Medina found that touching.

DOMBÁ'S RECEPTION IN XINGU PARK AND HIS RETURN TO HOSPITAL SÃO PAULO

In August 1997, when Dombá returned to Hospital São Paulo for a biopsy after a routine checkup revealed high levels of creatinine,[22] we interviewed him again. He told us about his joyful return to Xingu Park in May 1997, and why he was now back at the hospital:

When I left São Paulo, the Suyá people knew I was coming home. I flew straight to Brasília and from there to Diauarum [Indigenous Post]. When the plane was about to land, I saw a whole bunch of people waiting for me, my father and my brothers, Wetague, Temakati, and Sonkotg. My father started crying when he saw me, and he said, "I am so glad you are back!" Everyone was happy. The women roasted fish and prepared *beiju* for me.[23] It was so late I could only leave for Ricó [Dombá's natal village] the next day.[24]

In the morning we loaded the boat with all the goods I had brought with me from São Paulo: blankets, beads, a brand-new TV set, sugar, and coffee. In two hours we were there. We arrived at Ricó, where everyone was waiting for me at the shore. No one recognized me, though. They still thought that I was someone else. "Are you yourself?" they kept asking me. "Is it really and truly you?" Imagine! My own people did not recognize me, my very own relatives! My sister, Gaisarin, said, "Oh, you've been away for so long. And now that you have a stranger's *iturutö* [kidney], we no longer recognize you. Is it really you, my brother?"[25] She cried and hugged me. Finally she said, "I told my husband to look after you very carefully, and I can see he did! You look a little bit different, but you sure look fine!"

I made sure I brought home plenty of gifts for my brother-in-law: pairs of shorts and pants, shirts, suitcases, and a backpack. I had already gifted Taruaki; all she asked for was sewing thread. And I don't have to give anything to my father. So [after the gifting] people wanted to know all the details, especially who I got the kidney from. I told them that the doctors wouldn't tell me, and that the only thing that they had promised me was that it was from a young white man. So now I have to accept that the Suyá think I am now also part white. But even so, they still like me a lot. Then, my brother-in-law had to check me up entirely to make sure no evil animals had made their way into my body. He prayed and smoked and said I was OK. Then they told me the sad news about Dombeti's illness, and how he is now turning into a witch.[26]

We asked Dombá how he was feeling and how his latest medical exams had gone:

Well, I was feeling OK, and it was time for my checkup. But I had a fever during the last two weeks, so when I got here [to Hospital São Paulo] they checked my creatinine and saw that it was high. The doctors told me I needed a biopsy, to stick a needle in my new kidney and take a little part of it out to look at it. My wife started crying: "Not another hole! That's exactly what those evil witches from the Alto [Xingu] need!" Because you know how witches will take advantage of any little opening in your body and—*zup!*—the next thing you know, they are inside you. When that happens, there is no way out of it, and you die.

So I told my wife, "Send another radio message to my brother-in-law and have him come here right now!" So, she did, and that evening I heard the familiar knock, knock on the window of my bedroom on the tenth floor of the Hospital São Paulo. Actually I heard *two* knocks, because a nurse also came in. She looked around and saw the window open, and she asked me if I had done that. I said yes, and she asked why. I was about to tell her, and I suddenly realized that I shouldn't. She just wouldn't believe me! So I kept quiet and told her I was hot. The *pajé* was looking over her shoulders as she took my temperature and blood pressure.

As soon as the nurse left I said, "Brother-in-law, I need your help again. These doctors are going to open up my body tomorrow, and I need you here to make sure nothing evil will come inside me." My brother-in-law said, "Don't worry. I will stay by your side. Now tell me about your dreams." I said that I had only dreamed of the doctors with white masks and white clothes, with knives in their hands, operating on the dead fellow that gave me his kidney. I tried to see the dead man's face, but he had no face,[27] and when I looked hard enough, I could see that it was me! So I knew for certain that the dead man has transformed himself into me and he no longer exists as himself. "You are all right," my brother-in-law said; "you don't have to be afraid any more." And I was certainly relieved to hear that. The next day my biopsy turned out fine. The white doctors said that my kidney is just fine after all [despite their fears of a rejection crisis]. So you can see why when my brother-in-law tells me something, I always believe him.

NARRATIVE OF THE SUYÁ *PAJÉ* INTONI

Intoni, Dombá's shaman and brother-in-law, was from early childhood a man recognized by all for his sensitivity and kindness toward other people. These were the traits that lead him to become and to be accepted as a healer and *pajé* for the small group of Suyá living in Ricó village in Xingu Park. Over the years that Mariana worked with the Suyá, Intoni was a close collaborator, serving as a key witness in the Suyá land-claims case, at which he gave strong testimony of the spiritual charter for the Suyá territory. On one of her returns to Xingu Park in 1998, Mariana asked Intoni about his understanding of Dombá's illness and his role in his brother-in-law's recovery.

The following is a fragment of a very long transcription beginning with an account of how Intoni became a healer, which we have had to reduce considerably. Intoni's ability to metamorphose into various powerful creatures allowed him to routinely fly as a *xexéu* from the Xingu Park in central Brazil to São Paulo to visit and treat Dombá.

FIGURE 6.4. Mariana Ferreira with Intoni, Dombá's brother-in-law
and Suyá shaman.

This is how it went on with my brother-in-law [Dombá]. He started
getting kind of sick, feeling pain in his limbs. The *xexéu* brought a lot
of medicine for him, and I gave it to my brother-in-law, but it didn't do
him any good. Nothing [no disease object] would come out of him,
either. It was as if I couldn't really see what was going on with him, as
if a cloud were covering over his body. The *xexéu* was helping out, and
at night, in its dream, it saw something: "Look, there is a coconut inside
of him, but it is small [wasted]. It is a *caraíba* [white man's] thing, but I
will try to take it out."

The *xexéu* flew up to the *hwintuktö* plant and started scratching the
root with its beak. It threw the root into clean water and picked up the
root mixture in its beak to rub into my brother-in-law's [Dombá's] soft
spot. I flew far, far away, because Dombá was in São Paulo, at a *caraíba*
hospital. And when I got there, I saw the white coconut in his belly; too
big for a bird's beak, and too heavy to carry away. It was a white
coconut all right; it showed up in their machine. My brother-in-law
told me that he saw the picture that this x-ray machine took of the
coconut. The doctor said, "It is his *iturutö* that is sick; the *iturutö* is the
disease." But how was I going to take the kidney out? The coconut is
way too big for the bird's beak. I can't handle that. So the doctor must
cut it open with a knife in an operation and take it out. The *xexéu* was

telling me that if we take that coconut out, the hole would be way too big to leave it open, and we would have to close it up somehow. You know how big those coconuts can get. So the doctor thought of putting another coconut in its place.

Now, how would a *xexéu* ever be able to find another coconut? That is something for a *caraíba* [white man] to do, because to cut someone up with a knife and swap his kidney is something an *agatonkere* [shaman] does not do. The *xexéu* said, "The *caraíba* doctor is willing to help, so let us help him, too! We will let him cut, operate, extract the coconut, and put another one in its place. And, meanwhile, we will drop medicine in Dombá's mouth and on his soft spot to calm down his soul, so that it doesn't leave the body. We will control his soul."

But do the *caraíba* really know what they are doing? That's what worried the people the most, because the *caraíba* know how to operate, but they don't understand anything about the soul or the spirit. They always say things like *Spirits don't exist!* At their hospitals nobody is there to talk to the patients' souls. There are only injections, pills, medicine to spread on the skin. And machines, lots of machines. So the *agatonkere* will help. I spent the whole time helping my brother-in-law, telling him, "You will get better. You will not have bad dreams. When you dream of ["with"] an animal, you will call on me, because I will discover which animal is doing you harm. You will call me and I will help you." This is what I told Dombá over and over again.

The *xexéu* came back telling the Suyá people that the *caraíba* doctor had taken a coconut out of another man to place it in my brother-in-law. How do the *caraíbas* do that? How do you take an *iturutö* out of somebody to place it in another person? Where is the dead man's soul? Is it wandering around here in our village, trying to find its missing part? These are the questions that the people were asking. "The doctors said it was the best kidney they could get," I told them. But the women wanted to know, "Why did the young man die?" Romdó explained: "The white men don't have *agatonkere*, that's why they die a lot. So the young man died; he is dead. And now his *iturutö* belongs to my son." "'But where is the *iturutö*?" The people wanted to know. "How is it attached to him?" Dombá's wife explained over the radio how the doctors did it. The people wanted to know everything. His own father, Romdó, wanted to know everything too. Because at first he would not accept the operation and the idea that they would take his kidney out and put another one in its place.

In my dream, I can see the young man who died, but I cannot see his soul. It just left! And his kidney is not really a coconut, but a real kidney, an *iturutö*. It is alive, it is full of blood, it is life! I can see it going around and around in my hand, like a bug or some other little animal. I blow on it with the smoke from the king vulture's tobacco. Now it is calming down. I see Kokowá [Dombá's wife] in the hospital

spreading the healing *hwintuktö* on his stomach. She spreads the medicine I have dropped from my beak, and I blow the vulture's smoke on
it. The kidney calms down and stops circling around. It is finally still
and quiet in my hand. "You can lie still," I tell it, "because now you are
going to have a new owner. You have to get used to him. Now you are
inside a Suyá body, and you can't keep going around crazy like that."
So I had to talk a lot to this new kidney, making it understand.
Whenever it starts getting a little wild, the *xexéu* brings medicine for
it, and I blow it into the wound.

Now I see the doctor stitching my brother-in-law all up! I can see it!
The people are saying, "Don't leave it hanging out like an ugly thing!
Close up the opening! Do a good job!" But the doctors really know
their stuff, and they stitch the kidney up inside. The body is all smooth;
the kidney is quiet, and there is no more disease. The disease is gone!
My brother-in-law is cured! When he flew back from São Paulo, everybody saw him. And now all the people believe in me once again.

So this is how I care for people. This time I worked hard with the
caraíba doctors, and we did a good job together. In my dreams I am
always flying. I fly because I am a bird; you know that. I am a *xexéu*,
and I can fly. I can see disease; I can see people's souls. I know the spirits
of all the water animals, the ones that circulate in your body looking
for an opportunity to eat up your soul. I am *agatonkere*, and I know all
these things because I know all their songs, all the animal songs—the
tucunaré's [*Cichla ocellaris*], the bee's. And I sing their songs, and I
show their songs to the people so that everyone learns how to sing.
People are using tape recorders now, so they won't forget these healing
songs that I teach them. Because it is in singing these songs of the animals that I make my people well.

CONCLUSION: DOMBÁ'S SPIRIT KIDNEY

Spirit or soul loss, among the Suyá, usually results from an act of sorcery
by an envious witch and/or from a serious bout with illness or disability.
During Dombá's prolonged illness, Dombá's father, his brother-in-law, and
Dombá himself searched constantly for his spirit. A vulnerable person's
spirit may wander from one location to another until it eventually decides
to reenter the body. Because Dombá was seriously ill, and especially when
he was under anesthesia, he ran the risk of his spirit leaving his body permanently and taking up residence with a different form of matter, human
or not, animate or not, such as a plant, a rock, or an animal (Seeger
1985:197, 226). For the Suyá, as for many other Amazonian peoples, all
sentient beings (even animals) are human and possess a soul. All see themselves as humans and are believed to possess human subjectivity. Likewise, all

parts of human bodies possess spirit matter. In this sense Dombá's new kidney is a "spirit kidney," facilitating the interaction between Suyá and non-Indian souls.[28]

Moreover, in Suyá cosmology all beings are classified as either predators or as prey. Whites, like jaguars, are among the "top predators." Because he survived his transplant with a white man's kidney, Dombá is especially empowered. As an Indian with a white man's *iturutö*, Dombá acquired certain characteristics (both good and bad), including some of the predatory power of whites, without himself turning into a white person. Both Dombá and his substance group have inherited some characteristics of the young white male from whom Dombá received not only a kidney but also parts of the dead man's soul and his spirit double, who entered Dombá's body during his dream/vision. White/not white, body/spirit, living/dead—the transplant process provoked a central paradox for Dombá and his close kin, but one that they are learning to live with and benefit from.

The choices that Dombá, now 45 years old, has made in relation to his health and medical care have affected his wife and children, his father, Romdó, his brother-in-law, Intoni, and the other individuals who belong to his substance group. Dombá's transplant continues to affect them all. One could say that they are a transplanted community. To this day, Dombá and his substance group must all follow special dietary and other medical recommendations sent via short-wave radio to Xingu Park by Hospital São Paulo physicians and medical staff. But even this Dombá accepted with his characteristic calm and tranquillity as something new to be lived through with the help of his *pajés* and their cosmic knowledge and vision.

Finally, the kidney transplant enhanced Dombá's ceremonial power, because of the knowledge he gained from his close and intense interaction with his father, Intoni, and their animal doubles. During his surgery and recovery Dombá dwelled successfully with the animal world. This alone qualified him for ascendancy into the highest spiritual and ritual status among the Suyá. Dombá would have very likely become a ceremonial leader, a *merokinkande*, like his father, Romdó, or a *pajé*, *agatonkere*, like his brother-in-law Intoni.

EPILOGUE

Unfortunately, Dombá and his spirit kidney did not survive. The sad news of Dombá's passing reached us in 2004.

NOTES

1. This description in based on interviews by Nancy Scheper-Hughes with more than 60 dialysis patients from private and public clinics in Recife, Salvador, Rio de Janeiro, and São Paulo, Brazil, between 1996 and 2001.

2. Cyclosporin (Sanimmune Neoral) is a strong immunosuppressant drug that prevents organ rejection by interfering with the body's natural immune response, essentially shutting it down. This renders the transplant patient vulnerable to opportunistic bacterial, fungal, or viral infections. Because of an increased risk of skin cancer, patients taking cyclosporin must avoid direct exposure to the sun and wear protective clothing outdoors. Many posttransplant patients complain of cyclosporin-induced side effects, including loss of appetite, chronic nausea, hair growth, bleeding gums, chronic diarrhea, blurred vision, and tremors. Because prolonged use of the drug can cause kidney failure and liver problems, as well as hypertension and anemia, all transplant patients need to be closely monitored. Blood pressure is usually measured on a monthly basis, and kidney function, especially creatinine levels, is tested through frequent blood and urine tests.

3. Margaret Lock (2002) reviews this fascinating history in her book *Twice Dead: Organ Transplantation and the Redefinition of Death.*

4. Based on her multisited research in nine countries and as cofounder and director of Organs Watch, a research and medical human-rights project housed at the University of California, Berkeley, Scheper-Hughes has argued that the extension of transplant capacities to new areas and to new populations, often through new markets in bodies and body parts, has led to a radical commodification of the body and exploitation of the poor, the socially marginal, and the politically vulnerable. (See Scheper-Hughes 2002, 2004b.)

5. Cross-matching is testing for the presence of anti-HLA antibodies in the blood of patients awaiting a transplant. These antibodies are directed against the HLA antigens, cell-surface proteins that create a unique personal signature for each of us. These antibodies may be created whenever we are exposed to another donor's cells—blood or platelet transfusions, during pregnancy (where the donor is the fetus presenting the father's HLA antigens), or after a previously failed kidney transplant. A transplant in the presence of these antibodies can be quickly destroyed by the patient's immune system, and that is obviously a tragic waste of a precious organ. Cross-matching is done by mixing the prospective donor's T cells with the prospective recipient's serum. If antibodies are present, they are detected by their property of binding to the patient's cells via several different kinds of assays.

6. Fieldnotes and interviews from the files of Nancy Scheper-Hughes's multisited research project (1997–2002) "Medicine, Markets, and Bodies."

7. This process continues to the present day. The Brazilian military has taken advantage of old laws allowing the construction of military bases in Roraima on the border of Venezuela and Guyana that are now threatening the survival of Yanomami Indians (*New York Times,* October 1, 2002, p.1, A10).

8. *Diauarum* means "black jaguar" in Kaiabi, a Tupi language.

9. Body decoration is especially important in Amerindian societies where clothing is little used. Painting, tattooing, scarification, piercing, and the use of ear and lip disks and arm, knee, and ankle bands shape and express the individual body-self and the social body of indigenous peoples in Brazil, and of the Suyá in particular. See Conklin 1997; Ferreira 2001, 2002; Ferreira and Suhrbier 2002; Lopes da Silva 2000; Seeger 1985; Suhrbier and Ferreira 2001; van Velthem 2002; and Vidal 2000.

10. At the time of Dombá's initiation, Suyá elders were in disagreement as to whether or not they should follow the recommendations of the Villas-Bôas brothers that they erase all obvious signs of Indianness so as to more easily "integrate" themselves into the white man's world. In the Villas-Bôas' opinion, lip disks were particularly "ugly," as they gave the Suyá a "wild" appearance and also "rotted their teeth" (Ferreira 1994:28–42).

11. The *xexéu* is a small black-and-yellow bird, similar in appearance to a crow. The *xexéu* has a "double," its magical twin, which can inhabit the bodies of powerful shamans and carry them in bird form to the distant places where the shaman's skills are needed.

12. Birds are considered the most "bland-smelling" creatures and therefore very powerful within Suyá cosmology. And of all birds, the hummingbird is the "strongest of all animals" and the most precious to the Suyá, because the hummingbird first discovered water for the group. (See Intoni's narrative on the origin of water, plants, and foods in Ferreira 1994:15–18.)

13. The cayman is a small alligator.

14. Music is a central feature of Suyá ritual life. Curing chants (*sangere*) use metaphors to create a relationship between an animal and a specific trait (stillness, in this case) and, by association, between the animal and the human patient—as when the quiet and stillness of the cayman under water is transmitted to the feverish and shivering patient (Seeger 1985:25–26).

15. The Suyá classify animals in terms of smell. The strongest-smelling animals are considered the most dangerous, whereas the least odorous are considered harmless and friendly to humans. The categorization of nature and the world in terms of smell provides an important key to understanding Suyá knowledge and cosmology. (See Seeger 1985:92–105.)

16. The cheapest plywood and cardboard coffins made in Brazil that are distributed by hospitals for charity patients are sealed tight with nails. Not only Brazilian Indians but poor people from the rural northeastern Brazil prefer to keep the coffins unsealed so that the soul can easily escape and begin its journey to the next world.

17. FUNAI operates a Casa do Índio in a rented house in São Paulo, as the foundation does in other large cities also. The Casa do Índio is a place to house Indians before or after they have been treated for a serious illness at a hospital.

18. *Hwintuktö* is a small plant with a pungent, sweet smell. The plant is crushed in the hands, and the pulp is rubbed on children and adults who are weak or suffer from convulsions (Seeger 1985:103).

19. The Portuguese expression that Dombá used, *sonhar com,* conveys the notion that one is virtually "with" the people one dreams of, and in this regard is close to the Suyá understanding of dreams.

20. Properly speaking, the Suyá practice neonaticide, which in most traditional contexts is a form of postpartum abortion in the absence of other alternatives. The ethnomedical literature addressing the practices and meanings of neonaticide and infanticide is extensive, rich, and contested. It cannot be treated here with any degree of the care that it deserves. An article by Lynn Morgan (1998), "Ambiguities lost: Fashioning the fetus into a child in Ecuador and the United States," is, however, a good place to begin. Several chapters in the volume edited by N. Scheper-Hughes (1987) *Child Survival: Anthropological Approaches to the Treatment and Maltreatment of Children,* also discuss this issue.

21. São Paulo has a regionalized waiting list that monitors the procurement and distribution of organs. However, these good intentions are constantly interrupted by the power of individual surgeons and large hospitals. In 1997 organs were allocated to the transplant center, not to patients, and surgeons sometimes switched the patients designated to receive the allocated organ (interview by Scheper-Hughes with the head of São Paulo's Center for Transplants, July 1997).

22. Creatinine is the end product of creatine metabolism, found in muscle and blood and excreted in urine, and used to assist the body's acceptance of the new organ.

23. *Beiju* are manioc cakes made of pure manioc starch and water.

24. The Ricó village is located on the margins of the Suyá-Missu River, which is a tributary of the Xingu River.

25. Gaisarin, Dombá's sister, is married to Intoni, the *pajé* Dombá refers to as "my brother-in-law."

26. We have omitted this part of the narrative because it is not directly related to Dombá's story. After being cured by a *pajé* from the Alto Xingu, Dombeti began having bad dreams and visions, and was thus taken by the Kamaiurá people to be trained as a *pajé* in their village. The Suyá feared that he would be made into a witch and thus be used by the Kamaiurá as a scapegoat for local misfortunes.

27. This is a wonderful commentary on the anonymity and invisibility of the donor. But Dombá himself said that although he was curious, he really did not want to know very much about the man who would be having, as it was, such a great influence over his life and the lives of the members of Dombá's substance group.

28. According to "perspectivism," a cosmological model that accounts for the ontological differences of the various beings that inhabit the universe, all sentient beings, be they spirit, animal, or human, possess a soul, a human subjectivity (Viveiros de Castro 1996). It is in this sense that we claim Dombá's new kidney is a spirit kidney.

REFERENCES

Agamben, Giorgio. 1998. *Homo Sacer: Sovereign Power and Bare Life.* Stanford: Stanford University Press.

Coelho, Vera Shattan. 2000. Doação presumida e sistema de transplante no Brasil. In *Políticas do corpo e o curso da vida,* ed. Guita Grin Debert and Donna M. Goldstein, 83–88. São Paulo: Sumaré.

Cohen, Lawrence. 1999 Where it hurts: Indian material for an ethics of organ transplantation. *Daedalus* 128(4): 135–66.

———. 2002. The other kidney: Biopolitics beyond recognition. In *Commodifying Bodies,* ed. N. Scheper-Hughes and L. Wacquant, 9–29. London: Sage. [Originally published as *Body and Society,* vol. 7 (2001), nos. 2 and 3.]

Conklin, Beth. 1997. Body paint, feathers, and VCRs: Aesthetics and authenticity on Amazonian activism. *American Ethnologist* 24(4): 711–37.

Davis, Selton. 1977. *Victims of the Miracle.* Cambridge: Cambridge University Press.

Descola, P. 1998. Estrutura ou sentimento: A relação com o animal na Amazonia. *Estudos de Antopologia Social* (Universidade Federal do Rio de Janeiro) 4(1): 23–45.

Ferreira, Mariana Leal. 1994. *Histórias do Xingu: Coletânea de depoimentos dos índios Suyá, Kayabi, Juruna, Trumai, Txucarramãe e Txicão.* São Paulo: Núcleo de História Indígena e do Indigenismo/Fundação de Amparo à Pesquisa do Estado de São Paulo/FAPESP.

———. 1996. Firewater: The life-history of Pocá Kayabi in central Brazil. *Terra Nova: Nature and Culture* 1(2): 4–14.

———. 1997. When 1 + 1 = 2: Making mathematics in central Brazil. *American Ethnologist* 24(1): 132–47.

———. 1998a. Perícia histórico-antropológica na terra indígena Wawi, estado do Mato Grosso. Judicial Court of Mato Grosso, court case no. 95.00013967-7, Cuiabá, Mato Grosso.

———. 1998b. Silver fragments of broken mirrors. *Terra Nova: Nature and Culture* 3(1): 4–15.

———. 2001. Shamanic knowledge and power in Brazilian court cases in the new millennium. In *Ethnobiology and Biocultural Diversity: Proceedings of the Seventh International Conference of Ethnobiology,* ed. J. R. Stepp, F. S. Wyndham, and R. K. Zarger, 43–52. Athens: University of Georgia Press.

———. 2002. Tupi-Guarani apocalyptic visions of time and body. *Journal of Latin American Anthropology* 7(1): 128–69.

Ferreira, Mariana Leal, and Mona Suhrbier. 2002. The poetics of Guarani art in the face of hunger and scarcity. *Paideuma: Mitteilungen zur Kulturkunde* Frobenius-Institut, Frankfurt a.M.) 48: 145–64.

Gregor, Thomas. 1988. Infants are not precious to us: The psychological impact of infanticide among the Mehinaku Indians. Stirling Prize Paper, Annual Meeting of the American Anthropological Association, Phoenix, Arizona, 16–20 November.

Gruzinski, S. 1988. *La colonisation de l'imaginaire. Sociétés indigènes et occidentalisation dans le Mexique espagnol.* Paris: Gallimard.

Hugh-Jones, S. 1996. Shamans, prophets, priests and pastors. In *Shamanism, History and the State,* ed. N. Thomas and C. Humphrey, 32–75. Ann Arbor: University of Michigan Press.

Jimenez, Marina, and Nancy Scheper-Hughes. 2002a. Doctor vulture: The unholy business of the organ trade. *National Post* (Toronto), 30 March 2002, B1, pp. 4–5.

———. 2002b. Europe's poorest sell their kidneys. *National Post* (Toronto), 29 March 2002, A1, pp. 12–13.

Lock, Margaret. 2002. *Twice Dead: Organ Transplantation and the Redefinition of Death.* Berkeley and Los Angeles: University of California Press.

Lopes da Silva, Aracy. 2000. The *akwẽ-xavante* in history at the end of the twentieth century. *Journal of Latin American Anthropology* 4(1): 212–37.

McDonald S. P., G. R. Russ, P. G. Kerr, and J. F. Collins. 2002. ESRD in Australia and New Zealand at the end of the millennium: A report from the ANZ-DATA registry. *American Journal of Kidney Disease* 40: 1122–31.

Morgan, Lynn. 1998. Ambiguities lost: Fashioning the fetus into a child in Ecuador and the United States. In *Small Wars: The Cultural Politics of Childhood,* ed. Nancy Scheper-Hughes and Carolyn Sargent, 58–74. Berkeley and Los Angeles: University of California Press.

Overing, J. 1990. The shaman as maker of worlds. *Man* 25: 601–19.

Rosaldo, Renato. 1989. *The Anthropology of Truth.* Boston: Beacon.

Scheper-Hughes, Nancy, ed. 1987. *Child Survival: Anthropological Approaches to the Treatment and Maltreatment of Children.* Dordrecht: Reidel.

———. 2000. The global traffic in organs. *Current Anthropology* 41(2): 191–224.

———. 2002a. Bodies for sale—Whole or in parts. In *Commodifying Bodies,* ed. N. Scheper-Hughes and L. Waquant, 1–8. London: Sage. [Originally published as *Body and Society,* vol. 7 (2001), nos. 2 and 3.]

———. 2002b. Commodity fetishism in organs trafficking. In *Commodifying Bodies,* ed. N. Scheper-Hughes and L. Waquant, 31–62. London: Sage. [Originally published as *Body and Society,* vol. 7 (2001), nos. 2 and 3.]

———. 2004a. The cutting edge: Trans-Atlantic transplants. CLAS Newsletter, Center for Latin American Studies, University of California, Berkeley, May, pp. 14–17, 44.

———. 2004b. Parts unknown: Undercover ethnography of the organs-trafficking underworld. *Ethnography* 5(1): 29–73.

Scheper-Hughes, Nancy, and João Guilherme Biehl. 2000. O fim do corpo: Comercio de orgãos para transplantes cirúrgicos. In *Políticas do corpo e o curso da vida,* ed. Guita Grin Debert and Donna M. Goldstein, 49–81. São Paulo: Sumaré.

Scheper-Hughes, Nancy, and Margaret Lock. 1987. The mindful body: A prolegomenon to future work in medical anthropology. *Medical Anthropology Quarterly* 1(1): 6–41.

Seeger, Anthony. 1985. *Nature and Society in Central Brazil: The Suyá Indians of Matto Grosso.* Cambridge, Mass.: Harvard University Press.

——. 1987. *Why Suyá Sing: A Musical Anthropology of Amazonian People.* Cambridge: Cambridge University Press.

Shepard, Glenn. 1999. Pharmacognosy and the senses in two Amazonian societies. Ph.D. Dissertation, Department of Anthropology, University of California, Berkeley.

Suhrbier, Mona, and Mariana Ferreira. 2001. A poética da fome na arte guarani. *Revista do Museu de Arqueologia e Etnologia* (Universidade Federal do São Paulo) 10: 211–229,

United Network for Organ Sharing [UNOS]. 2002. OPTN/UNOS board revises kidney policy to boost minority transplants. Press release, 14 November.

Vainfas, R. 1995. *A heresia dos índios: Catolicismo e rebeldia no Brasil colonial.* São Paulo: Companhia das Letras.

de Vasconcelos, Maria Odete. 1995. Contribuição ao estudo antropológico do doador renal. Dissertation presented to the postgraduate program in anthropology, UFPE, Recife.

van Velthem, Lucia. 2002. "Feito por inimigos": Os brancos e seus bens das representações Wayana do contato. In *Pacificando o branco: Cosmologias do contato no Norte-Amazônico,* ed. Bruce Albert and Alcida Ramos, 000–00. São Paulo: UNESP.

Vidal, Lux B. 2000. O mapeamento simbólico das cores na sociedade indígena Kayapó-Xikrin do sudoeste do Pará. In *Antropologia, história e educação: A questão indígena e a escola,* ed. Aracy Silva and Mariana Ferreira, 209–20. São Paulo: Global.

Viveiros de Castro, E. 1996. Os pronomes cosmológicos e o perspectivismo ameríndio. *Mana* 2(2):115–44.

Wright, R., and J. Hill. 1992. Venancio Kamiko: Wakuenai shamana and messiah. In *Portals of Power: Shamanism in South America,* ed. E. J. Landon and G. Baer, 257–86. Albuquerque: University of New Mexico Press.

PART II

Localizing Policy and Technology

7   Genomics, Laissez-Faire Eugenics, and Disability

MARGARET LOCK

It is well known that the eugenics movement set in motion by Charles Darwin's cousin Francis Galton was actively embraced by the Nazi regime in order to give a thin layer of purported scientific verity to the practices associated with "racial hygiene." What is perhaps less well recognized is that many supporters of eugenics in the early part of the twentieth century were progressive-minded socialists, among whom Emma Goldman, George Bernard Shaw, H. G. Wells, and Margaret Sanger were prominent.

These writers and activists recognized the eugenics movement as a foundation for social reform. H. G. Wells claimed, for example, that "the children people bring into the world can be no more their private concern entirely, than the disease germs they disseminate, or the noises a man makes in a thin-floored flat." For Wells eugenics was integral to public health (Kevles 1995:92). Similarly, Margaret Sanger wrote in the 1920s: "Those least fit to carry on the race are increasing most rapidly. . . . Funds that should be used to raise the standard of our civilization are diverted to maintenance of those who should never have been born" (1922:98). In its early years the birth-control movement strongly supported Sanger's position, and a 1940 joint meeting of the Birth Control Federation of America and the Citizens Committee for Planned Parenthood was entitled "Race building in a democracy." The eugenics movement, explicitly bent on weeding out the "feeble-minded" and "degenerates," gained support during the depression, and many geneticists were directly involved in it (Paul and Spencer 1995). As Philip Kitcher points out in his book *The Lives to Come* (1996), from the outset the eugenics movement made assessments about genetic worth, and by extrapolation it questioned the very existence of certain individuals. This position was inextricably associated with a belief that the elimination of poor genes was justified for the good of society at large. The only method available to carry out the elimination of such genes was to enact policies that permitted political control over the reproductive lives of individuals designated as a burden to society.

Eugenics was part of a long line of utopian movements evident throughout the centuries that sought explicitly to dispose of unwanted peoples deemed as having little or no value. More often than not such people were visibly different, making them easy targets for banishment or other means of disposal. In this essay I will argue that, despite laws passed since the late 1940s in connection with human rights, including disability-rights acts, continuities with the past in which certain lives are deemed of less worth than others remain evident. Today, unlike in the past, interventions that may result in a neoeugenics are usually masked by a rhetoric very different from that of the early twentieth century, one in which individual choice is dominant and in which the role of government is rendered invisible. A further significant difference is that the new technologies of molecular genetics and germline engineering permit a calculated manipulation of human reproduction that has never before been possible. The crude techniques of forced sterilization are, in most countries, a thing of the past, and it is now pregnant women and their partners who make crucial decisions about pregnancy outcomes.

THE STIGMA OF DIFFERENCE

Many of the dilemmas that pregnant women have to face up to in making decisions about what action, if any, to take after hearing the results of tests that provide information about the fetus they are carrying have already been made explicit in the general field of disability research. Lying behind such dilemmas are always assumptions about what should be recognized as normal and what as abnormal. The grounds on which such moral decisions are made are, however, relatively rarely explicitly examined. Closely associated with such decisions are concerns that are more likely to be explicitly examined, about suffering and whether it can or should be avoided. The research of Gail Landsman involving the mothers of disabled children, in which she highlights the conflicts that the majority of mothers face, is illustrative. On the one hand, physical impairment is medicalized today. By definition this means that it is individualized and recognized as, in effect, an abnormality best handled by medical professionals. Mothers who participate in this medicalization are to some extent at least participating in an ideology of normalization, one in which the body of the child will be resculpted through medical technologies in order that the child may pass as healthy rather than being "burdened" with physical or mental difference. But Landsman found that many mothers would rather not know about the medical options—in their estimation the child is "normal enough" without medical assistance, and aside from providing essential basic medication when necessary, such mothers preferred to stay away from medicalized assistance. Landsman suggests that an affiliation can be detected among the mothers who fall into this latter group with the social world of disability activists. For them the acceptance or rejection of disability by the medical world and by the public at large is understood as a matter of politics and societal attitudes. The medicalized language of individual impairment and of deviation from normality is anathema to them and does not enter their vocabulary (Landsman 2005). Clearly, not all parents of disabled children are willing to buy the "unnatural histories" that are assigned to their children by the medical world (Rapp and Ginsburg 2001). However, many mothers are conflicted, because no matter how much they believe that society must change they do not want their own children to suffer prejudice and discrimination. Nor do they want to be made fully responsible for the condition or care of their children. Medicalization holds out the hope of a cure in the future; it expunges guilt by neutralizing the problem as amoral and entirely medical, and it sets the process in motion whereby mothers may obtain financial help and social support when necessary.

A case study from Japan illustrates some of the key conflicts experienced by parents of disabled children in connection with societal prejudice. Living in Tokyo, Mrs. Doi, the mother of a four-year-old girl with neurofibromatosis, confided in me that her husband and the four grandparents of her daughter have been fully engaged in doing all they can to help the child. She added that she is lucky because such support is still unusual in Japan and family shame is often associated with the birth of a sick or disabled child (Lock 1993). The grandparents have not only actively encouraged Mrs. Doi and her husband to get the best medical help available, but they have also extended themselves to actively take over some of the care of their grandchild. Mrs. Doi did not hesitate to tell me that she wishes a genetic test had been available at the time she became pregnant.[1] She is very impressed by the mothers she meets at the genetics clinic and how, in her words, they are "doing their best for their children," but she believes that she might well have chosen to have an abortion if she had known about the suffering and prejudice her daughter would face growing up in Japan. Yumiko is stigmatized and ostracized by her peers because of numerous brown pigmented blotches all over her face and body that cannot be hidden. Mrs. Doi is concerned not so much about future illness that may be in store for her daughter, but above all about the effects of this discrimination that both Yumiko and she herself experience in public places. Parents of children in the kindergarten that Mrs. Doi's daughter attends have told their children not to play with Yumiko, and several mothers communicated directly to Mrs. Doi that they were concerned about infection and refused to believe that Yumiko's condition was not contagious. They hinted in not too veiled a fashion that Mrs. Doi had no right to expect that her child should come to school at all. Mrs. Doi is angered by these mothers, but recognizes that they are simply exhibiting the values common to many people in Japan that discriminate against her daughter and others like her. She is adamant that, until public attitudes change, children who exhibit visible signs of difference, and their parents, will never be at ease. Mrs. Doi believes that her life has been enriched in very many ways through loving, caring for, and raising Yumiko, but she is so distraught at the social stigma that Yumiko is subjected to that she longs for a medical miracle, and on bad days believes that she did wrong by bringing Yumiko into the world.

THE HYPE/HOPE OF GENOMICS

For the space of a decade, during the 1990s, a good number of influential scientists argued that mapping the human genome was the "medical miracle" that so many people living with or caring for people with illness and disability were waiting for (Gilbert 1992). It is now clear, five years after the mapping was essentially completed, that we still await that miracle. Meantime screening and testing of genes has become increasingly accepted as part of everyday life, at least in the so-called developed world.

It is also disturbing to read that claims are being made to improve global health equity through the "harnessing" of genomics. Efforts should be made, it is argued, to stop the emergence of a "health genomics divide," and that investment must come about to ensure that the developing world is not left out, as is already the case with information technology and agricultural biotechnology (Singer and Daar 2001). The hope is that investment will permit economically strapped countries to develop and conduct their own genomics initiatives. It would be reassuring if, at a minimum, there was some indication that genomics for the developing world would go ahead hand in hand with the provision of clean water and sewage disposal, an adequate food supply, massive debt relief, and equal access to basic health care, and without interference by those local governments already notorious for corruption and infamy. But no doubt those of us who exhibit doubts about a rush to genomics for the developing world will be accused by some of paternalism.

LAISSEZ-FAIRE EUGENICS

Over 20 years ago, the historian of science Edward Yoxen pointed out that we have witnessed a conceptual shift that was not present in the language of geneticists prior to the advent of molecular genetics. While the contribution of genetics to the incidence of disease has been recognized throughout this century, it has only been since the 1960s that the notion of "genetic disease" has come to so dominate discourse that other contributory factors are often obscured from view (Yoxen 1982). Fox Keller (1992) argues that it was this shift in discourse that made the human genome project both reasonable and desirable in the minds of many involved researchers. In mapping the human genome, the objective was to create a baseline norm, but the result is one that corresponds to the genome of no living individual, so that we all, in effect, become deviants from this norm (Lewontin 1992). Moreover, with this map now in hand, the belief of many involved scientists is that we are rapidly moving into an era in which we will be able to "guarantee all human beings an individual and natural right, the right to health" (Fox Keller 1992:295). Fox Keller cites a report put out by the Office of Technology Assessment in the United States in which it is argued that genetic information will be used "to ensure that . . . each individual has at least a modicum of normal genes"—this is characterized in the report as a "eugenics of normalcy" and is grounded on the belief that "individuals have a paramount right to be born with a normal, adequate hereditary endowment" (Office of Technology Assessment 1988).

Although improvement of the quality of the human gene pool is being aired in documents such as these, as Fox Keller (1992:295) and others have pointed out, the language used is no longer one that focuses on social policy, the good of the species, or even the collective gene pool. We are now in an era dominated by the idea of individual choice in connection with decision making relating to health and illness. Genetic information will furnish the indispensable knowledge that individuals need in order to realize their inalienable right to health. A laissez-faire eugenics—a "utopian eugenics" (Kitcher 1996)—is already in place, one that depends upon decisions that individuals and families make, usually about abortion, on the basis of the results of genetic testing and screening programs. The iron grip of Foucault's microphysics of power (1980) is at work.

It is now agreed by virtually everyone that the eugenics of the first part of the twentieth century was grounded in invalid science, and its practices are roundly criticized. However, the social cost of treating and caring for "defective" children is still made explicit when justifying the implementation of screening programs. The State of California explicitly introduced maternal serum α-fetoprotein screening for all pregnant women more than a decade ago in the hope of reducing the number of infants born with neural tube defects and thereby saving costs (Caplan 1993). The 1990 guidelines of the International Huntington Association make it clear that it is acceptable to refuse to test women who do not give a complete assurance that they will terminate a pregnancy if the Huntington gene is found. As Paul and Spencer (1995) point out: "Those who made this recommendation certainly did not think they were promoting eugenics. Assuming that eugenics is dead is one way to dispose of deep social, political and ethical questions. But it may not be the best one."

Human eugenics is a fact of life because of consumer demand, a 1989 editorial proclaimed in *Trends in Biotechnology*. We are encouraged to believe that the public is pushing the scientists. This is the case in connection with some monogenetic diseases that have devastating effects on afflicted children. Certain involved families, often as part of advocacy groups, work actively together with clinicians and scientists to raise funding for research and to elevate public consciousness about the disease in question—such activities have been described as a form of "genetic biosociality" (Rapp et al. 2001). But other research has shown that only between 15 and 20 percent of people designated at risk for genetic disease, or for carrying a fetus believed to be at risk for a genetic disease, have made use of testing (Quaid and Morris 1993; Beeson and Doksum 2001), and others, when tested, have ignored the results (Hill 1994; Rapp 1999). So here too conflicts can easily be detected among people who are potentially implicated by the knowledge being produced as a result of the new genetic technologies.

In any case, as pointed out by Daniel Kevles (1984), who has written extensively on eugenics, the ability of scientists to meet most of the desires and hopes of consumers is still a long way off, despite the rapid progress being made in locating genes, or markers for them, on chromosomes. As more knowledge is accrued and we become increasingly aware of the complexities of gene-gene, gene-protein, and gene-environment interactions, it is undeniable how little we know. Even the mechanisms of some of the "straightforward" genetic diseases that follow well-defined Mendelian inheritance patterns are proving to be only sketchily understood. For one thing, we are often unable to predict disease severity that may range from mild to devastating. And until recently it was assumed that if someone had the gene for Huntington's disease it would inevitably be expressed, but now it is known that this is not always the case.

Beyond these technological limitations, the social consequences of genetic testing and screening can easily backfire. The sickle-cell screening programs set in place in the 1970s in the United States, often with active support from the African-American community, reveal in retrospect how programs designed to reduce suffering through genetic interventions can go badly wrong when this type of information gets into the hands of employers and school boards and is used to reinforce exclusion and racism (Duster 1990). Questions about who should have access to the results of genetic screening and testing remain unanswered, and firm policy recommendations have not yet been made; nevertheless screening for sickle-cell disease is currently mandatory in 33 of the 50 United States.

Another troublesome example is that of the screening program set up by the Colorado school board to detect Fragile-X syndrome. Guidelines for testing for the involved gene were issued in 1994 by the American College of Medical Genetics. The guidelines included recommendations that all males and females with any physical or behavioral characteristics of the syndrome, individuals with a family history of the disease, and those asymptomatic individuals deemed to be "at risk" for this disease should be tested (American College of Medical Genetics 1994). The incidence of this disease, associated with mental impairment and mild learning difficulties or hyperactivity (but often assessed as in the normal range: Brown et al. 1993), is estimated to be about one per 1,500 males and one per 2,500 females (Warren and Nelson 1994). In common with a good number of other so-called genetic diseases, the involved genes exhibit "incomplete penetrance": that is, for unknown reasons, by no means will all individuals with the genotype manifest the disease. It is estimated that about 20 percent of males and 70 percent of females with the mutation express no symptoms, making the designation "at risk" extremely problematic. Moreover, the severity of symptoms varies enormously, and cannot be predicted. Benefits from therapeutic and educational interventions have not been shown (Caskey 1994).

In 1993 a Fragile-X testing program had been put in place in the Colorado public school system as part of an effort to develop an inexpensive test that could be used as a model for a national program (Hubbard and Wald 1993). The project, funded by Oncor, a private biotechnology company, was carried out by a university/industry consortium, and was explicitly designed to save later public expenditure on children with mental deficits. Before the program was set up, a report was published by the Colorado Health Sciences Center and the University Business Advancement Center that argued that screening could enhance economic efficiency.

Estimated cost to families and also public expenditure used for care of Fragile-X patients were carefully calculated, and the conclusion was that "the savings to the state would be tremendous" from implementation of a screening program (Lauria and Webb 1992). Screening was not done in a clinical setting and, Nelkin notes, was driven by economic and entrepreneurial interests. Further, there are no known therapies for the condition once identified. The consequences for the lives of those children who tested positive was significant, not the least of these being discrimination against them by health-insurance companies. Nelkin points out that many parents actively supported screening for the Fragile-X gene and that a significant number of them, particularly mothers, initially experienced relief once their child's so-called behavioral problem was identified as genetic; parents could no longer be found wanting for the condition of their child (Nelkin 1996:538). However, after two years, the anticipated number of cases had not come to light, and the program was deemed uneconomical and suspended (Hubbard and Wald 1993:124).

Even though extreme caution would seem to be in order in connection with the new genetics, we forge ahead rapidly toward making genetic testing and screening routine (Beeson and Doksum 2001). In support of an expansion of these technologies is the argument that people will be able to make rational choices about their marriage partners and about abortion, thus avoiding bringing diseased children into the world. There is no doubt that screening programs in connection with, for example, thalassemia and Tay-Sachs disease have brought enormous relief to some families (Angastiniotis et al. 1986; Kuliev 1986; Mitchell et al. 1996), and the Cuban government reports success with a screening program for sickle-cell disease (Granda et al. 1991).

Counseling of young people who are screened and found to be carriers of these genes is offered in all such programs. Success is measured in terms of reduction in the incidence of the disease, achieved by means of genetic tests given to mothers deemed to be at risk as a result of screening of themselves and their partners as teenagers, followed by abortion when the fetus is found to have the unwanted gene. Reduction of thalassemia and Tay-Sachs disease has been very significant as a result of the screening programs in Montréal that have been in existence for over 25 years. It is reported that many involved families state that without such a screening program they would not have had children for fear of the disease, but that they are now at ease in the knowledge that their children will be spared great suffering (Mitchell et al. 1996).

One program based in New York that has tested more than 50,000 orthodox Jews in many parts of the world handles things a little differently.

This program, unlike those in Montréal, does not inform teenagers who are tested about their own status as a carrier for Tay-Sachs disease because of the associated stigma. When a couple who have been tested plans to get married, they may contact the rabbi in charge of the program, and he will inform them confidentially if their match is at risk for producing diseased offspring. Such couples then are given counseling. Couples designated as not at risk, on the other hand, are not informed whether either one of the partners is a carrier, and the program has been criticized as a result of this policy as paternalistic (Ekstein 1995).

Rayna Rapp's research in various settings in New York shows poignantly how the decisions that women and their partners must make as to whether to terminate wanted pregnancies are rarely made without pain and misgivings. She also demonstrates how genetic counselors unwittingly encourage certain women, whom they believe will not be able to take on the burden of a sick or disabled child, toward pregnancy termination—this is in spite of the fact that the fundamental guidelines of all genetic counseling is that it should be "nondirective" (Rapp 1999:59). Willis (1998) reminds us that abortion politics will affect the implementation and spread of screening technologies, with those countries and organizations where "right to life" campaigners are the most vocal having a direct influence on policy making. Certain advocates of gene therapy and germline engineering claim that when these technologies are routinely used abortions will be avoided and, moreover, that "bad genes" will be disposed of entirely. Clearly this is self-promoting hype, because genetic manipulation will not be available for by far the majority of the people in the world for the foreseeable future. But among those women who are increasingly required to undergo genetic testing during pregnancy, in those cases where an "abnormality" is found, a wanted pregnancy can, in the space of a short time, turn into a terrifying experience fraught with decisions that must be made, the consequences of which will be felt for ever.

A recent critique of prenatal genetic testing put out by people involved with disability rights points out that a major difficulty with such testing is inherent to all forms of discrimination: namely that a single trait stands in for the whole. In the case of prenatal testing "a single trait stands in for the whole (potential) person. Knowledge of the trait is enough to warrant the abortion of an otherwise wanted fetus" (Parens and Asch 1999:S2). Nancy Press has argued that "by developing and offering tests to detect some characteristics and not others, the professional community is expressing the view that some characteristics, but not all, warrant the attention of prospective parents" (Press 2000; Parens and Asch 1999:S2). However, none of the individuals who contributed to the report were categorically opposed to prenatal testing for devastating diseases such as Tay-Sachs.

GERMLINE ENGINEERING

For some scientists involved with the new genetics, testing and screening of genes is a cumbersome way of dealing with the havoc that may be wrought by the inadvertent transmission of genes through reproduction. Enhancement technologies are increasingly discussed, including gene therapy and human germline engineering. For the rest of this chapter I want to consider germline engineering. When people discuss this particular technology, they very frequently get agitated, but not usually, as one might predict, about inequalities of access to its possible benefits, or about an inappropriate use of scarce resources. Just about everyone who participates in discussions relevant to germline engineering realizes that what has up until now been thought of as an unassailable boundary between nature and culture could be permanently transformed by such interventions. For this reason many individuals, involved geneticists among them, believe that germline engineering is an insidious threat to the social order, although others believe that we are on the verge of making scientific progress to an extent we have never before witnessed. It is pertinent to consider, while implementation of this particular technology continues to be banned, how arguments for and against its incorporation into the armamentarium of the new genetics are being constructed.

Germline engineering involves the manipulation of germinal cells—eggs and sperm. In practice this means tinkering with fertilized eggs shortly after their formation while cells are at the "totipotent," or undifferentiated, stage. When an embryo is genetically manipulated in this way, the modification will be copied into every single cell of the adult, including the sexual cells. Unless we learn how to reverse-engineer the ensuing generation of fertilized eggs, this transformation will be passed along to all future generations. Germline engineering in effect produces a eugenics, not of individuals, but of entire genealogies—a eugenics of normalcy that implicates future generations.

Animated discussion in connection with such engineering reveals two points about which virtually all involved scientists appear to be in agreement. First, the technology, once off the ground, will be simpler and more manageable than the much more demanding sister technology of gene therapy. Before germline manipulation can be carried out, a safe, reliable way of delivering genes to a human embryo still has to be found, but the majority of scientists believe that this is a not too distant possibility and, once accomplished, will be replicable without much difficulty. Several hundred experiments have already been made with gene therapy—that is, with somatic-cell as opposed to germline modifications—but so far with little success and with the untimely death of at least one subject. Virus vectors are used to deliver new genes to every cell of the human body, and they must do so without causing untoward side effects if the therapy is to be successful. It is assumed that this delivery of replacement genes can be much more easily handled in embryos at a very early stage of development, as would be the case with basic germline engineering.

Second, there is general agreement that germline engineering is better characterized as an enhancement technology rather than as a therapy or even as genetic modification. In other words, germline engineering is not primarily about the elimination of specific diseases in living individuals, or even the abortion of embryos deemed "undesirable." Germline engineering will constitute in effect not a "negative" but a "positive" eugenics, one expressly devoted to the improvement of the "race." Children, enhanced as embryos, will be in possession of genotypes that they ordinarily would not have possessed.

Aside from these points of agreement, scientists currently arguing vociferously for and those arguing against germline engineering sit in two firmly opposed camps. This opposition is characteristic of a stark divide readily apparent during the past 200 years, throughout modernity, with respect to the relationship of science to ethics—a point to which I will return below.

ARGUMENTS IN FAVOR OF GERMLINE ENGINEERING

In June 1998 a one-day symposium was held at UCLA as part of the Science, Technology, and Society program in the Center for the Study of Evolution and the Origin of Life. This symposium, entitled "Engineering the human germline," was subsequently published as a book of the same name (Stock and Campbell 2000) and involved nine scientists in addition to the two organizers, Gregory Stock and John Campbell, both of whom work in what can broadly be described as the philosophy of science. Some superficial disagreement emerged among participants as to the potential dangers associated with manipulation of the germline, but no disputes of an epistemological kind erupted during the event. This group was overwhelmingly in favor of germline engineering (with one notable exception, French Anderson, the physician who had carried out more somatic gene-therapy

protocols than anyone else to that date) and declared that once the technology was available it would rapidly become "compelling" to "large numbers of parents" who would want to ensure that their offspring had the best
of all possibilities for their future lives.

The symposium organizers made clear the dramatic nature of what was
being discussed: "Germline engineering touches at the very core of what it
means to be human. It palpably extends human power into a sacred realm,
once mysterious and beyond reach . . . it makes us look at how far we wish to
intrude in the genetic flow from one generation to the next" (Stock and
Campbell 2000:3–4). Perhaps the most outspoken participants were Daniel
Koshland, Jr., past editor of *Science* and a professor of molecular and cell biology, and James Watson, Nobel Prize winner and past director of the National
Center for Human Genome research at the National Institutes for Health.

In discussing germline manipulations, Koshland commented: "The
demand for gene enhancement therapy will probably be very large, to give
your children a better chance of success in the world" (2000:27). Earlier he
had noted that "if the criterion [we use] is that children should turn out to be
at least as good as their parents, my guess is that germline engineering will
compete very well with those conceived the natural way. And if we make this
criterion that the children should be up to their parent's expectations, then I
think that the engineered child may have a good edge over the child conceived
in the normal way" (2000:26). When considering possible danger associated
with this technology, Koshland argued that "there is no such thing as absolute
safety in the world," and noted that the normal birth process is risky. He
added, "if germline engineering is designed to be no more risky than 'normal'
birth then the benefits will clearly outweigh the risks" (2000:26).

French Anderson stated at the original UCLA conference in 1998 that
"none of us wants to pass on to our children lethal genes if we can prevent
it, and that's what is going to drive germline gene therapy . . . you are not
going to pass on a lethal gene to your child if you can have a simple, safe
treatment that prevents it." (*Engineering the Human Germline* 1999:34).
This statement does not appear in the book based on the symposium proceedings, where Anderson is much more cautious: "We know so little about
the human body and so little about living processes, we would be unwise to
attempt genetic engineering to try to treat, much less 'improve,' the human
zygote or embryo" (2000:48). Between the upbeat time of 1998 and the
publication of the book on germline engineering two years later, 18-year-
old Jesse Gelsinger had died as a result of gene therapy (*New York Times*
1999). Although French Anderson was not his physician, he clearly felt
implicated in this event.

When discussants at the symposium turned to the issue of informed consent and possible harm to future generations, they were on the whole in agreement with the argument put forward by John Campbell that technology could be designed to solve this problem: "I think that if people are really concerned about consent we could take a human chromosome or a segment of it and put on a lock. None of those genes would have any effect until a person took an artificial hormone pill to unlock the cassettes and give him or herself the new engineered phenotype" (*Engineering the Human Germline* 1999:13). Germline engineering will not, it seems, override individual choice. But who will judge whether the interests of society should override individual choice? Questions such as this were not raised at this gathering, but in the book French Anderson (2000:47) once again sounds a cautious note:

> There needs to be societal approval prior to the first attempt at
> germline gene transfer. Almost all medical decisions are made between
> the patient and his or her physician. . . . Our rationalization for this is
> that 'my body belongs to me.' But our genes do not belong just to our-
> selves. The gene pool belongs to all of society.

Symposium participants briefly took up the question of the "sanctity of the gene pool." James Watson commented: "If we could make better human beings by knowing how to add genes, why shouldn't we do it?" (2000:79). This was followed by a superficial examination of "what *really* is normal?" An ensuing discussion about "seizing control of our own evolution" culminated in comments about how it is difficult to sustain an argument for the "sanctity" of the human gene pool. Watson (2000:85) interjected with the comment:

> I can't indicate how silly I think it is [the sanctity of the human gene
> pool]. I mean, we have great respect for the human species . . . but . . .
> [e]volution is just damn cruel [a similar comment had been made by
> Francis Galton 100 years earlier] . . . we should treat other people in a
> way that maximizes the common good of the human species.

Koshland (2000:26) was equally indignant at criticism of germline engineering:

> We should start, perhaps, with the question raised by some who say we
> shouldn't tamper with the germline. I frankly don't understand these
> people. Where are they living? We are already altering the germline
> right and left. When we give insulin to a diabetic who then goes on to
> have children, we are increasing the number of defective genes in the
> population. No one is seriously suggesting that we refuse to give life-
> saving drugs to genetically disadvantaged people.

ARGUMENTS AGAINST GERMLINE ENGINEERING

The other side of the debate is succinctly set out in a 1992 position paper published by scientists all participating in the Council for Responsible Genetics (CRG), located in Boston. They start out by criticizing the genetic reductionism present in the assertions of those in support of germline engineering, and then go on to outline the technical pitfalls and dangers associated with this particular technology. These authors argue that we may in fact already be modifying the germline inadvertently while doing experiments with somatic gene therapy.

The CRG confronts unexamined ethical assumptions built into the discussions in favor of germline engineering, including the likelihood that such technologies will go only to the economically privileged. But the council is even more concerned about the assumption that "the value of a human being is dependent on the degree to which he or she approximates some *ideal* of biological perfection," together with the assertion that "all limitations imposed by nature can and should be overcome by technology" (Council for Responsible Genetics 1992:1). The council's position is: "To make intentional changes in the genes that people will pass on to their descendents would require that we, as a society, agree on how to identify 'good' and 'bad' genes. . . . Any formulation of such criteria would necessarily reflect current social biases" (ibid.).

The CRG is unconditionally opposed to germline engineering for three reasons: first, because its target is "future" people rather than relieving the suffering of those of us already alive (in other words, there is no clinical justification for germline engineering); second, because people will increasingly be seen as "damaged goods" if they fall short of a technologically achievable ideal; and third, no accountability toward future generations is taken into consideration. However, the council is not opposed to further discussion of this technology and does not declare that it is categorically opposed to it for all time.

THE GHOST IN THE MACHINE

The division between these protagonists reflects the divide already visible 200 years ago for which history has made Denis Diderot primarily responsible on the one hand, with Jean-Jacques Rousseau situated on the other side. For the followers of Diderot, the "Encyclopedists," as they came to be known, science in effect usurps ethics and is charged with formulating and implementing the goals of mankind and society. Human "nature" belongs entirely to the realm of biology, and science will deliver what is needed. This has come to be known as the "Standard View" of technology (Pfaffenberger 1992), the position taken by those individuals currently in favor of germline engineering.

Rousseau, in contrast, argued that ethics are autonomous and not only are irreducible to science, but exercise tutelage over it. Rousseau believed in perfectibility, but above all that humans have the freedom to make choices. He came to represent the position that there are in effect two cultures, one of humanism, distinct from and in some ways superior to the other, that of scientific endeavor. Participants in the CRG fall for the most part into the Rousseauian camp. In a paper published in the medical journal *The Lancet*, three members go further and make it clear that in their opinion discussion limited to existing values and conditions is not sufficient, nor are the usual parameters of bioethics. We must search, they argue, for new ways to debate and monitor these technologies, because they will affect the lives not only of individuals, but of entire communities and future generations (Billings et al. 1999).

But the perceived threat posed by several biomedical technologies whose use is at present banned or carefully circumscribed—cloning, clinical use of fetal tissue, the introduction of animal genes and organs into humans, and germline engineering, among others—is experienced not only because of their potential effect on future generations. These technologies represent for many the possibility of a radical break with our "natural" evolved selves and with what sets us apart from the rest of nature, our very "humanness." It is salient to observe how two well-known geneticists have chosen to deal with this criticism.

French Anderson, for example, in an article in *Human Gene Therapy*, sets out by defining what for him is a "normal human being." He divides humans into two unequal component parts: those characteristics and features that are measurable, and the part that "all of our quantitative measurements will fail to define: perhaps it could be called a soul." A soul cannot be examined under a microscope, declares Anderson, nor can it be assigned a quantity. He believes that this is the "subjective, non-measurable, spiritual aspect . . . of a human being," what makes the whole greater than the sum of the parts. Anderson then argues that "if what is uniquely important about humanness (not about individual humans but about humankind as a whole) is *not* defined by the physical hardware of our body, and since we can only alter the physical hardware, it follows that we cannot alter that which is uniquely human by genetic engineering" (1994:758). Anderson takes comfort from this conclusion and believes that he should be free to go ahead with genetic manipulations, although it is possible that he has modified this position in light of the poor track record of gene therapy.

Steve Jones, professor of genetics at University College, London, in a self-declared effort to show the extent to which we can tinker with nature without worry, insists that to speculate about mind and its origin is largely futile. He makes this argument in a recent book, in which he writes that "genes make brains and brains make behavior" (1999). Jones, like Anderson, resorts to the equivalent of Gilbert Ryle's ghost in the machine to justify his line of argument: "The birth of Adam," he writes, "whether real or metaphorical, marked the insertion into an animal body of a post-biological soul that leaves no fossils and needs no genes." As a reviewer of Jones's book notes, "this is almost identical to a line in the recent encyclical about evolution written by the Pope" (Evans 1999).

What is disturbing about these commentaries is that geneticists who embrace this type of thinking, by setting off mind, soul, humanness, or spirituality as distinct from the physical hardware of our bodies, are able to rationalize a determinism that justifies genetic manipulations of all kinds. Our souls will emerge unscathed, but our genomes will be suitably enhanced. One intransigent continuity from early modernity has survived intact, it seems: the idea of a stable, internalized, authentic subjectivity; a subjectivity that constitutes our uniquely human heritage, while our material bodies, along with the rest of the animal world, are constituted entirely from nature.

The philosopher Erik Parens, criticizing Anderson's paper, argues forcefully for keeping body and soul together; for recognition that our "humanness is within—not beyond—the reach of genetics, and for recognition of complexity." In contrast to both Diderot and Rousseau, and to those scientists arguing openly for and against germline engineering, ethics should not be compartmentalized from science, Parens (1995) insists, nor should it be privileged. In another paper, Parens (1998) makes it clear that he is concerned that we may impoverish ourselves through efforts at enhancement and inadvertently reduce the diversity upon which we as humans have always flourished. I would add that we appear to be intent on creating not a "brave" new world, but a bland new world of sameness. The spectrum of what counts as normal is narrowed considerably.

It has been pointed out by several commentators that critical discussion about genetic engineering is filled with inflammatory declamations about "playing God," "interfering with nature," and so on, and that this type of language usurps any possibility of conducting useful discussion (Boone 1988; Bonnicksen 1994). Even when debate is moderated, participants in symposia continue to talk past each other. On the one hand are those critics who insist that the scientific claims in favor of germline engineering are inaccurate and that the complexity of gene-gene and gene-environment interactions are grossly underestimated. It is also often argued by these same critics that even though the technology is feasible it is "medically irrelevant," because a similar end result can be achieved for individual cases (but not for future generations) by using preimplantation diagnosis with selective embryo transfer. We should therefore opt for the less grandiose intervention (Winston and Handyside 1993).

On the other hand, ethicists in their discussions frequently black-box the technology itself and associated biological manipulations, and set out the importance of creating an international ethical framework on the basis of which policy decisions will be made. It is recognized by these protagonists that an ethics of individual rights is no longer sufficient, and there is discussion about communitarian ethics and "transnational harmonization" leading to an international "normative code" (Knoppers and LeBris 1991:361). These ethicists are concerned, rightly, that if no international standards exist, then procreative tourism will become common; but they rarely take into consideration inequalities in access to health care or recognize divisions among scientists, or how problematic are some of the scientific claims made by them.

A third line of criticism points out that in an era of repeated cutbacks in health-care systems, individuals are made increasingly responsible for their own health and for that of their offspring. The elderly, those with disabilities, and the mentally impaired are characterized at times in official documents as "burdens" on society. This rhetoric is not as far removed from Nazi Germany as we would like to think, argues Alan Petersen (1998). The bioethical rhetoric of the "right to know" and "informed choice," the assessment of risks and benefits associated with various medical interventions, and a focus on family health compound the problem, deflecting attention away from the conditions of differential access to services that prevail in so many countries, and above all from the social and political factors implicated in disease incidence (Lippman 1998; Lock 1998a, 1999; Petersen 1998)

The new genetics has enabled many families to avoid suffering, but there is plenty of evidence that it has increased anxiety for many more by furnishing people with information about their genes or those of their spouses, parents, siblings, or offspring about which they would rather not know. Uncovering the dilemmas and competing value systems associated with the new genetics that directly affect reproduction and family life is important. Paul Rabinow (1999:12) urges social scientists to focus on the larger picture, however, and argues that "values and opinions proliferate as a matter of course in democratic, consumer capitalist societies." Rather than focusing initially on competing value systems, he insists that we should pay attention to the new forms—the new assemblages—that precipitate these value conflicts.

Technology is central to this story, and it is well recognized that major changes are taking place today in the scientific representation, intervention, and manipulation of life forms. Analysis of these new forms of thought and practices cannot be divorced from the social and political contexts in which they emerge, nor can a consideration of their effects on social as well as individual life. Assessing the effects of the application of new biomedical technologies, including the new genetics, for individuals, families, communities, social relations, and for future generations, before the technologies are institutionalized, is a demanding task. The discursive practices, politics, rhetoric, undisclosed interests, and goals associated with these technologies need careful scrutiny. Such a critical perspective is made urgent now that the private sector is increasingly involved in funding and determining what technologies will be developed and marketed.

The pervasive idea of perfectibility of the body through human intervention—a utopia of health based on the management of individual genomes—motivates some researchers associated with the new genetics, but not all of them, as we have seen. The rhetoric used to justify enhancement of the human genome by at least two of those geneticists who believe in perfectibility makes use, as we have seen, of fossilized assumptions about souls and spirits. This rhetoric is designed to deflect criticism that the scientists are playing God. (Such criticisms are, of course, reiterations of much older Judeo-Christian debates, reformulated in light of emerging technologies.) Highlighting the plurality of forms and practices at local sites that the new genetics and other technologies take, both at home and around the world, despite widely shared scientific premises, is an important task for social scientists. (See, for example, Handwerker 1998; Lock 1998b, 2001). This activity has continuities with the classical anthropological task of making the strange familiar and lays bare the pervasiveness of pluralism and diversity of thinking. But equal emphasis should be given to making the familiar strange—to asking why, for example, particularly in North America, flying in the face of all that we know about molecular biology and population genetics, so many people are apparently captivated by a genetic reductionism as the best means to bring dignity to humankind and to ease all the pain and suffering in the world. We must also ask why a regime of laissez-faire eugenics, one grounded in individual interest, is already firmly institutionalized when there has been rather little discussion of what might be in the best interests of those individuals with disabilities or other forms of visible difference, of society at large, or the world as a whole.

The anthropologist finds herself "situated, like a trickster, in between different moralities and epistemes" (Pels 2000:136) when investigating the social implications of discourse and practices associated with emerging biomedical technologies. This is particularly so when participating in policy-making arenas, into which anthropologists are increasingly being drawn, albeit often with reluctance. We will not make the horrible mistakes that Margaret Sanger did (although she was after all acting as a woman of her time); we will insist that attention is paid to complexity, hierarchies, and inequalities, and take a reflexive position about the production of both scientific knowledge and bioethics. The ethnographic method is crucial for exposing moral conflicts, unexamined assumptions, and what counts as valid knowledge—insights from ethnography create tension at policy-making venues, but this is all the more reason why such insights must be put on the table.

NOTE

1. A genetic test is now available in Japan for neurofibromatosis, but it is not routinely used for all pregnant women.

REFERENCES

American College of Medical Genetics, Working Group of the Genetic Screening Subcommittee of the Clinical Practice Committee. 1994. Fragile-X syndrome: Diagnostic and carrier Testing. *American Journal of Medical Genetics* 53: 380–81.
Anderson, French. 1994. Genetic engineering and our humanness. *Human Gene Therapy* 5: 755–60.
———. 2000. A new front in the battle against disease. In *Engineering the Human Germline*, ed. Gregory Stock and John Campbell, 43–48. Oxford: Oxford University Press.
Angastiniotis, Michael, Sophie Kyriakidou, and Minas Hadjiminas. 1986. How thalassaemia was controlled in Cyprus. *World Health Forum* 7: 291–97.
Beeson, Diane, and Teresa Doksum. 2001. Family values and resistance to genetic testing. In *Bioethics in Social Context*, ed. Barry Hoffmaster, 153–79. Philadelphia: Temple University Press.
Billings, Paul R., Ruth Hubbard, and Stuart A. Newman. 1999. Human germline gene modification: A dissent. *The Lancet* 353: 1873–75.

Bonnicksen, Andrea. 1994. Demystifying germ-line genetics. *Politics and the Life Sciences* 13(1): 246–48.

Boone, C. K. 1988. Bad Axioms in genetic engineering. *Hastings Center Report* 18(4): 9–13.

Brown, W. Ted, G. E. Houck, A. Jeziorowska, F. Levinson, X. Ding, C. Dobkin, N. Zhong, J. Henderson, S. S. Brooks, and E. C. Jenkins. 1993. Rapid Fragile-X carrier screening and prenatal diagnosis using a nonradioactive PCR test. *Journal of the American Medical Association* 270(13): 1569–75.

Caplan, Arthur L. 1993. Neutrality is not morality: The ethics of genetic counseling. In *Prescribing Our Future: Ethical Challenges in Genetic Counselling*, ed. Dianne M. Bartels, Bonnie S. LeRoy, and Arthur L. Caplan, 149–65. Hawthorne: Aldine de Gruyter.

Caskey, C. Thomas. 1994. Fragile-X syndrome—Improving understanding and diagnosis. *Journal of the American Medical Association* 271(7): 552–53.

Council for Responsible Genetics Human Genetics Committee. 1992. *Position Paper on Human Germ Line Manipulation*. Boston: The Council for Responsible Genetics.

Duster, Troy. 1990. *Back Door to Eugenics*. New York: Routledge.

Ekstein, Josef. 2001. The Dor Yeshorim story: Community-based carrier screening for Tay-Sachs disease. *Advances in Genetics* 44: 297–310.

Engineering the Human Germline. 1999. Proceedings of a Symposium, University of California, Los Angeles, March 1988.

Evans, Dylan. 1999. Evolutionary matter over mind. *Guardian Weekly*, Sept. 30–Oct. 6, p. 16.

Foucault, Michel. 1980 *The History of Sexuality*. Vol. 1, *An Introduction*. New York: Vintage.

Fox Keller, Evelyn. 1992. Nature, nurture, and the human genome project. In *The Code of Codes: Scientific and Social Issues in the Human Genome Project*, ed. Daniel J. Kevles and Leroy Hood, 281–99. Cambridge, Mass.: Harvard University Press.

Gilbert, Walter. 1992. A vision of the grail. In *The Code of Codes: Scientific and Social Issues in the Human Genome Project*, ed. Daniel J. Kevles and Leroy Hood, 83–97. Cambridge, Mass.: Harvard University Press.

Granda, H., S. Gispert, A. Dorticos, M. Martin, Y. Cuadras, M. Calvo, G. Martinez, M. A. Zayas, J. A. Olivia, and L. Heredero. 1991. Cuban programme for prevention of sickle cell disease. *The Lancet* 337: 152–53.

Handwerker, Lisa. 1998. The consequences of modernity for childless women in China: Medicalization and resistance. In *Pragmatic Women and Body Politics*, ed. Margaret Lock and Patricia A. Kaufert, 178–205. Cambridge: Cambridge University Press.

Hill, Shirley A. 1994. *Managing Sickle Cell Disease in Low-Income Families*. Philadelphia: Temple University Press.

Hubbard, R., and E. Wald. 1993. *Exploding the Gene Myth: How Genetic Information Is Produced and Manipulated by Scientists, Physicians, Employers, Insurance Companies, Educators, and Law Enforcers*. Boston: Beacon.

Jones, Steve. 1999 *Almost like a Whale: The Origin of Species Updated.* London: Doubleday.

Kevles, Daniel J.1984. Annals of eugenics: A secular faith, I. *The New Yorker,* Oct. 8, pp. 51–115.

———. 1995. *In the Name of Eugenics.* Cambridge, Mass.: Harvard University Press.

Kitcher, Philip. 1996. *The Lives to Come: The Genetic Revolution and Human Possibilities.* New York: Simon and Schuster.

Knoppers, Bartha M., and S. LeBris. 1991. Recent advances in medically assisted conception: Legal, ethical and social issues. *American Journal of Law and Medicine* 27(4): 329–61.

Koshland, Daniel, Jr. 2000. Ethics and safety. In *Engineering the Human Germline,* ed. Gregory Stock and John Campbell, 25–30. Oxford: Oxford University Press.

Kuliev, A. M. 1986. Thalassaemia can be prevented. *World Health Forum.* 7: 286–90.

Landsman, Gail. 2005. Mothers and models of disability. *Journal of Medical Humanities* 26: 121–39.

Lauria, David P., and Mark J. Webb. 1992. The economic impact of Fragile-X syndrome on the State of Colorado. In *1992 International Fragile X Conference Proceedings,* ed. R. J. Hagerman and P. McKenzie, 48–52. Dillon, Colo.: Spectra.

Lewontin, Richard. 1992. The dream of the human genome. *The New York Review of Books,* May 28, pp. 31–40.

Lippman, Abby. 1998. The politics of health: Geneticization versus health promotion. In *The Politics of Women's Health: Exploring Agency and Autonomy,* ed. Susan Sherwin, 64–82. Philadelphia: Temple University Press.

Lock, Margaret. 1993. *Encounters with Aging: Mythologies of Menopause in Japan and North America.* Berkeley and Los Angeles: University of California Press.

———. 1998a. Situating women in the politics of health. In *The Politics of Women's Health: Exploring Agency and Autonomy,* ed. Susan Sherwin, 48–63. Philadelphia: Temple University Press.

———. 1998b. Perfecting society: Reproductive technologies, genetic testing, and the planned family in Japan. In *Pragmatic Women and Body Politics,* ed. Margaret Lock and Patricia A. Kaufert, 206–39. Cambridge: Cambridge University Press.

———.1999. The politics of health, identity and culture. In *Self, Social Identity and Physical Health,* ed. Richard J. Contrada and Richard D. Ashmore, 43–68. New York: Oxford University Press.

———. 2001. Eliminating stigmatization: Application of the new genetics in Japan. In *Cross-Cultural Perspectives on Reproductive Health,* ed. Carla Makhlouf Obermeyer, 253–76. Oxford: Oxford University Press.

———. 2002. *Twice Dead: Organ Transplants and the Reinvention of Death.* Berkeley and Los Angeles: University of California Press.

Mitchell, John J., Annie Capua, Carol Clow, and Charles R. Scriver. 1996. Twenty-year outcome analysis of genetic screening programs for Tay-Sachs and b-thalassemia disease carriers in high schools. *American Journal of Human Genetics* 59: 793–98.

Nelkin, Dorothy. 1996. The social dynamics of genetic testing: The case of Fragile-X. *Medical Anthropology Quarterly* 10(4): 537–50.

New York Times. 1999. Day for the human side of gene therapy. Friday, Dec. 10, p. A19.

Office of Technology Assessment. 1988. *Mapping Our Genes.* Washington, D.C.: Government Printing Office.

Parens, Erik. 1995. The goodness of fragility: On the prospect of genetic technologies aimed at the enhancement of human capacities. *Kennedy Institute of Ethics Journal* 5: 141–51.

———. 1998. Is better always good? The enhancement project. *Hastings Center Report* 28: 24B–40B.

Parens, Erik, and Adrienne Asch. 1999. The disability rights critique of prenatal genetic testing: Reflections and recommendations. *Hastings Center Report* 29: S1–S22.

Paul, Diane B., and Hamish G. Spencer. 1995. The hidden science of eugenics. *Nature* 374: 302–4.

Pels, Peter. 2000 The trickster's dilemma: Ethics and the technologies of the anthropological self. In *Audit Cultures: Anthropological Studies in Accountability, Ethics, and the Academy,* ed. Marilyn Strathern, 135–72. London: Routledge.

Petersen, Alan. 1998. The new genetics and the politics of public health. *Critical Public Health* 8(1): 59–71.

Pfaffenberger, Bryan. 1992. Social anthropology of technology. *Annual Review of Anthropology* 21: 491–516.

Press, Nancy. 2000. Assessing the expressive character of prenatal testing: The choices made or the choices made available? In *Prenatal Genetic Testing and the Disability Rights Critique,* ed. Erik Parens and Adrienne Asch, 214–33. Washington, D.C.: Georgetown University Press.

Quaid, K. A., and M. Morris. 1993. Reluctance to undergo predictive testing: The case of Huntington disease. *American Journal of Medical Genetics* 45: 41–45.

Rabinow, Paul. 1999. *French DNA: Trouble in purgatory.* Chicago: University of Chicago Press.

Rapp, Rayna. 1999. *Testing Women, Testing the Fetus: The Social Impact of Amniocentesis in America.* London: Routledge.

Rapp, Rayna, and Faye Ginsburg. 2001. Enabling disability: Rewriting kinship, reimagining citizenship. *Public Culture* 35: 533–56.

Rapp, Rayna, Deborah Heath, and Karen Sue Taussig. 2001. Genealogical disease: Where hereditary abnormality, biomedical explanation, and family responsibility meet. In *Relative Matters: New Directions in the Study of Kinship,* ed. Sarah Franklin and Susan MacKinnon, 384–409. Durham: Duke University Press.

Sanger, Margaret. 1922. *The Pivot of Civilization*. Washington, D.C.: Scott-Townsend.

Singer, Peter A., and Abdallah S. Daar. 2001. Harnessing genomics and biotechnology to improve global health equity. *Science* 294: 87–89.

Stock, Gregory, and John Campbell, eds. 2000. *Engineering the Human Germline: An Exploration of the Science and Ethics of Altering the Genes We Pass to Our Children*. Oxford: Oxford University Press.

Warren, Stephen T., and David L. Nelson. 1994. Advances in molecular analysis of Fragile-X syndrome. *Journal of the American Medical Association* 271(7): 536–42.

Watson, James. 2000. The road ahead. In *Engineering the Human Germline*, ed. Gregory Stock and John Campbell, 73–98. Oxford: Oxford University Press.

Willis, Evan. 1998. Public health, private genes: The social context of genetic biotechnologies. *Critical Public Health* 8(2): 131–39.

Winston, R. M. L., and A. H. Handyside. 1993. New challenges in human in-vitro fertilization. *Science* 260: 932–36.

Yoxen, Edward J. 1982. Constructing genetic diseases. In *The Problem of Medical Knowledge*, ed. P. Wright and A. Treacher, 144–61. Edinburgh: Edinburgh University Press.

8 Why Am I Not Disabled?

Making State Subjects, Making Statistics in Post-Mao China

MATTHEW KOHRMAN

As Ma Zhun pushed open the doors that chilly morning and shuffled her way into a branch of Beijing's Xuan Wu district government, her goal was simple: to get a disabled person's ID card so that she could keep her job. Ma Zhun made this very clear, first in a gentle conversational tone and finally in a loud declaration. Like many people I observed during the spring of 1995 visiting Xuan Wu district's *canjiren lianhehui* (an agency commonly translated as the Disabled Persons' Federation), Ma Zhun had been sent by her employer. Those in charge of the state-owned enterprise for which she worked, a small money-losing engine factory, told Ma Zhun that her only chance of keeping her job, of not being laid off like 35 percent of the factory's other employees, was for her to get a disability ID. That spring, the Beijing government had sent out directives demanding that all work units in the capital document that at least 1.7 percent of their full-time staff were officially recognized disabled persons (*canjiren*), or else the work units would face stiff fines. So, like many others in the capital at that time, Ma Zhun was informed by her bosses that either she must get a disability ID card or they would dismiss her and hire someone who had one.

That was the same message delivered to Wang Liming, who I had observed the previous afternoon stopping by the Xuan Wu district's federation office. Wang showed up in the late afternoon, around 5:00 P.M., as two of the office's five staff were packing up to head home. Wang gestured to Cadre Chen and then placed on Chen's desk a set of papers that included a medical report from a nearby hospital and a set of wallet-sized photos. Cadre Chen looked over everything, asked a few background questions, took Wang's fingerprints, and then instructed him to come back two days later to pick up his ID.

Ma Zhun's visit to the Xuan Wu office went far less smoothly. Over a 30-minute period she struggled in vain to convince Cadre Chen that she was entitled to receive an ID. Ma stated over and over that, in an industrial accident a decade earlier, she had lost the toes on her right foot and thereafter had had difficulty walking. On the second telling of the story, Ma unlaced her shoe and showed Cadre Chen her foot as well as the wooden block she kept in the front of her shoe to help her walk. But Cadre Chen was unmoved. Holding a federation manual in hand, he repeatedly told Ma that whether or not she could walk easily did not matter. If she was only missing toes on one foot, she did not meet the state's standards for *canji*, and so she could not have an ID. Just before she left the office, Ma made this terse statement:

> Where did your *canji* standard come from? It doesn't make any sense. If that damned industrial machine that fell on my toes ten years ago had cut off more of my foot and I had trouble walking just as I do now, I'd be able to get an ID. But because my foot isn't more mangled, I have to lose my job. That's stupid. If someone can barely walk, why doesn't that count as *canji*?

In this chapter, I explore the questions posed by Ma Zhun. I will also extend these questions, for as I have learned over the last decade while conducting research on disability in China, addressing queries like Ma Zhun's requires that one go beyond just asking why the Chinese government created criteria in the late twentieth century for *canji*, how they did so, and why the resultant criteria are highly physiological in orientation. Indeed, it requires one to address a broader anthropological conundrum: how and why at the close of the last millennium some of the most powerful institutional artifacts of modernity—nation-states—came to define, standardize, and medicalize aspects of human existence under and within a relatively new social category: that is, disability.

This may strike some as strange. Why associate the existence of disability with the relatively recent phenomenon of the nation-state? Have there not been women, men, and children with disabilities since time immemorial? As contributors to the quickly growing scholarly sphere of disability studies have documented, although people since the beginning of recorded history have suffered from what have been locally understood as disparate forms of bodily dysfunction and disfigurement, in fact it has only been within the last few decades or so that disparate conditions of bodily difference and dysfunction have been aggregated and standardized under a universalizing biomedically framed category called "disability." Disability scholars like Lennard Davis, Deborah Stone, and Henri-Jacques Stiker have

shown that such processes of aggregation, standardization, and medicalization have played out at different speeds and in different ways from location
to location. They have further documented that the processes have been
closely linked to modernity, particularly the growth (initially in Europe
and North America) of the nation-state as the preeminent unit of mass
political organization and, in turn, the nation-state's dependence on the
growth of biomedical, legal, and educational institutions (Stone 1984; Davis
1995; Stiker 1997).

Recently, a small but growing number of researchers have been examining these topics outside North America and Western Europe. Not surprisingly, their findings, although cursory, seem to fit with our general
anthropological portrait of how the proliferation of institutional structures
constitutive of the modern nation-state has coincided with, if not under-
written, the expansion of a wide variety of bodycentric regimes of knowledge and practice in localities around the world during the twentieth
century. For instance, after surveying disability research done up to the
mid-1990s, Whyte and Ingstad argue that the existence of a "framework of
state, legal, economic, and biomedical institutions" (1995:10) greatly
explains how and in what localities disability has been concretized as a
locus of societal intervention and identification. Stated more explicitly,
Whyte and Ingstad assert that, in locales where such a framework remains
weak, popular recognition of disability or local language equivalents are
generally inchoate. Where such a framework is strong, by contrast, community members often acknowledge disability as a universally applicable
condition, one that maps onto various types of bodies, and they expect disability to be a site for at least some degree of social assistance, political
action, and identity formation.

Whyte and Ingstad's broad-sweeping assessment, whatever its overall
validity, prompts several questions closely aligned with those raised by Ma
Zhun and of vital importance to medical anthropology. If the recent and
ongoing emergence of disability as a space of psycho-somato-social production is contingent on the proliferation of modernist institutional frameworks, including those constitutive of nation-states, by what means might
these institutional frameworks formally fix boundaries around what is disablement and what is not? By what processes might such institutional
apparatuses make disablement not just more perceivable in local contexts
but codified, so that some locally understood differences and alterities are
included and some excluded?

No doubt there are many ways to investigate these matters. To do so,
however, and remain attentive to Ma Zhun's original queries, our focus

must be cast on a distinctive set of processes. These are processes of numerical abstraction and biomedical reduction—namely, epidemiology—that medical anthropologists have examined at length, but rarely in regard to disability and rarely in terms of Chinese cultural contexts. Yet, when thinking about the category of disability in contemporary China, why examine epidemiology? The denial of a disability ID to Ma Zhun that day in the mid-1990s occurred largely because her body did not fit criteria created some ten years earlier for an epidemiological exercise. In the mid-1980s, in coordination with several international organizations, branches of China's party-state crafted those disability criteria for what is called the 1987 National Sample Survey of Persons with Disabilities. This survey reputedly was China's first "nationwide" count of *canji* adults and children. It was a mammoth undertaking, one that collected data on more than 1.5 million people residing in 424 rural and urban communities distributed throughout China's provinces and autonomous regions. And by the time it was conducted, after several years of preparation, the 1987 survey had become a decidedly biostatistical study, one informed by several internationally anointed standards for what is and what is not disability.

Why did the 1987 survey occur? Why in the mid-1980s did the Chinese governmental elite decide that it was important to count the "disabled" in more than 400 communities of the People's Republic of China (PRC)? And, as they were preparing the survey for launch, how did their reasoning for mounting it shape the ways they defined disability?

ARGUMENT, AIMS, AND CAVEAT

By describing the assemblage and execution of China's 1987 National Sample Survey of Persons with Disabilities, I explore how disability in China has become an extension of what Ian Hacking (1981:25) has described as modernity's preoccupation with enumeration. In several essays and a full-length monograph, Hacking provides a history of the expansion in Europe of a "fetishism for numbers" (1981:24; see also Hacking 1990). He focuses on a period of tremendous development and sociopolitical enthusiasm for statistics, the early 1800s. That period, Hacking documents, did more than just trigger the "avalanche of numbers" (1981:22) that in so many parts of the world has come to structure contemporary life. Statistics during that epoch was an extension of and further enabled the proliferation of what we have come to know through Foucault's writings as "biopower": a regime that emerged in Europe, one that under the imprimatur of humanism placed new social, legal, political, and scientific focus on freshly fashioned bodily categories and that came to exert unprecedented influence over people's lives through these categories (Foucault 1979:138–46). As Hacking shows, it was to a significant degree via enumerative developments—most specifically, statistical moves to identify and count ever more detailed bodily distinctions—that biopower created its normalizing gazes, its gradations of standards for what constitutes everything from normal and abnormal behavior to proper and improper ways of dying. Stated more succinctly, with the help of statistics biopower strove at once to know, manage, and make its subjects (Hacking 1982). ·

But then and now, what has driven biopolitical processes of enumeration, standardization, and normalization? There is no single answer to this question, and to a large degree the factors involved are always context-specific, because biopower is never the same from place to place and from epoch to epoch. That said, according to Hacking (1981:15), in Europe of the 1800s, enumeration of bodily difference was significantly spurred by one of the central artifacts associated with biopower's growth, the modern nation-state. Not only was quantification frequently "an overt political response of the state" to quell restlessness among its citizenry, Hacking says (1982:281), but it was also a technology for justifying state expansion. State officials in Europe promoted numerical inquiry of bodily "deviancy" in part because such inquiry could help substantiate that the state was needed to perform important palliative and curative functions, that the state must be expanded so those functions could be carried out more effectively, and that state authority was unquestionably legitimate.

In this chapter, I develop an argument vis-à-vis Hacking's ideas. The perspective offered by Hacking no doubt deepens our understanding of how statistics can fuel standardization of, and attention to, disability in many societies in recent years. But when examining disability's enumeration in late-twentieth-century China, one must look beyond just a vague notion of state formation and expansion. One must take into consideration a more specific although certainly related matter. One must consider something Hacking makes little mention of: government agents' own identity making.[1] For complicit with the statecraft of concretizing disability as a new somatosocial realm (one that may act as a bulwark against dissent and as a lever for government expansion), what significantly fueled statistical inquiry of disability in China in the 1980s was how elite government actors themselves were incited to negotiate their identities in relation to conflicting imperatives and discourses. Just as important as expansionary impulses of the nation-state, if not more so, was how government representatives were compelled to manage their own subject positions vis-à-vis a complex set of sociohistorical forces.

By developing this argument, I hope to answer more fully Ma Zhun's questions. I also harbor two additional aims. The first is to promote greater dialogue between, on the one hand, disability scholars, many of whom until now have overlooked the workings of enumeration (cf. Davis 1995), and on the other hand, a group of anthropologists, most of whom have largely ignored disability but who in recent years have been exploring linkages between statistics and transnational forces of state formation (Anderson 1991; Horn 1994; Appadurai 1996; Gupta 2001). Second, I hope to help fill a lacuna in China studies. Several observers have noted that statistics in the PRC, like statistics generated in possibly all cultural contexts, are often as much the product of political exigencies as they are of rigorous inquiry (Tien 1991; Huang 1996; AFP 1998; Merli 1998), and other China scholars have shown that the PRC's party-state has used statistics to concretize new social categories and policies (Gladney 1991; Lee 1998; Schein 2000),but little inquiry has occurred in the PRC that focuses on the relationship between statistics and the subject making of enumerators. (Cf. Greenhalgh 2005.)

Before continuing, at least one caveat is in order. The development of statistics in China—more specifically, statistical inquiries into the category of *canji*—has a complex and long history. Complexity and historical depth, however, are no excuse for inattention. Elsewhere, I plumb genealogies having to do with *canji* classification and enumeration as far back as the fourteenth century (Kohrman 1999). That stated, I hope readers will understand my need to pass over those longer genealogies here.

READYING A NEW FORM OF ENUMERATION: THE 1987 NATIONAL SAMPLE SURVEY

To some readers, particularly those with significant knowledge about China, it might seem quite obvious what drove the Chinese government in the late 1980s to design and conduct a large survey of disability and to create China's first government-sanctioned nationwide disability criteria. The primary engine driving this large survey was the needs of an institution emerging from within China's party-state in the 1980s. The institution to which I am referring is the China Disabled Persons' Federation, into whose office Ma Zhun hobbled that frosty Beijing morning.

Founded in March 1988 amid great fanfare in the Chinese and international media, the China Disabled Persons' Federation is today a vice-ministry within the People's Republic's governmental apparatus. And, like nearly all governmental ministries within the PRC, the federation has a set of formal and well-publicized objectives. Those objectives are threefold: to represent the common interests of all Chinese citizens with disabilities, to protect their legal rights and interests, and to mobilize social forces to serve them.

Yet the federation has had other agendas that need to be noted. These cannot be found anywhere in the federation's mission statements but have been made quite clear to me by federation officials during my research.[2] One agenda has been to develop the federation's own infrastructure as rapidly as possible. Since its founding in 1988, the federation has been racing to expand from a small office within China's Civil Affairs Ministry to a full-fledged ministry in its own right. And on the surface, the federation has been quite successful on this front, at least initially. Within only six years of its launch, the federation already possessed more than 45,000 chapters nationwide (Chu et al. 1996). What drove this early flurry of federation building? To a sizable degree, the source was a fleeting treasure: privileged links to China's paramount leader, Deng Xiaoping. The federation was founded by Deng Xiaoping's eldest son, Deng Pufang, in the last decade of Deng's life. Owing to Deng Xiaoping's ill health and his advanced age when the federation was launched, it was understood by all that the clock was ticking for the fledgling institution. Federation staff understood that, as quickly as possible, they needed to transmute their treasure, their somatosocial capital of patrilineal affiliation to the nation's leader, into more durable administrative structures so that their institution, their own bureaucratic authority, and their disability advocacy would continue to exist long after Deng Xiaoping's death and the subsequent decline of Deng Pufang's influence.

Another agenda of the federation that is absent from its mission statement but closely tied to its institution-building efforts has been helping to maintain the legitimacy of the Chinese Communist Party (CCP) in the post-Mao era. As is well known, following Mao's death in 1976, the Party embarked on a major sea change under Deng Xiaoping's direction. It increasingly based its legitimacy on its ability to oversee the growth of market-oriented economics and the replacement of Maoist forms of production and public assistance. To see how Deng Pufang and his staff have shrewdly positioned their institution as a buoy for the post-Mao party-state, one need only read the federation's own publicly circulated documents. In such documents, Pufang and his staff openly assert that federation succor for a newly identified needy sector of the population—that is, the *canji*—not only provides the CCP an important boost to its moral status but also serves as an innovative damper against popular anger over rising inequality and the decline of Maoist guarantees (Deng 1995).

In the mid-1990s, shortly after I began research on the federation's early formation, several members of its leadership talked to me about how their various agendas helped prompt disability enumeration in China in the 1980s. They said that when Deng Pufang and his staff first became involved in the business of disability assistance in the mid-1980s, when they began placing themselves in the dual roles of disability and party-state advocates, they quickly came to recognize that they needed to produce specific kinds of knowledge to launch the federation and speed its expansion. Most important, they needed to produce criteria delineating what their institution's target population was—that is, who China's disabled were—and they needed to produce irrefutable statistical information about that population's special conditions. With such information in hand, the federation leadership could more easily justify to China's vast citizenry, people both inside and outside government, why the People's Republic required a high-profile national *canji*-assistance organization.

Thus, from what has been explained so far, it would seem that Hacking's arguments about the relationship between statistical enumeration, biopower, and the formation of state bureaucracy are quite incisive. Clearly, the push to produce statistical information about disability in China in the 1980s was tied to the production of state bureaucracy and the maintenance of CCP authority. Yet, there are clearly many matters that remain unaddressed by this approach. For instance: Why did Deng Pufang become personally invested in institutionally assisting the disabled? Why in the 1980s did federation and other party-state officials place such a special premium on statistical knowledge about disability rather than other kinds of knowledge? And, finally, why did these officials come to believe that they needed to produce disability criteria that were particularly bio-medical in orientation?

To answer these questions, specific sociopolitical processes at play in the 1980s need to be highlighted. Mao had died only a short time before (in 1976), and the Cultural Revolution (1966–76) was still fresh in people's memories. For these and other reasons, many within China were then in the midst of intense deliberations about matters of identity politics—specifically, how China and its people measured up to other nations in terms of "development" (*fazhan*), both economic and civilizational. Significant segments of China's leadership and citizenry were extremely worried that what they were increasingly calling the "lost ten years" of

Maoist radicalism had caused China to lag even farther behind other nations in the race for modernity, that the Cultural Revolution had left China shamefully "backward." It was against this backdrop of developmental angst that Deng Xiaoping began promulgating not only his market reforms but also his Open Door policy. A primary goal of this policy, as most readers know, was to strengthen China by giving its people greater access to some, but certainly not all, of what wealthy countries were then billing as their most progressive and most novel techniques for social and economic advancement.[3]

It so happened that, just as the Open Door policy was being launched, disability and disability advocacy were receiving precisely that type of billing. Owing to a number of forces—for example, emergent rights discourses, changing public-health imperatives, medical developments, and legislative moves—several of the world's wealthiest countries were increasingly treating disability as a key signifier of a new sociopolitical movement. In the early 1980s, the "disability movement" was infused with distinctive developmental and globalist orientations when the United Nations mounted its International Year of Disabled Persons in 1981 and subsequently its Decade for Disabled Persons (1983–92).

How did Deng Pufang—the oldest son of one of the most elite of China's twentieth-century officials—come to interact with this purported movement? We know a sizable amount about Deng Pufang, unlike most children of high-ranking CCP officials, in large part because the federation's leaders have deemed his story an effective creation myth for their institution. I have written about the Deng Pufang story at length elsewhere (Kohrman 2003), so I do not delve into it deeply here. In outline, as commonly presented by federation hagiographers, Deng's story is about the maturation of a nationally minded disability advocate whose identity was forged by elite pedigree, tragic circumstance, and historical contingency. A pivotal period of this maturation began in the mid-1960s, when Mao and his supporters labeled Deng Xiaoping and other high-ranking CCP officials "enemies of the people." Shortly thereafter, Deng Pufang was imprisoned by Maoist radicals at Beijing University, where he was a graduate student. After several months of captivity in a university building, Deng Pufang tried to commit suicide by throwing himself from a third-floor window. The fall shattered his spine, leaving him paralyzed from the chest down. In the ensuing years, Deng Xiaoping was reinstated as head of the party-state. Following the Open Door policy's launch, visiting U.S. physicians arranged for Deng Pufang to be flown out of the country and receive extensive orthopedic surgery free of charge at the Ottawa Civic Hospital.

Deng's Canadian clinical care did more than allow him to sit up again. It prompted him to establish a new persona, his hagiographers tell us. Treated with medical care unavailable anywhere in China and exposed to discourses about disability that then were being championed by a growing number of international organizations, Deng Pufang had an "epiphany" in Canada: he realized he must commit himself to being a leader in the area of disability assistance and use his pedigree to garner public support for China's disabled. As his main hagiographer explains, Deng realized that he had no choice but to quickly leave Canada and propel himself into a life of advocacy so that China's disabled might also benefit from advanced forms of rehabilitation care and "the gospel" (*fuyin*) of disability assistance (Qin 1992:244).

However ideological these representations are, however much they have enabled federation staff to use (and at times abuse) Deng family authority for institutional expansion and political-economic gain, it cannot be denied that they are contingent on notions of identity formation.[4] And whatever the factuality of Deng's Canadian epiphany, it is clear that, not long after his return from Ottawa, his presence in the area of disability advocacy began to be felt in institutional ways across China. By the mid-1980s, he oversaw the founding of the China Disabled Persons' Welfare Fund (*zhongguo canjiren fuli jijinhui*) and raised enough money through the fund to build a large rehabilitation research center and hospital in southwest Beijing. According to my informants within Deng Pufang's staff, shortly after the welfare fund's launch, the staff determined that, to assist China's disabled persons significantly, they would need to do far more than build a technologically advanced medical facility in Beijing. They would need to create a nationwide advocacy organization, one with offices at every level of the state apparatus and in every administrative territory of the country.[5] The staff also determined, as already mentioned, that they would need specific knowledge: detailed information about China's disabled.

To understand what prompted China's 1987 National Sample Survey of Persons with Disabilities and structured its *canji* criteria, however, one must look beyond the story of Deng Pufang and his federation. For almost a dozen agencies of China's party-state were involved with the decisions to launch and develop the 1987 survey.[6] Some of these organizations began working on disability enumeration several years before Deng Pufang's group entered the mix. What were some of the means by which members of these other agencies were drawn to disability quantification and prompted to mount the 1987 survey?

Again, it would seem that the interplay of national and transnational forces was pivotal. And as far as I have been able to tell, the United Nations (UN) was an important catalyst for those interactions. As the 1980s unfolded, China's central-government officialdom became increasingly eager to interact with the UN, particularly to have it help assess China's socioeconomic situation.[7] Faced with such enthusiasm and given the UN's ongoing global disability campaigns, Beijing's UNICEF office invited the former director of UNICEF's U.S. committee, Norman Acton, to come to China for two weeks in 1981 in order to assess China's disability infrastructure. Following his fortnight in China, Acton submitted a consultancy report in which his primary recommendation was for the Chinese government to conduct a detailed "household survey . . . to obtain more complete information about the prevalence of disability among children" (1981:11). A few months later, this recommendation was amplified by the UN General Assembly. It passed a resolution declaring that "developing countries" should create methods of "data collection" on various disabilities "to be used as essential tools and frames of reference for launching action programs to ameliorate the condition of disabled persons" (United Nations 1990:iii).

Not long thereafter, China's National Statistical Bureau, in conjunction with several other government offices, carried out a survey of children aged one to 14 living in 137,000 households across China. Among other things, this survey found that, of those children surveyed, 1.4 percent were "obviously and seriously unhealthy."[8]

According to people I interviewed—people who ran the survey of children—the idea of building an organization like the Disabled Persons' Federation was not part of their motivation. Rather, the key factors stimulating the survey of children, these enumerators explained, was the PRC's then new Open Door policy and how the UN's disability initiatives piqued identity politics that were circulating through and structuring the Chinese polity. As already mentioned, these were identity politics informed by modernist perspectives that framed China, at best, as a "developing country" and, at worst, as "backward."

In the early 1980s, with the growing strength of the Open Door policy, many high-ranking Chinese officials increasingly interacted with visiting foreign dignitaries who, prompted by the UN's Year and Decade programs and the General Assembly's pronouncement, repeatedly asked epidemiological questions about China's disability situation. Much to their frustration, these high-ranking Chinese functionaries had no way of answering the foreigners' questions, because China's government had never made disability an object of significant nationwide study. And as one of the surveyors of disabled children told me: "To stem this problem, to stop China from losing face, we felt our only choice was doing a big study based on the most scientific of international techniques."

Not long after the survey of children was conducted, officials within China's Ministry of Civil Affairs informed Beijing-based UN representatives that the Chinese government had decided to do something the representatives had not expected. The Chinese government planned to do a far more ambitious study of disability, the one ultimately called the 1987 National Sample Survey of Persons with Disabilities. Why, so soon after the survey of children, did the Chinese state make this decision? As I have come to learn, at that juncture Deng Pufang's unfolding interest in establishing a disability-advocacy institution had started to play a role in decisions about disability research. But an equal if not stronger impetus for the decision to conduct a large national survey was the fact that, for many Chinese officials, the 1983 survey of children allowed them not to "save face" but instead to "lose face." This again had to do with Norman Acton, specifically with something Acton had written two years earlier.

When the UN was preparing to launch its 1981 International Year of Disabled Persons program, it asked Acton to help draft UN Secretary General Kurt Waldheim's opening speech for the campaign. That invitation occurred no doubt because Acton was not only a former UNICEF official but also then director general of Rehabilitation International (RI), an organization that had been pivotal in the globalization of various disability-advocacy discourses and practices during the twentieth century. In his contribution to Waldheim's speech, Acton inserted a statistical figure that he hoped would have a serious effect on the development of disability provision worldwide. As Acton explained to me, he wrote that 10 percent of the world's population was disabled. This 10-percent figure was not altogether new; Acton and others at Rehabilitation International had been citing it for more than a decade. But as Acton further noted to me: "This 10-percent figure was not a rigorously derived rate. It was something we at RI largely invented. Based on limited evidence, we created the figure. We wanted to have a weapon to make people respond to our issue. People don't tend to think an issue is big unless you have big numbers."[9]

Because it was included in Waldheim's speech, Acton's 10-percent figure was reproduced frequently from 1981 forward.[10] And in the ensuing years, given modernism's fetish for numbers and given that Acton's 10-percent figure carried the UN's imprimatur, his prevalence rate took on tremendous normative authority.[11] How the 10-percent figure (together with the survey of children) influenced many Beijing officials is something I began to grasp only after interviewing New York–based UN staffers. As one of these staffers explained to me:

> The 1983 survey of children made many [Chinese officials] terribly embarrassed and frustrated, so much so they tried to hide their results from us. The UN and Rehabilitation International hoopla had sent a message to the Chinese that their 1983 result would be around 10 percent. And they didn't get 10 percent. They didn't get anywhere near to 10 percent. They got 1.4 percent.

In light of such embarrassment, it is not surprising then that the Ministry of Civil Affairs in the mid-1980s asked the State Council to approve and finance a far more ambitious national sample survey or that the council quickly agreed.

PREPARING AND LAUNCHING THE SURVEY

Yet with approval in hand, the new survey's Leadership Group had a "tough job ahead," as its director obliquely quipped in an April 1985 *China Daily* report (Chen 1985). Not only did the survey's Leadership Group have to organize and conduct a survey large enough and complex enough to satisfy envisioned international norms of scientific validity, but it also had to guarantee a final prevalence rate that would offer China the maximum benefit. And according to a number of people involved in the survey, there were conflicting pressures that made it very difficult to discern what figure was best for the nation. On the one hand, the 10-percent rhetoric created pressure for a certain kind of number. If the survey's rate did not fall at or above 10 percent, some within China and in international circles might view the Leadership Group (and by extension the CCP and China) as unable to handle basic scientific methodologies and thus as backward and incompetent.

On the other hand, there were powerful forces within China militating against a 10-percent or higher figure. For example, some within the government thought a figure of 10 percent or higher might be damaging to the CCP's authority. Because of how many across the PRC historically viewed *canji* (and its more idiomatic cognates *canfei* and *feiji*) as shameful and to be hidden, and because of the related erstwhile "sick man of Asia" concept,[12] a prevalence rate of 10 percent or higher could potentially call into question the very ground on which the CCP rested its legitimacy in the early 1980s: the purported successes of Mao's revolution.

The differing exigencies—some pressing for 10 percent or more, some pressing for less—had several effects on how the Leadership Group handled the survey. Before noting some of these, I should point out an important facet of my research. Although our meetings occurred in the informal settings of their and my Beijing residences, and we talked warmly about each others' families and friends, Leadership Group members were often wary if not reluctant about describing the processes by which they designed their survey. Unless I introduced a fact about the survey I had learned elsewhere, most Leadership Group members were extremely reticent in what they said and tended to take pains to describe everything they did as having been structured by unanimity and the most rational of scientific techniques.

As time has passed since those meetings, I have become even more convinced that these interlocutors' reticence and obfuscation were related to matters of identity making. Specifically, my interlocutors were struggling to craft their subject-positions as highly able cosmopolitan scientists and caretakers of the PRC's image while confronted, in the highly politicized setting of Beijing, with the troublesome intersection of two locally and translocally acknowledged realms of otherness, two realms of alterity often viewed as suspect and potentially dangerous in China and in many other sociopolitical settings. Not only were my Leadership Group interviewees being confronted with the "foreign investigator," but they were also being confronted by a foreign investigator asking questions having to do with the "abnormal body."

Because of the challenges of conversing with Leadership Group members, much of what I ultimately learned about their design work came through chance encounters with people who contributed to the 1987 survey in ancillary ways. One example of how such chance encounters deepened my understanding relates to the way the Leadership Group defined *canji*. In the end, the 1987 survey gathered data on five categories of *canji*: *tingli canji* (hearing disability), *zhili canji* (intellectual disability), *shili canji* (visual disability), *zhiti canji* (physical disability), *jingshenbing* (mental illness).[13]

Initially, Leadership Group members indicated to me that they had chosen these categories early in the design process after consulting a variety of "foreign standards." Yet because of a chance conversation in Beijing during the spring of 1995 with a psychiatrist, Dr. Liu, I learned that the final decision on this five-part definition was far more complex and far more political than group members wanted me to know and that it occurred very late in the survey design stage. Dr. Liu and, subsequently, others explained that the Leadership Group, after consulting a number of countries' national disability criteria, settled on the first four categories quite quickly. But they included mental illness only after intensive lobbying by elite Chinese psychiatrists.

The main reason the psychiatrists pressed to have mental illness included, it would seem, was their wish to expand psychiatry's institutional strength. According to Dr. Liu, the psychiatrists concluded that the soon-to-be-established federation, under the tutelage of Deng Pufang, would probably grow into a powerful institution and that, as a medical discipline, psychiatry would enjoy far greater nationwide support if allied with the federation than if it simply remained affiliated with the Ministry of Health. The psychiatrists succeeded in having mental illness included in the survey by getting Deng Pufang to take up their cause. The main argument they pitched to Deng was built around three themes: the optics of modernity, national identity, and foreign assessment of China. As Dr. Liu has explained, he and his colleagues convinced Deng by asserting that having mental illness excluded from the survey would make China seem out of step with modernity, since Western governments considered the quality of care offered the mentally ill a measurement of "civilizational development."[14]

According to one high-ranking Ministry of Civil Affairs official who later spoke to me somewhat grudgingly about this matter, the survey's Leadership Group did not want mental illness included, because the soon-to-be launched federation did not want to be responsible for and associated with a socially identified group—the mentally ill—that many in China and the Chinese state have long viewed as unpredictable and thus threatening to social order. Another reason for avoiding mental illness, the same civil-affairs official implied, was that the Leadership Group saw the mutability of mental illness as challenging to their subject-positions as government scientists, as people charged not just with conducting rigorous research but with the vexing need to make sure their research reflected well on the state:

> Back then, the survey group just thought that the concept of mental illness was too broad and mutable. Not only is mental illness hard to diagnose, but a person may be mentally ill one day, and then tomorrow they might be okay. . . . The Leadership Group felt that disability had to be things . . . that were not only permanent but easy to grasp and control [*zhang wo*]. Only that way could they ensure that their disability research came out right and was good for the nation.

Beyond what categories of disablement were to be included or excluded, the desire to manage data production carefully also had a strong influence on how each category was ultimately defined. During one of my research trips to New York City, I learned from a UN official that initially the survey's Leadership Group did not plan to organize their study around a biomedical vision of the body. Instead, to determine whether or not people were *canji*, the Leadership Group at first planned to outfit its local data gatherers with a relatively idiomatically worded and social-function-oriented questionnaire.[15] This questionnaire was short-lived, however, largely because it produced a disability prevalence rate of 13 percent during a pilot implementation in the mid-1980s. That left the Leadership Group quite disturbed. According to a UN official: "When they got 13 percent [in their pilot], my New York office started getting constant phone calls from them in which they said, 'We got 13 percent. It's too high.' They were very uncomfortable. They thought, 'Oh my lord, now everybody is going to think we have too many disabled.'"

As a result, the Leadership Group, under advisement from a number of international consultants and Ministry of Health officials, decided that internationally recognized and biomechanically based orientations should play a much more central role, and they accordingly changed their methods. This new emphasis influenced not only how each category of disability was defined but also who would ultimately designate a research subject's disability status. In their revised methodology, the Leadership Group required that local, government-employed, biomedical practitioners be enlisted. These clinicians were required to examine each person whom nonmedical surveyors deemed potentially disabled and then make a designation (Di 1987).[16]

These definitional and methodological revisions bring us back to one of the questions raised by Ma Zhun highlighted at the beginning of this chapter: Why does someone in China who is unable to walk well not merit a disability ID? Ma is ineligible for *canji* certification because the revisions that occurred shortly before the survey was conducted involved a remapping of *zhiti canji* (physical disability) in terms of corporeal integrity and mechanics. What is more, she is ineligible because the shift to a more biomaterial approach allowed the Leadership Group to insert several provisions at the end of the new *zhiti* criteria. One of these provisions states that "loss of forefoot with the heel intact" will not be recognized as a physical disability (Di 1989:1478). Why were these provisions added? As explained to me by a key Leadership Group member, the provisions were born of the same reasoning that guided much of the survey's design: "Being that we were scientists and government officials, our duty was ensuring that the survey struck the best balance between good science and China's social and political needs. That provision, the one about the forefoot, we felt accorded with both of those goals."

This statement, however, does more than highlight once again a main point made throughout this article, that the identity formation of the survey's designers was instrumental for *canji*'s enumeration and codification in the 1980s. It also helps us recognize that we would be mistaken to portray such identity formation narrowly as simply the outcome of Western hegemony. Indeed, as I have tried to convey during the course of my discussion, the reasons why and how enumerators focused on *canji* in China in the 1980s, although certainly structured by modernist discourses and practices, many of which were originally developed in North America and Western Europe, were not willy-nilly determined by Euro-American domination. Rather they were the product of enumerators struggling to negotiate their way through a historical array of thorny political, economic, and moral issues, and this array was as much local as translocal, as much national as transnational.

FINAL ACCOUNTING AND ANXIETIES

Curiously, not only did China's State Council almost never have a chance to approve the Leadership Group's final criteria as the People's Republic's new nationwide disability standards, but the 1987 survey's results also were almost never released. To understand all this, one must know more about the final stages of the Leadership Group's work.

Once their revised two-step methodology was created and their earlier functional criteria were jettisoned, the Leadership Group was at long last ready to conduct the survey. And so, in early 1987, the group's locally based research teams descended on neighborhoods across China. With great specificity, the Leadership Group's published *Survey Report* describes that the research teams entered 424 communities and determined that 77,345 of their research subjects possessed one or more kinds of disability. But something that cannot be known by reading the report's 29 capacious volumes is that this final count, the tally of 77,345 disabled people, initially made many of the Leadership Group members very upset. Why? Given that the total number of research subjects was 1,579,000, the sum of 77,345 meant that the Leadership Group's carefully planned survey produced a national disability prevalence rate of only 4.9 percent. And as a senior public-health scholar in Beijing explained to me, that rate caused the Leadership Group members to fret they would be viewed as "backward, unscientific, and out of step with reputedly universal standards of disability quantification."

Not surprisingly, the Leadership Group considered shelving their results. That they finally released the survey's data in December 1987 and petitioned the State Council to certify their criteria had very much again to do with the interplay of the local and the translocal. After the results were tabulated and the 4.9-percent figure was generated, the group's director, Li Zheng, began seeking out foreign-trained statisticians, a number of whom were either foreign nationals or Chinese citizens recently returned to China from overseas. The ostensible goal of these visits was to hear what such experts thought about the group's data. But according to at least one of the sought-out PRC experts I interviewed, "it was also quite clear the goal was to see how, in the eyes of international experts, the data reflected on the professionalism and competence of the Leadership Group."[17]

In addition to the role played by such processes, that the data were released and the criteria certified in all likelihood also had a great deal to do with the imperatives of the then embryonic federation. On December 7, 1987, China's State Council and the National Statistics Bureau formally accredited the 1987 survey. Then, two days later, on December 9, the State Council drew on the survey's data extensively when it announced to the Chinese public that it was founding the Disabled Persons' Federation. And from that moment forward, federation officials have constantly invoked and celebrated the "scientific validity" of the survey. As they have gone about building broader bureaucratic and financial support for themselves and China's disabled, they have cited the survey's data repeatedly.

CONCLUSION

Of course, at this juncture, it is unlikely that someone like Ma Zhun knows much about the inner workings of the 1987 survey that I have described. And given the institutional and identity politics undergirding so much of the 1987 survey, it is unlikely that Ma Zhun will know much anytime in the near future about the moves of standardization, medicalization, and subject making outlined here. To be sure, over the last two decades, more and more people in China have been encountering disability statistics because of the federation's purposeful circulation of them in China's mass media. But because, like most government agencies around the world, the federation requires the local and translocal legitimacy afforded by empiricism's supposed remove from social processes, few people in China are likely to know anytime soon why it is that someone like Ma—someone deemed disabled by her employer and told to get a disability ID or lose her job, someone who cannot walk easily—cannot get a disabled person's ID. Few people will know why, at the same time that disability is becoming more and more a recognized form of being, one spanning several types of long-acknowledged alterities (for instance, blindness, deafness, and mental illness), it has been defined by China's party-state largely in terms of a narrow range of biomedically informed standards and not in terms of discourses more amenable to everyday human experiences, such as social functionality or occupational need.

Before concluding, I would like to emphasize that the point of this chapter has not been to criticize a specific research effort. Rather, my goal has been to highlight processes by which such research is made manifest. My goal has been to show how a research project like the 1987 survey can be shaped by elite subject making as much as by political economic needs of a nation-state. Hall (1985) and Agamben (1998) have encouraged us to move beyond Foucault's capillary portrait of biopower to examine how biopower proliferates within state structures. Yet to do so, as I have tried to show here, we need to not just focus on institutional structures within nation-states, their internal administrative logics, or the internationalist structures that may animate them (such as NGOs, globalizing discourses of development, worldwide campaigns of social justice, colonial histories, and flows of scientific knowledge). We must go further and examine more fully the actors that animate institutions of nation-states, the figures for whom any given nation-state is not just a vague political steward but a workplace, a set of professional duties, a set of turf battles, and a locus of identity making. We must examine how, for state officials—many of whom are also "researchers"—locally and translocally informed processes of biopolitics and identity formation are mutually constitutive.

I believe there are vitally important things at stake in pursuing this type of scholarship. In a sociopolitical setting like post-Mao China and no doubt many others, the people who formally codify disability and create government assistance programs for the disabled usually live at great experiential remove from bodily alterity and other forms of otherness. Nearly all of the people who orchestrated the 1987 survey achieved their political authority well in advance of the 1980s through processes—education, professionalization, and political training—that demanded that they have lives largely free from any question of deviance, difference, and otherness. And as I have tried to highlight, for a number of those people the ongoing need to demonstrate a high level of ability and to conform to perceived international normalizing benchmarks of scientific competence and national respectability were important factors in how they framed disablement—as much as, it would seem, if not more so than, say, any experientially motivated form of empathy.

For disability to become a more pluralistic arena of biosociality and destigmatization, it is vitally important that scholars examine biopower. But we must not just fall back on a vague understanding that biopower is expansive, that it is becoming omnipresent and multiply sedimented. Rather, we must investigate who the figures are that design and institutionalize new biopolitical arenas and why and how they do so. Only then can people in sociopolitical settings like the PRC or elsewhere more fully "reclaim disability," to borrow and redirect a phrase of the disability scholar Simi Linton (1998). Only then can people, their families, and others who struggle on a daily basis with meanings and practicalities overlapping with matters of dysfunction and bodily difference, and who are potentially subject to the expanding humanitarian gaze of emergent disability-advocacy organizations, take greater control over how that gaze works, how inclusive it is, and what benefits it actually provides.

NOTES

1. To be sure, Hacking discusses many a person in his writings about statistics. For instance, in his volume *Taming of Chance* (1990), Hacking comments at length on the works of Condorcet, Durkheim, and Peirce, who were each quite influential in promoting quantification as a key component of European governance and social thought in the nineteenth century. That noted, Hacking gives little attention to the processes of identity formation that these types of figures were encountering on a daily basis or how such processes may have shaped their work.

2. My inquiry into the federation's formation began in the early 1990s as part of my doctoral research and has involved several research trips to China, the longest lasting 20 months.

3. Of course, the Deng Xiaoping regime did not design the Open Door Policy with the idea of allowing all "foreign" discourses and practices into China. In particular, the Deng regime marked for exclusion "foreign" sociopolitical forces it deemed at odds with the Chinese Communist Party's retention of political preeminence.

4. During the 1980s, one of the primary ways the Disabled Persons' Welfare fund raised money was through the Kanghua Corporation. Created by the fund ostensibly to finance disability assistance, Kanghua is now known as one of the more notorious examples of post-Mao elite corruption. Drawing on special trade privileges granted it because of its disability-assistance mission and its association with the Deng family, Kanghua ballooned in size during the mid-1980s and was involved in a wide variety of highly lucrative import-export schemes. The Party leadership shut down Kanghua not long after quashing the 1989 democracy movement because student protesters had so publicly denounced Kanghua and its ties to Deng Pufang.

5. When the Disabled Persons' Federation was founded in the late 1980s, the Welfare Fund became a subordinate branch of the federation. Although the federation and the fund can be seen as China's first nationwide organization specifically providing services to "disabled persons" (*canji ren*), at least two organizational structures predated it and served allied categories of people. The first is the China Association for the Blind, Deaf, and Mute. Established in 1960 out of smaller organizations, the association's history dates to before the founding of the People's Republic and is rooted in Western educational approaches to visual and auditory limitations, many of which were initially introduced into China by U.S. missionaries. In 1988, the association (along with the schools it had established) was absorbed by the Disabled Persons' Federation. The second organizational structure of note is part of the military. In the 1930s, the Red Army began providing benefits to injured soldiers. In 1950, the military expanded its entitlement infrastructure and started extending specialized health care to "revolutionary crippled soldiers" (*geming canfei junren*). In the late 1980s, as part of the Disabled Persons' Federation's attempt to dissociate the government from what the federation leadership considered to be a derogatory term (i.e., *canfei*), "revolutionary crippled soldiers" was changed to "revolutionary injured and disabled soldiers" (*geming shangcan zhunren*).

6. The agencies that participated in the 1987 survey Leadership Group included the Ministry of Public Health, the National Statistics Bureau, the National Planning Commission, the National Education Commission, the Public Security Bureau, the Ministry of Finance, the State Council's National Census Leadership Group, the Association for the Blind, Deaf, and Mute, and the Disabled Person's Welfare Fund.

7. Joe Judd, UNICEF's representative in Beijing during 1984–85, told me Chinese government officials with whom he interacted were extremely eager for engagement, and specifically that they "seemed hungry to have us serve as their eyes, to assess where they stood internationally."

8. "Obviously and seriously unhealthy" included children loosely defined as seriously congenitally deformed, blind, deaf, and mute, and those who were postnatally disabled (for example, as a consequence of polio and encephalitis: Social Statistical Section of the National Statistical Bureau 1985).

9. One official in the UN Statistical Division, to whom Acton has also made this admission, has commented to me that "Norman thought 10 percent would both stimulate disability activism around the world and give it lots of clout. . . . His 10-percent figure was prompted by nothing other than political expediency."

10. For instance, in 1992, the office of the UN Secretary General drew upon Acton's figure in a large glossy brochure produced by the UN to mark the culmination of the Decade of Disabled Persons (Boutros-Ghali 1992:2).

11. Not surprisingly, that normative authority strongly affected the way many governments like China's responded to the UN call for national disability surveys. In several countries, so strong was the idea of 10 percent that not only did local statisticians sometimes hide their newly conducted disability

surveys whose results did not closely approach 10 percent, but some of these statisticians subsequently took their most up-to-date population figures, applied a 10 percent rate, and published disability statistics based on that equation (UN Statistical Office, personal communication, January 28, 1996).

12. The exact source of the concept "sick man of Asia" (*dongya bingfu*, which accurately translates as "East Asia's sick man") is unclear. The concept is usually associated with the century following the Opium War period (circa 1840–60), when large sectors of what is now the PRC were controlled by European, North American, and Japanese colonial forces. The concept was built around social-Darwinian notions (common during that period and still latent within much contemporary modernist discourse) that health, racial strength, and modernity coevolve. After the Opium War, the concept was used by both Chinese and colonial forces to describe Chinese people and the then nascent Chinese nation-state as weak, backward, and economically torpid. The concept is still regularly invoked in China, most often by Chinese nationalists to highlight China's past humiliations and to emphasize recent forms of "progress." For a discussion of how *canji, canfei,* and *feiji* have been linguistically framed in years past and how they have been negatively coded, see Kohrman 1999, especially pages 67–81.

13. The English-language translations provided here are those that are usually provided by the Disabled Persons' Federation's own translators.

14. This information was also conveyed to Drs. Michael Phillips and Veronica Pearson during a formal interview they conducted in the early 1990s with one of the leaders of China's psychiatric community (Michael Phillips, personal communication, March 16, 1995).

15. This questionnaire was filled with loosely worded queries about social adaptation and self sufficiency (e.g., "Is that person able to see well enough to differentiate ideograms on a newspaper?" "Is this person able to bathe?").

16. This revised approach was ultimately approved by China's State Council and made the basis of the Disabled Persons' Federation's official standards for *canji.* During the 1987 survey's implementation, the type of assessment government-employed biomedical practitioners were expected to carry out when evaluating a person's disability status, of course, differed on the basis of the category of disability under consideration. In general, however, the move toward a biomechanically based orientation was particularly significant in terms of the categories of physical, visual, and hearing disabilities. In the case of *tingli canji* (hearing disability), for instance, potential candidates for disabled designation were assessed mainly in relation to a decibel system. For *shili canji* (visual disability), candidates were primarily assessed in relation to the radius of visual field as measured in mathematical degrees and the best-corrected visual acuity as measured by the Monoyer's decimal scale. In the case of *zhili canji* (mental disability), potential candidates were assessed mainly in terms of IQ (intelligence quotient) as defined then by the WHO and to a lesser degree in terms of the American Association on Mental Deficiencies Adaptive Behavior Scale (AAMD 1970). For mental illness, candidates were persons

understood to suffer for more than one year from "(1) psychosis associated with organic diseases of brain and body; (2) toxic psychosis including alcohol- and drug-dependencies; (3) schizophrenia; and (4) affective paranoid reactive schizo-affective and periodic psychosis." The 1987 survey literature does not detail what methods were used for diagnosing these forms of mental illnesses. The literature makes clear, however, that for the purposes of subsequent "international comparisons," the WHO's Social Disability Screening Schedule was used to grade mental illnesses as more or less severe (Di 1989:1474–82).

17. One of Li Zheng's statistical consultations involved travel to UN headquarters in Manhattan. There, he and other group members talked at length with quantitative specialists in disability research. One of these specialists described what transpired: Li and his entourage came to tell us they were considering quashing the survey because they wanted 10 percent and they didn't get it. We carefully looked over everything they brought. We then told them that, as far as we were concerned, the survey was just fine, that they had proven themselves highly effective researchers, and that they shouldn't worry about not getting a rate closer to 10 percent. (UN Statistical Office, personal communication, January 28, 1996).

REFERENCES

AAMD. 1970. *Adaptive Behavior Scales.* Washington, D.C.: American Association on Mental Deficiency.

Acton, Norman. 1981. Report of Joint UNICEF/Rehabilitation International mission for a preliminary examination of childhood disability in the People's Republic of China, Mar. 9–21, 1981: Rehabilitation International. New York: United Nations.

Agamben, Giorgio. 1998. *Homo Sacer: Sovereign Power and Bare Life.* Trans. D. Heller-Roazen. Stanford: Stanford University Press.

Agence France-Presse [AFP]. 1998. China warns against "fabricated" statistics. Jan. 10.

Anderson, Benedict. 1991. *Imagined Communities: Reflections on the Origin and Spread of Nationalism.* New York: Verso.

Appadurai, Arjun. 1996. *Modernity at Large: Cultural Dimensions of Globalization.* Minneapolis: University of Minnesota Press.

Boutros-Ghali, Boutros. 1992. Foreword. In *The United Nations Decade of Disabled Persons: A Decade of Accomplishment (1983–1992),* 2–3. New York: United Nations.

Chen, Guanfeng. 1985. Survey on disabled aims at better care. *China Daily,* Apr. 26.

Chu Shuowei, Zhou Xuezhu, Liu Shulan, Wang Jin, Yuan Ping, and Liao Guozhen, eds. 1996. *Zhongguo canjiren shiye nianjian (1949–1993)* (Almanac of efforts on behalf of persons with disabilities [1949–1993]). Beijing: Hua Xia.

Davis, Lennard. 1995. *Enforcing Normalcy: Disability, Deafness, and the Body*. London: Verso.

Deng Pufang. 1995. *Deng Pufang tongzhi zai dibazi quan guo canlian gongzuohuiyi shangde jianghua* (Comrade Deng Pufang's speech at the Eighth national Disabled Persons' Federation working conference). Beijing: China Disabled Persons' Federation.

Di Ya, ed. 1987. *Quanguo canjiren qiuyangdiaocha gongzuoshouce* (Research manual for the 1987 National Sample Survey of Disabled Persons). Beijing: National Sample Survey of Disabled Persons Office.

———. 1989. *Zhongguo 1987 nian canjiren chouyangdiaocha cailiao* (Data from China's 1987 Sample Survey of Disabled Persons). Beijing: Office of the National Sample Survey of Persons with Disabilities.

Foucault, Michel. 1979. *The History of Sexuality*. London: Allen Lane.

Gladney, Dru. 1991. *Muslim Chinese: Ethnic Nationalism in the People's Republic*. Cambridge, Mass.: Council on East Asian Studies, Harvard University.

Greenhalgh, Susan. 2005. Missile science, population science: The origins of China's one-child policy. *China Quarterly* 182: 253–76.

Gupta, Akhil. 2001. Governing populations: The integrated child development services program in India. In *States of Imagination: Ethnographic Explorations of the Postcolonial State*, ed. Thomas Blom Hansen and Finn Stepputat, 000–00. Durham: Duke University Press.

Hacking, Ian. 1981. How should we do the history of statistics? *I and C* 8: 15–26.

———. 1982. Biopower and the avalanche of printed numbers. *Humanities in Society* 5(3–4): 279–95.

———. 1990. *The Taming of Chance*. Cambridge: Cambridge University Press.

Hall, Stuart. 1985. Signification, representation, ideology: Althusser and the post-structuralist debates. *Critical Studies in Mass Communication* 2(2): 91–114.

Horn, David G. 1994. *Social Bodies: Science, Reproduction, and Italian Modernity*. Princeton: Princeton University Press.

Huang, Yasheng. 1996. The statistical agency in China's bureaucratic system: A comparison with the former Soviet Union. *Communist and Post-Communist Studies* 29: 59–75.

Kohrman, Matthew. 1999. Bodies of difference: Experiences of disability and institutional advocacy in modern China. Ph.D. dissertation, Department of Anthropology, Harvard University.

———. 2003. Authorizing a disability agency in post-Mao China: Deng Pufang's story as biomythography. *Cultural Anthropology* 18 (1): 99–131.

Lee, Sing. 1998. Higher earnings, bursting trains and exhausted bodies: The creation of travelling psychosis in post-reform China. *Social Science and Medicine* 47: 1247–61.

Linton, Simi. 1998. *Claiming Disability: Knowledge and Identity*. New York: New York University Press.

Merli, M. Giovanna. 1998. Underreporting of births and infant deaths in rural China: Evidence from field research in one county of northern China. *China Quarterly* 155: 637–55.

Qin Yan. 1992. *Deng Pufang de lu* (The Deng Pufang road). Taiyuan: Shu Hai.

Schein, Louisa. 2000. *Minority Rules: The Miao and the Feminine in China's Cultural Politics.* Durham: Duke University Press.

Social Statistical Section of the National Statistical Bureau. 1985. *Zhuo zhuang cheng zhang de zhong guo er tong: 1983 nian quan guo er tong qiuyang diao cha cai liao* (Growing into sturdiness: Data from the 1983 National Sample Survey of children). Beijing: National Statistical Bureau Press.

Stiker, Henri-Jacques. 1997. *A History of Disability.* Trans. W. Sayers. Ann Arbor: University of Michigan Press.

Stone, Deborah. 1984. *The Disabled State.* Philadelphia: Temple University Press.

Tien, H. Yuan. 1991. *China's Strategic Demographic Initiative.* New York: Praeger.

United Nations. 1990. *Disability Statistics Compendium.* Statistics on Special Population Groups. Series Y, No. 4. New York: United Nations.

Whyte, Susan Reynolds, and Benedicte Ingstad. 1995. Disability and culture: An overview. In *Disability and Culture,* ed. Benedicte Ingstad and Susan Reynolds Whyte, 3–32. Berkeley and Los Angeles: University of California Press.

9 Seeing Disability and Human Rights in the Local Context

Botswana Revisited

BENEDICTE INGSTAD

The issue of rights for people with disabilities has lately entered the international agenda of human rights. To what extent are their human rights insured in various countries and cultures, and what may be done to improve an assumed situation of abuse and neglect? There are several forces behind this development.

Partly as a result of successful lobbying by organizations of people with disabilities themselves (mainly those from the more developed countries),[1] the idea that disabled people should be secured equal rights with other citizens and full participation in society has been disseminated to most countries of the world. These advocates have strongly voiced concerns about their own rights and as an act of solidarity become engaged in fighting for disability rights globally.

The work of the United Nations has been of great significance in making disability rights a global issue. In 1983, the UN General Assembly signed its World Program of Action Concerning Disabled Persons, followed by the Decade for Disabled Persons (1983–92), in which "full participation and equality" were the stated goals. A global meeting was held midway through the decade to assess the impact so far, and it was suggested that a guiding philosophy should be developed to indicate the priorities for action in the years ahead (United Nations 1994).

Following this meeting, draft outlines for a declaration on disability rights were presented twice (by Italy and Sweden) to the UN General Assembly but were rejected. The (unofficial) reason was that one did not want the Universal Declaration of Human Rights (United Nations 1948) to be weakened by too many separate declarations for minority groups. More officially it was said that existing human-rights documents guaranteed persons with disabilities the same rights as others.

237

However, a working group was established to recommend effective measures to realize the goal of "full participation," and in 1993 the General Assembly in a resolution adopted the Standard Rules on the Equalization of Opportunities for Persons with Disabilities (United Nations 1992).[2] Out of 22 rules, 12 are concerned with preconditions and target areas for equal participation. These concern the following areas of life: awareness raising, medical care, rehabilitation, support services, accessibility, employment, income maintenance, and social security, family life, and personal integrity (including marriage, sexuality, and parenthood), cultural activities, recreation (including sports), and religion. These rules offer an international instrument with a monitoring system to help make sure they are effective. The monitoring system is implemented through a UN special rapporteur, advised by a panel of experts. Thus there is indeed a universal standard, accepted at the highest international level, for the achievement of human rights for persons with a disability.

Following this, various donors—nations and NGOs—have put assistance to people with a disability on their agendas. In 2000 a resolution calling for a convention was passed at a world NGO summit on disability in China, and in 2001 the General Assembly of the UN adopted a resolution that established the Ad Hoc committee to consider proposals for an international convention to establish the rights of people with disabilities (Light 2004).[3]

Moreover, in this time of heightened attention to human rights, scientific advances in genetics and the global discourse on bioethics have sharpened the discussion of the human value and rights of people born with a physical or mental abnormality (Ash 2001; see also Lock, this volume).

This chapter is concerned with the importance of understanding the issue of human rights for persons with a disability in a local context, and especially in the context of poverty. While some needs are more or less universal, others differ with localities and culture. What is perceived as a problem in one culture or community may not be seen as such in another, and measures to improve the situation for persons with disabilities in more developed countries may have different (unintended) effects in other parts of the world. If (one of) the function(s) of "rights" is to secure the material and spiritual needs of persons with disabilities, we must take such matters into consideration. Not doing so presents the risk that groups and individuals who do not fit the UN prototype of "a person with a disability" will fall behind in development. Since this prototype is largely based on the picture created by activist groups from the so-called developed countries and supported by elite activists in developing countries, the Standard Rules may not fit well either those who are severely multi-handicapped or poor rural people with disabilities in developing countries.

In an introduction to the edited volume *Human Rights, Culture and Context,* Richard Wilson describes human rights as "one of the most globalized values of our time" and goes on to say that "human rights are among the few utopian ideals left" (Wilson 1997:1). In the discourse of disability and human rights, what does this mean? Is there a global agreement as to what the rights are of persons with a disability? And are these ideals really utopian? In this chapter I will first look into a possible global agreement— what we may call "universal human rights." I will then turn to the question of their applicability. Are there really issues here that are universal and valid cross-culturally, or do we first of all have to consider the situation of persons with a disability in terms of the cultural context in which they live? Finally I will discuss the role of the (anthropologist) researcher in the field of disability and human rights.

The position I take in this chapter is that of advocating for an anthropology of disability that widens the perspective from the American- and European-inspired Standard Rules to one that takes in the lived experiences of people with disabilities in various cultural settings. The Standard Rules are without doubt needed and appropriate on a global level as a first step toward full recognition of rights and citizenship for people with disabilities worldwide (Rioux 2002). However, all standardized schemes or guidelines, whether in the form of manuals for Community-based Rehabilitation or classifications of disabilities or Standard Rules stand the danger of being more or less culturally inappropriate when faced with real-life challenges. We must be careful about forcing issues that are important for us upon people with a disability in other countries. We must also be aware of the possible existence of human-rights issues of importance to them that we have not seen, or of (unintended) consequences of commonly accepted issues. We thus need an anthropology of disability and human rights that sees disability in context.

As an anthropologist who has worked for almost two decades in rural Africa, I do see some dangers involved in the way universal human rights for people with a disability are being promoted in developing countries. I strongly believe that anthropology has a contribution to make by bringing forward the lived experiences of disabled people who cannot themselves participate at the negotiation tables and government offices where decisions affecting their lives are being made.

BOTSWANA REVISITED

I shall begin my argument by taking the reader on a trip to Botswana in order to revisit some people with disabilities who live there. I met these people for the first time in 1985–86 when I did a study of the implementation and effects of the WHO program Community-based Rehabilitation (Ingstad 1997). I revisited some of them in 2002 in order to find out what had happened to them, and—with the issue of "disability rights" in the back of my head—to see how current international debates are relevant to the present life situation of these people. To my knowledge this is so far the only long-term follow-up of people with a disability in a developing country.

I was able to make these visits together with my former assistant from 1984–85, Patricia Ntonge. This greatly helped me, both in the tracing of old informants and in reassuming contact. We were on the whole treated as old and very welcome friends. Having only two weeks at our disposal, compared to two years previously, the study is limited in many ways. We had to restrict the number of people revisited to those who were reachable within a few hours' drive from the capital. Previously we had been in contact with a hundred disabled people from 95 households, living within the borders of a huge district called Kweneng, stretching from near the capital, Gaborone, toward the east and into the Kalahari Desert toward the west. We were able to trace the whereabouts of 46 previous informants. Of the remaining 54 we know nothing. Out of the people we traced, 12 were dead. Ten were not reachable for various reasons. In total we managed to meet and interview 24 persons with a disability or their close kin (in cases where the person with a disability was not able to talk). In the following brief account of our findings I will discuss these meetings along some of the dimensions that are most prominent in the discourse of rights for disabled persons: the rights to life, health care and care in general, marriage and children, education, work, and a decent standard of living.

LIFE, DEATH, AND (HEALTH) CARE

The death of 12 out of 46 people (26%) within a time span of 16 years may seem like a high mortality. However, in considering this we should also keep in mind that Botswana is in the midst of an HIV/AIDS epidemic with a death rate that has increased very rapidly within the last few years. As we shall see from the discussion of having children, girls with a disability seem to be at high risk for casual sexual encounters and thus at risk for HIV. We were given the reason for the death in eight cases. We found that one woman had died from old age; actually she had lived much longer than we had expected when we saw her before, probably due to loving care from her daughter. One child had fallen into a bucket and drowned. Two men who were paraplegic after mine accidents had died from infections. Three multi-handicapped children had lived with their grandmothers at the time of our first meetings. Upon the death of the grandmothers they had been transferred to the care of their mothers and had died sometime afterwards. Nobody seemed to know the reason; they "just got sick and died," and nobody seemed to know exactly when. One woman, Neo, speechless and with a learning disability, had died in an epileptic seizure, leaving behind a young son (born after our first meetings) who was also a "slow learner" and suffering from epilepsy. Her caring and very concerned family had brought her to the clinic, but the injection she got there had not worked, and she died on the way to the hospital where she had been referred.

What can we gather from these stories concerning the right to health and care? Since independence (1966) Botswana has developed a primary health-care system that, at least in theory, is supposed to reach everybody within walking distance. But what about those who cannot walk, or who lack other means of transport? Even in the more developed countries people suffering from paraplegia struggle with sitting sores and urinary infections. It was therefore no surprise to find that these two young men had not survived long in surroundings where bacteria thrive in heat and dust. The clinics and health posts are only equipped for the basic health services, and it is not likely that the (frequently changing) staff have any training concerning the special health needs of people with paraplegia.

Status epilepticus may be hard to treat even if it happens close to a well-equipped hospital.[4] People with epilepsy in Botswana usually get medication and are followed up by the decentralized psychiatric services. But the medication is fairly standardized and lacks the sophistication and possibilities for individual adjustment that we see in more developed countries. Thus complete absence from seizures can rarely be counted upon. Neo's family however did the best they could by transporting her to the nearest health services as soon as it appeared that the seizures would not stop. She had been living with a married elder sister and her family, consisting of her husband, three unmarried daughters, and their small children. Another sister with a similar disability, as well as Neo's five-year-old disabled son, were also included in the household. The sister said that the family preferred to live in the countryside because there they could get nourishing milk for the children. On questioning who would take care of the child when she herself died, her daughters stated very firmly that this would be their responsibility, and one they would take on gladly.

It may not be ruled out that the child who drowned in the bucket did so due to neglect, although we have no information to indicate such circumstances. Neither can we completely rule out the possibility that the three severely multi-handicapped children who died after they moved from their grandmothers to the care of their mothers were neglected to the point of dying from a potentially curable illness. However, it is more interesting to try to understand the potential implications of such a move. All three women were single mothers who had left their disabled children with their own mothers in the village while they were working in the capital. They were the main providers for the village households. Upon the grandmothers' deaths these women found themselves in a situation of being alone with the care from which they had previously been relieved, and thus being seriously impaired as far as income-generating activities were concerned. To what extent these worsened circumstances influenced their ability to provide the disabled child with nourishing food and proper health care we may only guess.

The examples show us that surviving with a disability in a rural African setting may to a large extent depend on social and structural factors. If the health-care system is properly equipped and health workers trained to give the extra care that people with a disability may need, the chances are there. If the caretaker has enough time and resources to dedicate herself (because it is most often a woman) to the task, the chances are good. Thus life chances for the people in my sample who had died could most likely have been improved by addressing issues such as the health-service delivery system, poverty, rural unemployment, and the necessity for rural-urban migration. Too often, however, such issues are turned into a question of caretakers' attitudes, thus blaming the problem on those who are suffering from scarce resources and the sorrow of losing a loved one.

Kaplan-Myrth (2001) touches upon the same problem when she describes the failure of trachoma prevention programs in Mali. She points out that disabling conditions of everyday life overshadow conditions of individual disabilities. And thus it becomes a mistake to blame failure of a program on individual attitudes of disabled persons and their caretakers. We must shift from an individual, often standardized focus to the understanding of the roots of disabling conditions such as poverty, failed policies, and the like.[5] Only by doing so are we able to understand the real causes of social suffering (Farmer 1999).

MARRIAGE AND CHILDREN

Out of the people we met and interviewed only one man was married, and one woman had a steady marriagelike relationship with a partner who was the father of her children. However, in evaluating this low number we have to take two conditions into consideration. The first is that out of the 22, as many as ten had a moderate to severe learning impairment, some also with physical impairments or epilepsy or both as additional problems. Second, we have to consider the fact that marriage is almost about to become an exception in Botswana. More and more women remain unmarried mothers in female-headed households, and men tend to be elusive figures who are more likely to provide (if at all) for their mothers and the children of unmarried sisters than for their own offspring (Ingstad 1997). Our one married man with a disability is thus exceptional in more than one way.

When we first met Kabelo in 1984–85 he was a friendly young man of about 18 who was selling vegetables along the road. His legs were spastic from cerebral palsy, and he could not walk. There was nothing wrong with his mental abilities, but he had never been to school. He did not use a wheelchair but preferred to ride around on a donkey, which had been given to him by an uncle. With some help from the same uncle in the beginning he had organized his small business by paying friends to go to Gaborone and buy vegetables wholesale for him to sell in his home village. With his small business he was the only provider for his widowed mother and two younger brothers in school.

We met him again in 2002 behind the council building. He came bicycling toward us at high speed with a wide smile on his face having heard that we were back to see him. His walking was much better, and he miraculously had managed to learn to ride a bike and to buy one for himself. The donkey was long ago dead, and he had been run out of business by the arrival of a supermarket in the village. However, he had managed to find employment as a messenger at the council. He was happily married to a (nondisabled) woman and the father of three (nondisabled) children who were all in school. The wife was also employed, and together they had built a nice house. Kabelo was clearly eager to tell us all this. He saw himself as a successful man and claimed he had never encountered any form of discrimination because of his handicap.

Kabelo's story confirms an impression from the first study (Ingstad 1997): that the decisive factor for whether persons with a disability in Botswana get married is the ability to provide for a family, and to a much lesser extent the disability as such. (Whyte and Muyinda make a similar point concerning Uganda in their chapter in this volume.)

The issue of children is a more complicated one. Out of 15 females whom we met or heard news of, eight had got one or more children since our first meeting (when most of them had been children themselves). However out of these eight women, three were quite severely mentally handicapped, and their mothers confirmed that they had been raped by men who were not handicapped themselves.

The family of Neo, who died in an epileptic seizure as we have seen, claimed that she had gotten pregnant after being raped in the bush when looking after goats. They did not know by whom. They only discovered her condition when she was about eight months pregnant, and when they tried to question her she only cried and cried. She gave birth to a beautiful boy who is now ten years old and the pride and joy of the aunt. Like his late mother he also has epilepsy and mild mental retardation. He refuses to go to school because he does not want to leave the aunt, and they do not want to send him because he just runs away and they are afraid he will get lost in the bush.

When we met Nana after all the years gone by she was a young woman in confinement after the birth of her first child. In spite of having cerebral palsy and a severe learning disability, she speaks quite well and is able to walk around on her own. The baby had been born by a cesarean section, and the doctors had tied her tubes at the same time. Her mother had agreed to this, but Nana had not been consulted. The mother said she understood Nana was pregnant when one day she found her naked. She was shocked at first and very much afraid that Nana would die during delivery, but now that the baby is born she is very happy and hopes that the child will grow up to take care of Nana. According to Tswana custom they went to the parents of the boy they suspected of the rape, but those chased them away saying that they were only out for their money. The boy said that if he ever heard someone call him the father of that child he would stab them with a knife. He was so ashamed of having had sex with a disabled girl.

Elizabeth had also grown into a young woman, though still developmentally delayed by a learning disability and with no speech. She got pregnant two years back, and her parents suspected a distant relative who had spent some days with them at the time—he too a somewhat "slow learner." The mother claimed this must have been rape since her daughter did not understand what had happened at the time. On suspecting that she was pregnant she took her to the doctor, but she did not really believe it could be so until the doctor confirmed it. The mother claimed she was terrified that her daughter would die during delivery. Therefore the doctor arranged for a cesarean operation at the hospital, and the tubes were tied at the same time—in agreement with the parents but without informing Elizabeth. The grandmother is very pleased with the little boy and had not worried that he would have a disability too. So far he seems fine. Elizabeth too is happy about her baby, although not able to take care of him much herself. She likes to hold him and cries if someone takes him away. The family has employed a maid to help with the baby and make sure Elizabeth is not raped again while the grandparents are out working.

The issue of rape in these cases is of course a matter of discussion. We do not know to what extent the girls themselves may have agreed in spite of clearly not having the knowledge to foresee the consequences. What we can conclude, however, is that girls like Neo, Nana, and Elizabeth are very vulnerable when it comes to possibilities for sexual abuse from casual sex partners, and thus in the Botswana context perhaps even more at risk for HIV/AIDS than the able-bodied population. They cannot negotiate for the use of condoms, and at the same time men probably see them as likely to be virgins and thus safe partners. There is also a belief that men may cleanse themselves from ritual pollution (which some people consider AIDS to be) by having sex with a virgin. For Nana and Elizabeth to have their tubes tied without being consulted is likely to be seen by the disability-rights movement as an abuse (Rioux 2002) but was an act of concern by the doctors and mothers, who feared for their health should they become pregnant again. Common to all three families, however, is the love they have for the children and their lack of worry about whether or not they will be disabled. The families were happy their daughters had survived the ordeal and hopeful that the children would provide for them in the future.

In addition to Nana, Neo, and Elizabeth there were a few cases (both in 1984–85 and in 2002) of mothers with severe mental retardation where we strongly suspect that their families had knowingly closed their eyes to the sexual relationships that were going on, or had even taken an active role in assuring that the girls got pregnant. Why would they do that? Perhaps out of a conviction that sexuality is a natural thing to which everyone should have the right—and thus in line with the ideology of the UN Standard Rules? More likely the explanation is one that was given independently from two of these grandmothers: *I was happy when I found out she was pregnant, because then the child can take care of both the mother and me when she grows up.*

To what extent this is fair to a child may however be a matter of discussion.

FIGURE 9.1. Disabled mother and her son on the lap of his proud grandmother.

EDUCATION

The discourse on education for people with a disability in Botswana has gone mainly along two lines. Since the late 1970s the government has emphasized the need to integrate children with disabilities in mainstream schools, while NGOs have developed special education, mainly with boarding facilities, for selected groups (deaf, blind, physical impairments) and also a few day-care (for multi-handicapped) and rehabilitation centers. Out of the 22 persons with a disability we visited in 2002, only one had finished form five in mainstream secondary school. One had failed form two and dropped out, while five had dropped out at various stages in the ordinary primary-school system. Four had been attending a special school for children with learning impairments, and three had attended special training courses at training centers for persons with physical impairments. In evaluating the dropouts from the ordinary school system we have to take into consideration that the dropout rate for children with no impairments is also relatively high. Only in one case did the mother tell us that the child had quit because the teachers and other students had laughed at her.

Thandi is a young woman with severe malformations of her legs, which makes her dependent on a wheelchair, or sliding on her buttocks, for moving around. When we first met her in 1984–85 she was not attending school, because she had not yet got a wheelchair. Her parents however wanted her to go to school, and after some discussion with the headmaster it was agreed that her siblings should bring her back and forth in a wheelbarrow. She finished primary school and was sent to live with a brother in Gaborone to attend secondary school. Unfortunately she failed form two, and because her parents could not afford to send her to a private school she returned to the village. At a later stage she had attended shorter courses in dressmaking and juicemaking at the training center for persons with a physical impairment.

Thandi is in many ways a typical example of persons with a disability who fail to utilize the mainstream school system to its full extent. Having the motivation and the ability, but lacking the economic resources and perhaps also the social support (her brother may have been busy with other matters), she gives up and returns to a village life, where she is not even able to utilize the special skills she has been given at the training courses. With some extra help and support she clearly could have gone further in the educational system.

On the other hand we have those for whom mainstream education is not an option, at least not in the crowded classrooms of most developing countries, where special education teachers are scarce. Job (and three of the others) had been attending a day-care center for severely multiply handicapped children that was opened in one of the larger villages after our 1984–85 fieldwork. Reaching the age limit of 16 he had to quit, but had learned the skills of sweeping and gardening and was able to make himself useful around the parents' compound without having to be supervised all the time. The family felt that the years at the center had been useful because he had become quieter and seemed satisfied, and the mother had been able to have a full-time job.

Job and his classmates would have had no chances in the mainstream Botswana school system, but in a sheltered environment with specially trained teachers they have thrived and learned skills that enable them to be useful family members in their special way. The point when they have to leave the center to make room for the younger ones is of course heartbreaking. Ideally such centers should be followed by placements in sheltered workshops or sheltered employment. But even when this is not the case, the fact that people like Job are able to make themselves useful after training, and to take care of their own hygiene without having a 24-hour watch on them, makes an enormous difference for their acceptance by the family.

EMPLOYMENT AND AN ACCEPTABLE STANDARD OF LIVING

Education alone is not enough, however. The most important issue is what takes place after (or without) education as far as employment or self-sufficiency is concerned. The council messenger Kabelo, whom we met above, was the only one of our revisited informants who had any formal employment. How he managed to get this job we do not know for sure, but it is likely that his charming and enterprising personality and a certain amount of social conscience among council officials were decisive factors. As long as special rights to employment for persons with a disability are not in place on a national basis, those persons may easily become losers on a labor market where even the most able-bodied struggle to find a placement.

However, the issue of employment should be seen in a wider family perspective; it is not only a matter of the individual with a disability. Elsewhere (Ingstad 1997) I have argued for the need to consider a family with a disabled member as a "disabled family." This means that sometimes the best help for such a family is to find employment for the father or mother of the child (or adult) with a disability. This was the case for Job's mother, who because of the day-care center, and later on his relative self-sufficiency, was able to work in the family business. This was also the case for the mothers of two of his former classmates who had found employment in the kitchen of the day-care center.

In an effort to create employment opportunities NGOs often set up training courses of shorter or longer duration, but seldom with any guarantee of employment or an appropriate income afterwards. This may create opportunities for personal enterprises but also lead to frustrations and disillusion for those who do not succeed.

Sara is in her forties, confined to a wheelchair by polio, and the single mother of three (nondisabled) children whom she has successfully supported through the educational system. When we first met her in 1984, she had just finished training in dressmaking at a rehabilitation center. She had been given a sewing machine and sent back to the village. Business was not very good, however, and collapsed completely when the machine broke down and nobody could repair it. She invested what little money she had made in buying *chibuku* beer wholesale and selling it from her house.[6] By 1985 the business was going well: she had built herself a new house and was the main supporter of her elderly parents. By 2002 she was still in the *chibuku* business and by now highly respected in her village as a successful woman. She was the member of several committees and played an active role in the home-based care program for AIDS patients.

Thandi, whom we have already met, also wanted to set up her own business. Like Sara she did not find dressmaking very profitable and gave up when the machine broke down. She wanted to start with juicemaking but had no money to invest in the machine she had learned how to handle. Neither was there a loan arrangement in place to help her. Thus she was sitting idle at home.

The Kgari family was the poorest of the poor when we met them in 1984. A total of five family members had various types of disabilities. One of the sons, a polio survivor, had received some training in shoe repair and was thus able to supplement the destitute ration they were receiving from the clinic. By 2003 three of the family members with a disability and both the old parents had died. The shoemaker was left, trying unsuccessfully to provide for his severely multiply handicapped sister. They were just as poor as before.

Mary was a bright young girl with a visual impairment who had finished secondary school for the blind and was hoping to go to Zimbabwe for training to be a switchboard operator. When we met her in 1984 she was back in her home village, way out in the Kalahari, far from everything she had learned to appreciate while in boarding school and with a braille Bible as her only pastime. She still had some hope left but was getting more and more disillusioned. The year after we learned that she had committed suicide.

These cases show us the range of outcomes of training for persons with a disability in our sample: from the successful businesswoman who gains respect in her community to the deepest poverty and despair. Common to most training for people with disabilities in Botswana is the lack of follow-up when it comes to equipment or loans which make it possible for people to practice their skills. It is also a problem that the skills taught are not always appropriate for the market or that the demand is very limited. Training gives hopes and possibilities for the future but also creates expectations that may be hard to fulfill. The Community-based Rehabilitation (CBR) program put in place in Botswana in the early 1980s should ideally follow up persons with disabilities and help them through the various "bottlenecks" they may encounter in their attempts to support themselves. However, while the CBR program is still in place—at least officially—most of our 2002 informants claimed that they had not met anyone who was interested in their situation since we were there last time in 1985.

None of the people in the 2002 sample knew anything about human rights or the discourse on rights for persons with disabilities. Out of common sense, however, they felt very strongly that people like them should be treated "just like anybody else," and many (but not all) of their stated needs were in line with what is called for by the Standard Rules. Only one of them had at any stage been in touch with an organization for people with disabilities (although there are several of them in Botswana), and this contact was disconnected when the social worker who had organized the local support group was transferred.

SO WHY DO WE NEED TO SEE DISABILITY IN A SOCIOCULTURAL CONTEXT?

Is being blind in Africa really so fundamentally different from being blind in Norway? This was a question from an anonymous reviewer to something I wrote recently. It made me think through the issue once more, and I came to the conclusion that yes, it is really fundamentally different (or at least it may be so)—not from the purely biomedical point of view perhaps, but from most other perspectives. It is generally accepted that social, cultural, economic, and physical conditions play at least as important a role as the medically defined impairment in generating a disability or handicap (whatever we choose to call it) for an individual. This is what has been called the "social model" of disability. Thus any planning to achieve equalization should clearly be founded on knowledge about the particular context in which a person with a disability lives. Unfortunately, this is not always the case. Seeing disability in context implies understanding disability not (as it once did) in one particular isolated cultural setting, but in contexts in which modern ideas about rights for persons with a disability coexist with possibilities, constraints, and beliefs imposed by the local physical, social, economic, and cultural setting.

Let me give an example. In my part of the world persons with a visual impairment will be trained to achieve independence from others, to live by themselves, to be able to move around freely with the help of a white stick or a dog. There are warning sounds at street crossings and other amenities. Such independence is something valued and seen as a right. In contrast, in 1984 I once followed a rehabilitation worker to visit a blind middle-aged woman in a Botswana village. The rehabilitation worker had been struggling for some time to train her to cook for herself and to walk alone in the village with a stick, the way the WHO CBR manual said she should do. When we came to the compound, we found the woman sitting together with a young daughter-in-law. On engaging them both in a discussion on why the woman refused to learn to walk with a cane, we were told that if she did walk around alone in the village like that, people would say that the family was not taking proper care of her. Besides, a white stick was quite unnecessary, since there would always be a small child around to lead her. Quite likely this task made the child feel important and promoted contact between generations, which tends to become a scarcity in other parts of the world. Actually, this lady had very little desire to be "independent" in our sense of the word. Rather, she saw her blindness as an opportunity to harvest the care, respect, and honored status from her children and grandchildren that she felt she deserved after a long life of caring for others. However, this attitude did cause considerable inconvenience for her children and in-laws, who lived in different villages and had to take turns staying to care for the woman.

My second argument concerns marriage. Sentumbwe (1995), who himself has a visual impairment, has shown from Uganda how blind men sometimes marry seeing women, while blind women most often marry blind men. Is this mainly a question of blind women being more disadvantaged than blind men? Or of a sexist society in which men, even when they are disabled, have more chances of choosing than do women? Or perhaps the blind women are looking for other qualities in life, like sharing similar life experiences with their husbands? If we automatically assume that for people with a visual impairment to marry each other is a sign of their being discriminated against, does this not in itself imply devaluation? As we see, different perspectives may provide very different interpretations of this situation. As seen from the revisits to Tswana families, the central issue is not necessarily one of the rights of a disabled person to be married, or to have a child, or both. There is also the issue of being protected from sexual exploitation or even (as in some Asian countries) unwanted arranged marriages to partners chosen for the main purpose of providing care.

Another example concerns the right to have children. In many societies to have a child is the key to achieving full personhood (or at least womanhood) in a society (Whyte and Ingstad 1995). Few people would dispute the right of persons with disabilities to have children if they feel they can care for them. But the matter may be more complicated than we think. Thus we may also include the rights of children into this picture. To what extent should the right of a person with a disability to have a child be weighed against the need of the child to have a secure childhood and an adult life in which obligation toward a disabled parent does not become too much of a disability in itself? In some contexts the right of a woman with a disability *not* to have a child by arrangement of the family, or in some cases rape, may be equally important as that of having children.

My final argument concerns the issue of education, another "right" adopted unconditionally on behalf of persons with a disability. When an African village mother refuses to send her seven-year-old son affected by Down syndrome to school, where classes of 40 to 60 students are taught by a teacher with very little formal training—is that "hiding" and "neglect"? Her fear is that the other children will tease him and that the teacher will beat him for not being able to follow the lessons. And can a government that is struggling to bring general education to its most remote corners be expected to provide for special attention to one or two children with (for instance) a hearing impairment living in a small remote village? Or do we have to accept specialized but segregated education that brings children from a large area together in a boarding school although it provides for little contact with their families (who cannot afford to pay the bus fare) and no opportunity for parents and siblings to learn sign language? Or are these children better off remaining at home with their families learning to look after the cattle?

In a case from western Greenland Nuttal shows how disabled children from remote areas are taken away by the school authorities and sent to a boarding school far from their families to get special education. Their teachers keep alive a myth that they are "dumped" and neglected by their families. The truth is, the families cannot afford to come to visit them. Nuttal tells a touching story of a boy, Nils, with a hearing impairment. His parents had taken him out of a local primary school in a remote village from which they felt he was not able to profit much. Instead he was being trained by his father to be a fully competent hunter until he was taken by the school authorities and sent to a boarding school far away. Nuttal concludes that "not only was Nils categorized as incompetent, but his family were also left feeling a sense of inadequacy and incompetence at being deprived of caring for him" (Nuttal 1998:192).

I personally see no easy answers to such dilemmas. They do however show us that the achievement of human rights in the form of "full participation and equality" for all people with a disability in this world is indeed a long way from being realized. As long as there are poverty and scarcity of resources, as long as there are political regimes that prioritize development of cities and armies above rural development and the eradication of poverty, they will remain utopian. However, just as important as the issue of attainability of the goals is the question of their applicability. As the examples have shown, the issue is not necessarily about what desirable goals are attainable but *which goals* are *desirable, in whose eyes,* and in accordance with *what ideology.* To understand this we have to see disability in context.

ANTHROPOLOGISTS AND HUMAN RIGHTS
FOR PERSONS WITH A DISABILITY

Roughly we may single out different roles for the anthropologist along a continuum defined by two poles. At one pole we find the role of the advocate for universal "rights" or standard rules and the implementation of studies that document how these are (and are not) achieved. This role often attracts researchers who have a disability themselves or in the close family. At the other pole we find the relativist, mainly oriented toward understanding disability as perceived by the people with a disability themselves. I will go for a middle way myself. I accept the need for universal principles as guidelines for governments in the work to improve the living conditions of citizens with a disability. But at the same time I will stress the need to consider these ideals (standard rules), to assess and question their applicability, and also their (possible) unintended consequences, in various cultural settings. A pamphlet on violations of human rights toward disabled people, published by four organizations of people with disabilities (Disability Awareness in Action 1998) to commemorate the fiftieth anniversary of the UN Universal Declaration of Human Rights,[6] is a clear example of lack of such consideration. One cannot make a cry of discrimination based on global statistics alone. We also need to know the context and to assess the assumed violations against the everyday life of everyone concerned, not only the individual person with a disability. For example, marriage rates of people with disabilities must be seen against overall marriage patterns in particular countries; literacy or illiteracy for people with disabilities must be seen against the general literacy and school attendance in the countries concerned.

Organizations of disabled people and their supporters have done an important job in promoting universal rights for people with disabilities. But in disseminating their message to the developing counties they stand the danger of allying themselves with a small elite of educated, urban or privileged people with disabilities. These people may not be in touch with real needs as perceived by the majority of their poor rural and disabled compatriots. Support from outside may strengthen these organizations' capacity for outreach activities, but there are also examples of such support leading to a struggle for scarce resources within an organization that eventually may be quite destructive for its course.

The discourses on human rights tend to carry with them a message of individualism. This may work well with the urban elite of people with a disability in developing countries but may be far removed from the reality, needs, and probably also desires of the rural, and often poor, disabled people of many developing countries. It may also lead to the alienation of local organizations, as the carriers of such messages, from their own grassroots, and may create undesirable oppositions between the people with a disability and their families and caretakers.

At the American Anthropological Association's 1992 conference in San Francisco, AIDS and gay activists were posting signs saying *These Natives Can Speak for Themselves*. This message is also brought forward by people with disabilities in the more developed countries. But we should also remember that there are other "natives" in this field who cannot speak for themselves. I am thinking about those who are too mentally affected to talk or reflect on their own situation and whose interests have to be represented by parents or siblings. I am also thinking about the people in developing countries who cannot read or write and who live far from the urban centers in which most of the discourse on "full participation and equality" takes place. Although it is of course an eventual aim that their voices should be heard, one cannot automatically assume that any representative from the global disability community can represent their case.

Advocacy for universal human rights by disabled people's organizations from the more developed countries may blur their vision for the perspectives and needs of other "natives" and even sometimes work in contradiction to the interests of those supposedly represented by their advocacy. The agenda of the activists from the more developed countries may not similarly touch upon the core problems for persons with a disability in the less developed countries. Thus for a poor hearing-impaired woman in a village in the Kalahari it is presently of little interest whether she is called "deaf," "disabled," or a "person with a disability." (She does not have the equivalent words in her language anyway.) Her agenda would more realistically be summarized as access to food and firewood, and care from her children tomorrow.

Similarly, for her young neighbor whose legs are paralyzed after a mining accident the issue of wheelchair accessibility is not very relevant, since the sand in the village is too deep for a wheelchair to get around. In any case he is quite mobile, sliding on his buttocks with wooden clogs tied to his hands to protect him from getting sores. Neither does the issue of independent living concern him much for the time being. What he wants is some sort of work he can do at home in order to contribute to the economy of his parents, with whom he finds it natural to live as long as he is not married. What he needs even more are locally based health-care workers who are trained to take care of his special medical needs on short notice. And if he marries—which depends more on his family's ability to pay a

FIGURE 9.2. Homemade assistive devices: a woman using rubber thongs to protect her knees for walking.

bride price (*lobola*) than on his looks and ability to walk—the young couple is likely to spend the first years of marriage living with his parents until they can establish their own compound close to them.

We see from this that the promotion of human rights for persons with a disability in developing countries first of all must be an integrated aspect of general development programs with the aim of eventually empowering the (often) poor people to speak for themselves. Such programs, *together with* an awareness of "disability rights" may give persons with a disability the chance of developing their skills and abilities in the local community where they belong with their friends and family.

Moreover, we need more research that sees disability and human rights in context. We need to find out the implications of advocating universal concepts of "rights." To what extent do these fit (or not fit) into different cultural and socioeconomic contexts? To what extent are they of importance to those who do not know about them (or are unable to read and write) and thus cannot consciously use them in a struggle for equality? This is a different but equally important type of advocacy.

Thus we may conclude that both universalism and relativism recommend themselves to the ethnographer interested in human rights for people with a disability. Universalism makes comparison possible (Wilson 1997:3), but in painting the "grand pictures" we stand the danger of losing the nuances and cultural sensitivity that make "rights" and "standard rules" applicable beyond the policy level. Relativism grants precedence to immediate contexts and creates sensitivity to diversity created by such factors as political economy, culture, gender, degree and kind of disability, and family situation. In the discourse on anthropology, human rights, and disability we have to be aware of the strengths and the weaknesses of both approaches.

Relativism in itself has its dangers, in that governments who oppose the application of rights for people with disabilities in their policies may actively use it for their purposes. Arguments such as *Why should disabled children have the right to schooling when education is not compulsory for other children in this country?* have been encountered in developing countries as an excuse for not providing for teacher's salaries in schools for children with a mental impairment. Universalism as advocated through the global NGO network of persons with a disability is important and necessary to raise national and global awareness, but it may work contrary to the good intentions if not complemented by the necessary understanding of— and adjustment to—the local cultural context.

Anthropological perspectives and research into the field of disability and human rights may help both planners and activists to avoid the pitfalls of these two perspectives, and thus create a knowledge base that takes into account the variety of life situations of people with disabilities worldwide. Research should contribute by providing activists with good arguments, but should not be driven by activism to the extent that it becomes blind to the fact that even the work of activists and organizations by disabled people themselves may be interesting topics of research.

NOTES

A shorter version of this chapter was presented at the meeting of the American Anthropological Association in Chicago 17–21, 1999.

1. For some types of impairments such groups are organized in global networks.

2. Whereas a declaration binds the UN member states, a resolution is not binding but serves as a guideline.

3. In 2006 (after this chapter had been completed) agreement was reached on the text for a Convention on the Rights of Person with Disabilities, thus bringing the process one step further.

4. Status epilepticus is an epileptic seizure (most often) with loss of consciousness that does not stop by itself after a short time.

5. WHO prevention programs as well as many other programs for targeting people with disabilities are often standardized to fit all countries and cultures.

6. *Chibuku* is a thick, porridgelike alcoholic drink, packed in paper cartons, which is driven out daily in big trucks from the brewery and sold to private enterprisers in the villages. It represents one of the few possibilities to invest money in business locally, but is also a severe threat to the health of the population.

7. Disabled Peoples' International, Inclusion International, World Blind Union, World Federation of the Deaf, World Psychiatric Users' Federation.

REFERENCES

Ash, A. 2001. Disability, bioethics and human rights. In *Handbook of Disability Studies*, ed. G. L. Albrecht, K. D. Seelman, and M. Bury, 297–326. London: Sage.

Disability Awareness in Action. 1998. Are Disabled People Included? Freeways Print.

Farmer, P. 1999. *Infections and Inequalities: The Modern Plagues*. Berkeley and Los Angeles: University of California Press.

Ingstad, B. 1997. *Community-based Rehabilitation in Botswana: The Myth of the Hidden Disabled*. Studies in African Health and Medicine, vol. 7. Lewiston: Edwin Mellen Press.

Kaplan-Myrth, N. 2001. Blindness prevention in Mali: Are improvements in sight? *Disability Studies Quarterly* 21(3): 91–103.

Light, R. 2004. A report from the third session of the UN Ad Hoc committee on a comprehensive and integral international convention on the protection and promotion of the right and dignity of persons with disabilities. *Disability Tribune* June–July: 5–8.

Nuttal, M. 1998. States and categories: Indigenous models of personhood in northwest Greenland. In *Questions of Competence: Culture, Classification and Intellectual Disability*, ed. R. Jenkins, 176–93. Cambridge: Cambridge University Press.

Rioux, M. H. 2002. Disability, citizenship and rights in a changing world. In *Disability Studies Today*, ed. Barnes C., M. Oliver, and L. Barton, 210–27. Cambridge: Polity.

Sentumbwe, N. 1995. Sighted lovers and blind husbands: Experiences of blind women in Uganda. In *Disability and Culture*, ed. B. Ingstad and S. R. Whyte, 159–73. Berkeley and Los Angeles: University of California Press.

United Nations. 1948. Universal Declaration of Human Rights. New York.

————. 1994. *Standard Rules on the Equalization of Opportunities for Persons with Disabilities.* New York.

United Nations Resolution 1990/26 of May 1990.

Whyte, S. R., and B. Ingstad. 1995. Disability and culture: An overview. In *Disability and Culture,* ed. B. Ingstad and S. R. Whyte, 3–32. Berkeley and Los Angeles: University of California Press.

Wilson, R. A., ed. 1997. *Human Rights, Culture and Context: Anthropological Perspectives.* London: Pluto.

10 Moral Discourse and Old-Age Disability in Japan

JOHN W. TRAPHAGAN

Japanese discourse about old age emphasizes family-centered provision of health care to sufferers of dementia and other disabling illnesses and conditions associated with the aging process. Expectations for care in old age have historically centered on provision of support within the context of multigenerational families, particularly in the form of coresidence with the family of one's eldest son. In practice, this has meant that the eldest son's wife actually provided the vast majority of physical care of elder members of the household, ranging from general help with activities of daily living to long-term care of bedfast elders. That a female family member will be the primary care provider in the event that a disabling condition arises in old age remains widely assumed; between 80 and 90 percent of all care providers to disabled elderly in Japan are women (Sodei 1998).

However, it is no longer assumed that the caregiver will be a coresident daughter-in-law. Although many Japanese continue to express a preference for virilocal residence in which women who marry successor sons reside with their husbands' parents and provide care to them should the need arise, it is increasingly common for parents to prefer having care provided by a daughter living close by, even while encouraging virilocal residence for a male offspring, or to prefer coresidence with a daughter (and her family) rather than a son and his family. This is due, in part, to the fact that daughters are often perceived as being likely to provide better care for elder parents than daughters-in-law, who may well lack emotive bonds to their in-laws. (See Traphagan 2004.) Nonetheless, whether she is related by blood or by marriage, it is normally the role of a woman to provide care to her parents or to her in-laws, should the need arise.

Through the expectation or desire that a coresident daughter or daughter-in-law will provide social support and health care to elder parents, in one sense the contemporary Japanese family continues to function as an old-age "insurance" provider along the lines Nakane (1967) describes more specifically for the stem family in rural Japan during and prior to the 1960s.[1] While people are less able to depend upon this form of old-age "insurance" than they were in the past, the idea that the family *should* provide such social support persists, and the idea that in the current social milieu the government needs to provide such support is often presented as something of a lament. The notion of filial coresidence, as Akiko Hashimoto points out, is a central feature of a *habitus*[2] in which security in old age is structured around notions of protection and predictability, rather than ideas of autonomy and independence that are more typically associated with many Euro-American societies (Hashimoto 2000:20). Filial coresidence provides a form of security that maximizes predictability and certainty, because it grounds expectations about care in the emotive and moral bonds that connect members of a family (Traphagan 2004). For Japanese coresidence implies a commitment on the part of coresident adult children such that, should care for acute or disabling conditions (or both) be required, the parent can legitimately expect to depend upon the child for provision of that care at home.

Despite the continued importance of this pattern to elder care in Japan, the number of households consisting of either a single elderly person or elderly couples has been rising for several years. And many young and middle-aged women who live with in-laws or their biological parents work outside the home, thus limiting the amount of time they can devote to caring for the older generation. For women contemplating marriage (particularly to eldest sons), ambiguities related to values about the direction of responsibility for care—"Should I care for *my* parents or my *husband's* parents?"—have contributed to refusal on the part of some women to provide care to in-laws or, for many others, ambivalence about providing care to agnatic relatives (Traphagan 2004). This tension is particularly strong when contemplating the provision of care for a disabled parent as opposed to a disabled in-law.

This chapter focuses on two issues as they relate to disability in old age in Japan. First, I am interested in exploring the cultural construction of disability in Japan as it relates to old age, and second, I will consider how disability in old age is structured in terms of a moral discourse that taps into cultural conceptualizations of activity and effort that are used in defining a "good person" and how this discourse is used by the state to rationalize the shifting of some expenses related to elder care to individuals (Lock 1993; Traphagan 2000a). More specifically, I will argue that disability in old age in Japan needs to be understood in terms of a moral discourse of elder care that is tied to values of self-effort and self-actualization. Disability among the elderly, whether it is expressed in the form of senility, bedriddenness, or difficulties with carrying out activities of daily living (ADLs), is presented through government rhetoric as the antithesis of self-actualization and carries with it the stigma of antisocial behavior. However, a discontinuity exists in the public discourse related to the care of disabled elderly in that, on the one hand, the newly promulgated long-term-care insurance program (*kaigo hoken*) is directed toward assisting in caring for the disabled elderly while, on the other hand, a rhetoric of nonuse of this program has emerged at the local level as a means of discouraging people from actually accessing it. At the core of this discourse is the moral (and moralized) balance between legitimate dependence and overdependence upon family members, particularly women, or government services for provision of care.

THE AGED NORTH

The northernmost six prefectures of Japan's main island of Honshū—Akita, Aomori, Fukushima, Miyagi, Iwate, and Yamagata—are collectively referred to as Tōhoku, a region that Japanese associate with a rural past, traditional values, and the farm families that symbolically represent an idealized Japan in which filial coresidence is the norm and individuals aspire to live according to that norm. Known for its snow-topped mountains and wide expanses of green rice paddies, the region is one of the main agricultural areas of Japan, producing rice, apples, and dairy products; but it has also become increasingly industrialized as manufacturing facilities for cars, semiconductors, watches, and other products have become common—a trend that has been observed in several parts of rural Japan (Dore 1978). The region is also well known for the agedness of its population. For example, in Akita Prefecture between 1975 and 1995 the proportion of the population over the age of 65 increased from 10 percent to 21 percent, and projections are that it will increase to 37 percent by the year 2020. For some of the smaller towns in the prefecture it is anticipated that the proportion of people over 65 will approach 50 percent by the same year (Akita-ken nōgyō kyōdō kumiai chuō kai 1999:5; see also Traphagan 2004).

As noted above, throughout Japan residence patterns have been changing along with the aging of the population. The proportion of the elderly population living either alone or only with a spouse has been on the increase for several years, moving from 8.5 percent to 13.2 percent of the elderly population living alone between 1980 and 1999 and 19.6 percent to 32.3 percent living only with a spouse over the same period of time. At the same time the percentage of elders living with children has dropped from 69 percent to 50.3 percent. Perhaps more telling is the fact that the percentage of elders living with married children has dropped from 52.5 percent to 31.2 percent while over the same time period the percentage of elders living with unmarried children has actually risen from 16.5 percent to 19.1 percent. This has profound implications for providing care to disabled elderly and elderly with difficulties with ADLs, because in many cases there are no coresident family members to assist in providing care. (See Raymo and Kaneda 2003 for a discussion of Japanese residence patterns.)

In this chapter, I will focus on elder care as it has been developed and experienced in three locales within the Tōhoku region, which I have been visiting for fieldwork since 1994. Kanegasaki and Mizusawa are located in the Kitakami River basin along the main rail and highway corridor through the north and are about 500 kilometers from Tokyo. Both municipalities have major agricultural areas; thus many of the people with whom I spoke were from farm families. Mizusawa, however, is a city of more than 60,000 people and serves as a business and entertainment center for the immediate vicinity, and most of my time in Mizusawa has been spent in an urban neighborhood where few residents have any connection to farming. In the summer of 2000, I was located in a town about 10 kilometers outside Akita City, which has close to 300,000 residents and is one of the major cities in the Tōhoku region. Much of the data for this chapter come from ethnographic interviews with caregivers, government workers and bureaucrats involved directly with elder-care programs, and older people themselves who were receiving various forms of care from family members, private care providers, or government care providers. In several cases, interviews focused on families in which filial coresidence was either being contested or was not possible due to issues such as the location of work for the child. I also have spent a considerable amount of time participating in elder activities and engaging in casual conversation about issues related to growing old.

Even with declining coresidence, throughout Tōhoku multigenerational households are common, particularly among families that engage in some degree of farming activity or are engaged in other family-based enterprises such as a shop or a medical or dental clinic. Before moving into a discussion of care for the disabled elderly, however, it is necessary to give some thought to how "disability" and being "disabled" are conceptualized in the Japanese context.

DISABILITY IN JAPAN

As one moves about Japan, whether in the megalopolis of Tokyo or out in the rural countryside, with the exception of some elders who have difficulty walking, it is unusual to see disabled people moving about in public spaces. As Hayashi and Okuhira note (2001:855), only 20 years ago, it was still considered normal to confine disabled persons to institutional settings for life. While there has been a significant disability-rights movement in Japan since the 1980s, throughout much of the modern period (since the mid-nineteenth century) disabled persons have experienced life either confined to home or segregated into institutional settings that removed them from public view and awareness (Hayashi and Okuhira 2001:857). This situation has improved considerably, but public facilities and transportation continue to have access problems, such as insufficient elevators and escalators in train stations, that inhibit mobility. In some cases, renovations are incomplete or seem oddly thought out—several subway stations in Tokyo have escalators that head toward the surface, but after departing the train one ascends the escalators only to find a long staircase without an escalator waiting at the end. I have often seen older people struggling to move up and down staircases in train stations, even in very modern stations for the bullet train. Moving through train stations is particularly difficult for elderly who are mobile but have some difficulty in walking or climbing stairs. People who use wheelchairs also encounter major problems in moving about and accessing public facilities—particularly older buildings. The concern over access was raised in a casual conversation I had with a group of wheelchair-bound tennis players at the local sports facility in Kanegasaki. As I chatted with them, they complained bitterly about the lack of laws to encourage easy access for the disabled in Japan and, perhaps rather idealistically, commented on how advanced the United States is in this respect.

In the beginning of his popular book *Gotai fumanzoku* (1998; literally, Five body parts unsatisfied), Ototake Hirotada writes autobiographically about his experience growing up without four of the five body parts equated with a normal human being in Japan (two arms, two legs, head). The word *gotai* is loaded with negative connotations in terms of how it represented the disabled in the past. Emiko Ohnuki-Tierney notes that those described as *gotai fugu*, meaning that their five body parts are missing or deformed, were seriously discriminated against in the past and "were thought to represent religious impurity" (1994:235).

Disabled from birth, Ototake presents his experience along the lines of these negative connotations, but positively, noting that he has in many ways benefited from his situation; thus he reacts against conceptualizations of himself and others like him as *shōgaisha,* a word commonly used for disabled persons in Japanese and the official term used by government organizations (Gottlieb 2001:987). The term *shōgaisha* implies someone who has an obstacle or obstruction in his or her life—an impediment to functioning as a normal person and having a normal life. While it has been adopted as preferential to more derogatory terms such as *mekura* (blindness, but also implying an ignoramus and illiteracy) or *kichigai* (used for intellectual impairment, but having the connotation of madness: Gottlieb 2001:985), the term is not without its own negative connotations. The character for the syllable *-gai-* means "hindrance" or "handicap" but can also indicate harm, injury, or damage and often is found in words with negative connotations such as *kōgai* (pollution), *satsugai* (murder), and *heigai* (vice). The extent to which Japanese actually associate these meanings with the term *shōgaisha* is debatable. When confronted with the meaning of *gai* one informant stated that the connection had never occurred to her in reference to the term *shōgaisha.* However, as Gottlieb points out, concern about such an association was sufficient that it motivated then NHK director Nohara Masao to take issue with the term in the journal *Rihabiriteishan Kenkyū* (Rehabilitation Research) in 1982 (Nohara 1982; Gottlieb 2001:987).

In contrast to this concept, Ototake does not view his lack of a complete body as an obstruction to a normal life and presents a detailed account of how he has lived a normal life, even while spending it within the confines of a wheelchair. In his childhood, he attends a regular school, rather than a school for the handicapped (*yōgo gakkō*), although this is not without some resistance from school officials, and with the involvement of his peers enjoys group activities such as outings to Mt. Fuji and baseball. As an adult, he has a career working on behalf of disabled people, wears fashionable clothing, and is a contributing member of society (Ototake 1998).

Ototake's experience is important because it points out the conceptualization of *shōgaisha* as people who are in some way blocked from normal activities and normal lives. *Shōgaisha* are a class of person distinct from normal persons and also distinct from others (specifically, from the elderly) who also may experience cognitive or physical impairment. Indeed, the word *shōgaisha* is not typically used for an elderly person who is confined to a wheelchair, bedridden, or otherwise experiencing functional impairment. Rather than being blocked from specific activities such as walking, being a *shōgaisha* connotes being blocked from having a normal life—that is, a life in which one marries, has a career, has children, and grows old.

As Whyte and Ingstad indicate in their introduction to *Disability and Culture,* in the Western world the term "disability . . . implies a deprivation or a loss of a needed competence or qualification." This is differentiated from "inability," which suggests "an inherent lack of power" to do something (Whyte and Ingstad 1995:7–8). The concept of *shōgaisha* is closer to the meaning "inability" than "disability" understood in this sense. Disabled elderly are not *shōgaisha,* because they have already accomplished a normal path of life events; they were not blocked from becoming old; their physical conditions did not block them from marrying or having children or having otherwise normal lives. Instead, impaired or disabled elderly are described in terms of their specific condition, such as *netakiri* (bedridden) or *boke* (senile; Traphagan 2000a).

In short, concepts such as disability or handicap as they are used in North America do not map easily onto the Japanese context. Rather, disability has localized meanings related to specific classes of persons and their abilities to engage culturally circumscribed values associated with what it is to have a normal life. Being disabled involves a set of practices that are contingent and rooted in culture (Cohen 1998:6).[3] While they can be impaired, elderly in Japan cannot become "disabled" in the same sense that people who are, for example, blind or deaf from birth are disabled, because they were once enabled. As one informant, a woman in her late thirties, put it: "In general, *shōgaisha* is used when from birth or from an accident or illness or even unhappiness [*fukō*], part of the body of a person becomes inconvenient to use. However, for *netakiri* and *boke* elderly, those with cerebral apoplexy [*nōsottyō*] that causes problems such with walking, hand use, or speech—such as a stroke victim—we do not use the term *shōgaisha.*" Although not disabled in the same sense as *shōgaisha,* impaired elderly do represent a class of people who are differentiated from nonimpaired elderly and other nonimpaired people in Japan. Concepts such as *netakiri* and *boke* symbolically represent old people as bodies that are different from and deficient in comparison to normal bodies. As I have argued elsewhere (Traphagan 2000a), these are bodies that have unlearned or lost the capacity to function as social entities and to operate within the framework of interdependent relationships that characterizes normal behavior in the Japanese context. Conditions such as these are associated with a loss of self-identity and entrance into a life apart from or outside normative social behavior. *Boke,* in particular, represents a kind of social death in which the individual no longer is able to engage in the interdependent relationships—in which reciprocation for what one receives from others is expected and carries moral weight—that define normative behavior in the Japanese context. In one sense, the disabled elderly represent a class of people who are, to some extent, engaged in a form of antisocial behavior. They require constant attention and care but cannot return, cannot reciprocate, the care that they receive.

People who become *boke* or *netakiri* or both are at once viewed as objects of pity and as possibly having allowed their condition to develop as a result of insufficient effort in pursuing activities (such as hobbies, sports, or study) and engaging themselves in social contexts. More important than the onset of the condition itself is the perception that one has done all one can to prevent or delay the condition. In this sense, disabling conditions for the elderly have the potential of carrying moral stigma—having failed to remain sufficiently active to avoid a condition such as *boke* indexes insufficient effort. This, in turn, places one in a condition of overdependence upon others for care, and thus one becomes a burden, unable to reciprocate the help he or she has received. As Long points out, avoidance of becoming a burden on family at life's end is an important theme in the social construction of a good death in Japan (Long 2001:273). Hence, identification with one of these categories of decline forms an attribution of what Cohen (1995:317) refers to as "difference or discontinuity to an old person, or to old people as a group," that implies a deleterious change in which the embodied state of functional decline carries with it not only the ontological, biomedically reified condition, but a culturally circumscribed moral stigmatization of the aging and aged body. Cohen (1995:326) argues that in Banaras, India, this moral discourse of aging is not simply a matter of the individual. The behavior of the senile elder indexes a bad family, or a family in which children fail to sufficiently care for their parents or are not sufficiently devoted to them. Thus, the weakened elder body becomes a pointer to a bad family.

In the Japanese context, the failure is more directed toward the individual than to his or her family, although the family is implicated in situations where an elder is living alone and lacks coresident or nearby family to provide care. Although overdependent and burdensome behavior carries social stigma in Japan, this should not be construed as meaning that all forms of dependency are interpreted as being burdensome. Indeed, as noted earlier in the chapter, there are legitimate forms of dependency in old age, and these forms of dependency are an important component of Japanese kinship ideas. A degree of later-life dependency upon family is expected and legitimate, while overly autonomous behavior is both discouraged and stigmatized (Kiefer 1999:201). The point where normal dependency begins to deteriorate into what is termed *meiwaku*, a sense of dependency that implies the burdening of another, signals a change not only for the elder but also for those who must provide care. Within the context of the multigenerational household, the presence of younger members who must provide continuous care can become a source of significant stress for elders, who may feel that they have traversed the line between normal dependence and burdensome behavior.

SOCIAL SERVICES AND THE DISABLED ELDERLY

Pressures of outmigration from rural areas, a generally low total fertility rate in Japan (which has been under 2.0 since the mid 1970s and was approximately 1.4 in 2000), and contested ideas about who is responsible for providing elder care have contributed to the creation of alternative approaches to family-provided care. In the event that one lacks a potential caregiver living nearby or coresiding, there are several forms of institutional support available. These include home helpers, day-care or day-service centers,[4] short-stay facilities, nursing visits, hospitals, and nursing homes.

There are a variety of both public and private programs that provide full-time and part-time day care for older people. For example, in the town of Kanegasaki, the day-service center is open five days a week and provides services to approximately 150 elderly people. Once a week, participants are either bused to the facility or driven by family members, spending their time there from early morning until late afternoon. The program is oriented so that people from the same part of town visit the facility together on their specified day of the week. Administrators at the center indicated that older people were unwilling to make use of the center unless they could attend with preestablished friends from their own section of town.

The center consists of a large room in which there are long tables at which participants do crafts, eat lunch, and spend time chatting and a counter behind which employees of the center take care of administrative work. The room is brightly lit with windows constituting the entire south wall. There is also a small tatami-mat room in which there are placed low tables at which to drink tea and chat. This room is used as a nap area following lunch for those who want to take a rest. When they arrive in the morning, a nurse visits with all members, taking their blood pressure and pulse—this is a time for conversation with friends from the neighborhood. After everyone is settled in, one of the center's staff members will write the activities for the day on a blackboard and sometimes discuss how these activities are beneficial for maintaining health. Older people are often encouraged to drink milk—small cartons of milk are handed out every day at the center—because of the severe osteoporosis that afflicts many of the women in the area. (It is not uncommon to see a woman who is bent over at a 90-degree angle at the waist and unable to stand up straight.) Many of the activities in which people engage at the center involve eye-hand coordination, such as making paper dolls or ring-toss games, which are viewed as being beneficial in preventing or delaying the onset of senility.

In Mizusawa, in addition to government services there is a private day-care facility known as Seiwa-en. This facility is largely indistinguishable from the government-run center in Kanegasaki, with the exception that it not only includes day visitors, but also provides short-term and long-term stay services. Seiwa-en also services a larger population, accommodating approximately 360 people who pay for the entire cost of participation in programs or residence. Seiwa-en is attached to a large private hospital and like the center in Kanegasaki it has a large, well-lighted central room in which older people gather for group activities and for socializing. Once a year, at the summer festival of the dead known as *obon*, this room is decorated with a large red-and-white pole in the center of the room, and various games such as fishing for plastic fish in a small pool are set up, games typical of what one might find in the *obon* festival at the neighborhood park. A group from the woman's auxiliary whose hobby is Japanese dance comes and performs for the elders in attendance, and those elders who are able join in the dancing, while those who are unable sit in a circle around those who are dancing, and in some cases a worker may come and push a wheelchair-bound person around the pole along with the dancers. Beer is served to those who do not have a medical reason for avoiding alcohol (and sometimes a small amount is served to those who do), and various festival foods, such as fried noodles (*yakisoba*) are cooked on the spot for everyone to enjoy.

In contrast to the day-service center in Kanegasaki, those who make use of the day-care services at Seiwa-en can come every day of the week (the facility is open seven days a week) and can stay from around 9:00 A.M. until about 5:00 P.M. The facility can also accommodate 50 live-in residents, whose stay may be as little as a week or as long as a few years. (See Tables 10.1 and 10.2.) More than half of the residents of the facility have lived there more than six months, and a quarter have lived there for more than a year; those who have lived in the facility more than three months account for 76.5 percent of the facility's residents. Those who have been living in the facility for an extended period typically do not have family living nearby, and seven of the 47 people living at the facility as of July 1998 were on waiting lists for admission to nursing homes. Thus, they were in the process of making a transition to permanent life in an institutional setting. The following

TABLE 10.1 *Length of Stay Among Seiwa-en Day-Care Residents As of July 1998*

Duration	Number	Percentage
Less than 2 weeks	4	8.5
2 weeks–3 months	7	15
3 months–6 months	11	23
6 months–1 year	13	28
More than 1 year	12	25.5
Total	47	100

TABLE 10.2 *Living Arrangements of Seiwa-en Day-Care Users as of July 1998*

Family Living Situation	Number	Percentage
Solitary elderly	101	46
Multiple elderly	43	20
Elderly in multigenerational household	54	25
Other	19	9
Total	217	100

is a transcript of a segment of conversation from a focus-group meeting held with four long-term residents of Seiwaen, all women, and a case worker at the facility. This segment of the conversation focuses on the responses to a question about where family members are living.

MIE: My daughter is nearby, but she is living with her husband's parents, so I can't live with them. My two sons both live in Tokyo and are married. Because they live in apartments there is no chance of going to live with them, although I don't think I would want to leave Mizusawa.

KIFUE: My son often asks me to come and live with his family in Tokyo, but I don't want to go there. I wouldn't mind going to visit for a week or so, but I can't live there permanently. I don't like life in the city, and I don't think I would have any freedom if I lived with them.

MIE: The best place to live is, of course, at your own home. But this is scary. I worry that I will go off and forget to turn off the gas stove, and this is dangerous. It is scary. Also, shopping is a bit scary [could fall, etc.].

Although three of these women stated that the decision to move to Seiwa-en was their own (the other woman indicated that her son decided), in making this decision all of them were fundamentally confronted with an inability to access family-centered support. For example, Kifue's desire to avoid moving away from Mizusawa, where her friends live and where she has lived her entire life, inhibited her ability to access family support, even though it was apparently available to her if she had been willing to move to Tokyo. Kifue went on to indicate that part of her concern in moving to Tokyo was that she felt she would not get along with her daughter-in-law, thus suggesting that the decision was also related to conflict within the family concerning coresidence. In the case of Mie, although she has a daughter living in Mizusawa, there is no possibility of living with her, because she has married into another household in which she is expected to focus her attention on the needs of her coresiding in-laws. Mie stated that her daughter does bring supplies to her at Seiwa-en occasionally, but she cannot expect to coreside.

Of those who use the day-care service, two-thirds are living either alone or with another elderly individual (usually a spouse), and only 25 percent are living in multigenerational households. Hence, elderly persons without younger family members coresiding make the greatest use of the facility. The proportion of those from such elderly-only households is considerably higher than the general proportion of such households in the city's population; as of 1997 only 8.4 percent (891) of the total population over 65 (10,632, or 17.7 percent of the total population) were living alone. And individuals from multigenerational families account only for a quarter of those who make use of the facility. These data indicate clearly that the day-care service caters primarily to those who lack access to in-home family-centered support.

This tendency to support those who cannot access family-centered support is evident among those who reside at the facility, as well. As of 1997, of the 45 people residing at the center at the time the count was taken, six had been living alone when they entered, and seven were from two-person elderly households. In other words, 28 percent of the resident population was from one-person or two-person elderly households. Furthermore, one case worker indicated that many of the others were from two-generation households in which the younger generation were, themselves, either elderly or approaching old age, and she said very few are from three-generation households.

For those who experience difficulties with ADLs or who are providing in-home nursing care to a bedridden relative, the home-helper program

TABLE 10.3 *Residential Situation of Home-Helper Users in Kanegasaki, July 1998*

Type	Number	Percentage
Solitary	20	27
Elderly couple	5	7
Elderly in multigenerational household	11	15
Coresident with under 65	37	51
Total	73	100

provides home visits to assist with care provision. The home-helper program is not specifically intended for the elderly, although not surprisingly users of home-helper services are predominantly over 65. As of October 1998 in Kanegasaki, of 72 people using the home-helper service, only 12 were under the age of 65. The average age of users was 74.8, with 50 people between the ages of 70 and 90. According to government officials, as of July 1998 about half of those who received home help were living in elderly-only households. (See Table 10.3.) It is instructive, however, to consider the type of service received on the basis of living situation. Forty-four of those who use the home-helper service are receiving nursing care (for bedridden, frail, physically handicapped, blind, or demented individuals). Twenty-nine receive assistance with housework. Of those living in a household that includes a person under the age of 65, only six (14 percent) receive housework assistance; the remaining 38 (86 percent) receive nursing care.

Those households in which there is a coresident younger person are highly unlikely to receive assistance with activities of daily living. Instead, they receive nursing care, primarily in the form of bathing services, which is of particular importance in the Japanese context because Japanese typically bathe in deep tubs that are oriented vertically so that one cannot stretch out in the tub but sits in water up to the shoulders. Lowering and raising a person in and out of the tub is difficult physical labor, and at day-care or day-service facilities there is usually a bath that mechanically lowers and raises those who cannot get in and out alone. The home helpers operate a bath truck which contains a portable shallow bath that is body length.

In those households in which there is a female resident to provide assistance in activities of daily living, the home helpers visit the house to assist in bathing bedridden individuals. In all cases that I have observed, women who receive this form of home help are themselves over the age of 60 and have difficulties providing all the required care. These visits occur once or twice a week; thus the remainder of the time the coresident caregiver provides bodily cleaning through sponge bathing. The home-helper program is not aimed at providing a break for the regular care provider. Rather, when the home helpers arrive, the care provider, a daughter-in-law in all cases I have observed, assists with the process of lifting, bathing, and cleaning up.

SOCIAL SERVICES AS SAFETY NET

The above examples indicate that services like the home helpers and day-service and day-care programs largely function as a safety net when in-home, predominantly female-provided support of the elderly fails. Individuals who are living in elderly-only households tend to receive assistance with activities of daily living such as cleaning. Although some daughters-in-law contest their role as caregiver, the emphasis on female provision of care continues to be reflected in expectations about who should provide care. Indeed, this expectation is often overtly reinforced by governmental and other social-service institutions.

One woman, Erika, who was in her mid-forties when we discussed her experiences with caregiving, was very frustrated by her inability to obtain government home-care services to help with her bedridden mother-in-law. She had been working in a national department-store chain as a clerk when her mother-in-law, with whom she resided, became ill. Erika was living in the traditional multigenerational household, with one daughter still at home. Erika enjoyed her work in the department store and wanted to continue her job, although she was willing to reduce her hours; she was also concerned with income, because her daughter was approaching college. Her husband also had a job in a local company and worked full-time. Because she wanted to continue working, she went to the town hall to consult with the health division about obtaining home-helper services so that she could continue working. The family wanted to share the responsibilities of caring for Grandma as well as possible, although Erika was well aware that she would be providing most of the care. At the town hall, she was told that since she was physically capable of caring for her mother-in-law, it was unlikely that she would be able to make use of home-helper services:

"The expectation was that I would have to quit my job in order to care for my mother-in-law rather than receive services from the town." Erika went on to state that were there not a woman living in the household who could provide nursing care, it would have been possible to access home-helper services. "Care of bedridden elderly," she said, "is seen as the responsibility of the daughter-in-law [yome], and that takes priority over her interests and job."

The idea that services fill in gaps in family-centered care is not limited to the home-helper program, nor even to government-run services. Caseworkers at Seiwa-en indicate that the purpose of the facility is to function as an alternative when family-centered care fails or is unavailable. Although the maximum stay of any person living in the facility at the time of fieldwork was two years and two months, the facility is largely viewed as a temporary residence. As one Seiwa-en caseworker indicated: "We try to get people to return home, and the main purpose of the facility is to rehabilitate people to the point that they get to the level of being able to be cared for at home again." Indeed, from October 1997 through September 1998, of the 175 people who were resident in the facility for some period of time, 86.3 percent returned home rather than moving on to some other form of institutional living arrangement.

Programs such as the day-service center in Kanegasaki, which caters largely to older people who either are in wheelchairs or have restricted motor abilities, provide very limited relief to women who are managing in-home assistance with ADLs, because they are only available once per week. When asked to describe the purpose of the day-service center in Kanegasaki, the director of the center stated: "It gives women relief from caring for the elderly person so that they can go and take care of other needs of the household such as food shopping, buying diapers [for the care recipient], or house cleaning." Although there is a sense in which the center is seen as enabling women, the enabling function is largely directed toward household activities that cannot be carried out while caring for the elderly resident.

What these data suggest is that social services aimed at providing assistance to families with disabled or frail elderly in Japan are not culturally constructed and used as a means of enabling women to pursue interests or work outside the caregiver role, nor are they culturally constructed as a means of providing independence and autonomy for older people themselves. Rather, they are adapted to fit within the confines of traditional Japanese norms of social support to the elderly; norms that emphasize in-home female-centered provision of assistance and nursing care. Social services for the disabled elderly are organized around notions of security that emphasize predictability and certainty (Hashimoto 2000:20); these services come into play when that security is not available. Social services operate as a safety net to compensate for situations in which female-provided home-based support fails or is unavailable. If there is a coresident woman who is physically able to provide care, she may be forced to quit her job to provide care prior to receiving assistance from government programs like the home helpers. Private centers such as Seiwa-en can be accessed provided a family has sufficient income to pay, but these centers are still primarily organized to provide temporary care with the eventual return of the individual to the in-home-care environment.[5]

THE LONG-TERM-CARE INSURANCE PROGRAM

As the proportion of the elderly population, and particularly the proportion of older people who lack access to family-provided care, has increased, demand for social services has increased as well. Partly in response to this increased demand, the Japanese government proposed and initiated, beginning in 2000, a long-term nursing-care insurance program (*kaigo hoken*) as a means of coping with the rise in bedridden elders and others who need services ranging from minor assistance with activities of daily living (ADL) to those who experience dementia. The Japanese nursing-care insurance program is a social insurance program that was designed along lines similar to the long-term-care program enacted in Germany in 1994, which is the only other long-term-care insurance (LTCI) program to have been initiated in an industrial or post-industrial nation. As Campbell and Ikegami argue (2000:29), the LTCI program was developed in part to redirect the momentum that the Japanese elder-care system had gained with the Gold Plan, under which elder care had been managed in the 1990s and during which targets were set for major expansion of health and welfare services. Concern that Japan was moving in the direction of the costly Scandinavian entitlement-based system, in which a wide array of social services are funded by a combination of local and national taxes and only limited user fees can be charged, motivated the government to develop an alternative approach to providing elder care.

Services that the insurance program supports include in-home care, home visiting by health-care professionals such as nurses, home helpers, and physical therapists, and in-home counseling by public-health workers, doctors, dentists, and others. The program also supports in-home bathing services for the elderly, day-care service at elder day-care centers, short-stay programs at nursing homes, subsidies for the purchase or rental of equipment and for home renovations to help with ADL (handrails, Western-style toilets rather than the squat-toilets typical of older Japanese houses, etc.), and long-term institutional care (Mizu sōgō kikaku 1999). In general, the program covers all the services previously available under the Gold Plan and extends and expands many of those services.

The new LTCI program is financed as a social insurance program in which the national government funds 50 percent, and prefectures and municipalities fund 25 percent each. From the age of 40, Japanese pay universal mandatory premiums to support long-term care for those in need. Between the ages of 40 and 64, people pay a supplement to their regular health-insurance premium that is based on a percentage of salary and shared with one's employer. From age 65, premiums are deducted from one's public pension (Campbell and Ikegami 2000:31–32). In addition to the premiums, recipients of long-term care are required to pay 10 percent of the cost of care. This can amount to a sizable portion of one's income if one is elderly, particularly if one's income is limited to the national pension program (*kokumin nenkin*), which provides approximately 50,000 yen per month. As the scheme is currently organized, an elderly individual who has high levels of need may face expenses of up to 36,000 yen per month. This financial burden is problematic for poorer elderly, particularly women living alone, many of whom are those most likely to be using *kokumin nenkin* as their sole source of income. In a report in the *Japan Times Online* (Uranaka 2001), a 79-year-old man suffering from emphysema stated that his current copayments were approximately 7,000 yen per month. He received an oxygen tank, twice-monthly nursing visits, and home-helper visits to do household chores. Prior to the shift to the *kaigo hoken* system, he paid 500 yen per month for the same services—the cost differential had a significant impact on him, as his monthly pension income was only 80,000 yen. The problems are serious enough that as of November 2000, more than 80 municipalities had defied the central government by paying all or part of premiums for those over the age of 65 who have limited income, a practice that has generated a political debate concerning the organizing principle behind determining who is responsible for paying for *kaigo hoken* and whether the national or the local government should incur the expenses by waiving fees for some people (*Japan Times Online* 2000).

Although individuals are experiencing difficulties paying for services that were previously much less expensive, the larger picture also indicates that the costs to the national treasury associated with the program are considerable. Official estimates of the costs for *kaigo hoken* anticipate more than $70 billion in spending by 2010—an estimate that Campbell suggests appears to be unrealistically optimistic (Campbell 2000:96; Campbell and Ikegami 2003:21). Given the size of the program, underestimation of the costs involved with *kaigo hoken* may mean that serious problems loom for Japanese fiscal policy and the general system of providing health care.

MORAL DISCOURSE AND DISABILITY IN OLD AGE

It is within this context that use of the long-term nursing-care insurance program is being developed and in which an ambivalent rhetoric related to use of the program has emerged, a rhetoric closely tied to the political economy of aging in contemporary Japan. A wide array of posters, brochures, and informational seminars has been presented by government offices to encourage individuals to make use of the new program and to help navigate the complexities of services and costs related to the it.[6] While individuals and families are encouraged to access the program through these informational media, the rhetoric used by government officials, at least in some areas, focuses on discouraging older people's use of the program. This is perhaps most apparent during the short speeches that government officials typically give at the opening of activities for older people, such as cooking classes, calligraphy classes, or gateball tournaments.

One excellent example of this that I encountered was at a new senior center I visited in Akita Prefecture in the summer of 2000. The building has two large rooms for activities such as sewing and cooking classes and a woman's chorus. The center is available for use only by those over the age of 60 and is funded entirely by money from the national government. One government official, Sato-san, described the center as being part of the *kaigo hoken* program and as being intended to function as a preventive device so that older people will not need to make use of the insurance program. As Sato-san explained it: "The idea is that if people use this sort of facility for activities that will help them maintain health and to participate in activities to help them avoid becoming senile [*boke boshi*], fewer people will actually have to make use of the *kaigo hoken* system." Sato-san went on to explain that institutions like the senior center are intended as venues for encouraging good health and as a means of limiting fiscal expenditures by the government for the *kaigo hoken* system.

At the introductory speech given by the head of another elder-activity facility in town to a new cooking class at the center, the message of nonuse was made very clear when he stated: "The purpose of this center is to create healthy people so that there will be zero older people using *kaigo hoken*."[7]

In his speech, the director directly engaged the value of self-actualization through group activities; if older people have activities to do in group contexts—if they have an *ikigai* (a concept I will discuss in detail below, but which implies one's focus in life or raison d'être)[8]—they will be less likely to develop problems, such as *boke*, that will require use of the services. In the context of the class, this was put forth in a very practical way. Knowing how to cook nutritional meals can contribute to better health; indeed, there was a strong emphasis on the nutritional value to older people of the meal that they were preparing. The meal included fish (*sanma*), which we were told is very high in calcium, and asparagus with a dressing made with large quantities of mayonnaise, which, too, we were told is healthy because of large amounts of calcium.

Clearly, the idea of the meal was to provide food that would help in preventing bone loss. But the class itself was important as a context for self-actualization. The government bureaucrat who gave the opening words interpreted the meaning of the class in terms of having an *ikigai* as a means to avoid using *kaigo hoken*. Of course, the participants likely do not want to be in a situation where they need to make use of the major services available through the program, but it is important to remember that the program is not limited to major nursing care but also includes basic help with ADLs such as cooking and house cleaning. I have encountered several individuals like the woman quoted above who have wanted to make use of basic services such as home helpers but have been unable to do so because government officials were unwilling to provide the services requested.

For older people these facilities, and the activities related to self-actualization they encourage, are organized around the concept of *ikigai*. Japanese of various ages routinely talk about having an *ikigai*, but older people in particular often center many of their conceptualizations and assessments of quality of life in old age, and even their presentation of themselves as elderly, on the presence or absence of an *ikigai*. Having an *ikigai* is regarded in very positive terms. For example, in a conversation with Itoh, a man in his sixties, in which I asked about who among his neighbors seemed to be having a good old age and why, he responded: "Yes, there are people who are doing well; the best example would be those who are active in society and who have an *ikigai*. I think that Inoue Takeshi is doing very well, both from a social point and as an individual. He has been active in a variety of socially oriented groups and activities, and his travel is impressive."

Inoue was a man in his early nineties at the time of our conversation who had retired from a position in the government when he was 55 (at that time the mandatory retirement age) and had since that time traveled overseas 27 times for recreation. Inoue himself described his travels as his *ikigai,* and others clearly saw his focus on overseas travel as one of the most impressive aspects of his life and often attributed his having a clearly defined *ikigai* as being a main reason for his continuing to be in good physical and mental health. It is interesting and instructive to note that at the age of 92 Inoue had decided that a trip he had taken a few months before to Kyūshū, at the southern end of the Japanese islands, would be his last. In a discussion we had about this, he indicated that he was deeply concerned that no longer being able to travel, and thus having lost his *ikigai,* he was already beginning to falter cognitively and beginning to slide into senility. Indeed, the lack of an *ikigai* is often linked to having a particularly unhappy old age, characterized by physical and cognitive decline, and ending with being bedridden or even suicide. Those who are perceived as being at greatest risk for this outcome are those who live alone. As Chiba, a 65-year-old childless woman who lives with and cares for her bedridden husband put it: "For those who are living alone, they become tired, they do not have any *ikigai,* and they are very pitiful [*kawaisō*], and they decide to commit suicide." In order to avoid this fate, she makes use of social services available to assist in caring for her husband, thus giving her time to be involved in a variety of social activities such as a gardening club and the women's association in her neighborhood.

Like many widely used cultural concepts, *ikigai* is polysemous. In simple terms, it can mean one's purpose in life; it is something into which one throws oneself fully. However, this idea can be applied very broadly. A college student might describe drinking as his or her *ikigai,* while a woman in her forties might describe flower arranging that way. Virtually anything can be one's *ikigai.* Gordon Mathews provides a particularly useful explanation of the term as consisting of two components. First, it indicates a commitment to the group to which one belongs, as is clearly evident in the conflation of living alone and the likelihood of not having an *ikigai,* suggesting that without group participation having an *ikigai* is difficult. Indeed, the concept has a distinctly social aspect in that it usually implies some sort of group membership and interaction with others. At the same time, the term conveys a more inner aspect in that it means self-realization or self-actualization (Mathews 1996:17). These notions might seem contrasting in the Western sense, but for Japanese it is often through membership in a group and involvement with the activity or activities associated with that group that one can engage most effectively in self-actualization.

For older people, finding an *ikigai* often represents one of the most important goals in life and is strongly advocated by government officials and family members as a means to avoid a lonely, sad, illness-ridden old age. It is particularly important as a category of activity through which individuals can avoid the onset of disabling conditions such as *boke* and *netakiri*. So strong is the emphasis on finding an *ikigai* for older people in Japanese culture that it can actually become a source of stress that can become severe enough that, as Mathews (1996) notes, one may be brought to consider or actually commit suicide. This is particularly true for older men for whom work has formed their *ikigai* throughout adult life and from whom, due to mandatory retirement, work is often rather abruptly removed. These men, if they are unable to find a new *ikigai*, are often viewed as being at greater risk of developing disabling conditions.

Figure 10.1 provides an example of how the concept of *ikigai* is represented by government organizations in a widely distributed brochure available at the Kanegasaki town hall and in offices related to health and welfare. At the top, the brochure states *Ikigai Is the Source of Vigor*, following which it states Let's Aim at Becoming a Health Millionaire with *Ikigai!* Below these slogans are an elderly-looking couple busily engaged in their *ikigai*—gardening. Interestingly, I have rarely encountered older couples who pursue an *ikigai* together; rather they tend to prefer developing their *ikigai* within the contexts of groups consisting of their own sex.[9] The pamphlet goes on to describe a variety of different avenues for finding an *ikigai* and lists a wide array of possible activities that one can pursue, ranging from house cleaning to study to sports. The important feature of one's decision is to select an activity that one truly likes. The pamphlet concludes by identifying four steps to making an *ikigai:* search for something you like, find a friend for mutual encouragement, don't get tired out or impatient (go at your own pace), and keep hold of your aims.

In many respects, the behaviors encouraged through government publications on *ikigai* are not particularly different from the types of activities and behaviors encouraged within the framework of "successful aging" in the United States. However, the concept has important connotations related to being a good person. Having an *ikigai* is often equated with being active—with doing—and this concept, as noted above, is central in Japanese conceptualizations of the good person. A good person is one who is not idle, one who is actively engaged in self-building, particularly within the framework of social interactions. It is at this juncture that the understanding of *ikigai* is relevant to the narrative of nonuse that has begun to develop in relation to the nursing-care insurance program.

生きがいは元気の源

生きがいをもって
目指そう！
健康長者

監修／県立長崎シーボルト大学教授・小林美智子

FIGURE 10.1. Cover of pamphlet used to encourage older Japanese people to develop an *ikigai.*

In the attempt to connect the *kaigo hoken* program with the concept of *ikigai,* town officials are trying to encourage older residents to maintain their health. But there is more going on here. Both elements of the concept of *ikigai* are operating in this context: individuals can pursue activities that keep them healthy, but these activities are overtly placed in the moral realm by emphasizing pursuit of *ikigai* as a means of attaining the goal of zero participation in and dependence upon the LTCI program. By placing the concept of nonuse in the framework of self-actualization, nonuse takes on the character of a social responsibility. Government officials are deploying the concept of self-actualization through having an *ikigai,* a concept that has deep moral import, as a means not only to avoid the onset of disabling conditions but to avoid overburdening the system. Indeed, the by-product of nonuse is the possible reduction of the fiscal burden of *kaigo hoken,* spending for which is estimated to surpass ¥7 trillion ($70 billion) by 2008 or 2010 (Campbell and Ikegami 2003:27). The senior center discussed here functions as an institutional structure for channeling self-actualization or self-building through creating contexts for developing *ikigai*. This channeling of the activities associated with self-actualization exists and is enacted within the milieu of the politics and economics of an aging society and is constructed around concepts of the good person as active, giving his or her all, and socially engaged.

This is particularly important for understanding the cultural construction of elder disability in Japan. Facilities like the senior center in Akita are presented as being contexts through which individuals can engage in activities aimed at preventing or delaying the onset of disabling conditions such as *netakiri* or *boke*. These conditions, as noted earlier in this chapter, are in essence the antithesis of *ikigai;* the concept of *boke*, in particular, is associated with inactivity, a lack of energy and effort to engage in the behaviors, particularly those of a social nature, that represent basic ideas about selfhood in Japan. In this sense, we can see how disability and its prevention, through engagement with ideals of self-actualization or self-building as they are expressed in the concept of *ikigai*, are culturally constructed within the framework of a moral discourse of aging and disability. It is morally imbued activity in the form of *ikigai* that will give people the tools to stave off the onset of disability and thus avoid using *kaigo hoken*, even in a minimal way; and this has political and economic consequences for both the present and the future. Like participation in the activities that potentially can delay or prevent the onset of disabling conditions, nonuse of the program is not simply a matter of personal health and well-being, it is a matter of social responsibility.

The rhetoric of *ikigai* and the activities associated with it are a framework through which disability in old age becomes integrated into the moral discourse on aging in Japan, structuring disability in old age as the antithesis of activity and thus as socially irresponsible behavior. To become a disabled elder, as opposed to being *shōgaisha*, a condition over which one has no control, is associated with having failed to carry out one's responsibility to avoid overburdening one's family and society in general. Having an *ikigai* is one way in which an individual can maintain health and thus avoid becoming a burden (financially, socially, etc.) to society by becoming disabled.

Furthermore, the moralization of disability is closely connected to Japanese cultural ideas about the locus and nature of in-home and institutional elder care. Earlier in this chapter, I argued that institutionalized elder care is not structured around ideas of enabling those who have become disabled but instead is structured around ideas about filling gaps in home-based care. In one sense, it might be argued that by rehabilitating disabled elders to be able to return home there is an enabling function to institutionalized care. However, the basic goal is not that people be enabled to live at home on their own but that they be able to be *cared for* at home, and it is one's moral responsibility to make every effort to ensure that this happens.

Charlotte Ikels has pointed out that in China, while long-term care of the elderly is viewed as the responsibility of the family and is based upon values that emphasize obligations to parents, long-term care also needs to be understood as being structured in relation to the political economy of contemporary Chinese society (Ikels 1997:452). This holds in the Japanese case as well and has become particularly pronounced in light of the new longer-term-care insurance program. The overwhelming expense of the system, combined with the political environment that has emphasized the importance and challenges of coping with what has often been represented as Japan's most pressing policy concern—its "aging society" (*kōreika shakai:* Campbell and Ikegami 2000:28)—contributes to an ambivalent rhetoric about the use of the system. It also contributes to the tendency of government officials and political leaders to tap into long-standing moral conceptualizations of the good person as active and as giving his or her full effort to stay healthy both physically and mentally, particularly in order to avoid burdening others, whether the family or society in general. The manner in which use and promotion of *kaigo hoken* develops and the ways in which elder disability is managed in Japan's future present an important context for understanding the cultural construction of disability in old age and the intersection of political, moral, and economic discourse as the manifestations of population aging are expressed, experienced, and interpreted.

NOTES

Research for this chapter was supported by a Fulbright doctoral dissertation research grant and grants from the Wenner-Gren Foundation for Anthropological Research, the Northeast Asia Council of the Association for Asian Studies, the Michigan Exploratory Center for the Demography of Aging, and the National Institute on Aging (grant AG016111). I wish to express my thanks to these organizations for their financial support and also to L. Keith Brown, Patricia Maclachlan, and Willis Traphagan for comments on drafts of the chapter.

1. The nature and structure of the stem family has been one of the central themes of anthropological writing on Japan by both nonnative and native

social scientists; thus it is unnecessary to go into extensive detail on the topic here. However, discussion of a few main points about the stem family is important for understanding the centrality of the family in providing elder care in Japan. Commonly, within the stem family system, a single household unit is represented as consisting of three generations—the elder couple and their eldest son, his wife, and their children. Positions within the family/ household are hierarchically organized, with a considerable amount of power invested in the position of head of the family or household. Most frequently, succession to the headship is primogenitural; however sons other than the eldest often take on the role of successor when the eldest is unwilling or unable to succeed. In the absence of competent and willing male successors, it is common for an adult male—often a son-in-law—to be adopted into the household to take the role of successor. (This person is known as *mukoyō shi*.) In such situations, much of the power associated with the headship may well reside with the daughter, who is a consanguineal relative, rather than the adoptive husband; more important than succession itself is an emphasis on keeping the bloodline intact and maintaining intergenerational continuity over time.

2. The generative schemes that form the framework in which individuals think and act and that are inherent in a society and embodied by the members of a society (Bourdieu 1990).

3. Miles (2000) provides an interesting discussion of historical conceptualizations of disability in some Asian philosophical traditions, arguing that meanings of disablement associated with Asian cultures may offer a challenge to European models of disability.

4. Usually, those programs that are directly connected to the government are called "day-service centers" and those that are private are called "day-care centers."

5. On the basis of a study of day-care centers for children (Ben-Ari 1997), it is evident that institutions providing care at both ends of the life course function in the same way—as compensatory facilities to fill in gaps in home-centered, female-provided care.

6. There is considerable confusion among people concerning which services they are eligible for and how they can go about accessing those services. Recently, offices devoted to providing counseling about care and services options, as well as venues for voicing complaints, have been opening to help individuals and families deal with this confusion. Also, in any bookstore one can find numerous publications aimed at explaining *kaigo hoken*.

7. This example is also discussed in Traphagan (2006).

8. The syllable *-gai* in *ikigai* should not be confused with *-gai-* in *shōgaisha*. The kanji characters used for these sounds are different and have distinct meanings.

9. This may, in part, be a product of the fact that my fieldwork has been located in more rural areas; however, Japanese do tend to organize activities around membership in same-sex groups.

REFERENCES

Akita-ken nōgyō kyōdō kumiai chūō kai [Akita prefecture farming cooperative central association]. 1995. *Kennai shichōson betsu no nōka jinko to nōgyō rōdō chikara no dōkō* [Trends in city, town, and village farm population and farm labor strength within the prefecture]. Akita: Akita-ken nōgyō kyōdō kumiai chūō kai.

Aruga, Kizaemon. 1954. The family in Japan. *Marriage and Family Living* 16: 362–68.

Befu, Harumi. 1963. Patrilineal descent and personal kindred in Japan. *American Anthropologist* 95(6): 1328–41.

Ben-Ari, Eyal. 1997. *Body Projects in Japanese Childcare.* Surrey: Curzon.

Bourdieu, Pierre. 1990. *The Logic of Practice.* Trans. Richard Nice. Stanford: Stanford University Press.

Brown, Keith. 1966. Dōzoku and descent ideology in Japan. *American Anthropologist* 68: 1129–51.

———. 1968. The content of Dōzoku relationships in Japan. *Ethnology* 7(2): 113–38.

Campbell, John C. 2000. Changing meanings of frail old people and the Japanese welfare state. In *Caring for the Elderly in Japan and the U.S.: Practices and Policies,* ed. Susan Orpett Long, 82–97. New York: Routledge.

Campbell, John Creighton, and Naoki Ikegami. 2000. Long-term care insurance comes to Japan. *Health Affairs* 19(3): 26–39.

———. 2003. Japan's radical reform of long-term care. *Social Policy and Administration* 97(1): 21–34.

Cohen, Lawrence. 1995. Toward an anthropology of senility: Anger, weakness, and Alzheimer's in Banaras, India. *Medical Anthropology Quarterly* 9(3): 314–34.

———. 1998. *No Aging in India: Alzheimer's, the Bad Family, and Other Modern Things.* Berkeley and Los Angeles: University of California Press.

Dore, Ronald P. 1978. *Shinohata: A Portrait of a Japanese Village.* New York: Pantheon.

Bourdieu, Pierre. 1990. *The Logic of Practice.* Trans. R. Nice. Stanford: Stanford University Press.

Gottlieb, Nanette. 2001. Language and disability in Japan. *Disability and Society*16(7): 981–95.

Hamabata, Matthews Masayuki. 1990. *Crested Kimono: Power and Love in the Japanese Business Family.* Ithaca: Cornell University Press.

Hashimoto, Akiko. 1996. *The Gift of Generations: Japanese and American Perspectives on Aging and the Social Contract.* New York: Cambridge University Press.

———. 2000. Cultural meanings of "security" in aging policies. In *Caring for the Elderly in Japan and the U.S.: Practices and Policies,* ed. Susan Orpett Long, 19–27. London: Routledge.

Hayashi, Reiko, and Masaki Okuhira. 2001. The disability rights movement in Japan: Past, present, and future. *Disability and Society* 16(6): 855–69.

Ikels, Charlotte. 1997. Long-term care and the disabled elderly in urban China. In *The Cultural Context of Aging: Worldwide Perspectives,* 2nd ed., ed. Jay Sokolovsky, 452–71. Westport: Bergin and Garvey.

Japan Times Online. 2000. Districts waive care premiums for the elderly. Nov. 12.

Kiefer, Christie W. 1999. Autonomy and stigma in aging Japan. In *Lives in Motion: Composing Circles of Self and Community in Japan,* ed. Susan Orpett Long, Cornell East Asia Series vol. 106, 193–206. Ithaca: Cornell East Asia Series.

Kitaoji, Hironobu. 1971. The structure of the Japanese family. *American Anthropologist* 73: 1036–57.

Lock, Margaret. 1993. *Encounters with Aging: Menopause in Japan and North America.* Berkeley and Los Angeles: University of California Press.

Long, Susan Orpett. 1987. *Family Change and the Life Course in Japan.* Cornell East Asia Papers 44, China-Japan Program, Cornell University.

———. 2001. Negotiating the "good death": Japanese ambivalence about new ways to die. *Ethnology* 40(4): 271–90.

Mathews, Gordon. 1996. *What Makes Life Worth Living? How Japanese and Americans Make Sense of Their Worlds.* Berkeley and Los Angeles: University of California Press.

Miles, M. 2000. Disability on a different model: Glimpses of an Asian heritage. *Disability and Society* 15(4): 603–18.

Mizu sōgō kikaku. 1999. *Yoku wakaru! kaigo hoken.* [Understand well! Nursing-care insurance]. Tokyo: Takahashi Shoten.

Nakane, Chie. 1967. *Kinship and Economic Organization in Rural Japan.* New York: Humanities Press.

Nohara, Masao. 1982. Kokusai shōgaisha to masukomi no yakuwari: 21 seiki o mezasu "kotoba" no mondai [The International Year of Disabled Persons and the role of the media: The problem of language for the 21st century]. *Rihabiriteishan Kenkyū* 39: 40–43.

Ochiai, Emiko. 1997. *The Japanese Family System in Transition: A Sociological Analysis of Family Change in Postwar Japan.* Tokyo: LTCB International Library Foundation.

Ohnuki-Tierney, Emiko. 1994. Brain death and organ transplantation: Cultural bases of medical technology. *Current Anthropology* 35(3): 233–54.

Ototake Hirotada. 1998. *Gotai fumanzoku.* Tokyo: Kodansha.

Raymo, James M., and Toshiko Kaneda. 2003. Changes in the living arrangements of Japanese elderly: The role of demographic factors. In *Demographic Change and the Family in Japan's Aging Society,* ed. John W. Traphagan and John Knight, 27–52. Albany: SUNY Press.

Sodei, Takako. 1998. Role of the family in long-term care. *Keio Journal of Medicine* 47(2): A16–A17.

Traphagan, John W. 1998. Contesting the transition to old age in Japan. *Ethnology* 37(4): 333–50.

———. 2000a. *Taming Oblivion: Old Age and the Fear of Senility in Japan.* Albany: State University of New York Press.

————. 2000b. The liminal family: Return migration and intergenerational conflict in Japan. *Journal of Anthropological Research* 56: 365–85.

————. 2004. Curse of the successor: Filial piety versus marriage among rural Japanese. In *Filial Piety in Contemporary East Asia*, ed. C. Ikels, 198–216. Stanford: Stanford University Press.

————. 2006. Being a good rōjin: Senility, power, and self-actualization in Japan. In *Thinking about Dementia: Culture, Loss, and the Anthropology of Senility*, ed. Lawrence Cohen and Annette Leibing, 269–87. New Brunswick: Rutgers University Press.

Uranaka, Taiga. 2001. Cash, traditions standing between elderly and proper care. *Japan Times Online*. March 28.

Yomiyuri Shimbun. 2000. Kaigo hoken sutāto (Nursing-care insurance start). Apr. 1: 1.

Whyte, Susan Reynolds, and Benedicte Ingstad. 1995. Disability and culture: An overview. In *Disability and Culture*, ed. Benedicte Ingstad and Susan Reynolds Whyte, 3–32. Berkeley and Los Angeles: University of California Press.

11 Wheels and New Legs

Mobilization in Uganda

SUSAN REYNOLDS WHYTE

HERBERT MUYINDA

It is lively business as usual in the town of Busia. On the Ugandan side, right up at the border crossing to Kenya, music blares from the Trust Me Music Centre. Traders and travelers coming through the gate stop to make calls at the two smartly painted containers, one for MTN and one for Celtel, that serve as stations for the competing mobile-phone companies. Trucks, buses, and cars are lined up waiting to be let through, but cyclists and pedestrians stream across more freely. Everyone is carrying something—women with baskets on their heads, bicycle-taxi men in electric pink shirts with boxes of soap tied on the backs of their bikes, children lugging sacks. Among them are big hand-crank tricycles, expertly maneuvered by men with legs withered and useless from polio. Some are attended by small boys who give an extra push. Their tricycles are so constructed that they can carry a couple of sacks of cement, a few cartons of shop wares, or two jerry cans of diesel fuel underneath. Busia is famous for its *boda-boda* bicycle taxis. All over Uganda, a *boda-boda* is a bicyclist who can be hired to transport people or goods on his baggage carrier. The term originated in Busia, where cyclists shouted *Border! Border!* to attract customers. But it is the three-wheelers and not the two-wheelers that catch our attention and imagination as we start our work in September 2001. On the streets of Busia, they weave through the traffic, carrying a mattress, a five-gallon drum, or sometimes another disabled person on the baggage rack. The tricyclists are almost all men, some well dressed, others in ragged and dirty clothes. They seem to know each other: they shout greetings as they pass or sit chatting together at the side of the road.

In this chapter, we use the example of mobility-disabled people in Busia to make an argument that has more general relevance. We suggest that the realization of disability policy depends on linkages between national policy,

FIGURE 11.1. Giving a lift to a friend on the streets of Busia, Uganda. (Photo: Susan Whyte)

local situations, and the efforts and resources of social actors. We will show how the particular constraints and opportunities in one part of Uganda were experienced and exploited by people who desired social recognition. We concentrate on people for whom wheelchairs and "new legs" (calipers [leg braces], crutches, walking sticks) are part of a technology of mobilization that is potentially physical, social, and political. Our point is that a national (and international) disability policy and the efforts of disability organizations and programs are taken up (or not) by particular people in particular worlds. We believe that one important contribution of ethnographers is the elucidation of diversity, constraints, and resources so that policy makers and disability organizations can better address variation as they work to translate "paper rights" into opportunities, respect, and recognition.

The material presented here was assembled in 2001 and 2002 through interviews with 22 individuals with walking disabilities in Busia and Malaba (the border town in Tororo District just north of Busia), discussions in a general meeting of the Busia Disabled Association, interviews with four district officials, visits to three orthopedic workshops, interviews at the Kampala headquarters of two national organizations of disabled people, interviews with political representatives of disabled people on district councils, and reviews of Ugandan documents. In addition each of us brought to the project experience from other parts of Uganda. Herbert Muyinda had done a study on perceptions of disability in Busoga and on land-mine victims in northern Uganda. As a polio survivor himself and a resident of Kampala who travels regularly to other parts of the country, he follows disability politics and has a national overview. Susan Whyte has been doing ethnographic fieldwork in rural eastern Uganda at intervals since 1969. In the course of research on dealings with misfortune and inter-action with health-care providers, she has come to know families and people with disabilities who are poor and much less engaged with disabil-ity politics and programs. These other perspectives provide the background for our understanding of the situation in Busia and Malaba.

OPPORTUNITIES IN URBAN SPACES

Urban spaces provide opportunities not found in rural areas for people with disabilities. In the nineteenth century, town streets in industrializing countries were where people excluded from the manufacturing labor force could earn a living through marginal economic activities such as petty trade, crafts, entertainment, service occupations, and begging (Gleeson 1999:99–126). The sparse literature from Africa points to the possibilities that cities seem to offer for people who cannot succeed in agriculture.

Begging is a source of income that is practiced in urban, not rural, social space. Hoffman (2001) describes polio survivors who migrate to Accra to earn a living sitting on the streets asking for alms. Some form part of "traffic-light communities," which assemble where vehicles have to stop. Wheel-chairs are assets here, because they put the beggars at a convenient height for interacting with car passengers and allow rapid, efficient coverage of several cars in the space of a red light. In East Africa, beggars in big cities approach the *wabenzi*, the Mercedes-Benz drivers, where traffic is heavy and slow.

Van den Bergh (1995), whose study from western Tanzania is the only one we know that systematically compares options and "ligatures" (social linkages) for disabled people in rural, semiurban, and urban spaces in Africa, shows that the broader opportunities for trade, small business, and craftsmanship are the most important attractions of small towns and cities. The many people she interviewed who had been disabled by polio found that their chances of getting a tricycle and earning money were better in towns. In the roadside settlements they did not beg as some blind people did, but took advantage of markets and transport to engage in trade.

The accounts she gives of women and men with leg impairments resonate well with the stories we heard in Busia and Malaba. But the situation and the dynamics of the Ugandan border towns are different and provide important lessons about the local realization of global discourses.

In 1990 the cross-border trade was flourishing in Busia. The *magendo* era of large-scale smuggling of agricultural products to Kenya and manu-factured goods to Uganda had given way to a more regularized business scene. But there was still money to be made for those willing to bend the law or establish good relationships with customs authorities; these possi-bilities were discovered by people on three wheels as well as the *boda-boda* men on two. A Muslim businessman, Asumani Asad, is remembered as the pioneer who first used his wheelchair for trade and transport and went on to develop his capital, buy vehicles and buildings, and marry four wives. Word spread that there were opportunities; more and more men on tricy-cles began crossing the border to purchase commodities on the Kenyan side, bringing them back for sale at a profit in Uganda. Many were hired by shopkeepers in town who entrusted them with cash and a shopping order; some accumulated enough capital to buy and sell on their own. A few simply waited at the crossing point for customers who needed transport. All ben-efited from the fact that there was laxity at the border; disabled people passed freely through the barrier with their loaded tricycles—even though they ferried goods many times a day.

People came from many parts of Uganda to exploit this niche in the border economy, called by friends and relatives who told them: "Your fellow disabled are making money at the border. You better join them instead of sitting redundant in the countryside." Many who came did not yet own a tricycle. Some got loans from businessmen; some were helped by family members. Most worked and saved to purchase their own three-wheelers. Several started out being pushed across the border in wheelbar-rows to make purchases and bring back goods. Almost everyone we spoke to had bought tricycles somehow. Very few had received them as gifts from NGOs or religious institutions, in contrast to the physically disabled people Van den Bergh wrote about in western Tanzania.

In 1992–93 the Uganda Revenue Authority (URA) began to tighten up on the cross-border trade. The state campaign to increase revenue through strict collection of taxes and duties included tough moves against any activ-ities defined as smuggling. No exceptions were to be made for people with disabilities. URA officials began to "harass" them, demanding payment of duties and confiscating their goods. Their comparative advantage in the modest niche they had carved out for themselves was threatened. It was against this background that the Busia Disabled Association (BDA) was established in 1994. The membership then as now consisted almost entirely of men with leg impairments, and it undertook the interests of the tricycle transporters and traders. The leadership met regularly with URA officials to negotiate on behalf of the membership and intervened when members were in conflict with the authorities.

When we first interviewed the Busia tricyclists in 2001, a kind of modus vivendi seemed to exist, based on a common understanding: certain items are contraband, including fuel, but diesel and paraffin may be brought in discretely since there is no gas station in Busia and even government employees need these items; but no guns, no narcotics. The accepted convention was that tricyclists were bringing in "goods for household use," which is permitted. The URA officials knew the tricyclists—often by name—and by and large they knew the nature of their business. When new officers were posted, a representative of the BDA went to sensitize them about the situation of the disabled border crossers.

A year later, tensions were high. A revenue-protection unit, composed of army men, had been posted to Busia, and their style was harsher. There were many confrontations and even incidents of physical abuse of disabled people. The tricyclists were bitter, because they felt the crackdown hit them hardest. *Boda-boda* bicyclists could transport goods with impunity by using the *panya* (rat) routes, the small footpaths, all along the border. But tricycles have to use the official crossing on the tarmac road, and they are easy to stop: "They only discriminate against people with disabilities."

In 2002, together with Geoffrey Wandera and Yahaya Wangujo, elected representatives of disabled people in the district, we met with an army official from the Revenue Protection Services and the senior assistant revenue officer in their office at the border. They asserted that the tricyclists were not even locals, that they came from all over Uganda and were being used by businessmen to avoid paying taxes:[1] "And even if you are doing business for yourself, the law requires payment of taxes. The law is the same for all." They denied discrimination and said that people with disabilities were treated with greater leniency: "They imagine they have license to pass freely. They beg you to let them through, saying they have hungry children. Yet it is not allowed. But it becomes compromising. It's difficult personally to seize goods from a disabled person." Asked about the violent incidents, the military man from the revenue-protection unit blamed them on the tricyclists: "Disabled people are extremely violent. They fight for their goods, attack our men." The civilian revenue officer was more balanced, remarking that instances of violence must be investigated and that officials will be reprimanded if they make mistakes.

Afterwards, Wandera and Wangujo were critical, saying that the goods transported on three-wheelers are a minute proportion of what passes the border. Nothing is gained by a policy of zero tolerance against tricyclists. Better to concentrate on the big-time operators who smuggle cigarettes worth millions of shillings in their cars. As for the remark that the tricylists were not even from Busia: "Why can other people go anywhere in Uganda to work but not people with disabilities? They should set a good example by going home themselves. They are not from Busia either!"

Despite the continuing struggles of the tricycle transporters, the writing is on the wall. Not only have the Revenue Protection Services squeezed them so hard that many have given up since January 2002, but the future is even bleaker. Plans are to reestablish the East African Economic Community, and that will mean that their niche will vanish as customs and price differences disappear. Some men have already stopped the border business: the chairman of the BDA has now started a nursery school that employs two other disabled people. In Malaba, the border town to the north, there were never as many, partly because the border crossing is in a valley, making it hard to bring goods up by tricycle, and partly because this is the long-distance transit point, and business depends less on local shops. But in Malaba too, people had left and gone back home or elsewhere looking for better opportunities.

The border niche has been discovered by disabled people elsewhere in Africa too. Michela Wrong (2001) reports that in Kinshasa, where an entire population is working out ways to manage (*se débrouiller*) under difficult circumstances, tricyclists earn a living moving goods back and forth from Brazzaville on the river ferry. Their advantage is that disabled people get a discount on the ferries and the customs inspectors do not bother them. They too formed an organization, the Ngobila Beach Handicapped Mutual Aid Society, in an effort to earn a living without resorting to begging. And they too recognized the fragility of their niche when the finance minister announced a new policy on fares and customs that would stamp out "smuggling" by the tricyclists. The chairman of their society made a statement similar to one we heard in Uganda: "The state has never done anything for us. . . . And now they tell us we must pay just like everyone else" (ibid.:11). But how alike are the situations of tricyclists doing border transport in the two settings? In line with our emphasis on how people in local worlds appropriate resources and navigate constraints, we turn now to the particularities of national policy and district dynamics.

POLICY AND LOCAL INITIATIVE

When President Museveni visited Busia as part of his revenue campaign, he made a speech in which he said that smuggling on tricycles had to stop. Geoffrey Wandera, a man with impaired legs who walks with a cane, told us how he courageously spoke up to the president of the country to assert that they were disabled people trying to be self-sufficient, and not smugglers: "As long as the government provides no alternative source of income, we have to make a living as best we can." He sounded like his Kinshasa counterpart, but he spoke as a different person and in a different context. Ever since he finished senior secondary school, Wandera had admired and familiarized himself with the work of disability organizations and programs in Uganda. He speaks the language of disability rights, and he speaks as an elected representative of disabled people on the Busia District Council since 1997. In order to understand his position and the mobilizing potential of wheels and new legs, we must consider Uganda's unique recent history.

Shortly after the National Resistance Movement (NRM) came to power after years of civil war, 17 urban-based disability organizations joined together in 1987 to form the National Union of Disabled People in Uganda (NUDIPU). Established during the UN Decade of Disabled Persons, this umbrella organization was a conduit through which the new discourse on disability rights flowed into the country. More than that, it was a principal actor in nationalizing the international discourse and advocating a Ugandan version of disability policy and politics. Through its representation in the Constituent Assembly it insured that the fundamental law of the land specifically mentions disabled people. The constitution that was ratified in 1995 insures the rights of women, children, minorities, and persons with disabilities and requires the state to take affirmative action in favor of marginalized groups. Article 35(1) states: "Persons with disabilities have a right to respect and human dignity and the State and society shall take appropriate measures to ensure that they reach their full mental and physical potential."

Perhaps even more important, NUDIPU lobbied for the political representation that might keep disability issues on the agenda at all levels. The Parliamentary Act of 1996 provides special seats for disabled people: in the national parliament there are currently four regional seats and one earmarked for women with disabilities. Uganda is governed by a series of councils at levels from villages through subcounties and districts. The Local Government Act of 1997 requires that disabled persons be represented at every level, and politicians proudly point out that there are 47,000 disabled councilors in local government councils. Elections to the reserved seats at every level are through an electoral college organized within NUDIPU's membership structure. In order to take on this function, NUDIPU had to form branches in every district and at subdistrict levels—a massively ambitious move to bring disability awareness to every part of the country (Ndeezi 1999:26–27). Thus Wandera spoke not only as the PWD (persons with disabilities) representative on the district council, but also as an active member of NUDIPU. He was in close contact with the national organization and through them with national politicians who might promote the interests of the Busia Disabled Association. In fact it was his facilitation of NUDIPU workshops in Busia that had been important in creating interest in establishing the BDA in the first place.

This political organization is one part of the context in which the Busia tricyclists are able to use the discourse of disability activism. The other important component of Uganda's recent history is donor funding. Overall about half of the annual budget is covered by donors; the proportion is much higher in the areas of health and social welfare. Donors fund 99 percent of the expenditures of NUDIPU and other disability organizations in Uganda (Ndeezi 1999:38). The idiom of disability rights adopted by the government has been constantly reinforced by the donor-funded dissemination of ideas, resources, people, and language. Mostly the flow is from north to south, but funds have also facilitated south-south exchanges at international conferences. These "global" movements have been institutionalized in various forms. To the old rehabilitation and vocational-training centers like Kireka and Ruti have been added a new generation of special-education and assessment institutions. Danish International Development Assistance (DANIDA) funded the Uganda National Institute of Special Education, which trains teachers and rehabilitation workers at a beautiful complex near the national teachers' college. Schools for the deaf and the blind anchor and reproduce specific forms of communication and consciousness. The Norwegian Association of the Disabled supported a community-based rehabilitation (CBR) program implemented through government community-development officers. Geoffrey Wandera, who now speaks so articulately for rights not charity, did his apprentice and journeyman years in a CBR project funded from Norway. While these formative institutions constitute relatively fixed points, a plethora of national and local cross-disability and unidisability organizations form, endure, or fade. Some dissolve when the leadership is suspected of "eating" the money; some become dormant as members lose interest. Others, like the Busia Disabled Association, seem to flourish because they create or answer a need in their particular niche.

MOBILITY DEVICES

One might imagine that the first need of people who walk with difficulty or not at all is mobility devices and that the disability organizations or the training institutions provide for these needs. In fact, the technology of mobilization, in both the literal and the extended sense, is complicated. Well-known disability activists have developed appropriate technology for mobility aids working with people from the South (Werner 1987, 1998; Hotchkiss 1993, 2000). Looking at globalization and disability from the perspective of countries of the North, the spread of such technologies seems to offer solutions. But global flows of technology and artifacts take local twists and turns. The ethnographic project is to understand these crooked channels and the significance that a form of technology assumes in a local context.

An excellent example of this endeavor is Kohrman's (1999a) study of three-wheeled motorcycles for the disabled in Beijing. He shows how hand-crank tricycles first appeared on the urban scene in the early 1980s and how, like bicycles, they embodied modernity in the form of time-space compression. While the hand-crank tricycles were made at home or in small factories, the motorized versions were produced by the Chinese Rehabilitation Research Center, under the aegis of the China Disabled Persons' Federation headed by Deng Pufang, the son of Deng Xiaoping. The federation did not provide the motorcycles as a service (people had to buy them), but it nevertheless protected the rights of motorcyclists and was strongly supported by the urban men whose lives were changed by getting the motorized tricycles. In contrast, disabled people living in rural Hainan Province, where Kohrman also did fieldwork, did not have wheelchairs or other manufactured mobility aids and were largely unaware of the federation. Political mobilization for the disability organization and motorized mobility went together.

The politics of mobility devices in Uganda provide an instructive comparison. The Busia tricyclists and their association constitute a parallel, on a much more modest scale, to the Beijing motorcyclists. They bought their own vehicles and used the organization for advocacy and political mobilization. But before examining their movement in more detail, it is useful to place them within the wider context of the political lives of mobility devices.

There are no motorized tricycles in Uganda yet (though the Muzira Workshop in Kampala plans to produce one), and mobility aids are not for the most part manufactured by organizations of disabled people. In the mid-1960s the orthopedic workshop at Mulago, the national referral hospital, produced the first calipers and wheelchairs using local materials under the direction of an Irish orthopedic surgeon. In time, orthopedic workshops were established at regional hospitals in other parts of the country. Artificial limbs, special shoes ("surgical boots"), and crutches are made in these workshops. Like the rest of the national health system, the orthopedic departments lack resources and operate on a fee-for-service basis. Privatization is the tendency here as in other aspects of health care: private workshops began to appear in the 1990s. The first was started by a Church of Uganda bishop in Jinja. Two others are owned by technicians who are simultaneously employed in the public-hospital workshops. A fourth is operated by the Uganda National Association for the Deaf.

The largest manufacturer of wheelchairs in the country is the Muzira Workshop, whose yard lies near a major intersection close to Mulago Hospital. Their tricycles cost 250,000 shillings (about $125) in 2002. They get no subsidy and buy all material, mostly Indian-made and Chinese-made bicycle parts, on the open market. They supply tricycles to the orthopedic departments of the public hospitals, but their biggest customers are the donor-supported projects, including some in Rwanda and Congo. Sales to individuals depend on the season, said Fred Kitamirike: "Around Christmas there are many accidents on the road; three months later we get orders for wheelchairs."

Officially, supplying wheelchairs, calipers, and crutches comes under the rubric "service provision," and in today's decentralized Uganda it is supposed to be the responsibility of the districts. The district rehabilitation officer should facilitate people needing appliances by referring them to orthopedic workshops. But the districts have no funds to subsidize purchase of mobility devices—in 2002 Busia District was in debt to the regional hospital orthopedic workshop and unable to get more credit. The Tororo District rehabilitation officer was asking hopefully if we knew where she might get a tricycle donation; she had a client, a bright boy, who was getting discouraged with having to crawl to school. The rehabilitation officers, like many individual people with disabilities, must look for an organization or a sponsor to buy mobility aids.

Rights Not Charity, Solidarity Not Charity, Respect Not Pity are mottoes of the Ugandan as well as the international disability movement (Ndeezi 1999:8). But in a situation of scarce resources, the question is how to live up to Rule 4 of the UN Standard Rules on the Equalization of Opportunities for Disabled Persons: "States should ensure the development and supply of support services, including assistive devices for persons with disabilities, to enable them to increase their level of independence in their daily living and to exercise their rights." When donors step in to supply or subsidize devices, there are possibilities of charity and dependence, as well as personal favoritism in providing appliances. Supplying them can be a dilemma for disability organizations if it is not done in a transparent way (Larsen 2000:31). Nevertheless, for those who cannot afford to purchase appliances, sponsors and organizations are the only possibility. In her study in western Tanzania, Van den Bergh relates how people were given tricycles by missionaries, Lions and Rotary clubs, and NGOs. Those who managed to be sent for rehabilitation or training programs to other cities sometimes even received second tricycles (Van den Bergh 1995:179). There is thus a politics of positioning and networking in order to access mobility aids. In Uganda, there is also a conviction on the part of those who do not receive that the distribution is unfair and that leaders in organizations use the resources themselves or for their own family and friends. Because disability is on the national agenda, the provision of mobility aids can be very explicitly political.

Like any other valuable resource, mobility devices can be distributed as political favors or to insure support. The minister of agriculture promised to give a tricycle to Nubuwati Nsubuga when he saw her marching on her knees in the World Food Day parade in Busia in 1997. Geoffrey Wandera, by then a district councilor, followed him up, and she actually got her first wheels that way. During the 2002 campaign for the disability seat on the Tororo District Council, one candidate listed on her election manifesto the number of people for whom she had obtained tricycles, calipers, and surgical boots. The incumbent, Sara Kakai, told how she had mediated the distribution of devices from two organizations:

> I tried through NUDIPU—all women representatives on LC3s [county-level local council] got tricycles, calipers, and boots. The National Union of Women with Disabilities gave us two wheelchairs, two pairs of crutches, and one walking stick. I gave them to schoolgirls and one lady from Mazimasa. In Tororo when you give something, it must be on a tribal basis. [Tororo politics are always plagued by competition between the three main ethnic groups Padhola, Nyole and Teso, even when it comes to new legs.]

Examples like these show how different disability politics can play out in different settings. And it is not simply a matter of obtaining appliances.

Mobility aids need maintenance or replacement as well. The most dramatic case we heard concerned a Karamojong woman with an amputated leg who used to get into fights with people and beat them with her crutches. Once an opponent responded in fury, "I'm going to break your leg," and broke her new leg, her crutch. But for most people, it is not violence but simple wear that undermines their hard-won mobility. Those like Yahaya, who swing along using a long sturdy staff, can easily get replacements. But when tricycles, calipers, and boots go to pieces, one needs to pay an expert to fix them. As wooden canes and crutches wear down, their owners crouch lower and lower to use them.

STRUGGLES FOR RECOGNITION

The realization of a global discourse, a national policy, even the exploitation of a local niche like the border trade, cannot be comprehended only in terms of political economy. In order to understand what is happening in Busia and Malaba, it is important to explore what kinds of opportunities and social recognition were at stake and what constraints and resources affected people's lives.

Not having the full use of both legs is not as uncommon in Uganda as it is in wealthier countries. In the northern part of the country, civilians have lost limbs to land mines; years of war have produced soldiers who need new arms and legs; infected sores and other diseases can eventually maim people permanently. Most of all, the polio epidemics of the past have left people with sequelae of varying severity: some manage to walk with a limp, using a hand to brace a weak leg; others drag themselves along the ground or develop ingenious ways of moving by crouching and using their hands to lift their feet.

In rural eastern Uganda, as in some other parts of Africa, proverbs warn against ridiculing people with disabilities: "Disability can happen within a day [to you too]." One young man whose father had earned the nickname "New Leg" when he started to use a stick after going lame following an infection wrote on the door of his house: "Son of New Leg: Who laughs, let him laugh, who backbites, let him backbite, troubles will also catch him." These lines, based on a proverb to the same effect, imply that those who laugh may discover they were only temporarily abled. But they also suggest that people do mock those who cannot walk well, even as in this case those who are not severely disabled. It is easy to generalize from such examples and to assert, as some rehabilitation professionals do, that all people with mobility impairments are discriminated and marginalized.

But the challenge is to be more specific: in what respects? with what differences? in which situations?

The men who came to Busia and Malaba to earn a living said, when asked collectively at a general meeting, that people in town were more accepting of disability than those in the village. Political activism is supported by emphasizing difficulties and neglect. At the general meeting, one man said: "In villages we are discriminated and despised—a father who concentrates on his children with legs and looks at you as useless. Your brothers get married but don't contribute to your marriage. If you say something in your clan, they say you are a disability."

But when they spoke individually of their lives and why they came to town, they talked of being stuck in the village, where opportunities were few. The chance to extend their social being through going to school, earning a living, getting married, and having children was their immediate concern, as it is for most Ugandans. Although it is often said that parents do not value their disabled children, our interlocutors gave a more varied picture of their childhood. Kresent Jakait, doing tricycle transport in Malaba, was the eighth of ten children. He finished primary school but could not continue: "My parents loved me like the other children, but because of poverty they could not afford the school fees. My father gave me land, and I have a title deed." Opotot Samueli, also working at Malaba, says his two siblings went to school but he could not manage because of the distance. His father bought him a tricycle when he grew up and gave him three cows to marry: "My father loves me so much." (The chairman of the disabled association adds that it was the father who requested that his son be enrolled in the organization.) Baliddawa Patrick, the present representative for the disabled on the Busia Town Council, said that his father did not have money for school fees or a wheelchair to help him get to school: "The idea was to educate my able-bodied elder brother so that he looks after me in future." Baliddawa looked after himself by raising goats and poultry that he sold to get the fees to finally start primary school at the age of 16. Charles Mayende, who does long-distance transport from a trading center one hour by tricycle from the border, says he was eight when he got polio: "My uncle tried to take me to hospital but failed. Mother was caring, but Father didn't mind about me. At that time [the mid-1960s] it was like that. I never went to school."

Thus feelings about parents, and especially men's memories of the efforts and resources their fathers invested in them, were varied. People with disabilities themselves were sensitive to discrimination on the part of parents, even when their own parents had given them abundant love and what opportunities they could.

But no matter how our interlocutors recalled their childhood, all said that impairment of physical mobility limited their ability to earn a living in the rural areas. Clearing bush and tending banana plantations or fields of grain and cassava were physically very difficult. Some were able to cultivate small plots of vegetables or raise animals, but even these activities require a little start-up capital, which was even harder for them than for others to raise in poor rural areas. They could not hire out as day labor to others in order to get cash. As young men, they should have been establishing themselves, building their own houses, insuring resources to marry. Instead they felt "stuck," "redundant," "without anything to do." A few like Musa Nsubuga had been taken to learn a trade—tailoring or shoe repair. But without a sewing machine or tools they were not able to work.

A turning point in all the stories was coming to Busia or Malaba. Nearly every person told of being brought or being called by a relative; a few mentioned friends. Baliddawa recounted that his "cousin sister," who was selling food in the Busia market, on a visit home in Iganga told him: "You are suffering too much here; let's go to Busia—there is some work you can do and earn some money." He started out making paper bags and was encouraged to get a tricycle and go into the border trade by two friends who were also in the business. Wandera Fred was brought by his brother, a wholesaler at the market; at first he hired someone to push him in a wheelbarrow to buy goods for his brother across the border. Matavi Koucha tells how his grandfather came to his home in the village saying: "In Busia your friends [other people with disabilities] are making business to get something for their assistance—I want to take you there too." So people with disabilities came to town as most rural Ugandans do, with help from someone who offered a place to stay for a while and some contacts.

Like most rural Ugandans they came hoping for a chance to get on in life—to extend themselves through a livelihood that would enable them to establish and maintain a family. The intimate connection of physical and social mobility is underscored by the accounts of the traders and transporters. Getting to town in the first place allowed them to find some kind of work. Once they were able to buy a tricycle, other doors could be opened. One man was explicit: "The tricycle is your capital." It allowed them to cross the border on behalf of others and, if they were fortunate, to start their own businesses. Kakembo moved from hired transport to buying a plot and putting up a shop and later to running a restaurant. Baliddawa started bringing Kenyan milk across the border, and later went into buying and retailing Ugandan milk in Busia town. Many were still working for others, but nearly every man we spoke to had been able to marry.

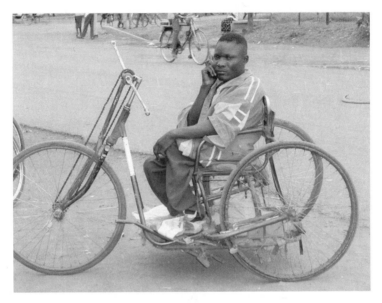

FIGURE 11.2. A tricyclist with his mobile phone, Busia, Uganda.
(Photo: Susan Whyte)

From Beijing, where an impaired body is disdained, Kohrman (1999a)
describes the difficulties encountered by disabled men in getting a wife. In
contrast, the Ugandan problem is the ability to support a wife, not the aesthetics or functionality of legs in themselves. A man who shows he can care
well for a wife can usually find one. (Wrong [2001] reports the same from
Kinshasa.) In conversations men said that they began to believe they could
marry when they came to town and saw that their fellow disabled were
earning a living and supporting wives. Almost all of the men we interviewed in Busia and Malaba had married nondisabled women. Some suggested that disabled men were better husbands, because they valued their
wives and provided well for them, especially when their wives gave them
children: "Able-bodied men don't invest enough in wives, because they
think they can easily get others." Laughing, Yahaya said that he had had
four wives and that women even left able-bodied husbands for disabled
men because they were stronger.

Listening to the tricyclists' accounts of coming to town, there was no
missing the satisfaction in their voices as they mentioned their families.
Wandera Fred says: "I married my wife in 1995—we had a wonderful wedding." This man who had started his Busia career in a wheelbarrow now
has two children, and he and his wife are building a brick house on their

own plot of land. Matavi Koucha puts it in a nutshell: "After my grandfather bought me a tricycle, I started ferrying commodities, and I realized life had changed tremendously compared to life in the village. The next was marriage. I married a wife after two years. We had a child in 1995, a second in 1997, and a third in 1999. Up to now I am still doing the same work to sustain the family." Again and again, as we talked with the tricyclists and visited their homes, we heard accounts of the ordinary desire for social being and the struggles of extraordinary bodies and persons to achieve it. They drew on nondisabled relatives and friends, and on their own resources of energy and will. But their struggles and achievements were intertwined with those of other men with disabilities like their own.

FELLOWSHIP

The example of other disabled people in the border business was inspiring. Not only did people like Koucha's grandfather bring word to villages, but disabled people who came to work for relatives in the border towns saw with their own eyes and in some cases were helped to start up in business by those who were already active. Ndomboli Peter came to work in his brother's shop and found that the commodities he sold were being brought by people on tricycles. He saved up and bought a tricycle too and became a successful businessman on his own.

The people who came to town were mostly from rural areas where they had not had other disabled people with whom to identify; only one or two had been to a rehabilitation vocational-training center where they were institutionally defined as people with disabilities. What was striking about the situation in Busia and Malaba was that communities of people who identified with one another on the basis of having a disability had taken shape relatively spontaneously. Neither special schools, rehabilitation programs, nor vocational training had brought people together. It was the existence of a niche and the common desire to create a better life that provided a foundation. A sense of identity developed that is reflected in the Ugandan English term "fellow disabled."[2] As Allamanzani Kakembo said when telling how he and his friend got started: "We saw our fellow disabled people working, but we did not know what to do. Our fellow disabled people taught us how to go about it."

Fellowship was institutionalized in the organizations of disabled people in Busia and Malaba. Under the leadership of people who had been inspired by the national discourse on disability, they embarked on plans for income generation as well as mobilization and advocacy. Many of the plans remain

FIGURE 11.3. The attendant at the bicycle spares shop operated
by the Busia Disabled Association. (Photo: Susan Whyte)

only plans waiting for a donor, like the project of constructing and charg-
ing for use of toilets and bathing facilities in Malaba. But subgroups have
formed around activities that bring people together, mostly of the same
kinds engaged in by other Ugandans. In Busia there is a mourning society
to assist members who have lost a relative. The Malaba Disabled Self-Help
Group has a "merry-go-round"—a fund into which all pay and that each
gets to use in turn. They also have a shoe-repair business, while their fellow
disabled in Busia have concentrated on a shop selling bicycle spares.

Fellowship looks inward toward interaction with one another. But it also
looks outward in that it involves the formation and assertion of an identity
and a political consciousness as people with disabilities. Several times we
heard people say with satisfaction: *There are no beggars in Busia; in other
towns you see people begging at mosques and on the street—here we say*

disability is not inability; we are earning a living without depending on charity. This rejection of begging does not preclude public displays of impaired bodies (a central feature in begging). But performances by members of the BDA are exhibits of alternative abilities, as in wheelchair races, or "cultural" shows of singing and dancing on hands and withered legs. These are ways of earning money and entertaining important visitors analogous to activities of women's groups in many Ugandan localities.

In its institutionalized form, fellowship involves emphasizing the commonality of disability over and above other social differences. As the BDA members said: *We come from all over and speak different languages, but we are in the same situation; we help each other; when a new person with a disability comes to town, we welcome him.* But political organization in order to represent common interests requires an effective spokesperson, and here social and cultural capital make a difference. The leader of the Malaba association is a woman even though most members are men. She explained that she was chosen because she was better educated and therefore better able to talk to visitors.

Political mobilization raises consciousness about injustices in general and not only about those against disabled people as a homogeneous category. The suspicion that better-placed people are channeling resources into their own pools is never far beneath the surface in Ugandan conversations. We heard many remarks about the possibility or probability that money intended for organizations of disabled people had been "eaten" before it reached its intended goal. Such insinuations were also made about well-placed persons with disabilities, for example in this short contribution at the BDA general meeting: "If you ask how many of us are well educated, only six or seven. This government told us to elect leaders, but they want educated people. And the educated ones don't feel for those who are not educated. Otherwise they would give the money meant for us. We who aren't educated don't have any voice."

There are differences among disabled people, even among the mobilized and motivated members of the Busia Disabled Association. And the BDA itself is dominated by men with tricycles and "new legs" in the form of sturdy poles and crutches. Where are the women? Where are those with other kinds of disabilities?

SOCIAL DIFFERENCE AND MOBILIZATION

The expectation that women are primarily farmers and homemakers whereas men should earn cash for family needs informed people's own explanations about the gender imbalance in the Busia and Malaba associations. The active core of these associations was composed of men who used their wheels and new legs to mobilize economically and politically. They said that disabled women were cared for by their own families or by their husbands; it was not so urgent for women to generate an income. In fact there were a few politically active women: Tabitha Itikine, the leader of the Malaba United Association for People with Disabilities; Sara Kakai, the women's representative for the disabled on the Tororo District Council. Three of the 13 people doing trade and transport at Malaba and one of the 28 in Busia were women. But as Margaret Sabano of Busia explained: "Most women with disabilities are still in villages It's hard to get a tricycle. I was lucky—my guardian bought one for me. Otherwise I'd still be in the village too." The difference between the situations of men and women is not absolute, but there is a clear tendency for men to be given and to (be forced to?) create opportunities that women do not have.

Both of us know examples from other settings in Uganda where women with walking disabilities are trying to mobilize support from parents and husbands. Women who lose legs to land mines in northern Uganda often find that they lose their husbands too, as men look for other wives who are better able to do the strenuous work of maintaining a home and family. Those like Elizabeth (Spittal and Muyinda n.d.) who are supported by their families count themselves fortunate. Elizabeth is not helpless; she took refuge in Gulu town and is sustaining herself selling charcoal in the informal sector. But she feels that her husband *should* have taken care of her: "I will never marry again, because if my husband who knew me and loved me before this injury can mistreat me . . . and still leave me . . . I do not think another man would want to care for me . . . he would not be committed enough to take care of me." Elizabeth looks forward to going back to her parents' rural home when the war ends.

Susan Whyte's friend "Natabo" in rural Tororo District, a polio survivor, is still living in her husband's compound, but she is bitter because he gives all his attention and resources to his younger and more able wife. He will not help her to replace her worn-out caliper nor even to rebuild her dilapidated house. She says she is only staying with him until her last child has grown up; then she will go back to her father's home.

Of the seven women we talked to in Malaba and Busia, only two were married. Both men and women said that it was more difficult for disabled women to marry: those who are educated or from rich families have better chances. Several had children by lovers who did not marry them; a few had been married and divorced. The pattern reported by Sentumbwe (1995) of blind women marrying blind men if they married at all did not hold for women with leg impairments. The immediate explanation was that they could not help one another if both were unable to walk. It may be that such "endogamy" is associated with special institutions: Sentumbwe's couples had met each other at schools for the blind. Most of our informants had not attended any disability-specific institution; the only "endogamous" couple, Musa and Nubuwati Nsubuga, had met at a vocational-rehabilitation school.

While most of the men had struggled to get their tricycles themselves, the women had been given theirs. Jetu Atine, a charismatic Christian like several of the disabled women, was given a wheelchair by a fellow Christian, a European named David. She did not ask for it; he brought it because he sympathized when he saw her crawling to church. Like Lucy Atiang, whom we met in Malaba, where she had come to get her tricycle repaired, Jetu was not an active member of her local disability organization. The lesson seems to be that wheels and new legs are necessary but not sufficient prerequisites for economic and political mobilization. The men who used theirs to earn a living supported their efforts by taking up political discourses and organizational forms that were available at that place and time in Ugandan history. The women were mostly not involved in the tough interactions with revenue officers that had motivated the traders and transporters to organize and keep working together.

In the rural parts of Busia and Tororo districts that we know, there are men with leg impairments engaged in enterprises in the small trading centers. George Lwakisa scoots on the ground, having lost the use of both legs after polio. But parked outside his combination drug shop and clinic he has a super-deluxe sports-model wheelchair that he got in Kenya, where he was working in a Red Cross orthopedic workshop. He can fold it and take it in a minibus taxi when he needs to renew his drug supply. Married and well integrated in his locality, he is not active in the disabled organization "because I have my business." With his various forms of capital (he is educated and has the only clinic in the trading center), he sees no need of political mobilization, unlike the entrepreneurs of Busia who were trying to create and sustain a business.

In small trading centers like the one where Lwakisa stays, and in the agricultural communities where the majority of Ugandans live, there are no concentrations of people with similar disabilities and common economic and political interests as is the case in Malaba and Busia. Sporadic meetings, occasional workshops, and unrealized plans are not enough to sustain the kind of mobilization that characterizes the tricyclist traders in the border towns. It is not only the lack of a critical mass, but the lack of a concrete benefit that makes it difficult to maintain enthusiasm. Moreover, there have been cases where people have paid membership fees for the local branch of their disability organization only to have the chairman or treasurer disappear with the funds.

The efforts of the National Union of Disabled Persons of Uganda to organize people for political representation all over the country right down to village level is impressive but fraught with problems. People who are poor and uneducated fall out of the process of mobilization for practical reasons. Elsewhere Whyte (2004) describes the difficulties encountered by Veronica, a blind rural mother, in trying to attend workshops to which she was invited in the county and district headquarters. It was not so much the fact of blindness that inhibited her mobility as it was the procedure of refunding transport expenses at the workshops rather than providing them ahead of time. She could not raise the money to pay the fare in the first place. Veronica had lost her sight after she was married and had children. For many years she did not know any other blind person. As efforts are now being made to establish an organization of blind people in her county, she is for the first time offered the possibility of a social identity as blind, and through the system of political representation as a person with a disability. But the urgent problems of life with an alcoholic and now seriously ill husband, eight children, and no money prevent her from enacting and enhancing that identity.

The fact that most representatives of the disabled on local councils have limb impairments that are not radically disabling (often a clubfoot or one leg atrophied from polio) does not go unnoticed. Gabiri, a man blind from birth who attended a special school and has been a subcounty councilor in Tororo District, says there are small disabilities (like having only one eye) and hardship disabilities (like "walking on your stomach" because you have no legs): "Now there are local council elections; those with small disabilities give out money, so they are chosen as representatives. People who are now standing have money and little disabilities. So I don't expect to win this time." Passing out money or other favors to gain votes in local elections is common practice in eastern Uganda. Gabiri simply expected the disabled candidates to do what "everyone" does. His point was the connection to the nature and severity of disability.

Current attempts to form or strengthen unidisability organizations reflect an awareness of this problem. In May 2002 we attended a meeting to choose officers of the new Tororo District branch of the Uganda National Association for the Deaf. Campaign statements in sign language were followed with intense interest, humor, and enthusiasm. The participants were by definition a select group of people who had been privileged to attend an institution where they learned sign language. But stronger uni-disability organizations can lobby in cross-disability ones to the advantage of less privileged people. In the recent NUDIPU organized elections for disability seats, word had come down to the rural village where Whyte works that the new councilor should be a deaf person. Charles, the man chosen accordingly, was not one of the deaf-educated like those at the Tororo meeting; he had his own form of signing, since he had never been to school.

It is not surprising that social differences are related to mobilization. In Pierre Bourdieu's terms economic, social, and cultural capital (even bodily capital) are fundamental for understanding how people appropriate symbolic capital—in this case the values, ideas, and possibilities in the disability movement and discourse (Bourdieu 1986). Pointing out that men like Wandera with ambulatory disabilities, education, and contacts to politicians and donor projects have more opportunities than blind uneducated rural women like Veronica is not meant to devalue the achievements that have been made in mobilization. Rather the task is to understand the positions of different kinds of people, their concerns, and the conditions for and interest in mobilization.

CONCLUSION

Analyses of the appropriation and practice of disability discourse and identity place varying weight on individual trajectories and social and historical contexts. Some scholars (e.g., Stiker 1999) trace the cultural and political history of impairment, institutions, and policies. Others focus on the lives of social actors and the ways in which they engage with a political movement or identify with others on the basis of a common disability. Kasnitz (2001) presents a life-course event-history method for analyzing leadership in the U.S. independent-living movement. Through the analysis of individual life histories her aim is to reach a more general understanding.

Our approach extends the work of these researchers by emphasizing the factors that emerge in a particular time and place. We started with a group (not just a category) of people who were working a specific niche in two border towns. In order to understand that niche we had to look at the recent political and economic history of that place, and the rural conditions and urban possibilities that brought these people to town. We tried to show what the Ugandan national policy on disability meant for these actors in that place. The technicalities of physical mobility, with wheels and "new legs," were necessary to other kinds of mobilization. While the struggle in countries of the North is about making public spaces accessible by changing the environment, the struggle for these people was to obtain the assistive devices that would let them get to those spaces.

Acknowledging the importance of fellowship, we were also sensible of social differences among the tricyclists themselves and between them and other people with disabilities. Physical mobility and economic enterprise were the basis for the development of a feeling of identity with peers, which was facilitated by national policy and the disability discourse imported through donor projects. The three-wheeling transporters and businessmen are a unique urban phenomenon, like the Beijing motorcylists described by Kohrman. But in another sense, and unlike their Chinese counterparts, they were not so unusual at all—husbands and fathers trying to support families. Their mobilization, in all senses of the word, was bound up with the possibilities of extending their sociality not only as people with disabilities but as people—full stop.

NOTES

1. The resident district commissioner shares the view that Busia is a mecca for disabled entrepreneurs. He told us that Busia has more disabled people than any other town in Uganda: "Even the tricycles here are different—all are modified to carry heavy loads."

2. This corresponds to a construction in Uganda's Bantu languages: e.g., Luganda *banange*, used to express similarity or identity as in "my fellow women," "my fellow clansmen," etc.

REFERENCES

Bourdieu, Pierre. 1986. The forms of capital. In *Handbook of Theory and Research for the Sociology of Education*, ed. J. G. Richardson, 241–58. New York: Greenwood.

Gleeson, Brendan. 1999. *Geographies of Disability*. London: Routledge.

Hoffman, Anke. 2001. Begging and handicap: A case-study of people with poliomyelitis in Accra. Masters thesis, University of Amsterdam.

Hotchkiss, Ralf D. 1993. Ground swell on wheels. *The Sciences* (New York Academy of Sciences), Jul.–Aug. http://www.nyas.org.publications/sciences/TOC_1993Jul.asp.

———. 2000. On wheels. *Public Culture* 12 (1): 43–50.

Kasnitz, Devva. 2001. Life event histories and the U.S. independent living movement. In *Disability and the Life Course: Global Perspectives*, ed. M. Priestley, 67–78. Cambridge: Cambridge University Press.

Kohrman, Matthew. 1999a. Grooming *que zi:* Marriage exclusion and identity formation among disabled men in contemporary China. *American Ethnologist* 26(4): 890–909.

———. 1999b. Motorcycles for the disabled: Mobility, modernity and the transformation of experience in urban China. *Culture, Medicine and Psychiatry* 23(1): 133–55.

Larsen, Kirsten Lund. 2000. *The Way Forward for Disability Support through Danish NGOs.* Copenhagen: Ministry of Foreign Affairs/DANIDA.

Ndeezi, Alex. 1999. *The Disability Movement in Uganda: Progress and Challenges.* Kampala: NUDIPU.

Sentumbwe, Nayinda. 1995. Sighted lovers and blind husbands: Experiences of blind women in Uganda. In *Disability and Culture,* ed. B. Ingstad and S. R. Whyte, 159–73. Berkeley and Los Angeles: University of California Press.

Spittal, Patricia, and Herbert Muyinda. N.d. *Socio-cultural and Economic Effects of Land Mines in Northern Uganda: Implications for Health Care and Rehabilitation of Land Mine Victims.* Kampala: Injury Control Centre Uganda.

Stiker, Henri-Jacques. 1999. *A History of Disability.* Trans. W. Sayers. Ann Arbor: University of Michigan Press.

Van den Bergh, Graziella. 1995. Difference and sameness: A sociocultural approach to disability in western Tanzania. Candidatus Politices thesis, Department of Social Anthropology, University of Bergen.

Werner, David. 1987. *Disabled Village Children: A Guide for Community Health Workers, Rehabilitation Workers, and Families.* Palo Alto: The Hesperian Foundation.

———. 1998. *Nothing about us without us: Developing Innovative Technologies for, by and with Disabled Persons.* Palo Alto: Health Wrights.

Whyte, Susan Reynolds. 2004. Disability: Global languages and local lives. In *Companion to Psychological Anthropology: Modernity and Psychocultural Change,* ed. C. Casey and R. Edgerton, 168–81. London: Blackwells.

Wrong, Michela. 2001. Out on a limb. *Transition* 88: 4–11.

Contributors

RENU ADDLAKHA is Reader at the Center for Women's Development Studies, Delhi. She conducted ethnographic fieldwork in hospital psychatric wards in India with particular reference to the treatment of women. Her areas of specialization include the sociology of medicine, mental illness and the psychiatric profession, anthropology of infectious diseases, bioethics, and disability studies. Currently she is engaged in research on gender and disability.

ADITYA BHARADWAJ is a Lecturer in Medical Sociology at the School of Social and Political Studies, University of Edinburgh, and has been a postdoctoral research fellow at Cardiff University for over three years. His principal research interest is in new reproductive, genetic, and stem-cell biotechnologies, and their rapid spread in diverse global locales ranging from South Asia to the United Kingdom.

VEENA DAS is Krieger-Eisenhower Professor and Chair of the Department of Anthropology, The Johns Hopkins University. She has worked on questions of violence, social suffering, gender, and subjectivity in South Asia, illuminating these issues through postcolonial and poststructural theory. Currently she is engaged in a collaborative study on health seeking and the burden of disease among urban poor in Delhi.

MARIANA L. FERREIRA is a Brazilian anthropologist interested in a physiology of oppression that connects indigenous peoples worldwide to diabetes, social inequality, and colonial trauma. She teaches anthropology and directs the Global Peace, Human Rights, and Justice Studies Program at San Francisco State University.

HILDE HAUALAND is a researcher at the Fafo Institute for Labor and Social Research in Oslo and a PhD student in social anthropology at the University of Oslo. She has been involved in research on Deaf and hard of hearing youth, and transnational connections in Deaf worlds. She is currently working on a project on disability, the labor market, information and communication technology, and welfare policies.

311

BENEDICTE INGSTAD is Professor of Medical Anthropology at the Institute for General Practice and Community Medicine, University of Oslo. Her research in Botswana, Norway, Yemen, and Kenya has focused on disability, family support, and national and international policies and programs. Currently she is doing a research project on disability and poverty in a cross-cultural/global perspective.

MARCIA C. INHORN is Director of the Center for Middle Eastern and North African Studies at the University of Michigan, where she is Professor in the Department of Health Behavior and Health Education, the Program in Women's Studies, and the Department of Anthropology. A medical anthropologist specializing in Middle Eastern gender and health issues, she has conducted research on the social impact of infertility and assisted reproductive technologies in Egypt, Lebanon, and Arab America over the past twenty years.

MATTHEW KOHRMAN, Assistant Professor in the Department of Cultural and Social Anthropology, Stanford University, has carried out extensive fieldwork in China. In his writings and research, he strives to engage various intellectual terrains such as governmentality, political economy, gender theory, critical science studies, narrativity, and embodiment.

MARGARET LOCK is the Marjorie Bronfman Professor in Social Studies in Medicine, and is affiliated with the Department of Social Studies of Medicine and the Department of Anthropology at McGill University. Her work in Japan and North America has focused on East Asian medicine, menopause, and organ transplantation. Her current research concerns the production of postgenomic biology and its translation and circulation among clinics, families, society, and globally, with particular emphasis on Alzheimer's disease.

HERBERT MUYINDA is an Assistant Lecturer in the Child Health and Development Center, Faculty of Medicine, Makerere University, Uganda. His main research interests are disabilility, conflict, sexuality and STDs, and poverty. He is currently a PhD student at the Department of Anthropology, University of Copenhagen, and is doing his fieldwork on disability, mobility, and violent conflict in northern Uganda.

NANCY SCHEPER-HUGHES is Professor of Medical Anthropology at the University of California, Berkeley, where she directs the doctoral program in Critical Studies in Medicine, Science, and the Body. Her work concerns the violence of everyday life examined from a radical existentialist and politically engaged perspective. She is currently engaged in research and action on the international traffic in human organs.

AUD TALLE is a Professor at the Department of Social Anthropology, University of Oslo. Her writings on pastoralism, gender, and social change are based upon long-term fieldwork in East Africa. She also has an interest in medical anthropology. Currently she is involved in fieldwork among Somalis in the diaspora.

JOHN W. TRAPHAGAN is Associate Professor of Asian Studies and Anthropology and Director of the Center for East Asian Studies at the University of Texas at Austin. His previous research has focused on aging and health in Japan, and he is currently conducting research on youth baseball in Japan and the United States.

MEIRA WEISS is Professor Emeritus, The Hebrew University of Jerusalem. Her research interests include critical anthropology of science, medicine and the body, violence, social suffering, death, human rights, and academic freedom. Her recent work concerns power and knowledge in the Israeli National Institute of Forensic Medicine.

SUSAN REYNOLDS WHYTE, Professor at the Institute of Anthropology, University of Copenhagen, has done extensive fieldwork in East Africa. Her areas of interest include the pragmatics of dealing with misfortune, health-care systems as social practice, the social lives of medicines, and family relations of chronically ill and disabled people.

Index

196–97; and disability in Israeli
society, 110–13, 122; and disability
rights activism, 197–98, 238; and
discrimination/oppression, 191–92,
195–96; and genomics, 192; and
individual choice, 193; limitations
of, 194; and medicalization of disability, 190–91
genital mutilation. *See* female
circumcision
genomics, 192, 193. *See also* genetic
testing
germline engineering, 198–207; arguments against, 202; arguments for,
199–201; and economic inequalities,
202, 205; and ethics, 202–3, 205; and
eugenics, 198, 199, 205, 207; and
human nature, 203–5
Ginsburg, Faye, 111, 112
globalism: and connections among
people with disabilities, 17–18; and
definitions of disability, 12, 57; and
disability rights activism, 4–5,
237–39, 294; and female circumcision, 57, 62–63; vs. local contexts,
9–11; and refugee experience, 58.
See also transnationality
Gluzman, Michael, 108
Goffman, Erving, 85, 86
Gotai fumanzoku (Ototake), 263–64
government policies: and citizenship,
23; and discrimination/oppression,
109, 122; and domestic citizenship,
128; and enumeration, 215–16,
231n1; and Japanese old-age disability, 261, 274–77, 283n6; and
Ugandan mobility-disabled people,
288, 290–92, 293–94, 309n1. *See
also* Chinese government definitions of disability; citizenship; social
service programs
Greil, Arthur L., 80, 82, 85, 86
Gupta, Akhil, 41

habitus, 260, 283n2
Hacking, Ian, 215, 216, 219, 231n1
Hall, Stuart, 230

Handbook of Disability Studies
(Albrecht et al.), 6
Hashimoto, Akiko, 260
hearing aids, 48
Helander, Bernhard, 69
hijab, 71
Hinduism, 93, 135
historical connections, 123–24n8,
129
HIV/AIDS, 240, 245
Hoffman, Anke, 289
Holland, Dorothy, 38, 48
Holzer, B., 9

IAC (Inter-African Committee on
Traditional Practices Affecting the
Health of Women), 63
ICF (International Classification of
Functioning, Disability, and Health)
(WHO), 13
ICPD (International Conference on
Population and Development)
(1994), 78
ICSI (intracytoplasmic sperm injection), 98
identity, 14–17; biosociality/biological
citizenship, 15–16; and Chinese
government definitions of disability,
216–17, 219–20, 221, 222, 228; and
citizenship, 21–22; and connections
among people with disabilities,
16–17, 41, 50; and definitions of disability, 231n1; and female circumcision, 73–75; and infertility, 79,
84–88; and liminality, 40, 48; and
play, 38–39; and refugee experience,
68–69; and social service programs,
14–15, 17; and technology, 18, 48.
See also connections among people
with disabilities
Ikegami, Naoki, 274
Ikels, Charlotte, 282
inaccessibility, 39, 109–10, 263. *See
also* discrimination/oppression
India, domestic citizenship in. *See*
domestic citizenship
India, infertility in. *See* infertility

Text: 10/13 Aldus
Display: Aldus
Compositor: International Typesetting & Composition
Printer and binder: Maple-Vail Manufacturing Group